Mysticism and Reform,
1400–1750

ReFormations

MEDIEVAL AND EARLY MODERN

Series Editors:
David Aers, Sarah Beckwith, and James Simpson

Mysticism and Reform, 1400–1750

Edited by

Sara S. Poor *and* Nigel Smith

University of Notre Dame Press

Notre Dame, Indiana

Notre Dame, Indiana 46556
www.undpress.nd.edu

Manufactured in the United States of America

Library of Congress Cataloging-in-Publication Data

Mysticism and reform, 1400–1750 /
edited by Sara S. Poor and Nigel Smith.
pages cm. —
(ReFormations: medieval and early modern)
Includes index.
ISBN 978-0-268-03898-4 (pbk. : alk. paper) —
ISBN 0-268-03898-8 (pbk. : alk. paper)
1. Mysticism—Europe—History. 2. Church history—Middle Ages, 600–1500. 3. Church history—16th century. 4. Church history—17th century. 5. Church history—18th century. I. Poor, Sara S., editor.
BV5077.E85M96 2015
248.2'209—dc23

2014049400

∞ *The paper in this book meets the guidelines for permanence and durability of the Committee on Production Guidelines for Book Longevity of the Council on Library Resources.*

Contents

Illustrations

Acknowledgments

Most of the essays in this volume grew out of a conference we organized at Princeton University in February 2008 ("Mysticism, Reform, and the Formation of Modernity"), which was generously funded by Princeton's Center for the Study of Religion (CSR) and co-sponsored by the Council for the Humanities, the Departments of English and German, the Program in Medieval Studies, and the Committee for Renaissance Studies. We are especially grateful to Robert Wuthnow, Jennifer Legath, and Anita Kline of CSR for their support. Invaluable to the organization of the conference were Tara Zarillo and the staff at Conference and Event Services, as well as our graduate student assistant, Alana King. We would like to thank all of our contributors for their cooperation and collaboration in developing the volume and special thanks go to Alana King and Prof. Dr. Franz M. Eybl for contributing essays after the conference.

The volume benefited greatly from the comments and suggestions of our anonymous reviewers, although, of course, any flaws remaining are ours alone. We are deeply indebted to the editors of the series ReFormations: Medieval and Early Modern (David Aers, Sarah Beckwith, and James Simpson) for their support of and enthusiasm for the project from the beginning. Special thanks go to Barbara Hanrahan (former acquisitions editor at University of Notre Dame Press) who shepherded the project from idea to accepted proposal and contract. We are even more grateful to our current editor, Stephen Little, at the University of Notre Dame Press, who has guided the volume through the review process with professionalism, integrity, and kindness. Finally, we both wish to acknowledge each other for the teamwork, fortitude, and friendship that made producing this volume together a truly enriching intellectual experience.

Sara S. Poor and Nigel Smith

Introduction

Sara S. Poor and Nigel Smith

There are times when mysticism seems more present in the public domain than at others. It can always be found in church history, in the continuing assessment of devotional tradition in parts of the Roman Catholic Church and its practice, and of course in many other world faiths. Mystical literature was one of the most distinctive components of medieval European piety, replete with a classic canon of texts, key authors, and devotional practices of which those texts were a part. It survives in that tradition and has been often reviled in Protestantism, much of which has had no time for it. It has nonetheless prevailed as a devotional practice and as a vast body of published writing that continues to be read and studied in religious and academic circles today.

Yet every so often mysticism sticks its head out of its cloister and into a larger world. Thus, at this difficult juncture in world politics, the well-known philosopher Simon Critchley proposes a "mystical anarchism" as, if not a total solution to today's political conundrums, then something of which we must take significant note. Critchley defines "mystical anarchism" as life lived with an "emphasis on secrecy, invisibility, and itinerancy, on small-scale communal experiments in living, on the politicization of poverty that recalls medieval practices of mendicancy and the refusal of work. What is at stake is the affirmation of a life no longer exhausted by work, cowed by law and the police."[1] While Critchley is skeptical of the millenarian expectation that has often accompanied medieval and early modern "mystical anarchism," "what animates it is a form of faith-based communism that draws its strength from the poor, the marginal, and the dispossessed."[2] Critchley is drawn to the thirteenth- and fourteenth-century "heresy of the free spirit" and how it offered a process of meditation by which an individual can overcome original sin and become one with God. The annihilation of self that this involves is, asserts Critchley, part of what he calls a communism that abandons private property and promotes social equality in a "politics of love, in which love is understood as that act of spiritual daring that attempts to eviscerate existing conceptions of identity in order that a new form of subjectivity [becoming one with God] can come into being."[3] Critchley latches onto the writings and career of Marguerite Porete, and the fact that she was burned at the stake in Paris in 1310 as a heretic. Her profession of mystical vision was identified as heresy and she died for it.

Critchley's account is very dependent on a small number of secondary sources, not least Norman Cohn's *The Pursuit of the Millennium* (1957). This means that his insights are only as good as these secondary sources. Cohn's tendency to run millenarianism and mysticism together would pose a problem for most historians today, and Critchley himself notices Cohn's prejudice against irrational creeds like mysticism influencing politics: he would have been thinking of medieval heresy and sixteenth-century Anabaptists in the context of Nazism and what it did to twentieth-century Europe. Critchley is openly angry with what he regards as a mischaracterization of the past in which Cohn plays into the heresy hunters' habit of casting immoral slurs on idealists: the allegation that the Brethren of the Free Spirit were really immoral libertines.

It is certainly the case that some forms of medieval mysticism have been associated with licentious behavior, not least because of their use of extremely erotic language, and their description of concepts of union with God, *unio mystica*, as indeed erotic. The Situationist philosopher Raoul Vaneigem treats this strain of mysticism as an attempt by pious people in the past to assert a genuinely creative devotion, over and against the repressive powers of national (or international) churches and the state, powers that are at least disciplinary and at worst violent. Cohn had seen a connection between the Brethren of the Free Spirit and the Antinomian Ranters of the English Revolution where in some written instances, a truly mystical awareness of self-becoming-God is to be found alongside a more enthusiastic sense of immediate and direct inspiration by the Holy Spirit, millenarianism, pantheism, and both free love and swearing as manifestations of God's love for his creatures. For Vaneigem the "orthodox" sexually sterilized mysticism of the Rhineland writers—Eckhart, Suso, Tauler, Ruysbroeck, Groote—was "revenge of the spirit for attempts to emancipate the body."[4]

But for Critchley the mystic's claim to union with God as a consequence of the annihilation of the self is nevertheless a powerful challenge to authoritarianism since it is in effect an empowering of the self that makes an external church entirely irrelevant. Moreover, the self is no longer an entity with property but part of a community that experiences all things as equal and not as possessions. While medieval inquisitors accused these mystics of using piety as a mask for lust, it is also possible to see in this tradition a manifestation of sexual communism in the name of the Holy Spirit and through an expressed sense of union with God.[5] Equally, such mystical enlightenment could come in the form of the sexual abstinence or chastity of groups like the Philadelphian Society or their nineteenth-century descendants the Shakers.[6] For some, taking such a position is to acknowledge that the mystic has arrived at a sense of *jouissance* that is itself something more than bodily passion and more than a "mere" claim for heavenliness.[7] It is at this juncture that medieval mysticism, defined as a form of contemplation that leads to an annihilation of the ego in order to experience a union with the Godhead, has been offered by Critchley as a solution to the shortcomings of many aspects of political action in our contemporary twenty first-century moment, be they liberal or authoritarian, and this is because such mysticism is understood, as we have seen, to be founded in a politics of love, which overcomes both pessimistic views of human potential (there will always be original sin) and a secular view that reason and law will always dominate compassion.

We open with this discussion of medieval mysticism's intrusion into twenty-first century discussions of political action because our interest in putting this volume together grows out of our observations in our respective fields of this same intrusion: the way that expressions of divine union and love in both the medieval and early modern periods have been closely intertwined with the mechanisms and politics of reform. While Critchley's lack of attention to the early modern cases of this "politics of love" should not be surprising, his starting point as a present-day thinker relying on a limited set of secondary sources, we note that the typical historiography of the Reformation has had this same blind spot. Yet we argue, and believe that this volume demonstrates, that mysticism's encounter with the Reformation helps us understand the ways in which the politics of love did flourish and develop in the very different territory of sixteenth- and seventeenth-century Europe. The apparent disappearance or great diminution of mysticism in the Protestant world after the Reformation used to be taken as an example of the arrival of modernity. The best that mystical literature could hope for would be antiquarian interest and eventual assimilation into European literature's Romantic vision. In 1973, however, Steven Ozment's book *Mysticism and Dissent* asked important questions about the connections between sixteenth-century theoreticians of the Reformation, especially Martin Luther, and such medieval mystics as Meister Eckhart and Johannes Tauler.[8] In the 1950s an early work by the Polish philosopher Leszek Kołakowski, translated into French in 1969, had made a case for a relocated mysticism, known through the proliferation of small-format printed books, promoting and defining a household piety that crossed the major confessional divide of the sixteenth century and that was very much a part of the Erasmian movement.[9] But since that time, the structures of our academic disciplines have very largely continued to rely on the notion of a complete break between the medieval and modern eras, or to see mysticism as already in decline in the fifteenth century.[10] Mysticism as a "trans-Reformation" phenomenon has been denied. However, as recent studies in history and literary history reveal, the "Reformation" was not experienced in such a drastic transformative manner in several different spheres, not least because the later Middle Ages itself was marked by a series of reform movements within the church.[11] As Ozment, and Leszek Kołakowski before him, began to explain, some reformers remained keenly and crucially interested in mystical literature.[12] Along these lines, we maintain that it is more accurate to characterize the history of early modern mysticism as one in which relationships of continuity within transformation occurred. The uses of mystical literature by the Antinomian Grindletonian sect of the 1620s and 1630s, for example, has been described as a reading of "their mystical sources through the spectacles of militant Puritanism in order to produce their own distinct and prophetic message. Defiantly Protestant, the Grindletonians claimed the legacy of the Reformation seen as they advanced perfectionist ideas that were anathema to the mainstream reformed tradition."[13] Rather than focus on the departures of the sixteenth-century Reformation from medieval traditions, the essays in this volume explore one of the most remarkable yet still underexplored chapters in its history: the survival and transformation of mysticism between the late Middle Ages and the early modern period.[14] We do not agree that the Reformation was "mysticism's failure," and hold that such pessimism—"Mysticism as a category cannot easily or unproblematically cross from the medieval to the early modern; it cannot carry the weight of this crossing while retaining its purity as a historical category"—is not only unwarranted but misplaced.[15]

The volume thus offers a reassessment of medieval mysticism as it makes its way across the imaginary divide constructed by the historiography of the Reformation. By mysticism we mean in particular the tradition of thirteenth- and fourteenth-century texts articulating affective piety, the *via negativa*, and the accompanying devotional practices. Within the ambit of this tradition, one important theme of historical continuity is the relationship between mysticism and the concept of religious reform. Mysticism after Luther was not, these essays argue, a quaint survival of a bygone era, merely a significant remnant of an old tradition in a post-reformed world, or, as Michel de Certeau would have it, a discourse predicated on a registering of the loss of unity and religious integration that was the Reformation.[16]

Rather, as the essays here show, later engagements with mysticism can be said to *respond* to and even *extend* the ideas of their medieval predecessors. In the writings of a mystic like Mechthild of Magdeburg (1210–82), for example, the experience of the divine is conveyed by and through multiple subject positions, which has the effect of subordinating the subject position of the mystic herself.[17] This openness with regard to subjectivity is the condition of possibility for later mystical expression, which, as Sarah Apetrei argues in this volume, created a space during the early Enlightenment for the exploration of radical political ideas, religious epistemology, human subjectivity, and the nature of God. Mysticism became no less than the means by which modern epistemological questions were framed: "something that in the medieval context is quite narrowly framed by the context of monastic practices of reading takes shape as a model for the experience of the self and the world."[18] As Euan K. Cameron shows in his essay, while mysticism's place in the array of different ways of knowing God (together with tradition, reason, and authoritative text) was upset by the confessional struggles of the sixteenth century, so that its status was troubled and associated with heresy in every confession, it nonetheless survived to hold its own particular place across Western Christendom.

It is the thesis of this volume that there is a relationship between this phenomenon—the persistence and longevity of mystical thinking—and the politics surrounding debates about how best to love God. In his disputes with the Anabaptists, Luther's aim was to limit the sphere in which, within new frames for thinking and feeling, the Bible could be interpreted. His fear was that a mystical reading of the Bible would function as a motor of destructive social revolution. In addition, mystical tradition and its texts could be used against Lutheran sola-scripturalism; in some instances, the witness of revelation turned the scripture into an allegory, contrary to the literalism beloved of the Lutherans. For his part, the mature Luther came to see mysticism as a dangerously self-centered as well as unscriptural practice, although earlier in his career, aspects of the *Theologia deutsch* had seemed to him and others to articulate his theology of justification.[19] A battery of further pre-, post-, and Counter-Reformation texts functioned in a similarly ambivalent way; this is a canon that is still being recovered.[20]

Some of the later texts in fact go beyond the old mystical synthesis and begin to look like documents of enthusiasm, and incorporated alchemical elements; Familist texts (those associated with Hendrik Niclaes) and especially Jakob Böhme's writings played a sometimes major role here as an influence, as we will see. The devotional writings of the Lutheran Johann Arndt (1555–1621), often seen as precursor of Pietism, also recuperated pre-Reformation mystical works.[21]

The early modern enthusiasts' bodily experience of divine presence can also be seen as an extension of medieval mystical writing in which the mystical union between the soul and God is experienced by and inscribed on a signifying body. By the late seventeenth century there would be new versions of female spirituality where the body would be regarded as a medium of religious experience in hitherto unarticulated ways, as Franz M. Eybl's essay in this volume shows with regard to Catharina Regina von Greiffenberg. Furthermore, self-experience would find expression in extremely learned literary, theological, and philosophical terms, but also elsewhere in contexts dogged by allegations of sexual scandal.[22] In this theological aesthetic (as was the case with some medieval mystics), pain plays a central role as a lens that concentrated mystical experience, making for some of the most compelling writing.[23] By making such claims for illumination, the enthusiast claimed to be where the mystic struggled to go but could never quite reach.

Perhaps not surprisingly, mysticism survived into the early modern period more readily inside domains where Catholicism remained dominant: notably in Spain, France, parts of the German-speaking world, and the Italian peninsula.[24] Much has been written of the career of mysticism with regard to its status within the Roman Catholic Church. New work in this area examines critical ruminations on mysticism from within the Roman Church, such as the German Jesuit Maximilianus Sandaeus's *Pro theologica mystica clavis* (1640).[25] The essays in this volume focus on mysticism in states that became Protestant, or where Protestantism was for some time powerful: the northern European areas of the Netherlands, the German principalities, and England. In these places, where the Reformation is perceived pervasively as a break or rupture with the past, the Reformation era and post-Reformation history of mysticism is far less well known or acknowledged.

In addition, the essays in this volume build on and expand the discoveries of scholarship on medieval mystical writings that have appeared during the past three decades. For example, there has been increased attention to mystical writings by twelfth- through fourteenth-century religious women.[26] A review of this scholarship reveals a central paradox relevant to our overall focus on the relationship between the articulation of divine love and political action: much interest in medieval women mystics and vernacular religious movements has focused on the transgressive or anticlerical sentiments often voiced in these texts.[27] However, while many of these individuals were transgressing cultural conventions in taking on the task of writing religious didactic texts, what they wrote was orthodox. The anticlerical sentiments were addressed to corrupt priests and to disingenuous worshipers. Mystics like Hildegard of Bingen and Mechthild of Magdeburg were not interested in *changing* doctrine, rather they were interested in a *return*—specifically, a return to *more* orthodox observance of religious practice.[28] Put another way, the impulse to reform that is often a central part of mystical writing seems transgressive because developing a personal relationship with God could be seen to bypass clerical mediation—it is this aspect of mystical discourse that captures Critchley's interest described above—but in particular the woman mystic often pursues this connection under the supervision of a confessor and in so doing, strives for a more conservative orthodoxy, a deeper embrace of religious practice and belief, not a break with doctrine. Moreover, this contradiction produces another: the impulse to reform in late medieval and early modern religious contexts has led to the emergence of vibrant cultures of literary production and exchange in which women play central roles. Reform is not necessarily about some kind of advance or progress; yet reform engenders writing and activism among women; reform is about conserving and observing orthodoxy, yet according to orthodox doctrine, women were not supposed to speak or teach. This aspect of the phenomenon of medieval mysticism among women is part of their appeal to post-Reformation figures. Not surprisingly, then, seven out of the twelve essays in this volume focus on mystical writing by women, for women, or about women. The increased literary production and circulation of devotional writing documented in the fifteenth century, especially in connection with women involved with the Observant Reform movement, has its analogue in the concerns of essays like Schepers's and Christensen's in this volume.[29] They chart later patterns of dissemination of mystical writing, much of it by women, but within the new context of broader circulation enabled by print and the risks that that new culture brought. While Eybl's essay explores Greiffenberg's version of the focus on the body as a medium for mystical experience, Wiggin's essay documents the ongoing problem associated with the inherent activism of women's radical embrace of mystical devotion—the problem of female speech that is so often marked by erasure and silence in the sources.

Despite some of the medieval sources' disclaimers about their agency or political aims, the essays in this volume tell the story of late medieval and early modern mysticism as inherently political (Marotti, Apetrei), proclaiming a politics of subjectivity (Gertz, Eybl, Wiggins, Largier) as well as problematizing the role of the image (Hamburger-Keller). For both time periods, mysticism provides ways to construct the self in the divine scheme of things that are alternative to the teachings of tradition, rational theology, and scripture. Within the medieval period, these alternatives could be contained within the dominant structures of the church in contrast to the dominant structures of belief offered by post-reformed national churches and the post-Reformation Church of Rome, all of which had problems accommodating mysticism. The essays here explore both these continuities and differences, and in so doing, challenge the terms in which the history of Western mysticism has been written.

While there has been a significant amount of scholarship on mystical writings in both medieval and early modern studies, very little has appeared that considers the two in conjunction with one another. The publication of James Simpson's provocative book *Burning to Read: English Fundamentalism and its Reformation Opponents* suggests that the time is ripe for a re-examination not only of what mysticism entails in both periods, but also of that to which it lays foundation.[30] Simpson makes a case for seeing sixteenth-century reformist rhetoric in England as a religious fundamentalism that had widespread violent consequences and not as the "grounding moment of liberalism" it has generally been taken to be. "Extremely powerful traditions of Western historiography," he argues, "continue to see this Lutheran moment as fundamentally positive and inspiring: the liberal tradition grounds itself in Luther's defiance as an individual against the power and threat of an institution" (23). Yet, as Simpson points out, Luther himself advocated asserting and defending his evangelism to the death even if the whole world were thrown into strife and confusion as a result (21). Similarly, much work on the mystical writers of the Middle Ages focuses on the radicalism of their retreat from institutional structures of thought and practice. As mentioned above, scholars have been drawn to and have perceived these moments of radicalism and resistance in religion without always acknowledging the not so attractive (or not so liberal) elements. Early modern mysticism was not usually connected with violence (although some of the early Anabaptists who did advocate and engage in armed conflict, such as Thomas Müntzer, cited mystical writers, and have been regarded as mystics);[31] it did, however, connect with practices of severe self-regulation, self-denial, or self-punishment that have much to do with medieval piety.

One recent study that does cross period lines is Michael Kessler and Christian Sheppard's 2003 edited collection *Mystics: Presence and Aporia*, which features theoretical discussions and coverage from Dionysius the Areopagite to Bataille as well as modern film and other media culture.[32] Authors and other figures not usually or mainly associated with mysticism find their place in the book: Aquinas, Joan of Arc, George Herbert, Hegel, Blanchot. While much about this book is novel and exciting, pushing the boundaries of what may be termed mystical, its broad approach seems to imply that nearly everything involves mysticism. Elsewhere we can see leapfrogging of the early modern period as contemporary perspectives are put into dialogue with ancient and mostly earlier medieval mysticism.[33] Other studies on the early modern period invoke mysticism as a sub-compartment of a dominant but finally very different theme: the making of absolutist monarchy.[34] The essays that follow aim to offer a more coherent picture: the centerground of Western mysticism, mostly apophatic, the understanding that the conscious self has to be "annihilated" in order for a believer to experience union with the godhead, as that tradition was put under pressure by major transformations of religious and social practice between the sixteenth and eighteenth centuries. They deal primarily with negative, or apophatic, mysticism, with the centrality of the mystical text to mystical practice, and, within the domain of the text, with the definition of the image. With regard to the latter theme, the interest is in the extent to which mystical experience defies imagery, and the way the image itself relates to personal interiority, as Hamburger and Keller argue. This collection thus reorders the understanding of mysticism at a crucial stage in its history—1400 to 1750—and offers it as a central component of both pre-modern and modern experience in the making. To that extent, there is in the essays dealing with the latter end of the collection's chronological coverage more than a hint that mysticism contributes to the role of religion in the formation of the early novel.[35]

The volume begins by asking: in what contexts did these transformations of mystical tradition belong? Euan K. Cameron shows that mysticism and the quest for mystical, intuitive illumination by the divine have never existed in isolation from other ways of knowing in Christian culture. At the end of the Middle Ages theologians were profoundly interested in the relationship between the different means of apprehending the divine. Tradition, reason, authoritative text, and the illumination of the Holy Spirit had their respective places. The Reformation debates disrupted this delicate balance between the different means to knowledge. In the controversies over scripture, tradition, and reason, personal illumination tended to lose credit. To Protestants it suggested a too familiar relationship between sinful humanity and God; for Catholics it threatened to disrupt the world of hierarchy and obedience that the Council of Trent consolidated. To both it carried a suggestion of dangerous sectarianism.

Yet in the world of confessional orthodoxy, dominated by theological systems, creedal formulas, and pastoral discipline, intuitive reaching for the divine kept its place. Cameron's essay reflects on the multiple trajectories that link late medieval and early modern religious epistemologies and explores the multiple pathways by which, after decades of dogmatic strife, the mystical instinct rediscovered itself in early modernity.

Precisely in this way Alana King shows how Meister Eckhart's notion of *Gelassenheit* (a state of detachment) survived in the later sixteenth-century Lutheran Valentin Weigel's work, retained in some ways, transformed in others, and so hidden (since Weigel's works were not published in his lifetime) that it only began to have an influence, and to raise objections among evangelical Lutherans, after Weigel's death. Weigel's notion of *Gelassenheit* meant that the center of reformation had to be the soul (where the loss of "self" took place), not the church or any other social institution. If such a reformation took place in those external places, war would be the only consequence. As King makes clear, Weigel's logic of mysticism meant that church and state were finally unnecessary to the work of salvation, and the former at least might be jettisoned. Of course such a challenging realization was a red flag to Luther, Calvin, and other magisterial reformers.

On the other hand, mysticism flourished in a thoroughly renewed way within the Catholic Church and in anticipation of the Counter-Reformation. In his essay in this volume, Kees Schepers explores the significance of the Saint Agnes Convent in the Netherlandish city of Arnhem, which in the seventeenth century became a center of fervent mystical culture that was firmly rooted in the works of the fourteenth-century Brabantine and Rhineland mystics Ruysbroeck, Eckhart, Tauler, and Suso. Focusing on a set of 162 sermons composed within and for the convent, Schepers shows how the practice of mysticism at this convent, in conjunction with the connection between the convent and the Cologne Carthusians, can be viewed as a kind of mystical renaissance. Schepers demonstrates also how the sermons develop inherited medieval mystical traditions by combining two types of mysticism that in the fourteenth century had been distinct—the Brabantine love mysticism of Ruysbroeck and the Rhineland speculative mysticism of Eckhart. The *Arnhem Mystical Sermons* clearly manifest knowledge and understanding of both traditions, and bring about a synthesis of these two schools of mysticism.

Schepers makes sense of this phenomenon in light of the Catholic revival stimulated in this region by the Carthusians. This movement started well before the official Counter-Reformation (but also through the period in which Arnhem would become part of the officially Protestant Dutch republic), and was directed not so much against the Protestant Reformation as at internal renewal. It gave birth not to modernity but, he maintains, to a mystical renaissance based on a newfound connection with the classics of late medieval Flemish and German mysticism.

The continued flourishing of Rhineland mysticism in the Netherlands of the sixteenth and seventeenth centuries is also Kirsten M. Christensen's interest. Her essay considers *The Right Path to Evangelical Perfection* (*Der rechte wech zo der evangelischen volkomenheit*), a collection of treatises and letters attributed to a beguine, Maria van Hout (d. 1547), in conjunction with a treatise on the Eucharist included in *The Paradise of Loving Souls* (*Dat Paradijs der lieffhavender sielen*), a set of mystical treatises that was published in Low German under the editorship of the Cologne Carthusians in 1532 and again in 1535 in Middle Dutch. Focusing on the letters to her confessor in *The Right Path*, Christensen shows how Maria is caught between the theologies of *imitatio Christi* (the wholehearted embrace of suffering as a way to union with Christ) and obedience to the church in the person of the confessor. Christensen discusses how the tension between these two poles emerges in Maria's discussions with her confessor about sacramental communion. In this text, and then further developed in the treatise in *Paradise*, Maria claims that the "Eucharistic presence of the Lord is constantly available" to those who have experienced mystical union even when they are not permitted to receive the actual wafer during Mass.[36] Christensen argues that this theology of the Eucharist acts as a counterbalance to her confessor and other clergy who tended to be overly controlling of women's devotional practices and especially of their access to sacramental communion. Christensen concludes her essay with a discussion of a devotional exercise on spiritual communion that is found in a manuscript from the convent discussed in Schepers's essay (Saint Agnes in Arnhem). This exercise can be seen as evidence of the circulation of Maria's writings, according to Christensen, and the dissemination of Maria's other writings by the Carthusians in this area attests to the importance and significance of this theology for the Catholic response to reformation. As Christensen deftly shows, "the Carthusians promoted Maria and the sisters of the Arnhem community as models of interiority and sanctity for a church that needed, most of all, to turn inward if it was to survive." Mysticism was the way to ground a healthy and necessary interiority that would have to precede any true reform, as a fit preparation for the Eucharist (itself regarded as a mystical experience, a direct physical encounter with Christ) or a spiritual substitute for it, and a means to resist false religion. Christensen's examination of both the reception context and the content of these texts thus reveals the fascinating extent to which mysticism had become, by the sixteenth century, a powerful tool for reform both of familiar devotional material and of the spiritual life of the Catholic Church.

That mysticism could be seen as a threat to the regulation of devotional life of both communities and individuals is evident a century later in women's writing that was a central part of the English Roman Catholic world. The great-granddaughter of Sir (or Saint) Thomas More, Dame Gertrude (née Helen) More combined in her life as a nun a rebellious and humbly submissive spirit, practical acumen and contemplative withdrawal from worldly preoccupations, saintly "idiocy" and intellectual rigor. The contemplative and mystical practices she learned from her spiritual mentor, the Benedictine Dom Augustine Baker (one of the key preservers of the medieval mystical canon), helped her resolve the contradictions in her life and empowered her devotion in peculiarly Catholic ways. Examining both More's own writings and Baker's biography of her, Arthur F. Marotti's essay discusses her personal practices of contemplation and mystical devotion, found in the posthumously published work *The Spiritual Exercises of the Most Vertvous and Religious D. Gertrude More . . . And Ideots Deuotions* (Paris, 1658), in the context of English Catholic exile culture and the traditions of mystical writing by which her devotional practices were shaped.[37] Like Maria van Hout before her, More struggles with the structures of authority and hierarchy within a church that also grants her the autonomy to experience God on her own. Marotti highlights specific aspects of her resistance to these structures, which clearly bears the traces of earlier mystics, but which takes on new significance within her situation as a Catholic exile.

Despite the attempts to exile Catholics and the religious practices associated with them after the Reformation in Protestant countries or regions, the role of women's piety in the practice and transformation of mysticism is evident within Protestantism, too. Beginning with an analysis of late medieval religious culture in England, Genelle C. Gertz argues that it privileges prophetic authority, both in vernacular religious texts and in models of sainthood, especially the lives of female saints. She goes on to consider the Reformation's seeming repression of this prophetic privilege, focusing on reformed conceptions of the Bible as the only source of revelation, and, in the context of lay response to scripture, Queen Elizabeth I's suppression of individual "prophesying" after sermons. Moving forward to the Interregnum, and the rise of sectarianism as well as the dissolution of the national church, Gertz takes up Quakerism's privileging of the "Inner Light" above scripture (although by no means accepted by all Quakers), what Geoffrey Nuttall identifies as the Puritan conception of the Holy Spirit separated from scripture, and revealed as the actual source of divinity rather than the text itself. Like Nuttall, Thomas Betteridge is right to worry that Quaker language might automatically be classified as mysticism, even in the case of an extremely enthusiastic Quaker like James Nayler. Nuttall saw nonetheless a relationship here and before raising his qualification query, Betteridge calls Quakerism "embodied mysticism."[38] Though Quakers' words derive from the Bible, they are understood to flow from God directly; they only sound like scripture because scripture has captured something of divinity. Finally, the essay discusses to what extent the Quaker conception of prophetic authority returns to, or recovers, late medieval understandings of prophecy or revelation. Should Quakerism be seen as the correction of Puritanism's trust in *sola scriptura*, and thus a consequence of Puritanism, or does it in some way recapture late medieval openness to visionary experience, especially extra-biblical forms?

Just as the Quakers developed a religion that redefined the role of women's relationships with men, so other groups within the Church of England in the later seventeenth century were marked by a new prominence of women as prophets and scriptural commentators, even as they propounded new theologies and cosmologies and explicitly returned to mysticism. Sarah Apetrei's chapter presents mystical theology as a vital force in the early English Enlightenment, tracing its influence from the Platonist revival at Cambridge through to the mystical movements of the early eighteenth century. Apetrei suggests that, far from representing a withdrawal from intellectual life and external affairs, mysticism created a space in which radical ideas about religious epistemology, human subjectivity, and the nature of God became possible. Apetrei focuses on the connections between three theologians of the later seventeenth century who drew together the threads of mystical and rational discourses: the Quaker George Keith, the Anglican and Tory Mary Astell, and Richard Roach of the Philadelphian Society. Based on this analysis, she argues that the same mystical currents that shaped some radical religion before and after 1640 also shaped Anglican theology, and formed an important context for some of the major controversies of the early Enlightenment in England.

Many of the subjects in Apetrei's discussion were familiar with or, in the case of the Philadelphians, disciples of the complicated and voluminous visionary writings of the Lusatian mystic Jakob Böhme (1575–1624).[39] Böhme's writings, translated into Dutch and English from the original German within four decades of their author's death, clearly caused a sea change in the way in which mysticism was understood and appreciated across Europe. It may be said that the extensive fusion of contemplative and practical, theological, alchemical, and medical elements, on such a prolix and to most readers mystifying scale, produced a *goût* for a new and absorbing mystical hermeneutics. "Theosophy" in the modern sense was born, and mysticism took a significant step further away from its roots in medieval monastic practice. Böhme incorporated the apophatic tradition within his eclectic synthesis, and while some of his earlier followers, such as John Pordage, Thomas Tany, and Thomas Tryon, have been intensely studied, we include here two essays that register the cultural transformation engendered by Böhme's writings, once his impact had begun to be felt in a wider way, no longer restricted to small groups of cult followers.[40]

A broader kind of mysticism also pervaded English Roman Catholic worship in the seventeenth century, one that was more akin to medieval bridal mysticism than the apophatic traditions taken up by the figures discussed up to this point. The "original psalm"—a pastiche of the Psalms and other biblical poetry—is strongly associated with post-Reformation English Catholic writing, in part because Catholics came to see vernacular metrical psalms as characteristically Protestant. They feature most prominently in the imaginative liturgies composed by John Austin, possibly for the Catholic literary circle centered on Tixall in Staffordshire. Published under the title *Devotions in the Ancient Way of Offices* in 1668, these achieved a wide circulation among Catholics, conforming Anglicans and—later—nonjurors, becoming one of the most popular devotional books of the late seventeenth and early eighteenth centuries.[41] Mimicking the breviary but directly addressing the plight of threatened religious groups, Austin's liturgies were intended for semi-public delivery and would have lent themselves well to the type of worship practiced by religious societies. His original psalms, in particular, seek to arouse a punitive spiritual intimacy among their users, which can be seen as substituting for auricular confession in an environment where priests were often hard to come by; Austin was associated with the Blackloist movement, the group of English Roman Catholics led by Thomas White who sought greater independence for English Catholics from both papal authority and the Jesuits, and demonstrates here its inventive concern to respond to England's particular challenges by empowering lay Catholics.[42]

Users who publicly repeated Austin's often merciless analysis of sinful thought-processes, several times a day, would have experienced a shared, heightened spiritual intimacy among themselves. This, in turn, would have fed off the qualitative distinction between psalms and other forms of religious verse; psalms were often perceived as a "seraphic" discourse that brought one uniquely close to the divine. Hence, Austin—like some modernist pioneers of free verse—shuns metrical convention in pursuit of a counter-cultural, transcendent experience so that the liturgy was enabling mystical experience to be public and shared yet with a very strong connection with private, incommunicable experience; but, true to his beliefs and environment, this was seen as being unachievable without continued penance.

Austin's writings were also part of religious worship and explicitly connected with bodily deportment during worship. Mystical literature that was undoubtedly part of the apophatic tradition was no less concerned with the body. Franz M. Eybl's essay deals with the conceptualization and interpretation of the body as a medium of spirituality in the Baroque mysticism of Catharina Regina von Greiffenberg (1633–94). These concepts of body-focused spirituality have been much neglected until now, but they are of central significance for the construction of mystical thought in the early modern period. Diverse currents of Baroque mysticism and Pietism develop forms of female spirituality in which the body functions as an important medium of religious experience, particularly experience of the divine in the self. Describing mystical experience as it affects or feels in the body is not new—this is quite common for medieval mystics—but here we see a much more specific sense of the body and its anatomy coming into play in the recorded experience of divine presence and absence. In this context the range of body experience includes intensified sensibility and emotionality, paralysis through loss of muscle control, anorexia, (visions of) stigmatization, (real or imagined) self-injuries, and experiences of pain, in particular internal organs as well as extraordinary images and concepts of self-redemption.

Eybl's essay provides a detailed account of the way the imagery and "presence" of the (female) body in language come to the fore in the work of Catharina Regina von Greiffenberg. Providing close readings of several of her most extraordinary poems and prose writing from the *Passionsbetrachtungen* (Meditations on the Passion), Eybl shows how Greiffenberg's poetry can be seen as a kind of literal staging of the bodily experience of mysticism in language. The poems are shown to have a pulsating rhythm akin to the back-and-forth of the mystical connection. Further, what has already been noted for some medieval mystical discourse associated with women, namely that the imagery and poetics take on an erotic cast, becomes more explicitly sexual in Greiffenberg's poetics. Eybl argues indeed for a "specifically female form of religious and esoteric representation" that is also described as a "very specific form of gendering." This is because, according to Eybl, Greiffenberg's understanding of female physical processes like procreation—an understanding reflected in the imagery of mystical interaction and union—corresponds to seventeenth-century conceptions of anatomy and the body. Eybl then concludes his essay by showing how the striking female imagery exhibited in her poems is excised in an edition of religious poetry produced just a few years later by Johann Reinhard Hedinger in 1702.

The traditions of Baroque mysticism and Pietism were present among the eighteenth-century German emigrants to Pennsylvania, and in particular the Ephrata community, where, incidentally, some of Jakob Böhme's works were first published in America.[43] Long obscured by the shadow of more famous men, the evidence for women's contributions in this context occurs at the intersection of what are now reinvigorated areas of scholarly inquiry: female religious authority and mystical experience in German radical Pietism, cultural transfer and encounters between religious radicals in the Old and New Worlds, and women's life worlds in colonial North America. Drawing on an array of manuscript and printed sources, Bethany Wiggin seeks to explore a nearly unknown early German colonist's mental and material universe.

In stark contrast to the case of Greiffenberg outlined by Eybl, Wiggin's essay traces fleeting glimpses of Marie Christine Sauer amid the crossfire exchanged between two of colonial Greater Pennsylvania's most well-known German-speaking residents: her sometimes husband, prominent Germantown printer Christoph Sauer (1695–1758; the first German-language printer and publisher in America), and her occasional spiritual leader, Conrad Beissel (1690–1768), founder of the Ephrata cloister. Emigrating from Germany in 1720, by 1726 the Sauer family had moved to a farm on the western frontier in Conestoga County, Pennsylvania, where they heard Beissel preach. In 1732 Marie Christine left her family to join Beissel's nascent community of religious celibates on the banks of Cocalico Creek, the settlement that became the Ephrata cloister. Marie Christine did not remain in the cloister, however, returning to her husband and spending the rest of her life with him.

Wiggin examines the conflicts among the German religious leaders in the area through various publications and reads them against the Ephrata chronicle, or "sisterbook," which is completely silent about Marie Christine's presence in the community, perhaps precisely because she left it. This approach to the material enables Wiggin to consider the paradox of women's participation in eighteenth-century religious movements and debates: "only in the chronicle's circular loops around that which cannot be said does the absence of Marie Christine Sauer take on any presence."

In the penultimate chapter, Jeffrey F. Hamburger and Hildegard Elisabeth Keller bring the central issues of the collection together as they explore the return to mysticism after the Reformation, a return motivated by a desire to address with more profundity the relationship between inner and outer selves or perceived states of being. This essay suggests approaching the relationship between mysticism and modernity by investigating the relationship between images and interiority. The history of interiority as it was constructed and cultivated in the Western mystical tradition grants images a critical role. Within the context of a spectrum of possibilities, the Reformation is often construed as an assault on the imaginative culture of late medieval Catholicism, and it is on this basis that it becomes possible to make connections between Protestantism and some of the more radical forms of medieval mysticism. To oppose the iconic and aniconic in this fashion, however, is too simple. The two conceptions of the image—inner as well as outer—remained as inseparably intertwined in Reformation polemic as in medieval mysticism. Focusing on the transition from the Middle Ages to modernity, and building on a selection of primary sources—sermons by Meister Eckhart, the debates of the Second Zürich Disputation, and some early modern emblems—the authors turn to issues of historiography and the semantics of the inner and outer image to provide a critique of the concept of interiority as it has been deployed in the historical discourse on mysticism, which, they note, is itself a modern term.

In all these debates, modern as well as medieval, the heart as the seat of true interiority provides the battleground. Interiority becomes something of a cipher, an empty space that both sides seek to occupy by expelling not only images, but also their opponents, whose placement outside the "truth" permits the individual to claim that interior space for herself. Just as the early Christians claimed that Jews saw only the letter, not the spirit, so too Protestants characterized Catholics as "Judaizers" mired in empty, exterior rituals. Protestants, in turn, quarreled among themselves as to who was the Judaizer and what was more important: eradicating exterior images or expelling them from the interior space of the heart. In all these debates, each side paradoxically laid claim to and reused imagery inherited from the other. Abandoning images was the watchword, yet the image of the heart persisted, indeed, proliferated. And the battle over inner space continues to this day. Such a focus points to the persistence of the importance of the meaning of imagery in mystical thought, even while the image itself is being radically eliminated, not so much as part of iconoclasm but as a necessary sensory obliteration that must come with the *Gelassenheit* that precedes *unio mystica*.

Finally, we come to Niklaus Largier's essay, which takes us from negative theology to modern aesthetics. In other recently published work, Largier has explained the influence of medieval mysticism on modern philosophy and literature, and the explicit fascination of some modern philosophers with the mystics, in a line that runs from Hegel to Heidegger and on to Derrida.[44] The connection of a rise of interest in mysticism as a response to the social and political turbulence of the earlier twentieth century is acknowledged in many studies.[45] The mystics, say the moderns, articulated modern subjectivity and described its relationship with God and nature. That inheritance was profoundly shaped by the early modern reception of mysticism, not least Luther's attempts to control or suppress some aspects of mystical teaching. Largier discusses late medieval attempts to delimit the practices of vernacular mystical hermeneutics and Luther's efforts to frame acceptable practices of reading the scriptures in his writings against the radical reformers. Largier thus focuses on the ways in which mysticism informed sixteenth- and seventeenth-century culture: ways that can be seen as both a continuation and a break with the medieval tradition. Luther was of necessity bridling discourses that honored the teachings of the sensations. By his action, they were elevated in the early modern period from a devotional to an epistemological framework. Luther achieved this transformation by defining mysticism through a constructivist model for the experience of the self and the world, and by playing the largest part in the severance of mysticism from its context of monastic practice, especially prayer, meditation, liturgy, and the reading of the scriptures. Luther was trying to limit a movement that was facilitated by vernacular scriptural interpretation and the invention of the printing press (just as were his own teachings). Devoid of their liturgical and hermeneutical location in monastic practice on the one hand, and from their inflammatory political eschatological meaning on the other (the *Schwärmer* interpretation of mysticism), these texts and the mystical practices of prayer and contemplation turn into something new, namely the basis for what we could call an experimental mysticism that is explored in its many forms from the sixteenth to the twentieth centuries. Since it no longer has its place within an authorized hermeneutics and since its subversive political and eschatological power has been neutralized through the distinction between secular and spiritual, the mystical tropes are set free to be used in a different realm, a realm that we could call an experiential supplement to the spiritual freedom of a Christian. Further examples in Largier's work are drawn from Eckhart, Porete, Gerson, Müntzer, Böhme, Angelus Silesius, Leibniz, Greiffenberg, von Klettenberg, Novalis, and Musil.

At the twentieth-century end of this line is also Georges Bataille, harnessing mysticism for its ability to go "beyond limits": "In Bataille's understanding the mystical texts do so in a response to the challenges of negative theology, focusing on the very practices that allow for the production of experience and for a phenomenology of experience where knowledge fails and always has to fail."[46] To engage in this kind of thought is always to fail to know. What did this mean in detail? The meditative practices of the high Middle Ages evolved, argues Largier, into the notions of mystical ascent in the later Middle Ages. Here prayer is understood to produce an overwhelming arousal of the affects so that one forgets why one is praying in the first place. Prayer is not for petitioning God but to reach a state of the soul's arousal, as purgation, illumination, and union are successively reached. These experiential states of awareness involve the senses of taste and touch rather than of sight, and constitute a regaining of perception lost at the fall. Furthermore, in the hands of the Franciscans, "a new affirmative mode with regard to sense experience itself and to an aesthetic justification of the world" was discovered. This was an emotional world, registering sensations of hopelessness and desolation as well as hope and joy. Consciousness for the mystic was denaturalized through prayer and then renaturalized as an aesthetic experience within the terms of the "phenomenology of literary affects." In the Baroque period, Largier argues, this phenomenology became a form of poetic experimentation that was also an "art of living" and then part of eighteenth-century philosophical discussion of the notion of the "art of the soul," of which we have several examples in the subject matter of this collection, before its eventual appeal to the decadents and their successors on account of the insistence that rationality must be exceeded in the name of experience.

There is something in negative theology that might be described as a very intensely accelerated reformation, one that the magisterial Reformation of Luther and Calvin found to be too much. But the apophatic tradition found its way through the Reformation, redefined and reshaped, engendering significant aspects of early modern politics and piety. Strikingly, it is also shown to play a role in establishing the building material of modern aesthetics. Mysticism is defined as precisely *not* to be the thing that was left behind at the great "break" that is called the Reformation. Indeed, as Largier's essay makes abundantly clear, quite the contrary is the case. Although we would not argue that mysticism is "everywhere," this book demonstrates the significant extent to which mystical discourse is not only an integral part of the intellectual history of the West but also deeply embedded in the way we talk about and understand ourselves today. In that respect, the place of mysticism deserves a more exacting framework of appreciation today, as it traveled into the modern world, than the recuperation of remote mystical theology or a more incendiary "mystical anarchism." Such a framework might help a "politics of love" to be acknowledged, understood, and even realized more broadly and effectively in our world, across confessions and between cultures.

Notes

1. Simon Critchley, "Mystical Anarchism," http://www.adbusters.org/magazine/102/mystical-anarchism.html, accessed May 11, 2012.

2. Simon Critchley, *The Faith of the Faithless: Experiments in Political Theology* (London: Verso, 2012), 11.

3. Critchley, *Faith of the Faithless*, 12.

4. Raoul Vaneigem, *The Movement of the Free Spirit: General Considerations and Firsthand Testimony Concerning Some Brief Flowerings of Life in the Middle Ages, the Renaissance, and, Incidentally, Our Own Time* (New York: Zone, 1994), 91.

5. Laurence Clarkson, *A Single Eye All Light No Darkness* (1650), in *A Collection of Ranter Writings from the Seventeenth Century*, ed. Nigel Smith (London: Junction, 1983), 169–72; and possibly also in the very obscure figurations of Joseph Salmon, *Divinity Anatomiz'd* (London: Giles Calvert, 1649), 7, 10.

6. See B. J. Gibbons, *Gender in Mystical and Occult Thought: Behmenism and its Development in England* (Cambridge: Cambridge University Press, 1996), 9, 152; Stephen C. Taysom, *Shakers, Mormons, and Religious Worlds: Conflicting Visions, Contested Boundaries* (Bloomington: Indiana University Press, 2011), chapter 3.

7. See Vaneigem, *Movement of the Free Spirit*, chapter 3; see also J. L. Davis, "Mystical Versus Enthusiastic Sensibility," *Journal of the History of Ideas* 4, no. 3 (1943): 301–19.

8. Steven E. Ozment, *Mysticism and Dissent; Religious Ideology and Social Protest in the Sixteenth Century* (New Haven, Conn.: Yale University Press, 1973).

9. Leszek Kołakowski, *Chrétiens sans Église: la conscience religieuse et le lien confessionnel au XVIIe siècle* (Paris: Gallimard, 1969).

10. Berndt Hamm, "Volition and Inadequacy as a Topic in Late Medieval Pastoral Care of Penitents," in *Reformation of Faith in the Context of Late Medieval Theology and Piety: Essays by Berndt Hamm*, ed. Robert James Bast (Leiden: Brill, 2004), 108.

11. Views of the English Reformation range from a revolutionary conclusion to a series of religious reformations, each successively demonstrating an evolution of the relationship between church, monarch, and Parliament.

Continuities in scholastic theology, political institutions, and poetic form are among those discussed in extant scholarship: see James Simpson, *Reform and Cultural Revolution: The Oxford English Literary History*, vol. 2, *1350–1547* (Oxford: Clarendon, 2004); idem, "English Reformations: Historiography, Theology, and Narrative," *Journal of Medieval and Early Modern Studies* 40, no. 3 (2010): 262–71. On the Continent, the fourteenth and fifteenth centuries saw the so-called Observant movement take hold in almost all of the existing religious orders and make many of the critiques of the church institution later attributed to Luther. For an overview, see the essays in Kaspar Elm, ed., *Reformbemühungen und Observanzbestrebungen im spätmittelalterlichen Ordenswesen* (Berlin: Duncker & Humblot, 1989).

12. Kołakowski, *Chrétiens sans Église*.

13. David R. Como, *Blown by the Spirit: Puritanism and the Emergence of an Antinomian Underground in Pre-Civil-War England* (Stanford, Calif.: Stanford University Press, 2004), 43.

14. A desideratum for future research expressed in the conclusion of a recent essay on Marguerite Porete by Juan Marin. Marin suggests that his "exploration of beguine theology helps us to begin to approach an unresolved dilemma: How, and why, did the medieval language of annihilation and deification haunt Europe even during the throes that gave birth to modernity?" Juan Marin, "Annihilation and Deification in Beguine Theology and Marguerite Porete's *Mirror of Simple Souls*," *Harvard Theological Review* 103, no. 1 (2010): 89–109, at 109.

15. Thomas Betteridge, "Vernacular Theology," in *Cultural Reformations: Medieval and Renaissance in Literary History*, ed. Brian Cummings and James Simpson (Oxford: Oxford University Press), 189–90.

16. Michel de Certeau, "Mystic Speech," in idem, *Heterologies: Discourse on the Other*, trans. Brian Massumi (Minneapolis: University of Minnesota Press, 1986), 80.

17. On Mechthild, see Sara S. Poor, *Mechthild of Magdeburg and Her Book: Gender and the Making of Textual Authority* (Philadelphia: University of Pennsylvania Press, 2004), and Amy Hollywood, *The Soul as Virgin Wife: Mechthild of Magdeburg, Marguerite Porete, and Meister Eckhart* (Notre Dame, Ind.: University of Notre Dame Press, 1995).

18. Niklaus Largier, "Mysticism, Modernity, and the Invention of Aesthetic Experience," *Representations* 105, no. 1 (2009): 37–60, here 40.

19. See Largier, "Mysticism, Modernity," 48.

20. See Ozment, *Mysticism and Dissent*; Nigel Smith, *Perfection Proclaimed: Language and Literature in English Radical Religion, 1640–1660* (Oxford: Clarendon, 1989), part II; Como, *Blown by the Spirit*; Ariel Hessayon, *'Gold tried in the fire': The Prophet Theaurau John Tany and the English Revolution* (Aldershot, Vt.: Ashgate, 2007).

21. See esp. Johann Arndt, *Wahres Christentum* (4 books, 1605–10); and Johannes Wallmann, "Johann Arndt und die protestantische Frömmigkeit: Zur Rezeption der mittelalterlichen Mystik im Luthertum," in *Frömmigkeit in der frühen Neuzeit: Studien zur religiösen Literatur des 17. Jahrhunderts in Deutschland*, ed. Dieter Breuer (Amsterdam: Rodopi, 1984), 50–74.

22. Burkhard Dohm, *Poetische Alchimie: Öffnung zur Sinnlichkeit in der Hohelied- und Bibeldichtung von der protestantischen Barockmystik bis zum Pietismus* (Tübingen: Max Niemeyer Verlag, 2000), chapter 2; Paula McDowell, "Enlightenment Enthusiasms and the Spectacular Failure of the Philadelphian Society," *Eighteenth-Century Studies* 35 (2002): 515–33; Nigel Smith, "Pregnant Dreams in Early Modern Europe: The Philadelphian Example," in *The Intellectual Culture of Puritan Women*, ed. Johanna Harris and Elizabeth Scott-Baumann (Houndsmill: Palgrave Macmillan, 2011), 190–201.

23. For example, Hildegard of Bingen, Mechthild of Magdeburg, Angela of Foligno, and Julian of Norwich.

24. For Spain, see, for example, Jessica A. Boon, *The Mystical Science of the Soul: Medieval Cognition in Bernardino De Laredo's Recollection Method* (Toronto: University of Toronto Press, 2012); for France, Michèle Clément, *Une poétique de crise: Poètes baroques et mystiques* (Paris: Honoré Champion, 1996).

25. Aline Smeesters, "Maximilianus Sandaeus, S.J. (1578–1656) as an Explorer of the Mystical Language," Renaissance Society of America, Annual Meeting, San Diego, April 4–6, 2013, Session 30111, *Program and Abstract Book*, 394.

26. A keyword search in the Princeton University library catalogue on "medieval women mystics" resulted in twenty-eight titles, one title from 1989, the rest from 1990 to the present (search made July 24, 2012).

27. For examples of this type of scholarship, see Ulrike Wiethaus, "Sexuality, Gender and the Body in Late Medieval Women's Spirituality: Cases from Germany and the Netherlands," *Journal of Feminist Studies in Religion* 7 (1991): 35–52; Elizabeth Alvida Petroff, *Body and Soul: Essays on Medieval Women and Mysticism* (New York: Oxford University Press, 1994); Monica Furlong, *Visions & Longings: Medieval Women Mystics* (Boston: Shambhala, 1996); Thérèse de Hemptinne and Maria Eugenia Gongora, eds., *The Voice of Silence: Women's Literacy in a Men's Church* (Turnhout: Brepols, 2004). It should be noted that as the discussion of women's mystical texts has become more accepted and even canonical, the scholarship has become increasingly sophisticated and nuanced.

28. Marguerite Porete is an exception, of course. She suffered execution because she would not refrain from circulating her book advocating a relationship with God that did not require the mediation of the church. Michael Sargent, "The Annihilation of Marguerite Porete," *Viator* 28 (1997): 253–79.

29. On the relationship between observance reform and manuscript production, see, for example, Werner Williams-Krapp, "Observanzbewegungen,

monastische Spiritualität und geistliche Literatur im 15. Jahrhundert," *Internationales Archiv für Sozialgeschichte der deutschen Literatur* 20, no. 1 (1995): 1–15. Williams-Krapp's thesis has since been qualified. Klaus Graf, "Ordensreform und Literatur in Augsburg während des 15. Jahrhunderts," in *Literarisches Leben in Augsburg während des 15. Jahrhunderts*, ed. Johannes Janota and Werner Williams-Krapp (Tübingen: Niemeyer, 1995), 100–159. See also the more recent Balázs J. Nemes, "*Dis buch ist iohannes schedelin*: Die Handschriften eines Colmarer Bürgers aus der Mitte des 15. Jahrhunderts und ihre Verflechtungen mit dem Literaturangebot der Dominikanerobservanz," in *Kulturtopographie des deutschsprachigen Südwestens im späteren Mittelalter: Studien und Texte*, ed. Barbara Fleith and René Wetzel (Berlin: de Gruyter, 2009), 157–214, who documents the devotional book production of a secular man. For an assessment of the English context, see A. I. Doyle, "Book Production by the Monastic Orders in England 1375–1530: Assessing the Evidence," in *Medieval Book Production: Assessing the Evidence*, ed. Linda L. Brownrigg (Los Altos Hills, Calif.: Anderson-Lovelace, 1990), 1–19.

30. James Simpson, *Burning to Read: English Fundamentalism and its Reformation Opponents* (Cambridge, Mass.: Belknap Press of Harvard University Press, 2007).

31. Hans-Jürgen Goertz, *Thomas Müntzer: Apocalyptic Mystic and Revolutionary* (Edinburgh: T&T Clark, 1993).

32. Michael Kessler and Christian Sheppard, eds., *Mystics: Presence and Aporia* (Chicago: University of Chicago Press, 2003).

33. See Louise Nelstrop with Kevin Magill and Bradley B. Onishi, *Christian Mysticism: An Introduction to Contemporary Theoretical Approaches* (Farnham, Surrey: Ashgate, 2009).

34. See, for example, Mitchell Greenburg, *Baroque Bodies: Psychoanalysis and the Culture of French Absolutism* (Ithaca, N.Y.: Cornell University Press, 2001), chapter 4.

35. On religious practice and the early novel, see Lori Branch, *Rituals of Spontaneity: Sentiment and Secularism from Free Prayer to Wordsworth* (Waco, Tex.: Baylor University Press, 2006), chapters 1, 2, and 4. A surprising association of mysticism with a much later novel is shown by Niklaus Largier, with his initial quotation of the decadent novelist Huysmans, in his contribution to this collection.

36. See Christensen's essay in this volume.

37. For Baker's work as collector and editor of mystical writings, including his worry that he would sink into obscurity of expression if he attempted an exposition of *The Cloud of Unknowing*, see Betteridge, "Vernacular Theology," 199–200; Elizabeth Dutton, "The Seventeenth-Century Manuscript Tradition and the Influence of Augustine Baker," in *A Cambridge Companion to Julian of Norwich*, ed. Liz Herbert McAvoy (Cambridge: Boydell and Brewer,

2008), 127–38; Nicholas Watson, "Despair," in *Cultural Reformations: Medieval and Renaissance in Literary History*, ed. Brian Cummings and James Simpson (Oxford: Oxford University Press), 356.

38. G. F. Nuttall, "Puritan and Quaker Mysticism," *Theology* 78 (1975): 518–31; Betteridge, "Vernacular Theology," 188–89.

39. See Serge Hutin, *Les disciples anglais de Jacob Bœhme aux XVIIe et XVIIIe siècles* (Paris: Éditions Denoël, 1960); Andrew Weeks, *Boehme: An Intellectual Biography of the Seventeenth-Century Philosopher and Mystic* (Albany: State University of New York Press, 1991); B. J. Gibbons, *Gender in Mystical and Occult Thought: Behmenism and its Development in England* (Cambridge: Cambridge University Press, 1996); Paola Mayer, *Jena Romanticism and its Appropriation of Jakob Böhme: Theosophy, Hagiography, Literature* (Montreal: McGill-Queen's University Press, 1999); Hans-Joachim Friedrich, *Der Ungrund der Freiheit im Denken von Böhme, Schelling und Heidegger* (Stuttgart: Frommann-Holzboog, 2009); Gerhard Wehr, *Jakob Böhme: Ursprung, Wirkung, Textauswahl* (Wiesbaden: Marixverlag, 2010).

40. See, for example, Smith, *Perfection Proclaimed*, chapter 5, 299–307; Manfred Brod, "A Radical Network in the English Revolution: John Pordage and His Circle, 1646–54," *English Historical Review* 119 (2004): 1230–53; Hessayon, *Gold Tried in the Fire*, chapters 11–12; Tristram Stuart, *The Bloodless Revolution: A Cultural History of Vegetarianism from 1600 to Modern Times* (New York: W. W. Norton & Company, 2007), 36–37, 61, and 75.

41. The nonjurors were those who refused to swear an oath of loyalty to William and Mary after the Glorious Revolution, maintaining that their oath to the ousted James II was still binding. They were largely High Church Anglicans and were sympathetic to the Jacobites, although they were not generally active supporters of the Jacobite risings of 1714 and 1745.

42. See Beverley C. Southgate, *Covetous of Truth: The Life and Work of Thomas White, 1593–1676* (Dordrecht: Kluwer Academic, 1993); Stefania Tutino, *Thomas White and the Blackloists: Between Politics and Theology during the English Civil War* (Aldershot, Vt.: Ashgate, 2008).

43. See Jakob Böhme, *Christosophia, oder, Der Weg zu Christo* (Ephrata, Pa.: Jacob Ruth, 1811–12). For further developments in the eighteenth century, see the new work of Michael Riordan, "Mysticism and Prophecy in Scotland in the Long Eighteenth Century" (unpublished Ph.D. diss., Cambridge University, 2014).

44. Largier, "Mysticism, Modernity."

45. See, for example, Paul Oliver, *Mysticism: A Guide for the Perplexed* (London: Continuum, 2009).

46. See Largier's essay in this volume.

1

Ways of Knowing in the Pre- and Post-Reformation Worlds

Euan K. Cameron

In Western Christian thought, it is at least as important to be clear about *how* one knows, as it is to be certain about *what* one knows. Very broadly, it can be (and has been) argued that there are four basic sources of religious knowledge acknowledged in Western Christianity, and indeed in many other faiths. First, there is the authority of sacred texts. Second, there is the collective witness and tradition of the religious community, including the tradition of how to exegete the sacred texts themselves. Third, there is human reason, properly applied within its limits to discipline and regulate the relationship between one proposition and another. Fourth, and finally, there is the experience of direct illumination of the Holy Spirit on the mind and soul of the believer.[1] None of these four approaches to knowledge is sufficient by itself; for most of history several or all of them have performed complementary, mutually enlightening and supporting roles in building up the body of theological knowledge. The claim to learn through direct divine illumination, however, tends to become increasingly problematical whenever those received certainties are brought into doubt. It thrives, relatively speaking, in the times when dogmatic debates have least impact on the political stability of the church. It loses most credibility, or exposes its adherents to greatest suspicion, in those epochs where disputes over doctrine cast the cohesion of the ecclesial community into doubt.

Dramatic challenges to the continuity and coherence of the Western tradition inevitably called forth challenges to the balance between different sources of authority. Naturally enough, one of the most radical of such challenges came from the sixteenth-century Reformation. Looking at the contributions to this volume from the perspective of a Reformation historian, one observes something of a chronological divide in the contributions between the later Middle Ages (even when those reach forward into the sixteenth century, as they do) and the great age of devotional writing, Protestant and Catholic, in the seventeenth century. The Reformation occupies an awkward and problematical point in the history of devotional literature. It is not so much a desert as a rough area of debatable lands, where the landmarks seem continually to be shifting. This chapter sketches a broad-brush, *longue durée* account of the history of the different means to religious knowledge from the Middle Ages to the seventeenth century. In so doing it proposes some reasons why the Reformation is both problematical and crucial to the story of mystical knowing.

Even in the period of the sharpest conflicts over the relative status of different forms of knowledge, there remained within Western Christianity a body of traditional literature in the area of mystical theology. Some of this corpus antedated the strife over ways of knowing and was available as common heritage to all the disputants. The Ur-texts for discussion of medieval mystical thought included the treatises *On the Divine Names* and the *Mystical Theology* attributed to the so-called Dionysius the Areopagite, probably written around the end of the fifth century. These lyrical and often enigmatic texts laid down some of the assumptions in the genre. Pseudo-Dionysius spoke of the "super-essential radiance of the Divine darkness"[2] to express the zone where

God was apprehended through contemplation after an ascent above and away from concrete images and specific propositions. He popularized the "negative approach" in mystical theology, where God was defined by an ascending hierarchy of negative statements. He stressed that God was neither a thing that could be perceived nor a proposition that could be understood.[3]

The next most important body of traditional material consisted of the monastic theological heritage of the period just before the flowering of scholasticism. Historians have traditionally divided this corpus into the Carthusian, Cistercian-Benedictine, and Victorine strands.[4] Clearly the author who exercised the greatest and most enduring influence in this area was Bernard of Clairvaux, especially though not exclusively in his sermons on the Song of Songs. The most striking attribute of Bernard's thought lay in its coherence as a complete theological system, within the limits of its period and setting. Human beings were called to a love of God that could only be attained by an ascent through the lower forms of love. This ascent involved leaving behind the "curvature" toward self-centeredness that derived from the fall. Faith and reason needed to work together to convert the soul to a sense of its true good and restore the lost "likeness" of God. This conversion process away from self could be most appropriately sought through the humility and discipline of the monastic life. After appropriate discipline, the monastic adept could come to know God in an ecstatic union where the soul was temporarily, briefly "liquefied" and appeared to lose its identity in that of God. It was important, however, that no matter how rhapsodic the language used, Bernard always preserved a certain theological restraint; he always remained aware of the cosmic distance between Creator and creature, and stressed that such distance could be only briefly bridged in this life.[5]

The Cistercian tradition of monastic theology aspired to comprehensiveness and balance, but even at its peak it was already forced to struggle for adherents with the first wave of the new scholasticism. Bernard criticized Peter Abelard for his excessive confidence in human reason; yet the future, at least in European academic theology, belonged to Abelard's approach more than to Bernard's.[6] There would persist through the Middle Ages a monastic, contemplative attitude to theology that resisted the speculations of the professional academics and the schools of mendicants; however, from the thirteenth century on it would be a subtext to a narrative that was largely being written elsewhere.

The real debate over ways of knowing in theology arose over the relative status of text, tradition, and reason in the later Middle Ages, and never really ceased until the Reformation. The colossal authority acquired, after his death, by Thomas Aquinas should never conceal the fact that he was very controversial in his own time and in the later Middle Ages. Thomas argued that reason, text, and tradition, all correctly and faithfully construed, would demonstrate the same truths in the body of revealed Christian theology. He wrote a striking monument to this kind of certainty in the *Summa contra Gentiles*, or *Summa against the Pagans*. The *Summa contra Gentiles* took the stance that the claims of Christian revelation regarding the cosmos and the relative status of God, the angelic natures, and humanity could be discerned from first principles using natural reason and philosophy; at the end of each chapter Thomas would demonstrate the claims made with a text from scripture, as a sort of QED flourish.[7]

In contrast to Thomas, many Parisian thinkers argued in the thirteenth century and beyond that the insights of Christian tradition and natural reason must, at best, exist in an uneasy, grating disharmony, exemplified by the stressful debates over such issues as the eternity of the world or the natural immortality of the soul.[8] The late medieval *Wegestreit*, or strife between realists and nominalists, focused on crucial questions of the relative competency of rational versus revealed truth. While followers of Thomas continued to argue that the divine dispensation was logical and therefore transparent to right reason, followers of the *via moderna* from William of Ockham on insisted that the presently observable rules of the game were merely conventional rather than necessary. If conventional, then arbitrary; if arbitrary, then accessible only through the revealed truths transmitted to the hierarchical church. The late Heiko Oberman added a vitally important nuance to this picture of the *via moderna*: the ways of God might be conventional and arbitrary, but in all ordinary circumstances the divine nature chose to operate through normal channels and methods (the *potentia ordinata*) and was therefore predictable in fact if not in principle.[9]

The strife of the ways, with its acute disagreements over the scope and use of human reason in theology, took place concurrently with the great age of late medieval mystical thought. Occasionally echoes of the *Wegestreit*, mapped, as it often was, onto the rivalry between Dominican and Franciscan friars, can be heard in the rivalries of different schools of mystics. Bernard McGinn associates Dominicans with an "intellective" and Franciscans with an "affective," or emotional, approach to mysticism.[10] However, the most neuralgic debates over mystical knowing in the later Middle Ages broke out over the precise limits to mystical union with the divine. A sort of theological cliché defined the differences between the "true" and the "false" mystics. "True" mystics were sensitive to the limits of human spiritual ascent; they were obedient and respectful toward the church; they recognized the need to practice conventional sacramental and devotional piety; they did not suffer from spiritual pride or arrogance. "False" mystics, whether called "free spirits," Beghards, Turrelupins, "friends of God," or anything else, contended that their spiritual insights transported them beyond the limits of mere mortals until their nature was effaced in the Godhead. In such rapture they would become incapable of sin; the ordinary means of human access to God through religious ritual would become irrelevant and unnecessary. They conceived themselves as being a spiritual elite far beyond the majority.[11] The problem with these ideal-types was that neither extreme actually corresponded neatly to any real mystics. They represented, perhaps, the idealized *positive* and *negative* images of Meister Eckhart and his followers. The negative image of "bad mysticism" was attacked by everyone—it was something "they" did, not oneself. One of the fiercest critics of "false mysticism" was Jan van Ruysbroeck. The "friend of God" Rulman Merswin, the most elitist and precious of the fourteenth-century mystics, criticized "false mysticism" in the same routine fashion.[12]

Real debates of course also took place between theologians over the relative scope of mystical theology. Possibly one of the most interesting arose around the polymathic and sensitive pastoral theologian Jean Gerson (1363–1429). Gerson, in his two treatises on mystical theology, attempted to set mystical theology on a solid and transparent scholastic foundation. He classified mystical experiences according to the range of human cognitive and affective powers.[13] *Cogitation* conducted in an orderly way aspired to the quality of *meditation*; *meditation* done really well might open the way to the insights of *contemplation*, the highest order of affective encounter with the divine.[14] Gerson then drew an extended and somewhat elaborate list of differences between speculative and mystical theology, rather to the advantage of the latter. Mystical theology was more accessible to all, brought mental calm rather than turmoil, and could not serve the mental vices as speculative or scholastic theology could.[15] Finally, in the theoretical part of his treatise Gerson warned, as did everyone else, against those who claimed too much for ecstatic love, believing themselves to be absolutely subsumed within the nature of God at a point where all distinctions were obliterated.[16] This entangled him in a dispute with the followers of Ruysbroeck.[17]

Despite the extremely positive view that Gerson gave of mystical theological experiences in *On Mystical Theology*, his attempt to find a neatly defined theological space for mystical experience seems to have been bitterly resented in certain monastic circles. A group of German monks at Tegernsee seems to have taken violent exception to Gerson's takeover bid for the territory of mystical theology, and drew Nicholas of Cusa into the debate by calling on him to advise them.[18] Consequently Nicholas of Cusa wrote his treatise *On the Vision of God*, which represented a fascinating attempt to merge with mystical theology many of the themes of Cusanus's *On Learned Ignorance*. The most intriguing aspect of Nicholas of Cusa's essay on mystical theology lay in his almost mathematical approach to the infinitude of God. God was absolutely infinite in all senses, which meant that all predicates applied to God—but not restrictively. Consequently human beings as "contracted" entities could not hope to apprehend the divine absolute directly.[19] Cusanus's Christology focused on Jesus Christ's ability to be at one and the same time the embodiment of the absolute and yet contracted into a human form, therefore to bridge an otherwise unbridgeable gulf.[20] Mystical insight came into play to the extent that human beings could only encounter the absolute God in the darkness of absolute incomprehensibility.[21] The only insight that mattered was to become fully aware of one's own human incapacity to know anything meaningful about God.[22]

For all the anxious debates over the precise scope of different kinds of theological insight, one should remember that the later Middle Ages in Europe witnessed perhaps the lowest level of real substantive theological disagreement for many centuries. Heresy in the fifteenth century possessed negligible political force outside Bohemia; in England, though Lollard dissenters certainly persisted in significant numbers, they posed little threat, intellectually or in terms of religious practice, to the ascendancy of traditional Catholicism as the fifteenth century wore on. After the closure of the Council of Basel in 1449, the political threats to the unity of the church were largely spent, as Pius II's decree *Execrabilis* (1460) and the failure of the anti-papal council of 1511 showed. Debates over means of access to theological truths, or over the rationale for received liturgical practices, attested to a remarkable amount of common ground over what should be believed and practiced.

The Lutheran Reformation changed all that, brutally and largely unexpectedly. As in previous centuries of debate, the focus shifted away from personal revelation to other more objective sources of authority. In the authentic part of his speech at his famous encounter at Worms in 1521, Luther declared that "unless I am convinced by the testimony of Scripture or evident reason . . . I am bound to the Scriptures which I have adduced and my conscience is captive to the Word of God."[23] In the debates over the early Reformation, the appeal to personal enlightenment was beside the point. In fact, the accusation of subjectivism, of insisting on one's private reading of the sources against the common witness of the church, constituted one of the most potent attacks made against the reformers. It was bad enough that the reformers insisted that scripture was self-authenticating and self-interpreting. *Sola scriptura* stood as a challenge to the allegedly continuous tradition of shared Catholic exegesis of the sacred texts. To traditional Catholicism, text and traditional interpretation co-inhered, and there could be no question of citing text against church any more than the opposite.[24] By 1547 the Council of Trent would explicitly embody this attitude to text and tradition in one of its most important decrees: "no one, relying on his personal judgment in matters of faith and customs which are linked to the establishment of Christian doctrine, shall dare to interpret the sacred scriptures either by twisting its text to his individual meaning in opposition to that which has been and is held by holy mother Church, whose function is to pass judgment on the true meaning and interpretation of the sacred scriptures; or by giving it meanings contrary to the unanimous consent of the fathers."[25]

All of Martin Luther's complicated responses to the issue of personal illumination have to be understood against the background of the Reformation crisis of authority and Luther's hard-won and tenaciously held belief in the absolute authority of the gospel revealed in the Word of God. Before discussing the few areas where Luther discusses mystical theology positively, it is important to understand why he remained so negative about many aspects of it. Very early in his career Luther confronted other, freer thinkers than himself who (in his eyes) took advantage of the space that his defiance had created. These people (the Zwickau prophets, Andreas Karlstadt, and Thomas Müntzer) claimed that their direct inspiration from the Almighty took precedence over Luther's scripturally based theology. The "spirits" laid claim to spectacular insights that transcended mere exegesis. In Luther's polemical treatise *Against the Heavenly Prophets* one sees occasional evidence that his attack on mystical insights was more than just generalized or hypothetical: "This is God's new sublime art, taught by the heavenly voice, which we at Wittenberg, who teach faith and love, do not understand and cannot know. This is the nice 'turning from the material,' the 'concentration,' the 'adoration,' the 'self-abstraction,' and similar devil's nonsense."[26]

In the same text Luther told a story of a visit to Orlamünde, where Andreas Karlstadt had intruded himself as the village pastor. Intended to demonstrate the ignorance and arrogance of Karlstadt's followers, the story ended by demonstrating something else besides:

> I must give an example of what I am saying to see whether Dr. Karlstadt might learn a bit himself and be ashamed that he teaches his disciples so well. When I was in Orlamünde . . . a man stepped forward who wanted to be the most wise among them and said to me, . . . "If you will not follow Moses, you must nevertheless endure the gospel. You have shoved the gospel under the bench. No, no! It must come forth and not remain under the bench." I said, "What then does the gospel say?" He said, "Jesus says in the gospel (I don't know where, though my brethren know it) that the bride must take off her nightgown and be naked, if she is to sleep with the bridegroom. Therefore one must break all the images, so that we are free and cleansed of what is created." So far the words of our conversation.
>
> "What was I to do? I had come among Karlstadt's followers and then I learned that breaking images meant that a bride should take off her nightgown, and that this was to be found in the gospel . . . Such idle pride had brought the man into all misfortune, and had pushed him out of the light into such darkness, that he gave as a reason for breaking images, that a bride should take off her nightgown . . . What though, if the bride and bridegroom were so chaste that they kept nightgown and robe on? It would certainly not hinder them much if they otherwise had desire for each other.[27]

Almost without doubt, what had happened in Karlstadt's preaching is that the erotic imagery of bride and bridegroom, which was such a staple of the mystical exposition of the Song of Songs, had infected the language of his critique of image-worship. For Luther, allegorical reading of mystical texts came to be associated with the dangerous arrogance of those who despised the Word in favor of their own personal insights.

A deeper theological reason, besides personal disdain and a horror for rival theologians, underlay Luther's reluctance and reserve toward mystical thought as practiced by others. So much medieval devotional practice focused on "improving" the human soul through focused meditation on the themes of the Christian drama. For Luther, all the language of spiritual self-improvement through devotional exercises had to be deeply suspect. In his 1519 *Sermon on Meditating on Christ's Passion*, Luther warned against meditating in a self-centered way, seeking our own benefit. He also warned the devout to think beyond the passion to the resurrection, and to use their awareness of the sufferings of Christ as a means to keep their own sense of suffering in proportion.[28] Once Luther's theology of justification had matured, he found the idea of progressive enlightenment aspired to by some mystics to be deeply dangerous. Lutheran theology of salvation always stressed that human beings remain rooted in the earthy and fleshly; we are covered with the righteousness of Christ and gradually, partially, and intermittently sanctified in this life; but the idea of ascending through ever higher states of ecstatic love while engaged in monastic *askesis* held less and less allure for Luther as time passed. It is not that mysticism *needed* to be linked with a theology of salvation based on monastic "good works": rather, according to the circumstances, that was how things looked in 1520.

However, one should return to the moment in his early career when Luther did appear to embrace a mystical text, the so-called *Theologia deutsch*. Luther issued a partial edition of this work in 1516 and a more complete edition in 1518, with a preface that praised this "German theology" in contrast to the Roman theology that he then opposed.[29] The *Theologia deutsch* included a number of themes that chimed relatively well with Luther's unfolding theology of justification. It set forth a relatively pessimistic view of human nature: the primary need of humanity was rescue from its sinfulness.[30] The work was strongly Christological: one must not forsake Christ to pursue one's own visions, and all spiritual experience must be consciously patterned on Christ.[31] The work set out a dialectic of being cast down and lifted up again, mortified and vivified, which would correspond fairly closely to the psychological experience of despair over sin and redemption through grace in Luther's thought.[32]

However, significant portions of the work embodied precisely the language of spiritual self-impoverishment and resignation that Luther would object to in others. Repeatedly the work entered the lists to debate with the "false mystics"; it shared in the clichés of Eckhartian intra-mystical polemic in a way that was simply not relevant to Luther's needs. Recently Bernard McGinn has quoted with approval the suggestion that the *Theologia deutsch* could be seen as a "central instructional manual of the Reformation."[33] It has even been claimed that its discussion of the "divinization" of the mystical adept should modify our view of what the Reformation taught in this area.[34] Those claims must surely be excessive. Steven Ozment's earlier claims for the work from 1973 seem much more balanced, especially where Ozment finds that Luther focused on the steps to salvation in the *Theologia deutsch*, but avoided its implications for anthropology and the possibility of union with God.[35] The explanation for Luther's expressions of approval must therefore be simple: in the moment of near-ecstatic relief that Luther experienced when he had worked out the definitive version of his theology of justification around 1518, that insight loomed so large and bright in his vision that it tended to bleach out the native colors of every other text Luther read. He read Augustine, Wessel Gansfort, the mystics, Hus, or the Bohemian Brethren and saw in them what he needed to see. On the other hand, those thinkers who swallowed the mystical theology whole and entire found themselves rapidly on the margins of reformed thought with the Anabaptists and Spiritualists.

Does this mean that the view of the magisterial reformers proposed here is of arid intellectual exegetes, unregenerate neo-scholastics who simply spat proof-texts at each other with no spiritual depth whatever? That must surely not be the case. However, one does need to handle the spiritual element in the early Reformation with considerable care. At various points leading reformers wrote that the text of scripture could only be interpreted in obedient listening to the Holy Spirit. Both Zwingli and Calvin—of all the reformers perhaps the most rational and least mystical in their theologies—argued that the Spirit of God was active in and through the business of working at scriptural exegesis.[36] However, claims made to draw close parallels between, say, the thought of Calvin and Bernard of Clairvaux do not entirely convince.[37] In reformed thought spiritual knowing and scriptural knowing overlapped, coincided, and reinforced each other. To have the Word without the Spirit was not really to have the Word at all.

On the other hand, to lay claim to the Spirit without the Word was even more dangerous. Luther, as Mark Edwards pointed out some years back, used the language of "spirit" in confronting his theological opponents. A bad theologian was one dominated by a bad spirit, a spirit undisciplined by reverence for the text. The same "spirit" might animate different and unconnected individuals with the same opinions.[38] At times Luther literally claimed that his opponents were possessed by demons. Again from *Against the Heavenly Prophets*: "It ought to surprise no one that I call him a devil. For I am not thinking of Dr. Karlstadt or concerned about him. *I am thinking of him by whom he is possessed and for whom he speaks*, as St. Paul says, 'For we are not contending against flesh and blood—but against the spiritual hosts of wickedness in the heavenly places' [Eph. 6:12]."[39]

German Reformation historiography has argued long and hard about where the "Reformation" ends and the "confessional age" begins. On the one hand the question is almost otiose. There is no clear or significant theological turning point, no "confessional turn" that clearly divides the first-generation reformers from their successors in the second and third generations. On the other hand, a profound difference in terms of psychological experience separated those who (1) discovered the insights of the Reformation in spiritual anguish and inner conflict; or (2) were born and raised into those insights once they had petrified into dogmas and been fashioned into redoubts to defend against all enemies.

The confessional era certainly did not lack inner self-awareness. Melanchthon and his followers argued over how in the experience of being sanctified the believer might apprehend and even participate in his or her own sanctification.[40] In the reformed tradition a vigorous literature developed around the so-called practical syllogism, where believers might attempt to introspect their own spiritual states and discern the actions of divine grace within them.[41] However, in all of this an often pernicious quest for ever more precise doctrinal definition was constantly at work. The more precision that theologians tried to achieve, the more conflicts tended to break out.

Interest in the mystical tradition revived in some corners of magisterial Protestantism as a reaction against the excessive quest for dogmatic definition. In the limited space remaining I wish briefly to discuss only two Lutheran instances, Johann Arndt from the very beginning of the seventeenth century and Gottfried Arnold from the very end of the same century. Johann Arndt (1555–1621) was trained in the most rigorous academic orthodoxy at Helmstedt, Wittenberg, Strasbourg, and Basel. However, his training seems to have provoked him to engage in a passionate critique of an over-intellectualized theology. In his *True Christianity* he expounded a set of prescriptions for the spiritual life, to be lived in humility and love.[42] In book III he observed that the modern notion of Christianity seemed to be to seek to acquire speculative theological insights, yet to know about God was not the same thing as to follow God.[43] At various moments in *True Christianity* Arndt seemed about to embrace a fully developed mystical theology: he quoted from Saint Bernard several times, spoke of the three stages of the spiritual life, and evoked the language of the Song of Songs.[44] He went on:

> This is that Darkness which is the Habitation of God, this is that Night, in which the Will rests sweetly in Union with the Will of God; and in which the Memory forgetteth all the Impressions of the Creatures. Then in a Moment does the divine Light strike the Understanding, heavenly desires inflame the will, and eternal Joys possess and fill the Memory; yet neither the Understanding, the

Will, nor the Memory, comprehend or retain the transcendent Joys with which they are visited of God. For this Perception is not lodged in the faculties of the Soul, but lies hid in the very Ground and Centre of it.[45]

However, it would be a mistake to read the many hundreds of pages of *True Christianity* as all equally suffused with mystical thought in this way. First, the evocations of Saint Bernard and the mystical tradition are not equally dispersed throughout the book; second, Arndt differed in several important ways from the later medieval mystical traditions. Whereas the abstraction from the material might in monastic mystical practice have entailed years of profound spiritual discipline and gradual ascent, for Arndt the abstraction from created things and their images was to be a daily exercise, a brief and salutary interruption from the round of existence in the physical world.[46] The abstraction from the physical was to be balanced with its opposite. Citing none other than Bernard of Clairvaux, Arndt firmly encouraged his readers to discover the Creator through created things, albeit looking through and beyond rather than at the material.[47] He warned people to have no pride in their own merit, to embrace the afflictions that they suffered, and to be compassionate for the faults of others. With such thoroughly practical and social feelings, one might recognize the presence of the Holy Spirit in oneself.[48]

Johann Arndt's work demonstrates that, even when an author embraced the medieval rhetoric of mystical enlightenment and approach to God, it was not possible, at least in this context, to return to the age before scholasticism. At most, Arndt belonged in a Protestant version of the world of Jean Gerson, where mystical insights were integrated into a more complex and inclusive understanding of theological cognition. A devotional and contemplative approach to the divine served not as an objective sufficient in itself, but as a specific corrective against certain trends in orthodox Lutheran religiosity. In the second generation Luther's spiritual struggles with the life of the monastery had become memory and legend. Justification by faith had become an intellectual system, where more and more stress was placed on the extrinsic quality of divine grace apprehended through faith forgiving human guilt, what is sometimes called "forensic" justification. Lutheran scholastics seem to have overbalanced their treatment of these intellectual notions in a way that Luther himself never did. Johann Arndt's appeal to devotion in general and the mystical tradition in particular, therefore, served a particular purpose: he called the mystics into play in order to redress the imbalances of a dogmatic, catechetical theology dominated by the intellectual apprehension of doctrine. Arndt's mysticism cannot be understood in any other context.

The late seventeenth-century radical Pietist Gottfried Arnold (1666–1714) reacted against dogmatic orthodoxy in a more visceral and more polemical fashion. His embrace of mysticism was more explicit and more assertive. His *Impartial History of the Church and Heresies*[49] of 1699–1700 argued that, from the very earliest years of the Christian church, the representatives of dogmatic orthodoxy were sometimes very bad representatives of the ethical and spiritual values of Christianity. Heretics might after all prove to have been gentler souls and better followers of Jesus. Arnold thus eroded the idea that all the right was necessarily on the side of the "orthodox." Arnold wrote a separate *History and Description of Mystical Theology* (1702),[50] parts of which were incorporated into later editions of his *Impartial History*. Mystics were to be found everywhere in the church, among the potentially heterodox in the early centuries, in England and the Rhineland in the fourteenth and fifteenth centuries, among the Lutheran Pietists and the Roman Catholic Quietists. This theological taste transcended confessional boundaries, and also had a habit of making dogmatic confessional theologians uneasy on all sides. As late as the work of Étienne Gilson one finds Catholic scholars of mysticism attacking the Quietists and their allies.[51] Both his attachment to mysticism and his individual attitude toward heresies led Arnold to an arresting and (for 1700) quite radical conclusion:

> The greatest commandment of our creator (which is love towards all people) has taught me to see the invisible universal Church, which according to the teaching of the theologians is not linked to a specific visible society, but rather is spread and scattered throughout the whole world amongst all people and congregations . . . The

> greatest shortcoming of historians is if they look to the honor and advantage of their own society by means of various spurious origins, and let the others look after themselves . . . It is very difficult, then, to say which of the external Church-congregations should be named as the true Church, and thus as the "mother" [of the faithful].[52]

For Arnold, ethical and spiritual goodness manifested themselves in an unpredictable and dispersed fashion among multiple churches or confessions. To make such a claim was to render moot a great body of confessional historical polemic. Since the Reformation, disputants had sought to prove how the reformers (or their opponents) were exclusively and absolutely right because they held correct dogma, rather than exhibiting Christ-like virtue. Arnold provoked a vigorous rebuttal from confessional orthodox Lutherans such as Ernst Salomon Cyprian (1673–1745), even beyond his own lifetime. Mystical indifference to dogma could not be allowed to impugn the essential rightness of the Reformation.[53]

No doubt there is and always will be a section of Christian and other religious sentiment that is particularly open to the attraction of mystical exercises and the quest for direct illumination. No doubt there will continue to be lines of development traceable from one mystical writer to another that cut across, transcend, or otherwise bypass the dogmatic movements in the broader church. A whole other subject—one explored elsewhere in this volume—concerns the way in which religious people lacking formal theological education processed their mystical insights, and the way that their spiritual directors sought to keep their visionaries within an orthodox path. Unlike many of the chapters in this volume, this essay discusses writers on mysticism who were overwhelmingly male. That in many respects regrettable imbalance reflects the particular role played in policing the boundaries of mystical writing by those scholars who also knew the academic theological disciplines through formal university education. The argument proposed here suggests that, first, the mode of knowing through direct illumination can only be seen in context if it is viewed in a dialectical relationship with the three other modes of knowing identified earlier, text, tradition, and reason. Second, it argues that whether obviously or not, the rise and fall of mystical literature in Western Christianity reflected larger and broader movements in the church and Christian thought. Mystical seeking will often, in one sense or another, arise as a reaction against dogmatic over-elaboration and over-definition: whether as an objection to the rise of scholasticism in the thirteenth century, or as a protest against the elaboration of catechesis in the confessional period. Mystical knowledge will always tend to fall into discredit in those periods where the finer points of belief and practice are contested and politically sensitive. To the extent that these claims may be true, it seems that the history of mysticism ought not to be written outside of the history of doctrine as a whole.

NOTES

1. This structure of knowledge has affinities to the so-called Wesleyan Quadrilateral of scripture, tradition, reason, and experience. See also W. Stephen Gunter et al., eds., *Wesley and the Quadrilateral: Renewing the Conversation* (Nashville: Abingdon, 1997). According to some commentators, Wesley regarded this approach as a descriptive rather than normative statement about how all religious knowledge is attained.

2. τόν ὑπερούσιον τοῦ θείου σκότους ἀκτῖνα.

3. For a widely accessible translation, see "Dionysius, the Areopagite," in *On the Divine Names and Mystical Theology*, trans. C. E. Rolt (London: Society for Promoting Christian Knowledge, 1951). See also Denys Turner, *The Darkness of God: Negativity in Christian Mysticism* (Cambridge: Cambridge University Press, 1995).

4. See esp. Étienne Gilson, *The Mystical Theology of Saint Bernard*, trans. A. H. C. Downes (New York: Sheed & Ward, 1940), 2 ff.

5. Gilson, *Mystical Theology of Saint Bernard*, esp. 22–60.

6. Gilson, *Mystical Theology of Saint Bernard*, 6 and 64.

7. The Latin text of the *Summa contra Gentiles* may be accessed through the website Corpusthomisticum.org at http://www.corpusthomisticum.org

/scg1001.html (accessed July 23, 2012) and following. The traditional English Dominican translation, slightly abridged, may be consulted at http://www2.nd.edu/Departments/Maritain/etext/gc.htm (accessed July 23, 2012).

8. For a preliminary discussion of the stresses in the University of Paris leading up to the condemnations of 1277 issued by Étienne Tempier, Bishop of Paris, see the *Stanford Encyclopedia of Philosophy* at http://plato.stanford.edu/entries/condemnation/ (accessed July 23, 2012) with references.

9. On *potentia ordinata*, see Heiko Augustinus Oberman, *The Harvest of Medieval Theology: Gabriel Biel and Late Medieval Nominalism* (Cambridge, Mass.: Harvard University Press, 1963), 30–45; see also W. J. Courtenay, "Nominalism and Late Medieval Religion," in *The Pursuit of Holiness in Late Medieval and Renaissance Religion*, ed. Charles Trinkaus and Heiko A. Oberman (Leiden: Brill, 1974), 37–43; Steven E. Ozment, "Mysticism, Nominalism and Dissent," in *The Pursuit of Holiness in Late Medieval and Renaissance Religion*, ed. Charles Trinkaus and Heiko A. Oberman (Leiden: Brill, 1974), 80–83.

10. Bernard McGinn, *The Presence of God: A History of Western Christian Mysticism*, 4 vols. (New York: Crossroad, 1992–2005), 4:337.

11. See, for example, McGinn, *Presence of God*, 4:402–4 and 4:426–27.

12. McGinn, *Presence of God*, 4:427.

13. Jean Gerson, *De Mystica Theologia*, in *Thesaurus mundi: Bibliotheca scriptorum Latinorum mediæ et recentioris ætatis*, ed. André Combes (Lucani [= Lugano]: In Aedibus Thesauri Mundi, 1958), 29–33.

14. Gerson, *De Mystica Theologia*, 51–65.

15. Gerson, *De Mystica Theologia*, 70–90.

16. Gerson, *De Mystica Theologia*, 105–12.

17. See the meticulous and hugely extended discussion of Gerson's response to Ruysbroeck in André Combes, *Essai sur la critique de Ruysbroeck par Gerson*, 4 vols. (Paris: J. Vrin, 1945–72).

18. Jasper Hopkins, *Nicholas of Cusa's Dialectical Mysticism: Text, Translation, and Interpretive Study of* De Visione Dei (Minneapolis: A. J. Banning, 1985), 11 ff.

19. Hopkins, *Nicholas of Cusa's Dialectical Mysticism*, 155–57.

20. Hopkins, *Nicholas of Cusa's Dialectical Mysticism*, 239 ff.

21. Hopkins, *Nicholas of Cusa's Dialectical Mysticism*, 159.

22. Hopkins, *Nicholas of Cusa's Dialectical Mysticism*, 179. Compare the discussion of Cusanus in McGinn, *Presence of God*, vol. 4, chapter 10.

23. Euan Cameron, *The European Reformation* (Oxford: Clarendon, 1991), 103 and notes.

24. See Cameron, *European Reformation*, chapter 9.

25. See Norman P. Tanner, ed. and trans., *Decrees of the Ecumenical Councils*, 2 vols. (London: Sheed & Ward, 1990), 663–65 and 664 for the quotation (the two volumes are consecutively paginated).

26. Martin Luther, *Luther's Works*, 55 vols., ed. Jaroslav Pelikan and H. T. Lehmann (St. Louis: Concordia, 1955–86), 40:117. Compare p. 148.

27. *Luther's Works*, 40:100–101 (abridged).

28. *Luther's Works*, 42:7–14, based on Martin Luther, *Luthers Werke: kritische Gesamtausgabe* (Weimar: Böhlaus Nachfolger, 1883–1948), 2:136–42.

29. The 1518 complete edition was *Eyn deutsch Theologia: das ist Eyn edles Buchleyn von rechtem verstand, was Adam und Christus sey, und wie Adam yn uns sterben, und Christus ersteen sall* (A German Theology: that is A noble little book on the correct understanding of what Adam and Christ are and how Adam shall die and Christ shall arise in us) (Wittenberg: Grünenberg, 1518). Multiple further editions followed in the next few years. For Luther's 1518 preface to the *Theologia deutsch*, see *Luther's Works*, 31:75–76.

30. McGinn, *Presence of God*, 4:397.

31. McGinn, *Presence of God*, 4:399.

32. McGinn, *Presence of God*, 4:399–400.

33. McGinn, *Presence of God*, 4:392–93.

34. Though one should also note that discussion of correlatives to "divinization" in Luther's thought has formed one of the key claims of the Finnish school of Luther studies associated with Tuomo Mannermaa.

35. See Steven E. Ozment, *Mysticism and Dissent: Religious Ideology and Social Protest in the Sixteenth Century* (New Haven, Conn.: Yale University Press, 1973), 14–60 and esp. 21–25 for the discussion of Luther.

36. Cameron, *European Reformation*, 138–39 and references.

37. One of the most ambitious works to this effect is Dennis E. Tamburello, *Union with Christ: John Calvin and the Mysticism of St. Bernard* (Louisville: Westminster John Knox, 1994).

38. Mark U. Edwards Jr., *Luther and the False Brethren* (Stanford, Calif.: Stanford University Press, 1975), esp. 200 ff.

39. *Luther's Works*, 40:149.

40. For the synergistic controversy, see Cameron, *European Reformation*, chapter 10, sect. 1.3 and references.

41. The classic text of the practical syllogism is William Perkins (1558–1602), *A case of conscience: the greatest that euer was; how a man may knowe whether he be the child of God or no. Resolued by the worde of God . . .* (London: Thomas Orwin, for Thomas Man and John Porter, 1592).

42. Johann Arndt's *Vier Bücher vom wahren Christentum* originally appeared in installments in the 1600s. Multiple complete editions appeared from 1610 on: *Vier Bücher von wahren Christenthum heilsamer Busse, hertzlicher Rewe und Leid uber die Sünde und wahren Glauben: auch heiligem Leben und Wandel der rechten wahren Christen* (Four books on [the] true Christianity of healing penance, heartfelt regret and sorrow over sins and on true faith: also on the holy life and transformation of the right, true Christian) (Magdeburg: Francke, 1610).

43. Reference is made here to Johann Arndt (1555–1621), *Of True Christianity, Four Books: Wherein is contained the whole Oeconomy of God towards Man; and the Whole Duty of man towards God. Written originally in the High-Dutch, by the most Reverend John Arndt* . . . , 2 vols. (London: D. Brown and J. Downing, 1712–14), introduction to book III, 2:307–8; compare book I, chapter 31, 1:283 ff.; and book I, chapter 39, 1:346 ff.

44. Arndt, *Of True Christianity*, introduction to book III, 2:306, 310; and chapter 6, 2:341.

45. Arndt, *Of True Christianity*, book III, chapter 6, 2:342.

46. Arndt, *Of True Christianity*, book III, chapters 12–13, 2:364 ff.

47. Arndt, *Of True Christianity*, introduction to book IV, 2:414 ff.

48. Arndt, *Of True Christianity*, book III, chapter 17, 2:381–83.

49. Original edition: Gottfried Arnold, *Unparteyische Kirchen- und Ketzer-Historie, von Anfang des Neuen Testaments biß auff das Jahr Christi 1688*, 2 vols. (Frankfurt am Main, 1699–1700). References here are to Gottfried Arnold, *Unpartheyische Kirchen- und Ketzer-Historien, vom Anfang des Neuen Testaments bis auf das Jahr Christi 1688, bey dieser neuen Auflage, an vielen Orten, nach dem Sinn und Verlangen, des Seel. Auctoris, vebessert* . . . , 3 vols. (Schaffhausen: druckts und verlegts Emanuel und Benedict Hurter, Gebruedere, 1740–42).

50. Gottfried Arnold, *Historia et descriptio theologiae mysticae seu theosophiae arcanae et reconditae itemque veterum et novorum mysticorum* (Frankfurt am Main, 1702).

51. See Gilson, *Mystical Theology of Saint Bernard*, 141–43 and, for example, his observation that "The spectre of Mme Guyon flits around a truth and makes the place uninhabitable."

52. Arnold, *Unpartheyische Kirchen- und Ketzer-Historie* (1740–42), 1:25–30, my translation.

53. See Scott Dixon, "Faith and History on the Eve of Enlightenment: Ernst Salomon Cyprian, Gottfried Arnold, and the *History of Heretics*," *Journal of Ecclesiastical History* 57 (2006): 33–54, based on Georgius Groschius and Ernst Salomon Cyprian, *Nothwendige Verthaidigung der evangelischen Kirche wider die Arnoldische Ketzerhistorie* (Frankfurt: Spring, 1745).

2

Gelassenheit and Confessionalization

Valentin Weigel Reads Meister Eckhart

ALANA KING

If the phrase "mysticism and reform" challenges the idea that the sixteenth-century Protestant Reformation is the only reform movement worthy of the name—both rethinking the Middle Ages as dynamic rather than static, and mysticism as this-worldly rather than purely other-worldly—it also raises the question of just what role mysticism played in the Protestant Reformation. For many, the phrase "Protestant mysticism" is a contradiction in terms:[1] "Entweder die Mystik oder das Wort" (either mysticism or the Word),[2] declares Emil Brunner.[3] The epigram to Brunner's work firmly aligns Protestantism with the Word: "Verbum est principium primum, Luther."[4] With the weight of Luther's authority behind him, Brunner suggests that mysticism is somehow not quite Christian—or at least not quite biblical—and thus has no place in Protestantism, which purports to be firmly rooted in scripture as Luther's principle of *sola scriptura* has it. Brunner writes: "Gott kommt zu uns, indem er *spricht*. Die Taten Gottes sind Kundmachungen, Euangelia. *Das* ist die Gegenwart des 'Numinosen': daß seine Gedanken kund werden. *Das* ist das Mysterium tremendum, daß er uns anruft" (God comes to us insofar as he *speaks*. The deeds of God are announcements, gospel. *This* is the presence of the "numinous": that his thoughts become known. This is the *mysterium tremendum*, that he calls us).[5] God does not make himself available to Christians via special experiences of the numinous and the *mysterium tremendum* (these words describe Brunner's understanding of mystical experience), but rather is *only* present through his call, his word, and his *euangelia*. To belong to Luther's "evangelical" camp[6] is to repudiate mysticism and respond solely to the Word.[7]

As Brunner's choice to introduce his argument with Luther's words suggests, the Wittenberg reformer's opinion on mysticism (as with so many of Luther's opinions) cast a long shadow.[8] Luther, it is true, read many of the texts now considered "classics" of the mystical canon—texts by Dionysius the Areopagite, Bernard of Clairvaux, Bonaventure, Jean Gerson, the (anonymous) *Theologia deutsch*, and Johannes Tauler[9]—but his relationship to these medieval authors is perhaps best characterized as ambivalent. Common features between these mystical texts and his own writings are counterbalanced by the elements that Luther either rejects or transforms so greatly as to make a break with the medieval sources.[10] For instance, Luther reports reading Tauler's sermons with avid interest,[11] and praised the *Theologia deutsch* for being more sound than scholastic theology,[12] while at the same time rejecting the idea of the *Seelenfunke* (*synteresis*)—so crucial to Tauler's theology and anthropology—that leads the soul to union with God.[13] Likewise, Luther praised Dionysius for articulating a negative theology that seemed to coincide with his view of God's hiddenness, but then sharply criticized the same writer for his presumptuous speculations that seemed to bypass (or to simply ignore) the crucified Christ.[14]

As important as Luther was for Protestantism, the fate of medieval mystical writers in the early modern era does not begin and end with him. Widening the scope of research on the sixteenth century in Germany, in particular to take into account the comparatively neglected second half of that century, shows that mystical texts did circulate more widely than a sole focus on Luther might suggest, and that they circulated in both orthodox and heterodox contexts. Furthermore, much of the previous scholarship on Protestant mysticism has proceeded by defining a set of ideas or motifs as mystical on the basis of medieval models (elevated as paradigmatic), and then trying to detect the presence or absence of these ideas in Protestant texts.[15] A more fruitful approach is a close reading of texts by Protestants that document an engagement with medieval texts, to discover how those medieval texts are retained or transformed, reclaimed or reappropriated.

The writings of the sixteenth-century Lutheran minister Valentin Weigel (1533–88) are one instance where medieval mystical writings—in this case the writings of Meister Eckhart—take center stage. Eckhart's writings were not well known in the sixteenth century,[16] making it unusual that a sixteenth-century author—and, as Brunner's and Luther's views on medieval mysticism suggest, a Protestant author at that—would give Eckhart such a prominent place. Weigel's treatment of Eckhart occurs, broadly speaking, in two phases: the first in which Weigel receives Eckhart's writings and the second in which he transforms Eckhart's ideas to serve as crucial arguments in his own theological projects.[17] In this essay, I examine this first phase and two episodes from the second phase.

Weigel's initial contact with Eckhart is documented in a short treatise from 1570, a text that essentially consists of Weigel's reading notes on sermons by Eckhart and Tauler, through which he becomes thoroughly acquainted with his medieval source material.[18] Here, Weigel zeroes in on the concept of spiritual poverty, including a nearly word-for-word transcription of Eckhart's sermon on that same subject.[19]

The key productive transformation of Eckhart's idea of spiritual poverty appears in his treatise on epistemology, *Der güldene Griff* (*The Golden Grasp*). Weigel's activity as a writer spanned the decades between the Lutheran Church first gaining a legitimate foothold in Europe under the terms of the Peace of Augsburg (1555) and its consolidation and empowerment under the protection of the respective rulers of various states throughout the sixteenth century. The transition from persecuted minority to established majority was a rocky one, the end-point of which was the publication of a document entitled the *Formula of Concord* in 1577. In Weigel's Saxony, all church ministers were required to acknowledge the force of this document with their signatures, at risk of losing their posts or even being exiled. Though many were in favor of the unity and calm that this *Formula* aspired to create, and though many agreed with the theology it promulgated, Weigel disagreed with a number of significant doctrinal points, and thought that the *Formula* chiefly had the effect of producing a *false concord*, where divergent opinions were not voiced out of fear.

True concord, as Weigel envisages it, was more difficult to attain, and it was to this end that Weigel took up Eckhart's notion of spiritual poverty. Weigel reimagines spiritual poverty as a means of generating agreement among a group hopelessly divided by dispute and debate, despite ostensibly belonging to the same denomination. In his treatment of spiritual poverty, Eckhart pushes the process of detachment beyond giving up possessions, knowledge, and desires to the point of abandoning one's very self, his goal being to return the soul to the unity it enjoyed with God before creation: the soul should be "as it was when it was not." For Weigel, this ultimate spiritual poverty has important epistemological ramifications. Abandoning the self entails abandoning the self's cognitive faculties, allowing God's own cognition to take over instead, leaving God to contemplate peacefully God's own self. In such a scenario, there cannot be, by definition, any disagreement or disunity, as the various selves abandon themselves and resolve into a single viewer (God) contemplating a single object (also God).

Eckhartian spiritual poverty makes another prominent appearance in Weigel's oeuvre, this time as practical advice for how Christians should behave in turbulent, discordant times. As is fitting for giving practical advice, Weigel takes up a pastoral form—the sermon. The sermon in question is part of his most controversial work, the *Kirchen- oder Hauspostille* (*Church or House Postil*), and treats the flight of the Holy Family from Herod's violent revenge on all the male children in Bethlehem. Weigel asks why God allowed this terrible slaughter to happen and why Christ did not intervene: surely the God incarnate need not fear an earthly king and be reduced to sneaking away at night to escape? Weigel reads the flight into Egypt as a defense of non-intervention in political affairs: it is better to refuse to be tempted into violence altogether by fleeing and hiding, which is not cowardice, but rather imitation of Christ himself. Just as Christ chose not to return Herod's violence with violence, a Christian should avoid intervening in earthly affairs because *any* intervention (even on the side of truth) can only increase conflict—never resolve it. Moreover, Weigel draws parallels between Herod's Judea and the Saxony of his own time, where corrupt priests, blinded by self-interest, cooperate with an earthly ruler to persecute the innocent and the faithful. Crucially, Weigel writes that the Holy Family knew that flight was the right choice because they had attained spiritual poverty. Weigel, then, borrows from Eckhart again, in the hopes of restoring peace and harmony to Lutheran lands: if the perfect concord that Weigel envisaged in *Der güldene Griff* is not to be attained, then at least Christians should imitate Christ in avoiding even more conflict by not joining the fray.

As his longing for harmony and unity suggests, Valentin Weigel had a strained relationship with the Lutheran Church. The outer facts of his career suggest a loyal son of the new Lutheran Church: he studied theology at Wittenberg (Luther's own university), was ordained a minister in 1567, and was charged with the spiritual care of the city of Zschopau in Saxony, where he worked until his death, mostly undisturbed by the Lutheran superintendents.[20] His writings (none of which were published in his lifetime, except for a single sermon) suggest a different figure altogether. Weigel rails against almost every aspect of the Lutheran Church, declaring it spiritually corrupt, in thrall to worldly rewards and the schemes of worldly rulers, given to cruel persecution of dissenters, and disgraced by the same bureaucratic spirit that Luther had so hated in the Roman Church.[21] Moreover, Weigel points to what he believes is a serious flaw in Luther's theology, namely that Luther emphasizes man's sinfulness to such a great extent that there is a danger of there being no fertile ground at all on which God's word might fall. Whereas Luther believed that the exteriority of salvation relieved man of the burdens of endless spiritual discipline, Weigel saw only indifference. As Weigel exclaims, "O du wilt dich behelffen mit der *iustitia imputatiua* und wilt dir den Tod Christi von aussen an zurechnen, seiner trösten, auf seine Kreuden zechen, ein unerstorben, ungetödet Leben füren, wie du es dann beweisset mit deiner Lehre und Wandel" (Oh, you would help yourself with the *iustitia imputativa* and would account Christ's death to yourself externally, comforting yourself with him, drinking at his expense).[22] If grace, for Luther, is *extra nos*, Weigel objects that Christ will remain external unless he is already there, or, more precisely, unless Christ had never been absent from the soul.

Weigel eventually came to understand the church as a purely spiritual community of true believers, rejecting entirely the idea that salvation was dependent on church membership. Unbaptized children, Muslims, and heathens were all potentially saved, provided they accessed the salvation they carried around with them by their very nature, in the ground of their souls, rather than needing to listen to sermons, to receive baptism or communion, or even to read the Bible.[23] This wholesale rejection of the worldly church apparatus—and especially the verbal (including liturgies of the word like baptism and communion) and textual aspects of church life—made Weigelianism into a fearsome heresy in the eyes of orthodox Lutherans, following the posthumous publication of Weigel's writings beginning in 1609.[24]

That Weigel came across Eckhart's writings in the first place is rather unusual; that he gives them such a prominent place in his own theological project is even more so. Conspicuously absent from the abovementioned list of mystical authors Luther was familiar with is Meister Eckhart—and frustratingly so for the contemporary reader, for whom Eckhart is the originator of the tradition of German mystical writing and one of the great German thinkers. Prior to Eckhart's triumphant return to the mainstream in the late eighteenth century,[25] his name was mentioned only sporadically in the early modern era, in part because his papal condemnation in 1329 hindered an enthusiastic and open appreciation of his ideas. Indeed, Eckhart's student Tauler was far more highly regarded than his teacher, and it was with the description of being "Tauler's source" that Eckhart's name was cited in the 1521 edition of Tauler that Weigel read.[26] That 1521 edition is the first appearance in print of a collection of Eckhart's German sermons, but only as an annex to Tauler's sermons.[27] Here, Eckhart's name appears neither on the title page nor in the volume's running titles, so a sixteenth-century reader's encounter with Eckhart's writings would only have been a by-product, so to speak, of an interest in Tauler.[28]

Following the publication of this rather successful book,[29] orthodox Lutheran theologians begin to react to Eckhart's ideas (albeit categorized under Tauler's name), finding specific fault with the Eckhartian notion of *Gelassenheit*. One such orthodox Lutheran, Matthias Lauterwalt,[30] though he does not use the word itself, describes how a person responds to God's call to salvation by withdrawing his thoughts into himself and away from all creatures, forgetting them entirely ("alle seine gedancken in sich abziehe von allen Creaturn / und derer gantz und gar vergesse") so that he forgets even his own self ("also / das er nicht von im selber wisset") and becomes empty ("lehr worden")—using, that is, the characteristic vocabulary that Tauler and Eckhart use to describe *Gelassenheit*.[31] Attaining this state, however, cannot happen in this life; Lauterwalt makes it clear that there is only one way to salvation, and that is by having faith in Christ. To seek other paths to redemption is to tempt the Lord by asking for extra divine intervention to achieve salvation in an irregular fashion.[32]

By contrast to Lauterwalt's lukewarm response to Eckhart and Tauler, Weigel enthusiastically embraced Eckhart's treatment of spiritual poverty in his first extant work, *Zwene nützliche Tractat, der erste von der Bekehrung des Menschen, der ander von Armut des Geistes oder waarer Gelassenheit* (*Two useful tracts, the first about conversion, the second about poverty of spirit or true Gelassenheit*).[33] In the second of the two tracts, Weigel copies almost the entire text of Eckhart's well-known sermon *Beati pauperes spiritu*, in which Eckhart formulates a demanding definition of spiritual poverty.[34] Understanding what Weigel makes of spiritual poverty is the focus of this essay, but for now I focus on Eckhart's sermon. Eckhart begins by setting aside what he calls outer poverty ("ein ûzwendigiu armuot"),[35] the giving up of earthly possessions, though he does concede that it is praiseworthy to live as Jesus lived on earth. Eckhart is more interested in an inner poverty ("ein inwendigiu armuot"), the spiritual poverty that Christ praises in the Sermon on the Mount, and, crucially, the spiritual poverty that grants access to the kingdom of heaven. Eckhart's definition of spiritual poverty proves to be far more complex than the simple formula by which he introduces it: spiritual poverty is wanting nothing, knowing nothing, and having nothing ("daz ist ein arm mensche, der niht enwil und niht enweiz und niht enhât").[36]

In the first of these three things—willing nothing—Eckhart demanded a greater sacrifice than other theologians might. It is not enough simply to desire only what God desires, to align one's own will with God's will, since this still implies the presence of will—the will to do God's will is still a will.[37] Nor is it enough to cease desiring frivolous earthly things and begin desiring lofty things such as eternity or even God himself ("begerunge hât der êwicheit und gotes").[38] Eckhart calls for the soul to be as free of willing and desiring as it was "when it was not," as Eckhart puts it ("sô sol er sînes geschaffenen willen alsô ledig stân, als er tete, dô er niht enwas").[39]

Breaking through to an uncreated or pre-created state is important to Eckhart because he conceives of creation as separation from God, which somehow diminishes both God and creature. Echoing Yahweh speaking to Moses from the burning bush, Eckhart says that before creation flowed out from him, God was simply what God was ("er was, daz er was"), but God is now God-in-creatures ("'got' in den crêatûren").[40] After creation, "God" is no longer the perfect end of creation ("sô enist er niht ein volmachet ende der crêatûre") no matter how great the God-in-creatures may still be.[41] Because, for Eckhart, God is both perfect and entirely "one," God cannot have any "distinction" in him that would mar this complete unity, whereas creatures must be either one thing or another ("this or that").[42] That is, God-in-creatures contains a distinction (God versus God's creation) that the soul must strive to break through into union.

Moreover, the creature is also somehow diminished by being created and therefore separated from God. When the creature existed in this union with God, it enjoyed a sovereign freedom not unlike God's own omnipotence. Speaking in the first person here, Eckhart proclaims that, when it was in God, the "I" was the cause of itself ("sache mîn selbes").[43] And like God, the "I" is perfect in itself, desiring nothing and lacking nothing ("dô enwolte ich niht . . . dô wolte ich mich selben und enwolte kein ander dinc").[44] In order to be truly perfected and blessed, the creature must not simply strive for union with God-in-creatures, but rather must also strive to return to this state before creation ("dô er niht enwas") and be united with God; the will is something created, the creature must give it up altogether.[45]

The second element of spiritual poverty—knowing nothing ("der [ist] arm, der nichts weiß")—calls for the creature to return its state of spiritual ignorance enjoyed by the creature before creation.[46] A person who is spiritually poor should be so bereft of all knowing that he does not even know that God is in him. Knowledge requires the knowing subject to be distinct from the object that is known, and there can be no distinction of any kind in such a perfect union with God. The soul could not take God as its object in order to know God because God is not an "other" nestling inside the soul, but rather is the soul itself ("dô der mensche stuont in der êwigen art gotes, dô enlebete in im niht ein anderz; mêr: waz dâ lebete, daz was er selber").[47] This ignorance of God is not a defect (a failure to be in possession of information about God, so to speak), but rather, knowledge of God is by definition an impossibility.[48]

The anthropological basis for the possibility of such an intimate union with God is what Eckhart calls a "something in the soul" ("einez ist in der sêle"), rather than from either knowing God or from loving God ("an bekennenne und an minnenne") as other theologians have taught.[49] This "something" is a relic of the soul's existence before creation and thus shares certain divine attributes. It is eternal (it has neither "before" nor "after") and perfect (it is not awaiting anything additional ["keines zuokomenden dinges"]).

In describing the third element of spiritual poverty—having nothing—Eckhart continues to develop this tension between distinction and unity. His previous opinion on possessions and attachments was that the soul should free itself from all of these so that it might hollow out an empty place ("möhte sîn ein eigen stat gotes") in which God might work ("dâ got inne möhte würken").[50] Eckhart has now revised this opinion, having realized that he had not taken spiritual poverty far enough. In this new position, the person pursuing spiritual poverty must relinquish even a self *in which* God can work.

Instead, the truly poor of spirit allow God himself to be the place in which God works ("daz er selbe sî diu stat, dar inne er würken wil").[51] God, concludes Eckhart, must be active in God's own self rather than a person's individual self, "ein würker in im selben," because preserving a separation between self and God is to hold on to distinctions ("underscheit"), which, as I discussed above, are entirely alien to God's unity and perfection.[52]

An interesting editorial interpolation by Weigel demonstrates that he has understood the logic of Eckhartian *Gelassenheit*. Later in the second tract, Weigel quotes from another Eckhart sermon, making the now-familiar argument that the soul must detach itself from all created things. Weigel then inserts a clause into this sentence that is not found in either the critical edition of the Eckhart sermon or the Basel Tauler edition before resuming the Eckhart quotation (I have put the words that Weigel added in italics): "Der Mensch, der sich allzumal liese einen Augenblick *inn gelassener Gelassenheit, das ist, das er nicht wuste, das er sich gelassen hette*, dem wurden alle Ding gegeben" (The person who gives himself for one blink of an eye to *abandoned abandonment, so that he did not know that he had abandoned himself*, to him were all things given).[53] The person who receives this reward is one who abandons himself in "gelassener Gelassenheit," clarifying that this doubling of Eckhart's term designates the height of *Gelassenheit*, when a person does not even know that he attained *Gelassenheit*. That this second-order *Gelassenheit* becomes the title of this small work is an indication of the importance of Eckhart's conception of spiritual poverty to Weigel.

In describing the kind of union achieved in absolute spiritual poverty, Eckhart left himself open to charges of heterodoxy. While many theologians did admit that the soul could be swept up into God in rapture, most were reluctant to argue that the soul is identical to God in union as Eckhart does, and would maintain that union cannot overcome the necessary distinction between creature and Creator.[54] Indeed, Eckhart's teaching on the union of man and God is one of the doctrines to which the Inquisition objected.[55] From both a theological and an institutional perspective, such a belief in the identity of God and soul is worrisome. The presence of a "something" in the soul that is the source of all blessedness is difficult to square with the corruption caused by original sin since it implies that original sin is an obstacle that can be obviated, and that blessedness is somehow also permanently in man's possession and does not have to be granted specially by God. Furthermore, Eckhart makes very little mention of the church as dispensing blessedness, even though he did not deny the necessity of the church and felt himself gravely misunderstood on this point.[56] Unsurprisingly, the idea that the soul should not desire anything at all, even holiness or salvation, was condemned—if the soul desires nothing at all, then there is no need for the church even to facilitate the attainment of blessedness.[57]

Three centuries after Eckhart's condemnation, Nicolaus Hunnius, an orthodox Lutheran theologian,[58] found himself in agreement with the medieval Inquisitors in objecting strongly to this same complex of ideas, which he, following Weigel's lead, terms *Gelassenheit*. Indeed, Hunnius identifies Weigel as the chief originator of the term, citing numerous examples from Weigel's texts. Hunnius allows that the Lutheran Church can accept a version of *Gelassenheit*, which he takes to mean nothing more than willingly converting, rather than stubbornly resisting God's grace.[59] Alas, he writes, Weigel taught a heterodox version of *Gelassenheit*, calling for people to give their minds, bodies, and senses to God completely, so that he can use them as he pleases.[60] Even worse is Weigel's claim that it is only in a state of *Gelassenheit* that man can receive divine teaching ("göttliche Lehre emphfangen"). Hunnius is clear about why he shudders at this kind of *Gelassenheit*: it denies the efficacy of the spoken word, spoken by an ordained minister, duly occupying an office which Christ himself instituted, and which is a kind of order established by God for instructing humankind toward its salvation. Such a malignant species of *Gelassenheit*, Hunnius concludes, can only be the work of Satan.[61]

This kind of *Gelassenheit* does not belong to the true (Lutheran) faith, so Hunnius ascribes it to his opponents instead, claiming that both Catholics and Anabaptists rely on Weigelian *Gelassenheit* to support extra-biblical practices (Catholics) or encourage insurgency

(Anabaptists).[62] Hunnius wages a war on two fronts, against outside enemies (Catholics) on the one hand, and against enemies within (Anabaptists and new Prophets) on the other.

Beyond rejecting Weigel's definition of *Gelassenheit*, Hunnius's drawing of boundaries according to denomination is precisely the logic that Weigel uses the idea of *Gelassenheit* to critique. Generating and maintaining doctrinal conformity became an urgent problem in Europe beginning in the sixteenth century, and modern scholarship has attributed this to the increasingly close integration of church and state that arose after the Lutheran schism removed the church from the administrative oversight of the Roman pope; in those territories, secular rulers stepped in so as not to leave the church leaderless. This body of scholarship has coined the term "confessionalization" to describe this logic, arguing that, although religion and politics had always been "structurally interlinked" in European society, in the early modern period, religion came to play a role in all areas of society, functioning as the "central axis" between state and society.[63] That is, the administration of the church was taken over by the princes of certain territories, which means that as doctrine became tied to particular territories under the formal leadership of secular rulers, doctrinal disagreements came to have political consequences, and, conversely, that doctrinal conformity was sought in order to maintain political unity.

The Peace of Augsburg in 1555 allowed the head of each territory to decide which religion would operate in his land (summed up by the phrase "cuius regio, eius religio"),[64] but even before 1555, the evangelical movement had, after parting ways with the Church of Rome, begun to transfer the administration of religious affairs over to the secular rulers. This involved giving the prince oversight over schools, as well as the universities where ministers were now trained in the new doctrine,[65] organizing the finances for the church by dissolving church property, setting up *consistoria* (staffed by both theologians and jurists) to carry out visitations of all the parishes, and publishing a *Kirchenordnung* for each realm that established a uniform liturgy.[66] The prince also commissioned confessional documents laying out what is to be believed, which members of the clergy were required to sign, as were some secular office-holders.[67] That is, confessional documents were not simply theological statements, but also served to regulate access to political and religious leadership in the early modern state.[68]

Weigel was a keen observer of this process of confessionalization (although of course he did not use that term), and documented its consequences throughout his work. He reports, for instance, reading reams of theological disputations, quickly growing tired of these endless quarrels (*scharmutzeln*). He frankly acknowledges that, rather than clarifying what true doctrine is, these disputations only made him less certain of what to believe. These quarrels, he reports, remind him of the confusion that reigned in Babel ("Ich sahe an wie ein verworren Babel es were bey uns").[69] The Babel allusion is apt since the spiritual transgression of the Babylonians (their hubristic building project) had *political* consequences (multiple languages that divided the peoples and ended their cooperation).[70] In Weigel's case, he means that theologians had begun resolving their doctrinal disputes by reporting each other to secular authorities, defeating their opponents not in open debate but rather by imprisonment or exile.[71] Moreover, the result of failure of the Babel project was humanity's inability to communicate across new language barriers; the impotence of words after Babel serves to reinforce Weigel's own skepticism about the centrality of texts and liturgy in church life.

Doctrinal squabbles intensified in the sixteenth century[72] not simply for their own sake, but also because the demarcation of confessional boundaries became the cornerstone of the state-building process, where the interrelation of church and state functioned as the "*Schlüsselmonopol* [key monopoly] within early modern state-building."[73] One crucial tool to achieve this was a new kind of document—the confessional document. The structure of the confessional documents served both to generate cohesion within the confession and to delimit one confession from another. For instance, the articles in the chief Lutheran confessional document, the *Formula of Concord* (1577), begin by affirming, in the first-person plural, what Lutherans believe and confess ("Wir gläuben und bekennen") and then by rejecting and condemning what other confessions believe ("Dagegen verwerfen und verdammen wir einhellig alle nachfolgende irrige Artikel").[74] The

Formula of Concord marked the high point in the drive toward confessionalization during Weigel's lifetime. A product of the cooperation of many Lutheran territories, the *Formula of Concord* was meant to unify Lutherans by providing an ultimate authority in matters of doctrine, backed by the authority of the secular rulers. Duke August of Saxony, for instance, had the document circulated throughout his domain, pressuring all theologians and pastors to subscribe to it. Refusing to sign, it was made clear, would result in dismissal from one's post, or even exile,[75] and so Weigel duly subscribed (though with regret).[76]

But if Weigel dismissed the *Formula* as creating a false peace by force rather than by true consensus, how does he propose to break through the religious disputes that so destabilized Saxony in the late sixteenth century? Not, Weigel makes clear, by attempting to come up with an ultimately authoritative (and ultimately persuasive) creed. The problem was not that the doctrinal statements produced until that point were in some way defective. Rather, Weigel identifies the cause of this conflict as individuals asserting their own interpretations,[77] and therefore he believes himself able to offer the appropriate pacifying solution: cut out the interpreting individual altogether. To this end, Weigel returns to Eckhart's ideal soul in a state of *Gelassenheit*; perfectly passive, entirely one with God, beyond ideas and words, beyond willful selfhood, and devoid of knowledge and concepts, such a soul does not simply add yet another interpretation into disputatious discourse, but rather moves beyond interpretations and opinions altogether.

Understanding how Weigel deploys *Gelassenheit* in the context of his critique of confessionalization requires a detour into his epistemological theories, which he set down in *Der güldene Griff*, composed in 1578, only one year after the signatures were collected for the *Formula of Concord*. Weigel argues that every person is naturally in possession of the entirety of both earthly and divine wisdom because God's spirit was implanted in all people at creation. In the traditional Genesis narrative, God turns clay into living creature by breathing a "living breath" into Adam (Gen. 2:7). Weigel supposes that God is more generous, implanting not only life but also the divine spirit as well ("sampt dem gottlichen geiste"), thus bequeathing Adam his eternal, heavenly wisdom ("der halben liget auch die ewige himlische weisheitt in ihme").[78] Weigel concludes that true knowledge of *all* things ("all erkentnis aller dingen") is to be found within each person already.[79]

Weigel thinks that knowledge about the world is gained in the opposite way that a contemporary reader would conceive of learning. The information found in books is not taken in or absorbed by the knowing subject; instead, pre-existing knowledge implanted by God "flows out" into books, which stand not as the source of human knowledge but rather as externalized monuments (excretions, almost) of this pre-existing knowledge.[80]

The fundamental principle of Weigel's epistemology is that knowledge comes from the knower and not the object known, and he repeats this formula often throughout the text: "alle dinge kommen von Innen heraus und nicht von aussen hinein."[81] As evidence for this counter-intuitive theory of knowledge, Weigel offers the fact that people disagree about almost everything. If the object were the source of knowledge, it would simply "impress" itself on the human brain and there would be no choice but to see the object for what it is.[82] Ultimately, Weigel is less interested in developing a theory about "natural cognition" than about what he calls "supernatural cognition."[83] There are a few key differences between natural and supernatural cognition. First, in natural cognition, the knowing subject actively pursues knowledge, reaching out to the object it wants to know.[84] Second, natural cognition relies on a distinction between the knowing subject and the object known.[85] Lastly, natural knowledge can only seek to know what Weigel calls "finite objects."[86] This category includes all created things, even abstract ideas or nonphysical entities. The example that Weigel chooses to illustrate his point—the Bible—is not idly chosen. The Bible, Weigel writes, is an instance of a finite object because it is a book that the reader can touch and see, but also because it is an idea and a message created by God, and the idea of it can be enclosed and comprehended (*begreifen* and *beschließen*, as Weigel writes)[87] in the reader's mind. Moreover, Weigel knows that it is a finite object precisely because people disagree about its meaning, which, in turn, is further proof for Weigel's theory that knowledge comes from the subject and not the object.[88]

Supernatural cognition, by contrast, is passive (*leidtlich*, as Weigel calls it), and the subject does not reach out for any object at all. God's grace causes a person to "stand still" (what he also calls "celebrating the Sabbath"), by which he means completely ceasing all cognitive activities.[89] Second, supernatural cognition only occurs in relation to an "infinite" or "incomprehensible" object. There is only one object in this class, and that is God.[90] And lastly, the components necessary for knowledge in supernatural cognition are collapsed into each other. Eye[91] and object are identical: they are both God. Because God is an infinite object, and the human mind is finite, it would be impossible for any mind to comprehend God except for God's own infinite mind. Moreover, because God is always present in the inner ground of the soul,[92] when God makes man's cognitive capacities cease by an influx of grace and pours his own eye into the void left behind by their cessation, eye and object can be identical. Man is no longer the eye that perceives, but rather God is himself the eye, and perceives himself through himself: "Droben ist bewisen worden, daß in der naturlichen erkentnis der mensche das auge selber sey, Aber allhier in der ubernaturlichen erkentnis ist der mensche nicht selber die erkentnis noch das auge, sondern gott ist selber das auge im menschen" (In the preceding it has been proven that in natural knowledge the human being is the eye itself. But here in natural knowledge the human being is never the eye or the knowledge; rather, God himself is the eye in the human being).[93]

Weigel has his favorite name for this ecstatic state: *Gelassenheit*.[94] The faithful, when they are reborn and become *gelassen*, receive an immovable foundation for their knowledge: "wer den glauben hatt, des grundt is unbeweglich" (Whoever has faith, his foundation is immovable).[95] Weigel means something very specific by this immovable ground, namely that a true Christian becomes a reliable judge of right doctrine. A person who is *gelassen* has the capacity to judge all sects to discern where God's spirit truly is: "er [der glaube] ist das Urteyl, dardurch alle seckten erkennet und geurteylet werden, er ist das auge, dardurch alle geister geprufen und gesehen werden" (faith is all things . . . it is the judgment by which all sects are known and judged . . . it is the eye through which all spirits are tested and seen).[96]

This is not simply an interest in discerning true doctrine for its own sake, but rather a way of disengaging from the logic of confessionalization altogether. Weigel begins by positioning the faith that makes the soul *gelassen* as "die meßschnure, das Winckelmaß, die richtschnure, der meßstabe, damit man das himlische Jerusalem abmisset, mitt ihren einwonern" (it [faith] is the compass, criterion, the measuring rod, [and] yardstick for measuring the heavenly Jerusalem with its inhabitants).[97] By comparison, the *Formula of Concord* describes itself as a "summarischen Begriff, Regel und Richtschnur, nach welcher alle Lehre geurtheilet und die eingefallene Irrungen christlich entschieden und erklärt werden sollen" (the summary content, rule, and standard, according to which all dogmas should be judged).[98] Weigel, then, intends his *Gelassenheit* to serve as the true plumb line (*Richtschnur*) by which truth in general—and doctrine in particular—is to be judged.

However, on closer examination, the conception of *Gelassenheit* that Weigel absorbed from Eckhart cannot serve as a plumb line or a yardstick at all. As I described earlier, *Gelassenheit* leads beyond language, beyond distinction, and beyond knowledge—hardly an obvious source for a confessional document since there would be nothing to write down and no words with which to write. Moreover, if God is without distinction, it is hardly possible to describe him in a series of articles of faith since language necessarily introduces distinctions. That is, Weigel does not turn to Eckhart because he thinks that, in a state of *Gelassenheit*, Christians might thereby receive any more accurate doctrinal information with which to win any doctrinal argument. He is not trying to get hold of a bigger stick with which to beat his enemies, so to speak, but rather is seeking to disengage from the battle entirely.

Weigel makes it clear that this is the only way for people to achieve concord and agreement, by the ultimate cessation of their minds and eyes—not by some kind of consensus reached by open discussion or by a better knowledge of facts, least of all by a document to be signed under duress.[99] Repositioned in a confessional context, Eckhart's idea of the spiritually poor person surrendering his individuality to such an extent that God works in God's own self in the person becomes, for Weigel, a way of circumventing the Lutheran ecclesiastical institution which, in his eyes, had become as corrupt as the Catholic one it was meant to replace.[100] Furthermore, because illumination from God occurs by replacing the self with God, not by the self receiving anything, all believers receive the same illumination and therefore all believers believe the same thing: no single person is especially qualified to testify to the truth since all believers are equally illuminated. In practical terms, a simple layperson has as much claim to the truth as an educated theologian or an ordained minister. Collapsing the duality between subject and object, and between self and God (in the spirit of Eckhartian *Gelassenheit*), eliminates any disagreement about doctrine or scriptural interpretation by definition because there are no individuals to disagree and nothing about which to disagree—only God's serene concord with himself.

Envisaging even the potential for such perfect harmony might have been a comfort to Weigel, though it does not immediately suggest how a Christian ought to participate in both secular society and in the church—especially to those who find themselves at odds with either of those two institutions. Weigel develops a more concrete idea of how a person who is *gelassen* would behave in a sermon from his *Kirchen- oder Hauspostille*, composed around the same time as the *Der güldene Griff*, patterned on the story of the Holy Family's flight from Egypt and Herod's slaughter of the innocents (Matthew 2). In this early episode in Christ's life, Joseph is informed by an angel of Herod's evil intentions toward Jesus and secretly takes his family away from Bethlehem; Herod retaliates by having all the male babies in Bethlehem killed.

Weigel gives the passage an unexpected meaning[101] by supplementing the set text with two scriptural snippets of his own, namely Christ's words of self-defense to Pilate ("Mein Reich ist nicht von dieser Welt" [My kingdom is not of this world]), and Christ's rebuke to his disciples for cutting off the ear of the soldier who tried to arrest him at Gethsemane ("Meynestu nicht, daß ich meinen himlischen Vater bitten köndte, daß er mir zuschicken köndte mehr dann 12 Legion Engel" [Do you not think that I could ask my heavenly father to send me more than twelve legions of angels?]).[102] These two passages are the key, writes Weigel, to understanding why Mary and Joseph avoided persecution by fleeing to Egypt, rather than defeating injustice by remaining in Bethlehem and calling on God to defeat Herod's soldiers. It was not cowardice to flee under cover of darkness. Rather, the flight to Egypt makes it clear, for Weigel, that Christ *chooses* not to intervene in political affairs—even if it is to protect the innocent from persecution, and even if Jesus, as the omnipotent God made flesh, is perfectly capable of doing so.

Christ chooses not to intervene because he is neither an Old Testament religious leader like Moses ("Priester nach Art deß Alten Testaments"), nor a political leader like Herod ("nicht ein Welt König, nicht ein Herr der zeitlichen Güter").[103] Rather, the flight from Egypt is a paradigmatic example of the New Testament model for Christian behavior ("die Art deß Newen Testaments").[104] The family is wholly reliant on angelic guidance (Matt. 2:13), and moreover, the new-born Jesus cannot even walk. He is utterly dependent on others for his safety, and thus illustrates the complete quiescence of the will that should characterize a true Christian.

For Weigel, this episode demonstrates that the Holy Family is not only materially poor, but also lacks what he calls self-will (or more literally, ownership of the will, "Eigenthumb deß willens").[105] Evasion, slipping away quietly at night, is the right thing for a Christian to do, and exemplifies the posture of the true believer, which Weigel again calls *Gelassenheit*. He describes the flight as an "Eigenschafft deß Glaubens Christi oder seines Evangelij," which is to be "ihme selber entnommen . . . und Gotte gelassen," to be "left to God" or "given over" to God.[106] Joseph and Mary have faith, and obey God's instructions to flee without grumbling ("ohne Murren")—and they do this "in Gelassenheit deß willens und der Güter" (in relinquishing the will and property).[107] Moreover, Weigel explicitly condemns those who take violent action in the name of their faith ("die jenigen sich Christi oder deß Glaubens rühmen, welche umb Land und Leute kriegen und Feldschlachten thun"); this is not at all in the spirit of faith ("gantz wider den Glauben"), and is a misreading of both scripture and

Christ's life.[108] Weigel turns the story of Jesus' escape from the murderous non-Christian king into a lesson about how Christ's followers must not use violence against fellow Christians.

Though commentators note Herod's inability or unwillingness to recognize that Christ is the Messiah, Weigel is more interested in the relationship between Herod and his religious advisors, after the fashion of the close cooperation of secular and religious orders in confessionalized states. Weigel emphasizes the extent to which Herod relies on the opinion of the *Schrifftgelehrten* (scriptural scholars) rather than the Magi or his own judgment, and, conversely, the extent to which these *Schrifftgelehrten* meddle in political affairs. This might be less objectionable to Weigel were the priests in Herod's court truly pious and able to recognize that the Messiah has appeared in their midst. They are as blind as Herod, however, and do not try to stop him when he resorts to violence—a sure sign for Weigel that they are corrupt and ungodly. Herod, furthermore, tries to struggle against God's providential ordering of worldly events by murdering the male children in Bethlehem. This amounts to an exercise of self-will, and insistence on keeping hold of his "Eigenthumb deß Willens." Like all faithless people, he remains "ihnen selbst gelassen," living only for himself ("lebete ihm selber") and not for God.[109] And in contrast to Mary and Joseph, who leave their home for an impoverished life in exile, Herod clings to his royal wealth, remaining in his "Eigenthumb der Güter." Taken together—the collusion of religious and secular authorities, the blindness of the supposedly pious priests, Herod's insistence on having his own way rather than God's—the *Ungelassenheit* of Herod's court and the priests represents (as Weigel states in no uncertain terms) the source of all conflict, the "Brunn aller Kriegen."[110]

Whereas Herod's *Ungelassenheit* leads him to take violent action, Weigel commends the *Gelassenheit* of those who take no action and do not intervene in worldly affairs. Weigel's Eckhartian concept of *Gelassenheit* helps him to reach the conclusion that reform does not mean modifying earthly institutions because this kind of change can only perpetuate suffering by causing wars: the only true reform is the reformation of the soul, its becoming *gelassen*. Despite the fact that Weigel hoped to imitate Christ by a peaceful and quiet evasion (in not publishing his works, for instance, or in not publicly leaving the church in protest), his definition of reformation had practical implications for both church and state that made him *non grata*: *Gelassenheit* means that neither church nor state is ultimately *necessary*. Unlike others who fought for the reform of the church, Weigel thought that a "Christian church" was a contradiction in terms.[111] That is, it is the very idea of an institutional church that is the problem, rather than any particular incarnation of the church. Through his reading of Eckhart's mystical texts, Weigel realized that a Christian's participation or nonparticipation in them is an indifferent matter, and can neither harm nor save a truly faithful Christian.

The puzzling conclusion that Weigel drew from his reflections on *Gelassenheit* was that outright duplicity was acceptable behavior for Christians. In a marked departure from the celebrated confessors and martyrs of the early church—and of Martin Luther's defiantly public statements of belief—Weigel allowed that neither priests nor parishioners need speak out against practices that were contrary to their beliefs, if doing so would endanger their safety.[112] It was enough to practice true religion in their *gelassene* hearts, secure in the knowledge that no exterior circumstance could diminish their faith, disrupt their intimate relation with God, or compromise their salvation. Of course, "duplicity" and "cowardice" were both terms that Weigel would most strenuously have rejected: rather than cowardice, Weigel saw turning the other cheek, and rather than duplicity, a pious desire to keep sacred wisdom safe from a hostile world.

On a final note, Weigel's desire to conceal his private beliefs behind an agreeable public face poses a particular challenge to historians. Strictly speaking, true esotericism would leave no material trace, making it impossible to write its history at all; alternatively, writing a history of esoteric theologies would proceed negatively, filling in the space around a self-effacing body of knowledge.[113] Unfortunately for Weigel, his wish to be known only to initiated kindred spirits was not honored, and the posthumous publication of his writings drew the fire he anticipated while he was still alive. Fortunately for the historian, however, Weigel's works have survived, and bring to light an unusual counter-current of thought in the sixteenth century—an engagement with mysticism, and specifically with Meister Eckhart. Ironically, the very writings that Weigel hoped to keep private also help illuminate the afterlife of the ideas of Meister Eckhart, a figure who (unlike Weigel, unintentionally) all but disappeared from the mainstream of Christian theology in the sixteenth century. Perhaps not entirely in the spirit of Martin Luther's *sola scriptura*, both the historian and the theologian must ultimately rely on the texts of absent authors.

NOTES

1. For an overview of Protestant disavowals of mysticism, see Karl Dienst, "Protestantische Mystik: Begriff—Geschichte—Kontexte," *Ebernburg Hefte* 31 (1997): 429–41.

2. Unless otherwise indicated, all translations in this essay are my own.

3. Emil Brunner, *Die Mystik und das Wort: Der Gegensatz zwischen moderner Religionsauffassung und christlichem Glauben dargestellt an der Theologie Schleiermachers* (Tübingen: J. C. B. Mohr, 1924), 5.

4. Brunner, *Die Mystik und das Wort*, 5.

5. Brunner, *Die Mystik und das Wort*, 5.

6. "Evangelical" was the name that Luther and his followers used for themselves, whereas "Protestant" and "Lutheran" were terms that others applied to them. Emphasizing the primacy of the *euangelia* is another way that Brunner indicates that Lutheran theology is true, and moreover, true because it is based on the evangelical speech act. Diarmaid MacCulloch, *Christianity: The First Three Thousand Years* (New York: Viking, 2010), 608.

7. Brunner also insists that union (a central theme in mystical texts) is nothing more than hearing and responding to God's word: insofar as a Christian accepts God's words, they become part of his person, which constitutes a kind of union. "Dieses Rufen hören, diesem unfaßbaren Sprechen Glauben schenken, diese Wahrheit, die all unsere Wahrheiten außer Kraft setzt . . . diese uns Fernste . . . als *unsere* geltende Wahrheit und darum als unser innerstes Wesen glauben, das ist das Teilhaben an Gott, von dem allein evangelische Gotteserkenntnis etwas weiß und wissen will" (Hearing this call, believing this incomprehensible speaking, this truth that disempowers all our truths . . . believing this truth that is farthest from us . . . to be *our* valid truth and therefore our most inner being, this is what it means to participate in God, in the only sense that is acceptable to the evangelical knowledge of God). Brunner, *Die Mystik und das Wort*, 6.

8. The literature on this subject is voluminous. See, for instance, Heiko Oberman, "*Simul gemitus et raptus*: Luther and Mysticism," in The *Dawn of the Reformation: Essays in Late Medieval and Early Reformation Thought* (Edinburgh: T&T Clark, 1986); Alois M. Haas, "Luther und die Mystik," *Deutsche Vierteljahrsschrift für Literaturwissenschaft und Geistesgeschichte* 60, no. 2 (1986): 177–207; Bernard McGinn, "Vere tu es deus absconditus: The Hidden God in Luther and Some Mystics," in *Silence and the Word: Negative Theology and Incarnation*, ed. Oliver Davies and Denys Turner (Cambridge: Cambridge University Press, 2002), 94–114; Steven E. Ozment, "Eckhart and Luther: German Mysticism and Protestantism," *The Thomist* 42 (1978): 259–80; idem, *Homo Spiritualis: A Comparative Study of the Anthropology of Johannes Tauler, Jean Gerson and Martin Luther (1509–1516) in the Context of their Theological Thought* (Leiden: Brill, 1969); Paul Rorem, "Martin Luther's Christocentric Critique of Pseudo-Dionysian Spirituality," *Lutheran Quarterly* 11 (1997): 291–307; Denys Turner, *The Darkness of God: Negativity in Christian Mysticism* (Cambridge: Cambridge University Press, 1995).

9. Oberman, *Dawn of the Reformation*, 140. Oberman points out that it is not clear that Luther even thought of them collectively as "mystical" authors belonging to a coherent body of thought, the category of mysticism being a much later innovation. Consequently, Luther could be said to have had no opinion on mysticism per se, but rather only on the individual writers. Luther distinguishes, for instance, between a "mystical sermon" by Tauler, presumably to contrast with Tauler's non-mystical sermons (140–41).

10. A number of scholars have argued that, on the contrary, there are many mystical elements in Luther. Berndt Hamm, for instance, argues that "Luthers ausgereifte Theologie, die man im Vollsinn des Wortes als 'reformtorische' bezeichnen kann, hat nicht nur eine mystische Seite oder Dimension und rezipiert nicht nur traditionelle mystische Motive, Bilder und Begriffe, sondern zeigt in ihrer Gesamtkomposition mystischen Charackter" (Luther's mature theology, which can be termed, in the fullest sense of the word, "reformatory," does not only have a mystical aspect or dimension, and does not simply receive traditional mystical motifs, images, and concepts, but rather has, in its entire composition, a mystical character). Berndt Hamm, "Wie mystisch war der Glaube Luthers?" in *Gottes Nähe unmittelbar erfahren: Mystik im Mittelalter und bei Martin Luther*, ed. Berndt Hamm and Volker Leppin (Tübingen: Mohr Siebeck, 2007), 242. However, Hamm then states that his argument depends on his redefinition of mysticism, a specifically Reformation faith-mysticism: "Man wird sich umgekehrt darauf einlassen müssen, bei Luther einem neuen Typ von Mystik, einer reformatorischen Glaubensmystik, zu begegnen, so wie es im Mittelalter wiederholt frappierende Neuaufbrüche der Mystik gab" (One will, however, have to engage with a new type of mysticism in Luther, a Reformation faith-mysticism, just as there were, in the Middle Ages,

striking departures in mysticism) (243). In particular, Hamm suggests that an inability to see that Luther's theology is fundamentally mystical is due to a view of mysticism that relies too strongly on Dionysius and Meister Eckhart. That Hamm argues for a constantly evolving mysticism, against a universal or trans-historical one, is interesting; however, Hamm is asking a different question (whether Luther pioneered a new kind of mysticism) than mine (how Luther related to medieval mystics). See also Carl E. Braaten and Robert W. Jenson, *Union with Christ: The New Finnish Interpretation of Luther* (Grand Rapids: Eerdmans, 1998); Bengt R. Hoffman, *Luther and the Mystics: A Reexamination of Luther's Spiritual Experience and His Relationship to the Mystics* (Minneapolis: Augsburg, 1976).

11. Steven Ozment, *The Age of Reform: 1250–1550* (New Haven, Conn.: Yale University Press, 1980), 239; Bernd Moeller, "Tauler und Luther," in *La mystique rhénane: Colloque de Strasbourg, 16–19 mai 1961* (Paris: Presses Universitaires de France, 1963), 157–68, at 159.

12. Martin Luther, *The Theologia Germanica of Martin Luther*, ed. and trans. Bengt Hoffman (Mahwah, N.J.: Paulist, 1980), 53–54.

13. Ozment, *Homo spiritualis*, 214–15.

14. Rorem, "Martin Luther's Christocentric Critique," 291–92.

15. Even Hoffman, who explicitly rejects this approach of dealing with mysticism en bloc as he calls it (Hoffman, *Luther and the Mystics*, 37–38), ultimately does just that, in statements such as "we are pointing out the essentialness of the mystical in the Reformer's justification experience" (218). Moreover, Hoffman defines mysticism as the "'experimental' and 'experiential' apprehension of God" (16) and sets out to document Luther's "experiences of the invisible" (218). To define mysticism as experiential is already to exclude the consideration of certain mystical writers from discussion—Dionysius and Eckhart in particular—whose writings, as Denys Turner argues, are chiefly to be understood as a critique of experientialism and mystical experiences. Turner, *Darkness of God*, 258–73.

16. Ingeborg Degenhardt, *Studien zum Wandel des Eckhartbildes* (Leiden: Brill, 1967), xvi.

17. Winfried Zeller writes that Weigel's interest in Eckhart is limited to his early writings. Although mentions of Eckhart's name and long quotations from Eckhart's sermons are not indeed found in Weigel's later works, the concept of *Gelassenheit*, which Weigel initially takes from Eckhart, continues to occupy a prominent place in Weigel's later writings, as this essay demonstrates. Winfried Zeller, "Eckhartiana V: Meister Eckhart bei Valentin Weigel: Eine Untersuchung zur Frage der Bedeutung Meister Eckharts für die mystische Renaissance des sechzehnten Jahrhunderts," *Zeitschrift für Kirchengeschichte* 57 (1938): 338.

18. Although this early work does not contain many of Weigel's own words, recent work has emphasized that note-taking (Blair), compilation and excerpting (Poor), and even footnoting (Newman) are all important textual practices for medieval and early modern writers, and should not be discounted as sub-literary or sub-philosophical. Ann Blair, *Too Much to Know: Managing Scholarly Information Before the Modern Age* (New Haven, Conn.: Yale University Press, 2010); Sara S. Poor, *Mechthild of Magdeburg and Her Book: Gender and the Making of Textual Authority* (Philadelphia: University of Pennsylvania Press, 2004); and Jane Newman, *The Intervention of Philology: Gender, Learning and Power in Lohenstein's Roman Plays* (Chapel Hill: University of North Carolina Press, 2000).

19. This early Weigel text is entitled *Zwene nützliche Tractate, der erste von der Bekehrung des Menschen, der ander von Armut des Geistes oder waarer Gelassenheit* (Two useful tracts, the first on the conversion of men, the second on spiritual poverty or true detachment), written in 1570. The second tract on "true detachment" contains Weigel's very close paraphrase of Eckhart's sermon on spiritual poverty; I discuss this work more fully later in this essay. There is no English translation as yet, but the tracts are reprinted in the critical edition of Weigel's works. Valentin Weigel, *Sämtliche Schriften*, 7 vols., ed. Will-Erich Peuckert and Winfried Zeller (Stuttgart: Friedrich Frommann Verlag-Günther Holzboog, 1966), 3:5–87.

20. Andrew Weeks, *Valentin Weigel (1533–1588): German Religious Dissenter, Speculative Theorist, and Advocate of Tolerance* (Albany: State University of New York Press, 2000), 5–17.

21. Weigel's most explicitly anticlerical piece is his *Dialogus de Christianismo*, in *Sämtliche Schriften*, 7 vols., ed. Alfred Ehrentreich (Stuttgart: Friedrich Frommann Verlag-Günther Holzboog, 1966), 4:3–158.

22. English translation cited from Weeks, *Valentin Weigel*, 139; German from Weigel, *Dialogus*, 4:112–13.

23. Weigel repeats this idea throughout his work, but see, for instance, Weigel, *Zwene nützliche Tractate*, 32–33; idem, *Vom Leben Christi*, in *Sämtliche Schriften*, 7:133.

24. Weeks, *Valentin Weigel*, 180.

25. See, for instance, Ingeborg Degenhardt, *Studien zum Wandel des Eckhartbildes* (Leiden: Brill, 1967); idem, "Meister Eckhart," in *Kindlers neues Literatur Lexikon* (1998), 5:19.

26. The short paragraph that prefaces the section of Eckhart's sermons in the first printed edition reads: "Folgen hernach etlich gar subtil und trefflich kostlich predigen, etlicher vast gelertter andechtiger vätter und lerer, auß denen man achtet Doctorem Tauler etwas seins grundes geno[m]me[n] habe[n]" (What follows are a few precious and very valuable sermons by several very

learned and pious fathers and teachers, from whom Doctor Tauler took some of his grounding, as one can see). Johannes Tauler and Meister Eckhart, *Joannis Tauleri des heilige[n] lerers Predig / fast fruchtbar zuo eim recht christlichen leben* (Sermons of Johannes Tauler the holy teacher, very fruitful for a truly Christian life) (Basel: Adam Petri, 1521), ccxlii.

27. This 1521 edition of Tauler's sermons, the so-called *Baseler Taulerdruck*, followed two other editions from 1498 and 1508, but Eckhart's sermons were not published in these earlier editions, except a set of four sermons misattributed to Tauler. Henrik Otto, *Vor- und frühreformatorische Tauler-Rezeption: Annotationen in Drucken des späten 15. und frühen 16. Jahrhunderts* (Gütersloh: Gütersloher Verlagshaus, 2003), 29–41.

28. The 1521 Tauler-Eckhart edition was the work of humanists in Basel and Augsburg who were sympathetic to the Reformation cause and published other Reformation-friendly volumes, circulating the sermons of the two medieval German authors in a Lutheran circle of readers. Because Eckhart was considered a secondary figure to Tauler, almost all the critical reception of Eckhart's writings in the sixteenth century occurs under the cover of Tauler's name (other than in Weigel, that is). On the printers involved in the Basel edition, see Christoph Reske, *Die Buchdrucker des 16. und 17. Jahrhunderts im deutschen Sprachgebiet* (Wiesbaden: Harrassowitz Verlag, 2007), 65–66; Frank Hieronymus, *1488 Petri: Schwabe 1988: Eine traditionsreiche Basler Offizin im Spiegel ihrer frühen Drucke* (Basel: Schwabe & Co Verlag, 1997), 138. On the Lutheran reception of Tauler, see Ernst Koch, "Taulerrezeption im Luthertum der zweiten Hälfte des 16. Jahrhunderts," in *"Der Buchstab tödt, der Geist macht lebendig": Festschrift für Hans-Gert Roloff*, 2 vols., ed. James Hardin and Jörg Jungmayr (Bern: Peter Lang, 1992), 2:124.

29. Otto, *Vor- und frühreformatorische Tauler-Rezeption*, 48.

30. Lauterwalt (1520?–1555)—or Lauterwald, as his name is more frequently spelled—studied at Wittenberg, then taught mathematics at the newly founded Lutheran university at Königsberg. Johann Samuel Klein, *Nachrichten von den Lebensumständen und Schriften Evangelischer Prediger in allen Gemeinen des Königreichs Ungarn* (Leipzig: Diepold and Lindauer, 1789), 185.

31. Matthias Lauterwalt, *Ein bedencken: Was zu halten sey von des erleuchten Herrn Doctor Johannis Taulers (seliger gedechtnis) Offenbarung* (Wittenberg: Veit Creutzer, 1553), 5–6. Lauterwalt's text is not paginated; the page numbers in this essay are my own.

32. Lauterwalt, *Ein bendencken*, 33.

33. Weigel, *Zwene nützliche Tractate*, 130; Weeks, *Valentin Weigel*, 65. To clarify a point of terminology, Eckhart usually referred to spiritual poverty as *abgescheidenheit*, though he sometimes also used the words *gelassen* and *Gelassenheit*. Weigel chooses the latter as his preferred equivalent for spiritual poverty,

as the title of the tracts indicates, *Armut des Geistes oder waarer Gelassenheit*, and this essay follows Weigel in using *Gelassenheit* as a synonym for spiritual poverty.

34. The pericope for the sermon is the opening to Jesus' Sermon on the Mount: "Blessed are the poor in spirit, for theirs is the kingdom of heaven" (Matt. 5:3, NIV).

35. Meister Eckhart, "Predigt 52," in *Die deutschen Werke: Meister Eckharts Predigten (25–59)*, 5 vols., ed. and trans. Josef Quint (Stuttgart: W. Kohlhammer, 1971), 2:486, hereafter referred to as DW. For an English translation of the sermon, see Meister Eckhart, *Meister Eckhart: The Essential Sermons, Commentaries, Treatises, and Defense*, ed. and trans. Edmund Colledge and Bernard McGinn (New York: Paulist, 1981), 199–203.

36. DW, 2:488.

37. The passage from Eckhart reads: "alsô lange als der mensche daz hât, daz daz sîn wille ist, daz er wil ervüllen den allerliebesten willen gotes, der mensche enhât niht armuot, von der wir sprechen wellen; wan dirre mensche hât einen willen, dâ mite er genuoc wil sîn dem willen gotes, und daz enist niht rehtiu armuot." DW, 2:491.

38. DW, 2:492.

39. DW, 2:491. Kurt Flasch points out that Eckhart is playing with time designations here ("spielt . . . mit den Zeitbestimmungen") since, strictly speaking, time is created as well, and thus there is no time before creation. Giving up ideas of before and after, past and future, also belongs to spiritual poverty. Kurt Flasch, "Predigt Nr. 52," in *Lectura Eckhardi: Predigten Meister Eckharts von Fachgelehrten gelesen und gedeutet*, ed. Georg Steer and Loris Sturlese (Stuttgart: W. Kohlhammer, 1998), 188.

40. DW, 2:492–93. Michael Sells points out that the quotation marks around the word in this passage are an editorial intervention, and that those listening to the sermon would have been left to sort out the difference between *got* and "*got*" on their own. Michael A. Sells, *Mystical Languages of Unsaying* (Chicago: University of Chicago Press, 1994), 1.

41. DW, 2:493.

42. Flasch, "Predigt Nr. 52," 186; Turner, *Darkness of God*, 162–67.

43. DW, 2:492.

44. DW, 2:492.

45. Of course, Eckhart is aware that the creature does still remain, in another sense, a creature, and it is only *insofar as* the creature is intellect that the creature is identical to God in a pre-created union. On the *inquantum* (insofar) principle, see McGinn, *Essential Sermons*, 54; Flasch, "Predigt Nr. 52," 194.

46. DW, 2:494.

47. DW, 2:495; Bruce Milem, "Suffering God: Meister Eckhart's Sermon 52," *Mystics Quarterly* 22, no. 2 (1996): 76.

48. Unfortunately, some passages of the *Basel Taulerdruck* have a number of small errors that are then taken over in Weigel's transcription. For instance, where Quint's text reads "diu werk gotes," the BT reads "den Weg Gottes," obviously either an error of a scribe in the manuscript lineage that the BT was based on, or a typesetting error in preparing the printed text. Likewise, the BT has "der muß arm sein alles seines eigenen Wesens" (he must be poor of all of his own being) where Quint has "der muoz arm sîn alles sînes eigenen wizzennes"—"wizzen" and "wesen," differing only by a minim or two, are easily confused if the scribe's hand were bad or the paper damaged. Virginie Pektas attributes this kind of error to Weigel, seeming not to have looked at the Basel edition that Weigel would have used. Virginie Pektas, *Mystique et philosophie: Grunt, abgrunt et Ungrund chez Maître Eckhart et Jacob Böhme* (Amsterdam: B. R. Grüner, 2006), 195–206. However, every one of these divergences from Quint's text originates in the Basel edition, and most of them, so far as I can tell, are what one might term "innocent" errors—misreadings of two very similar-looking words with different meanings—rather than a deliberate attempt to either change or play down any heterodox element in Eckhart's sermons since the changes are not applied consistently throughout a sermon. The sentence that confuses "wizzen" and "wesen," for instance, transcribes "wizzen" correctly in the second clause of the very same sentence. My opinion is that these errors make the Basel edition confusing in places, but that the form of the sermon is repetitive enough that most of what is omitted or distorted in one place is clearly transmitted in another, such that not only Eckhart's ideas but also his characteristic language are conveyed if the text is taken as a whole.

49. DW, 2:496.

50. DW, 2:499.

51. DW, 2:501.

52. DW, 2:502. Denys Turner calls this Eckhart's "apophatic anthropology." Turner, *Darkness of God*, 168–85.

53. Weigel, *Zwene nützliche Tractat*, 75.

54. Turner, *Darkness of God*, 142–48 and 164–67.

55. McGinn, *Harvest*, 150. In the papal bull *In agro dominico* (reprinted in Meister Eckhart, *Essential Sermons*), for instance, the relevant articles are 10 through 13 and the first of the additional objections. Article 13 reads: "Whatever is proper to the divine nature, all that is proper to the just and divine man. Because of that, this man performs whatever God performs, and he created heaven and earth together with God, and he is the begetter of the Eternal Word, and God would not know how to do anything without such a man" (78). The additional objection is: "There is something in the soul that is uncreated and not capable of creation; if the whole soul were such, it would be uncreated and not capable of creation, and this is the intellect" (80). See also Bernard McGinn, "'Evil-Sounding, Rash, and Suspect of Heresy': Tensions

Between Mysticism and Magisterium in the History of the Church," *Catholic Historical Review* 90, no. 2 (2004): 193–212.

56. McGinn, *Harvest*, 164.

57. *In agro dominico*, articles 7 through 9, in Eckhart, *Essential Sermons*, 78. Article 8 states: "Those who are not desiring possessions, or honors, or gain, or internal devotion, or holiness, or reward or the kingdom of heaven, but who have renounced all this, even what is theirs, these people pay honor to God."

58. Hunnius (1585–1643), a theology professor at Wittenberg and then superintendent of the city of Lübeck. During his time in that office, he had to deal with followers of Weigel and other suspected mystics and spiritualists—the group he calls, in the title of the work cited here, the "new Prophets." It is in arguing against their convictions that he deals with Weigel's work, which he believes to be a source for these disruptive new Prophets. See Theodor Mahlmann, "Hunnius, Nikolaus (1585–1643)," in *Theologische Realenzyklopädie*, 15 vols. (Berlin: de Gruyter, 1986), 15:707–9.

59. Nicolaus Hunnius, *Mataeologia Fanatica, oder Ausführlicher Bericht von der Neuen Propheten . . . Religion, Lehr und Glauben. Mit einer neuen Einleitung J.H. Feustkings* (Dresden, 1708), 146.

60. "Sie erfordern eine solche Gelassenheit, da wir alle unsere Sinne GOtt ergeben, daß er sie gebrauche, wie er will, und alle unsere Gliedmassen." Hunnius, *Mataeologia Fanatica*, 146.

61. The original text, in full, reads: "Durch die Gelassenheit wird die Ordnung zerrüttet und auffgehoben, welche GOTT uns zur Lehre fürgeschrieben, und deren sich die Christenheit allezeit gebrauchet hat: Das ist die mündliche Predigt, die Christus angeordnet" (Order is subverted and abrogated through *Gelassenheit*, and order that GOD prescribed for us, and which Christendom has always held by: And that is the spoken sermon, that Christ instituted). And "Nun hat ein jeder leicht zu ermessen: Wer sich in die Gelassenheit begiebet, das ist, in ein Vergessen sein selbst und aller Sinne, den mag man durchs mündliche Wort lehren, solang man will, er wird doch so wenig davon lernen, als ein Todter und ein Klotz . . . in solcher Gelassenheit, so ist unsers HErrn GOttes Lehr-Ordnung gäntzlich zerrüttet, auffgehoben und zu nichte gemacht: welches Werck einig und allein vom leidigen Satan seinen Ursprung haben muß" (Now each person can easily judge: Whoever gives himself into *Gelassenheit*, that is, into a forgetting of self and all the senses, he could be instructed by the spoken sermon for as long as one cared to teach him, and he would learn so little from it, as if he were a corpse or a clod . . . in this kind of *Gelassenheit*, our LOrd GOD's teaching order is completely subverted, abrogated, and reduced to nothing: which work can only have its origin from Satan himself). Hunnius, *Mataeologia Fanatica*, 150.

62. Hunnius, *Mataeologia Fanatica*, 151.

63. The original German of my English paraphrase reads: "Das Konzept der 'Konfessionalisierung' . . . beruht auf der Tatsache, daß in Alteuropa—im Mittelalter nicht anders als in der frühen Neuzeit—Religion und Politik, Staat und Kirche strukturell miteinander verzahn waren, daß unter den spezifischen Bedingungen der frühneuzeitlichen Vergesellschaftung Religion und Kirche nicht historische Teilphänomene waren, sondern das Gesamtsystem der Gesellschaft abdeckten und zentrale Achsen von Staat und Gesellschaft bildeten." Heinz Schilling, "Die Konfessionalisierung im Reich: Religiöser und gesellschaftlicher Wandel in Deutschland zwischen 1555 und 1620 (1988)," in *Ausgewählte Abhandlungen zur europäischen Reformations- und Konfessionsgeschichte*, ed. Luise Schorn-Schütte and Olaf Mörke (Berlin: Duncker & Humblot, 2002), 507.

64. Robert von Friedeburg, "Church and State in Lutheran Lands, 1550–1675," in *Lutheran Ecclesiastical Culture 1550–1675*, ed. Robert Kolb (Leiden: Brill, 2008), 361–410.

65. Marcel Nieden, *Die Erfindung des Theologen: Wittenberger Anweisungen zum Theologiestudium im Zeitalter von Reformation und Konfessionalisierung* (Tübingen: Mohr Siebeck, 2006); Ralf Thomas, "Die Neuordnung der Schulen und der Universität Leipzig," in *Das Jahrhundert der Reformation in Sachsen*, ed. Helmar Junghans (Berlin: Evangelische Verlagsanstalt, 1989), 120–24.

66. Anton Schindling and Walter Ziegler, *Die Territorien des Reichs im Zeitalter der Reformation und Konfessionalisierung: Land und Konfession 1500–1650*, 7 vols. (Münster: Aschendorffsche Verlagsbuchhandlung, 1990). Saxony was partitioned in 1485. Though Weigel was born and taught in Albertine Saxony, he studied at Wittenberg in Ernestine Saxony; both examples are relevant to this essay. For Albertine Saxony, 4:21ff. For Ernestine Saxony, 2:17ff.

67. Klaus Schreiner, "Rechtgläubigkeit als 'Band der Gesellschaft' und 'Grundlage des Staates': Zur eidlichen Verpflichtung von Staats- und Kirchendienern auf die 'Formula Concordiae' und das 'Konkordienbuch,'" in *Bekenntnis und Einheit der Kirche: Studien zum Konkordienbuch*, ed. Martin Brecht and Reinhard Schwarz (Stuttgart: Calwer Verlag, 1980), 351.

68. "Konkordienformel und Konkordienbuch bildeten nicht nur ein 'corpus doctrinae' . . . ; sie regelten auch gleichzeitig den Zugang zu Ämtern und Diensten des frühprotestantischen Territorialstaates und seiner Kirche." Schreiner, "Rechtgläubigkeit," 351.

69. Weigel, *Der güldene Griff*, 89.

70. Admittedly, in another sense the Babel allusion is not apt at all since, in fact, the building of the tower was perfectly successful. Were it not for God's intervention, the tower might have been built and the various peoples might have continued to cooperate, aided by their common language.

71. "Item do sahe ich wie einer den andern fur weltlicher obrigkeitt angabe, Incarcerirte, verlagte etc. von wegen der erbsund, des freien willens, der person Christi etc." Weigel, *Der güldene Griff*, 90.

72. An overview of these disputes can be found in Irene Dingel, "The Culture of Conflict in the Controversies Leading to the Formula of Concord (1548–1580)," in *Lutheran Ecclesiastical Culture 1550–1675*, ed. Robert Kolb (Leiden: Brill, 2008), 15–64.

73. Schilling, "Die Konfessionalisierung im Reich," 514. Schreiner and Schilling both note that the basis for this belief that political unity and societal harmony could be best achieved through religious unity, as summed up in the phrase "religio vinculum societas" (religion is the bond of society). Schreiner, "Rechtgläubigkeit," 351. On the development of the first confessional statements in the early church, and particularly on Emperor Constantine's involvement in the Council of Nicaea, see Gunther Gottlieb, "Confessio in der alten Kirche: Entstehung, Funktion, Inhalte," in *Bekenntnis und Geschichte: Die Confessio Augustana im historischen Zusammenhang*, ed. Wolfgang Reinhard (Munich: Verlag Ernst Vögel, 1980), 11–32.

74. *Concordia Triglotta: Die symbolischen Bücher der evangelisch-lutherischen Kirche* (St. Louis: Concordia, 1921), 776ff.

75. Inge Mager, "Aufnahme und Ablehnung des Konkordienbuches in Nord-, Mittel- und Ostdeutschland," in *Bekenntnis und Einheit der Kirche: Studien zum Konkordienbuch*, ed. Martin Brecht and Reinhard Schwarz (Stuttgart: Calwer Verlag, 1980), 274–75. Klaus Schreiner observes that the secular and religious leaders of the sixteenth century likely did not view the obligatory subscription to confessional documents as a measure designed to restrict freedom, but rather as a way to generate both religious and political consensus: "eine religiös und rechtlich qualifizierte Treuebindung gegenüber Gott und dem weltichen Herrscher." Schreiner, "Rechtgläubigkeit," 355.

76. Weeks, *Valentin Weigel*, 15–17.

77. James Simpson has investigated the negative consequences of affirming the primacy of the individual reader in sixteenth-century England. James Simpson, *Burning to Read: English Fundamentalism and its Reformation Opponents* (Cambridge, Mass.: Belknap Press of Harvard University Press, 2007).

78. Weigel, *Der güldene Griff*, 11. There is an English translation of this work: Valentin Weigel, "The Golden Grasp," in *Valentin Weigel: Selected Spiritual Writings*, trans. Andrew Weeks (Mahwah, N.J.: Paulist, 2003), 143–214.

79. Weigel, *Der güldene Griff*, 12. Unlikely as it might seem, Weigel does seem to mean that man has an innate knowledge of all the arts, crafts, and university learning.

80. "Uber das [earthly wisdom] hatt der mensche die ewige seele, durch das einblasen von gott, sampt dem gottlichen geiste, der halben liget auch die

ewige himlische weisheitt in ihme, daraus geschlossen wirdt, das alle erkentnis aller dingen, nicht aus den buchern genommen werde, sondern aus dem Menschen selbest her fliesset in den buchstaben" (Beyond that [earthly wisdom] the human being also has the eternal soul, from the inspiration by God, along with the divine spirit. For that reason the eternal celestial wisdom also lies within him, from which it can be concluded that all knowledge of all things is not taken from books, but rather flows out of the human being into the letter) (Weigel, *Der güldene Griff*, 11–12). Weigel, "Golden Grasp," 152. That Weigel demotes the written word from the source of all knowledge set him at odds with many Protestants who, following Luther, placed the utmost importance on scripture (*sola scriptura*).

81. Weigel, *Der güldene Griff*, 13.

82. Weigel concedes that external objects do play a role in our understanding but only as reminders of what we already know. Outer things are only there to jog our memories, books are there to testify to and refer us inward to the true Text—the wisdom God implanted in Adam. Weigel, *Der güldene Griff*, 39.

83. Weigel, *Der güldene Griff*, 48.

84. Weigel, *Der güldene Griff*, 48.

85. Weigel, *Der güldene Griff*, 49.

86. Weigel, *Der güldene Griff*, 49.

87. Weigel, *Der güldene Griff*, 19.

88. Weigel, *Der güldene Griff*, 85.

89. The passive state the soul must come to is not necessarily a pleasant or joyous one, but rather is "nothing less than dying," as Weigel writes ("nit weniger als in den todt gehen und sterben"). It is as if one is cast into hell or even seized with unbelief ("gantz im unglauben begriffen sein"). Weigel, *Der güldene Griff*, 55.

90. Weigel specifies that even an infinite object can still be viewed as an object (though the rest of the treatise is dedicated to ways of viewing God *not* as an object, as Eckhart admonished). He compares the incomprehensible object "God" to the ocean. The ocean is far bigger than the eye can take in at a single glance, but one part of it can still be looked at, and it is thus seen as an object but not "comprehended." Likewise, it is possible for the human mind to consider God as an object, so long as it is understood that the mind cannot possibly acquire complete knowledge of God this way, nor can it ever "comprehend" the infinite object (comprehend in the sense of "completely surround"). Aquinas also distinguishes between two meanings of comprehend ("*Comprehension* is twofold"), either to "completely surround" or rather to "attain, touch." Thomas Aquinas, *Summa Theologiae*, part 1, question 12, article 7.

91. Weigel identifies the "eye" as the seat of a person's identity. A person is not a body, but rather the sum of his talents and insights. He does not mean

the physical eye, but rather the inner eye. A smith is who he is because of his knowledge of metalworking, not because his hands are capable of working metal. Likewise, since my self is my eye, my self can be changed completely if my eye is replaced. Weigel, *Der güldene Griff*, 45.

92. "Eben das *obiectum* ist schon darinne, im Inwendigen grunde der seelen, Nemlich gottes Wort, Wille, gesetz, geist etc" (The *obiectum* is already inside, in the inner ground of the soul, namely God's word, will, law, spirit, etc.). Weigel, *Der güldene Griff*, 53. Here Weigel quotes Luke 17:21, one of his most frequently used proof-texts: "Das reich gottes ist Inwendig in euch" (the kingdom of God is within you).

93. Weigel, *Der güldene Griff*, 55. The English text is from Weigel, "Golden Grasp," trans. Weeks, 183.

94. Weigel, *Der güldene Griff*, 87. Here, Weigel identifies this ecstatic state in which God displaces the human eye to contemplate God's own self in man as being "gotte gelassen," and calls it a faith that God produces "in dem gelassenen Menschen."

95. Weigel, *Der güldene Griff*, 87.

96. Weigel, *Der güldene Griff*, 87; idem, "Golden Grasp," trans. Weeks, 203.

97. Weigel, *Der güldene Griff*, 87; idem, "Golden Grasp," trans. Weeks, 203.

98. *Concordia Triglotta*, 776–77.

99. Weigel calls this consensus among the truly faithful a *concordantz*, probably an ironic reference to the false consensus created by the *Formula of Concord*. "Doher findet sich in allen gleubigen eine *Concordantz*, ein glaube, ein Christus, ein gott, ein geist, ein Hertz, eine tauffe" (Then in consequence among all the faithful there is [to be] found one concordance, one faith, one Christ, one God, one spirit, one heart, one baptism). Weigel, *Der güldene Griff*, 50; idem, "Golden Grasp," trans. Weeks, 179.

100. Ozment, *Mysticism and Dissent*, 207.

101. Weigel is unusual in being preoccupied by the issue of whether Christ displayed cowardice in allowing the innocents to be slaughtered. In a lengthy sermon on this pericope, Luther never raises the issue of Christ's cowardice. At most, he dismisses the suggestion that the Magi ought to have reported back to Herod rather than going home by another way (because God could, of course, have protected the baby Christ with a miracle) as tempting God; God provided humanity with creation, which ought to exhaust natural means before demanding divine intervention. Moreover, in Luther's sermon, Herod is not considered as a secular ruler, but rather as a figure for the pope—any potential collusion between priests and potentate is thereby neutralized. Lastly, Luther writes that Herod deceived the priests, who are therefore not complicit in his plot to kill Christ, but rather are themselves victims of Herod's

wickedness. Martin Luther, "Das Euangelium am tage der heyligen drey künige," in *D. Martin Luthers Werke: kritische Gesammtausgabe*, 120 vols. (Weimar: Hermann Böhlaus Nachfolger, 1910), 10.1:555–728.

102. Weigel misattributes the two passages. The first is actually from John 18, the second from Matthew 26, not the other way around as he writes.

103. Weigel, *Kirchen- oder Hauspostille*, 73.

104. Weigel, *Kirchen- oder Hauspostille*, 73.

105. Weigel, *Kirchen- oder Hauspostille*, 73.

106. Weigel, *Kirchen- oder Hauspostille*, 75.

107. Weigel, *Kirchen- oder Hauspostille*, 76.

108. Weigel, *Kirchen- oder Hauspostille*, 76.

109. Weigel, *Kirchen- oder Hauspostille*, 76.

110. Weigel, *Kirchen- oder Hauspostille*, 78.

111. Leszek Kołakowski explores the development of this idea throughout the sixteenth and seventeenth centuries in great depth in his book *Chrétiens sans Église: la conscience religieuse et le lien confessionel au XVIIe siècle*, trans. Anna Posner (Paris: Gallimard, 1969). I am grateful to Professor Nigel Smith (Princeton University) for this reference. In the twentieth century, Weigel's ruminations on freedom of conscience in the context of a state religion might be productively read alongside the theology of another Lutheran dissident, Dietrich Bonhoeffer (1906–45). Bonhoeffer did not affirm duplicity for safety's sake as Weigel did, campaigning outspokenly against the Nazification of the Lutheran Church in Germany. Nevertheless, Bonhoeffer sharply criticized the Confessional Church for dispensing what he called "cheap grace." Instead, he hoped to liberate Christian discipleship from the church, advocating what he termed, intriguingly, a "religionless-secular" Christianity that has sloughed off the "outer garment" of the church, which, for Bonhoeffer, was the product of a historical circumstance, but which is not necessary to properly follow Christ. Moreover, Bonhoeffer reflected that a religionless Christian can then consider Christ as "the man who lives out of the transcendent," making "[Christ's] 'being there for others' . . . the experience of transcendence." Stephen Plant, *Bonhoeffer* (London: Continuum, 2004), 135; Ferdinand Schlingensiepen, *Dietrich Bonhoeffer (1906–1945): Martyr, Thinker, Man of Resistance*, trans. Isabel Best (London: Continuum, 2010), 353. Bonhoeffer thereby joins Weigel and Eckhart in examining how the incarnation destabilized the relationship between transcendence and immanence; examining how all three figures call into question or at least recast the role of the earthly church as a result might be an interesting avenue for future work on Weigel.

112. Weigel returns to this theme often in his work. See, for instance, Weigel, *Dialogus de Christianismo*, esp. 59–62; idem, "Ein Gespreche, wie ein Leyhe seinen Beuchtvatter uberzeuget, das der Priester an Gottes Stadt nicht Sunde vorgebe," in *Von der Vergebung der Sünden oder vom Schlüssel der Kirchen*,

Sämtliche Schriften, ed. Will-Erich Peuckert and Winfried Zeller (Stuttgart: Friedrich Frommann Verlag, 1964), 2:84–101.

113. Leo Strauss, *Persecution and the Art of Writing* (Glencoe, Ill.: Free Press, 1952). Here, Strauss proposes a provocative and problematic approach to interpretation, in which a text can mean anything if the reader suspects an author of writing a doubled text (inscribing a private, esoteric text within or behind the public text). For a discussion of Strauss, see, for instance, Ehud Luz, "How to Read the Bible According to Leo Strauss," *Modern Judaism* 25, no. 3 (2005): 264–84; Arthur Melzer, "On the Pedagogical Motive for Esoteric Writing," *Journal of Politics* 69, no. 4 (2007): 1015–31. Whether Strauss's hermeneutic is the key to Weigel's work is not the question here, especially since Weigel only published a single text in his lifetime, and so the distinction between exoteric and esoteric meanings cannot apply to his texts. Rather, Strauss's contentious essay does suggest some broader questions for future work on Weigel's writings, particularly about the role of authorial intention in interpretation, about how Weigel conceived of preaching and writing in the public sphere, and about the involvement of laypeople in theology. Moreover, Weigel himself thematizes the distinction between the exoteric (publicly confessed beliefs) and the esoteric (privately held beliefs) in texts such as his *Dialogus*, as well as his *Schrifflicher Bericht von der Vergebung der Sünden oder vom Schlüssel der Kirchen* (see in particular 54–55) and *Ein Gespreche, wie ein Leyhe seinen Beuchtvatter uberzeuget, das der Priester an Gottes Stadt nicht Sunde vorgebe* (esp. 84–85).

3

The *Arnhem Mystical Sermons* and the Sixteenth-Century Mystical Renaissance in Arnhem and Cologne

KEES SCHEPERS

In the second quarter of the sixteenth century eruptions of religious upheaval brought to light simmering doctrinal and church political conflicts that had been bound to burst out. All that was needed was a triggering event. When Luther wrote his Ninety-Five Theses in Wittenberg in 1517, he formulated a fundamental censure of the teachings of the Western church that inevitably led to divisions within the Christian world. Though Luther intended to be a renewer of doctrine, he unwillingly became a revolutionary. The wide-ranging practical consequences of his essentially "doctrinal act" solidified in the following decades and continue to this day. In the days of uncontrolled outbursts, however, the course of events was unpredictable and its outcome uncertain. Conflicting parties, reformers on all sides, played their roles with equal uncertainty over where this all would lead. In this context of fundamental conflict shocked conservatives were no less in the dark than ardent revolutionaries over what could realistically be achieved.

This period of turbulence and transformation forms the backdrop for the development of a particular type of mysticism within the context of Catholic reform. To understand this development it is important to distinguish between the phenomena of Counter-Reformation and Catholic reform. Predating the Counter-Reformation, which can be seen as the officially sanctioned offensive against the Protestants, was the movement of Catholic reform.[1] In this earlier period many Catholics still hoped to stifle the Protestant reform movement simply by showing that sincere spirituality was still alive within the Catholic tradition. This sixteenth-century Catholic reform was a highly fluid phenomenon, in which the forces of Catholic self-affirmation and renewal are difficult to distinguish from those of rejection and condemnation. Within this Catholic reform movement the mystical life had its radically spiritual niche.

During the second quarter of the sixteenth century, the bridges between the Catholic and reformation-minded worlds were starting to collapse. A region where the push for Catholic reform was particularly strong stretched from the Duchy of Guelders (or Gelre) in the Low Countries—with the principal city of Arnhem—down to the urban center of Cologne in the adjacent Rhineland. Key spiritual centers were the Saint Agnes Convent in Arnhem and the Charterhouse in Cologne. Only in the past few years has the importance of Arnhem as a leading center in the emergence of a new type of mysticism come to light.

Sixteenth-Century Mystical Renaissance

A sixteenth-century mystical renaissance was never formally declared or instigated, but it can be identified in retrospect, and the concept helps to connect seemingly separate phenomena. The Saint Agnes Convent in Arnhem and the Charterhouse in Cologne were both centers of a sudden re-emergence of mystical spirituality. The mystical life was lived with great passion by women in Saint Agnes, after a century of *Devotio Moderna* culture characterized by asceticism rather than mysticism. It was promoted with intensity by men in the Cologne

Charterhouse, who exchanged their introversion for extraversion in light of the historical circumstances prompting them to act. The mystically inclined women both in Saint Agnes and in secondary centers of spiritual revival such as Oisterwijck and Diest apparently maintained close relations with each other. They also wrote original mystical texts themselves.[2] They were, moreover, in close contact with the Cologne Carthusians, who for their part contributed to the mystical renaissance by editing and publishing classic mystical texts from fourteenth-century Brabant and the Rhineland, as well as contemporary vernacular texts, some of which were produced in Arnhem. From the symbiotic life of these groups of men and women a new mystical culture arose.

First, I introduce some aspects of the Saint Agnes Convent and its milieu, and then go on to present the leading proponents of Catholic reform initiatives from the Cologne Charterhouse. Finally, I focus on the Arnhem mysticism as expressed in the *Arnhem Mystical Sermons*.

A strong impetus for the exploration of the sixteenth-century mystical culture has come from the first close reading of the manuscript in which the *Arnhem Mystical Sermons* are found.[3] All 162 sermons are anonymous and the codex provides no clues as to its origin. In 2006 the manuscript was attributed to the Saint Agnes Convent on the basis of paleographical evidence.[4] Recently it was ascertained that the sermons themselves must also stem from Arnhem. The sermons of the sanctorale are unquestionably connected to the liturgical calendar of the diocese of Utrecht, and at least one sermon is linked to a specific devotion in Arnhem that is not found anywhere else.[5] Hence, we now know with certainty that the collection is not a translation from a lost or unknown collection in German or Latin. The collection has now been given the quite self-evident name of *Arnhem Mystical Sermons*.

Anchoring these sermons in the Saint Agnes Convent consequently led to the connection of other important sixteenth-century mystical texts to the same Arnhem milieu: *The Evangelical Pearl* and *The Temple of Our Soul*. There are close textual connections between these texts that need to be examined in depth.[6] Suddenly, Arnhem has become an eminent center of sixteenth-century mysticism.

In what follows, I describe the specificity of the mystical spirituality that the *Arnhem Mystical Sermons* articulate, as well as the other closely related texts. I start by sketching the immediate context out of which these sermons developed.

First a few words about ecclesiastical, cultural, and national boundaries. The organization of dioceses in the late Middle Ages was different from what it is today. During the period the Saint Agnes Convent flourished (second and third quarters of the sixteenth century), Arnhem belonged to the diocese of Utrecht, as it still does. The Utrecht diocese in turn was part of the archdiocese of Cologne. This is no longer the case; Utrecht is now an archdiocese itself.

Today, the Dutch province of Guelders and the region around Cologne belong to different countries, and the languages in Guelders and Cologne are clearly distinct: Dutch and German. In the sixteenth century, however, people throughout this region spoke closely related dialects. The region stretching from Guelders to Cologne was one contiguous cultural region. Thus, it was quite natural for Arnhem to have close cultural ties with Cologne.

Women in Arnhem

In the following discussion of the historical context of the Arnhem convent, I touch on three aspects of the life of the sisters in the Saint Agnes Convent: first, the external history and the communal life of the Saint Agnes Convent; second, the book culture as witness to its spiritual culture; third, the author of *The Evangelical Pearl* as possibly the most important person in the local spiritual network of the Saint Agnes women. Research into the external history and the communal life in Saint Agnes is greatly impeded by the scarcity of extant documents. Luckily, from what little documentation survived those tumultuous times, it is possible to sketch the broad outlines of the external history, although it remains unavoidably vague. In contrast and paradoxically, the innermost life of the sisters can be reconstructed with some precision from the *Arnhem Mystical Sermons*.

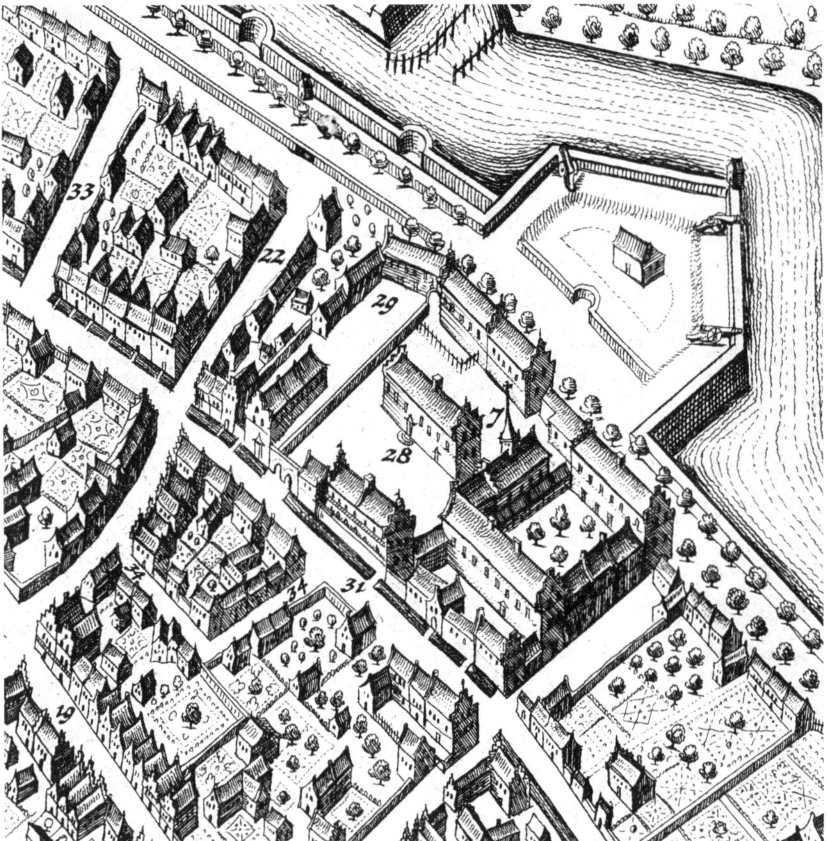

Fig. 3.1. The complex of the Saint Agnes convent in the center of Arnhem on a map printed in 1649 by Johannes Blaeu. Author's photo, courtesy of Ruusbroec Institute, University of Antwerp.

Saint Agnes Convent: History and Communal Life

The Saint Agnes Convent was located in the center of Arnhem, within the city walls (fig. 3.1).[7] It was founded in 1428 and existed until 1636. The convent had grown from a community of Sisters of the Common Life. At some time between 1420 and 1458 the members became tertiaries. Around 1460 the sisters adopted the Rule of Saint Augustine to become canonesses regular. This was a quite common trajectory for religious women in the fifteenth century. The convent was closely associated with, but never a member of, the Windesheim congregation, the monastic branch of the *Devotio Moderna*. We know that spiritual authority over the convent rested with monasteries belonging to the Windesheim congregation. Five confessors, sent out from the Albergen monastery, are known by name for the period from 1452 to 1525. Around 1560 the confessor was Nicolaas van Diepenbroick, who had come from the monastery of Bethlehem in the city of Zwolle.[8]

After 1580 a steep decline set in for the Arnhem convent. In that year Catholic life in Arnhem came to a halt. The authorities forbade Catholic worship to be carried out in public; Catholic institutions were abolished and their buildings confiscated, including the Saint Agnes Convent. Although the sisters of Saint Agnes were allowed to remain in the convent, no new novices were to be admitted. The number of nuns dwindled rapidly from one hundred in 1580 to a mere four in 1634.

The convent seems to have had its heyday in the second and third quarters of the sixteenth century. In those years a large number of the inhabitants, perhaps all of them, were of aristocratic and patrician origin. It is unlikely that this had been the case from the early days on, when the community consisted of Sisters of the Common Life, who normally were of more modest descent. It might well be that the prevalence of aristocratic daughters was typical for the convent in the sixteenth century.[9] In a letter concerning the Saint Agnes Convent, written by the Guelders Court (Hof van Gelre) located in Arnhem, it says that "in this convent numerous spiritual young ladies and religious women of good and distinguished nobility and daughters of other respectable citizens live together."[10] The social background of these sisters is a likely factor in the development of a sophisticated literary and mystical culture in the sixteenth century.

Charles of Gelre (1467–1538), Duke of Guelders, clearly took a strong personal interest in fortifying Catholic devotion in whatever way he could.[11] At his insistence, Frederik van Baden, bishop of Utrecht, added the feast of Lamentatio Mariae to the liturgical calendar of Utrecht in 1514.[12] Charles had the feast celebrated in Arnhem with great pomp and processions. He also asked the Windesheim congregation to include the feast in their calendar. The duke supported the feast in yet other ways: in 1515 he commissioned the printing of an *Officium beatae Virginis* in Paris, of which, unfortunately, no copies survive.[13] He further subsidized the printing of some small booklets of Marian and passion devotion.

As a result of these actions, Charles gained a reputation as an ardent (and even violent) defender of the Catholic Church. In this context it is important to note that in 1530 he wrote a letter to the Cologne theologians—in fact, the Carthusians—to express his support for the enormous edition project they had undertaken of the works of Denis the Carthusian (1402–71). The letter was included in the volume *Commentaria in omnes D. Pauli epistolas*, printed in 1533 at Quentell in Cologne.[14]

One of the confessors of Saint Agnes, Jan van Lochem, had previously been the prior of Albergen. During that period he wrote a journal, in which he touched on the affairs of Saint Agnes on numerous occasions. It is the most informative written source we possess about the life of that community.[15] The journal covers the years 1520–25, and we learn that Saint Agnes prospered spiritually at the time. There is an enlightening scene in Van Lochem's journal recounting a visit to the Arnhem community. Much to his delight he found the sisters admirably devoted to the religious life. I quote in translation from Latin an entry from the summer of 1522:

> When I returned from the Chapter meeting in Germany, I traveled straight to Arnhem as I had decided to conduct a visitation at the convent of the Sisters. It had been a year and a half, you see, since my last visitation, and the new rector had been in function for over a year. People urged me not to delay my visit any longer, especially since under a new rector there are often innovations against which appropriate measures must be taken. Before starting the actual visitation, I summoned the sisters individually, in the order in which they used to confess with me. As I questioned each of them about the state of the community, the peace among themselves and their discipline, I found—thank God—that the convent was in such good shape as I would like to find every-

> where. Therefore there was no reason to spend any more time on the visitation. I ended my investigation and called the sisters together. I urged them to persevere in this simplicity and sincerity. That put an easy end to my visitation, and after taking my leave I returned home, only to find that the Guelders' armed bands had arrived and wreaked havoc.[16]

Jan van Lochem's report paints a picture of a devoted community in perfect harmony. There is only a hint of religious turmoil in the expressed fear of undesirable "innovations." The peacefulness in Saint Agnes was definitely not a state of affairs that was commonplace in monasteries and convents at the time.

Some episodes in Van Lochem's journal serve to illustrate life's precariousness in the early sixteenth century. In 1521 Van Lochem's sister visited him at his monastery.[17] She had fled the village of Lochem, fearing the advent of the plague. After two weeks Van Lochem decided that it would be better if his sister returned home. She cried and objected, overcome with the very real fear of death. Van Lochem ignored her pleas and returned her to her village. Not surprisingly, she died of the plague within three weeks. The scrupulous prior agonized over the question whether she had made a timely confession; he had no second thoughts over having returned her to a plague-ridden village. Astonishing as it might seem that Jan van Lochem knowingly put his sister in mortal danger, it does reveal how utterly convinced he was that earthly existence is nothing more than an insignificant prelude to the symphony of eternal life. A prelude, however, that must be executed in the best way possible.

These were eventful and passionate times, which Huizinga could have portrayed in his *Waning of the Middle Ages*. In this period the region was scourged by both natural and manmade disasters, such as the bubonic plague, city fires,[18] icy winters, and incessant sectarian warfare—which had nothing to do with religion and everything to do with the lust for power and money. Two particularly life-threatening dangers were on everybody's mind: the Guelders wars and the plague.[19] Whoever managed to escape one threat could well fall victim to another. But on opening the codex with the *Arnhem Mystical Sermons* and reading these texts one finds complete serenity and peace, with rarely a suggestion, let alone any direct mention, of all this worldly commotion.

Book Culture

What remains of the manuscript collection of Saint Agnes is now scattered over libraries in the Netherlands, Belgium, and Germany. The original holdings of the library are unknown for lack of a book-list from the period.[20] Yet such a list must have existed since even modest books were of considerable value. We know that Alberta van Middachten, one of the daughters from a famed Guelders family, was *custos librorum* (keeper of books) in the mid-sixteenth century.[21] The books were divided into at least two groups. One extant manuscript was placed among the "best books;" therefore a second category of more ordinary books must have existed.[22]

In 1971 the historian Paul Begheyn published a list of twelve Saint Agnes manuscripts, compiled on the basis of ownership marks.[23] This list attests to a remarkable interest in the masters of fourteenth-century mysticism. The manuscripts contain works of Ruysbroeck, Eckhart, Tauler, and Suso. There are also works of Gerlach Peeters and Hendrik Herp (Harphius). It is quite remarkable to find all of these names in such a small collection. Surprisingly, no printed books are known from the collection of the Saint Agnes Convent.

The additional attribution of three manuscripts in the past few years, however, has suddenly allowed Arnhem to emerge as a center not just for the reception of mystical texts, but also of their production. First came the attribution of the so-called Gaesdonckse treatise manuscript.[24] It contains some contemporaneous mystical texts that were probably originally written in the Rhineland, though much remains unclear about them.[25] But only the attribution of manuscripts The Hague, 133 H 13 and 71 H 51 links Saint Agnes to the production of mystical texts. Both manuscripts lack ownerships marks, but the script has been recognized as belonging to Saint Agnes scribes.[26] Ms. 71 H 51 contains a large excerpt from *The Evangelical Pearl* and is the sole manuscript witness of that text. Earlier attempts to determine the provenance of the manuscript—of obvious importance because of this excerpt—have remained unsuccessful.[27] Several scholars read ms. 133 H 13 cursorily in the past century and noted the striking mystical nature of the sermons as well as the obvious correspondences with the works of Ruysbroeck, Tauler, and Eckhart. But the exceptional importance of the collection has become clear only as the contours of a mystical milieu in Arnhem have begun to appear.

A remarkable aspect of the book culture of the sisters is that they made handwritten copies of contemporary printed books dealing with mystical spirituality. A striking example is ms. Berlin, Staatsbibliothek zu Berlin—Stiftung Preußischer Kulturbesitz, 242/243 (a manuscript in two volumes). The two large folio-volumes contain a manuscript copy of the Tauler edition that was published, it is assumed, by Peter Canisius in 1543.[28] The Middle High German of the edition was translated into Dutch. The second volume also contains a translation of Gertrud of Helfta, *Insinuationum divinae pietatis libri v*, probably from the 1536 edition by the Cologne Carthusian Justus Lanspergius.[29] Another example is ms. The Hague, Royal Library, 71 H 51. The third codicological unit in this manuscript contains a translation of a printed book entitled *Hortulus devotionis*. This miscellany was compiled by an anonymous Cologne Carthusian, possibly the Brabant-born Gerard Kalckbrenner (1494–1566),[30] and printed in 1541.[31]

The case of ms. *olim* Münster, Paulinische bibliothek (Universitätsbibliothek), 698 is less certain. It contains the only known copy of a Middle Dutch translation of *Eden seu Paradisus contemplativorum*.[32] The Latin text was never published separately, but was included as the third book in the *Theologia mystica*, the edition of the works of Hendrik Herp by Dirk Loer in 1538.[33] Though we cannot be certain whether the translation was made from the printed edition or a manuscript version, given the fact that the three aforementioned works were indeed based on Cologne prints, it is quite likely that the same was the case here.

This choice of books provides interesting insight not only into the preferences of the sisters, but also into the way they acquired texts. Four manuscript texts are based on books printed in Cologne, in the edition of which Carthusians were in some way involved. The copies concern texts that either influenced Arnhem mysticism (Tauler, Eckhart) or expressed comparable mystical spirituality (Herp, Gertrud, *Hortulus*). It seems that the sisters were able to either translate the texts into Dutch themselves or have them translated for them. Finally, the fact that the books all came directly or indirectly from the Cologne Carthusians suggests that someone from Cologne brought useful texts to the attention of the sisters or even provided them with copies.

The Author of The Evangelical Pearl

The mystical aspirations of at least some of the Saint Agnes sisters were shared by other women, first and foremost by the anonymous author of *The Evangelical Pearl*. This vernacular work of fervent mysticism was first published in 1535.[34] The *Pearl* became a bestseller in four languages for three centuries.[35] It was a significant source of influence on late sixteenth- and seventeenth-century mysticism in France,[36] having been read, for example, by Pierre de Bérulle (1575–1629), Louis de Blois (1505–65), and Benoît de Canfield (1562–1611).[37]

Despite several attempts at identification, the author remains unknown.[38] The prologues in the earliest editions provide very unspecific information about the author. The prologue of the edition of 1542 certainly goes into detail and tells us she was a virgin who died in 1540 at the age of seventy-seven.[39] Still, her name and origin remain in the dark. It is almost certain, however, that she was a woman in or close (spiritually or geographically) to the Saint Agnes community in Arnhem, not just because the one existing manuscript excerpt stems from the Saint Agnes Convent, but, more important, because striking similarities exist between the mystical spirituality expressed in the *Arnhem Mystical Sermons* and *The Evangelical Pearl*.[40]

The genesis of *The Evangelical Pearl* is still obscure. The first edition of 1535 has come to be called "The Small Pearl" because shortly after publication of that text the editor, Dirk Loer, found a copy of a much extended version, which he published in 1537–38.[41] This version is called "The Great Pearl."[42] The version of "The Small Pearl," however, has parts of text that are not included in "The Great Pearl"; therefore the larger text is not merely an extension of the smaller.[43]

The *Pearl* consists of three parts with fifty-three, fifty-six, and fifty-eight chapters respectively.[44] McGinn calls it a mystagogical work and "the last masterpiece of medieval female mysticism."[45] The "valuable pearl" (Matt. 13:46) refers to the hidden treasure in the depths of each person: the potential mystical union with God. The entire work circles around this theme, in treatise-like exposés, reflections on the liturgy, meditations, spiritual exercises, and prayers. Spiritual poverty and *Gelassenheit* (detachment) are needed for God to be born in the depth of the soul. Ruh observes that in this respect the *Pearl* reveals the influence of Rhineland mysticism.[46] Particularly striking about the *Pearl* is that the author sometimes bursts out in passionate, highly personal excursuses. These are the passages in which she shows her exceptional literary talent. The *Pearl* covers all aspects of mystical life in depth and breadth: from the day-to-day practice of contemplative, religious life to the sublime experience of diving headlong into the divine abyss.

The same author allegedly also wrote *The Temple of Our Soul*, even though there are conspicuous differences besides remarkable correspondences.[47] *The Temple of Our Soul* was printed in a single edition in 1543, again with substantial involvement of the Cologne Carthusians, Dirk Loer in particular.[48] There are no surviving manuscripts. Whereas the *Pearl* was reprinted over and over again, the *Temple* seems not to have been a success. This might have to do with the fact that the *Temple* is exclusively concerned with the highest phase of the mystical life, whereas the *Pearl* provided material for every level of the spiritual life.

The *Temple* is an elaborate exposition on the mystical reliving of the life of Christ through the spiritualization of the events of the liturgical year in the "temple of the soul." The *Temple* clearly contrasts the temple of the soul to that of the material church: "In dyen tempel werden die hoochtiden gheviert ende hebben een voorbigaen, mer in desen werden si gheviert ende bliven daer weselic. In dien ist des jaers eens kermisse, maer in desen yst altoos stacie ende toevloeyinge der rijcheit ende der ghenaden Gods" (In that temple the feasts are celebrated and pass, but in this temple they are celebrated and remain in their essence. In that temple the dedication of the church takes places once a year, but in this the celebration and the flow of God's richness and grace are continuous).[49]

The anonymous author or authors of these texts must have been in contact with other individuals and groups, sharing similar spiritual desires. Some of them are mentioned by Kirsten Christensen in her contribution to this volume.[50]

Men in Cologne

The first printed edition of *The Evangelical Pearl* takes us to the second pole of the sixteenth-century mystical Renaissance: men in Cologne, more specifically Carthusians in the Saint Barbara Charterhouse. *The Evangelical Pearl* was first published in 1535 in Utrecht, with the substantial involvement of the Cologne Carthusians, and this involvement continued in the following editions that were published in Antwerp. Dirk Loer (†1554), a Cologne Carthusian from the Low Countries region of Brabant, edited the text and wrote a preface.[51] Gerard Kalckbrenner, originally from Hamont in the Low Countries, supplied introductory texts for *The Temple of Our Soul*.[52] Apparently the Carthusians were impressed with these vernacular works and deemed it useful to make them available through the printing press.

In these editions the introverted, mystical life of Arnhem women meets the activism of Cologne Carthusian men. We get a glimpse of the outside world in Dirk Loer's preface. It tells us how the text was perceived and put to use in a Catholic offensive. Loer praises the content of the work, explicitly mentioning the spiritual dangers that abound. Books like *The Evangelical Pearl* must be published, "op dat de luyde daer mede tegen de menichfoudicheit der luterscher boecken, die nu in allen hoecken opstaen om die sielen, godt betert, te verleyden, in den rechten ghelove gesterct ende inder liefden godes weder ontsteken mochten worden, die nu te hants by nae over al inder luyden herten vercout is doer tijtlicke liefden ende sinlike wellusten daer

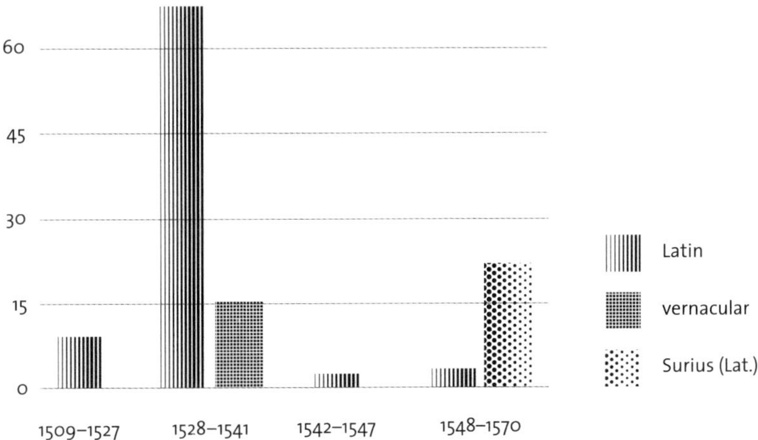

Fig. 3.2. The book production of the Cologne Carthusians.

si toegevuecht zijn" (so that through them—against the numerous Lutheran books that now spring up from all corners in order to allure souls, God forbid—people are strengthened in their true faith and inflamed once more in the love of God, which now has cooled off most everywhere in most people, because of the temporal love and sensuous lusts to which they adhere).[53] Religious people are portrayed as torn between the Lutheran heresy on the one hand and the lures of the world on the other.

The Evangelical Pearl is just one noteworthy item from the stream of texts that the Carthusians prepared for publication. It is interesting to note when this publication offensive peaked: well before 1545, and thus well before the official Counter-Reformation. Spurred on by the prior Petrus Blomevenna (1466–1536), the Carthusians started to present the textual reflections of inner life and spirituality to the outside world.[54] They put in print texts written by themselves, by contemporaries, and by exemplary authors from the fourteenth century. The publication campaign picked up steam just before 1525, with the bulk of books published between 1528 and 1538. Figure 3.2, for which the data were compiled by Gérald Chaix, shows the output of the Carthusians.[55] It is clear that the Carthusians did not need any official impetus to start spreading the word of Catholic devotion and mysticism.

Driving forces in this offensive were for the most part Carthusians originating from the Low Countries. From 1507 to 1566, under the Dutch priors Peter of Leyden and Gerard Kalckbrenner, at least two-thirds of the inhabitants were from the Low Countries.[56] One scholar goes so far as to call the Cologne Charterhouse a Dutch community.[57] For decades Dutch monks did indeed hold the most important offices in the Charterhouse.

I have already mentioned Dirk Loer, who as an editor-in-chief oversaw the monumental project of editing the plethora of texts of Dionysius the Carthusian.[58] Gerard Kalckbrenner spent a lot of his time and energy supporting circles of devout women in the Low Countries. A case in point is Maria van Hout, from the Brabant village of Oisterwijk, who in the past was accredited with the authorship of *The Evangelical Pearl.* Kalckbrenner even invited Maria and some of her disciples to come live in a house near the Charterhouse.[59] They eventually did so in 1545. Maria died in 1547. Other groups of devout and mystical women in places such as Den Bosch and Diest also received attention from the Cologne Carthusians and others sympathizing with their cause. Among them was Peter Canisius (1521–97), the first Jesuit from the Low Countries, who had studied in Cologne, and Nicolaas Esch (1507–78), priest of the Diest beguinage and former professor in Cologne.

A somewhat particular case is Laurentius Surius (1522–78). Because he was born in Lübeck and belonged to a later generation than Dirk Loer and Petrus Blomevenna, his work stands somewhat apart from that of his fellow Carthusians. He started working on his impressive oeuvre of translations of mystical and ascetical texts when the first period of intense editorial activity had already ended.[60] Important works that he translated into Latin are the opera of Ruysbroeck,[61] Tauler, and Suso.[62] The Latin translation of *The Evangelical Pearl* is also attributed to Surius.[63]

The most important person might well be Peter Blomevenna, also known as Peter of Leyden.[64] He was active as author, translator, and proponent of the new mystical devotion. His most significant translation is probably Hendrik Herp's *Mirror of Perfection*. He also wrote a polemical text, *Candela evangelica* (1526), in which he juxtaposes Lutheran doctrines (symbolizing darkness) with their refutations (the candles). From 1508 on Blomevenna was also the visitator of the Rhine Province (*Provincia Rheni*) of the Carthusian Order. This brought him very close to Arnhem, possibly even into Arnhem, since the border of the Rhine Province runs just east of the city.

Blomevenna brings us back to Arnhem, to the *Arnhem Mystical Sermons*. In these 162 sermons just one contemporaneous author is mentioned: Petrus Blomevenna. He is spoken of in a tone of veneration. The sermon on the feast of the Assumption of Mary states: "Mer inden derden dach, seit die heilige carthuser Peter van Leyden, is si opgenomen inden hemel ende heeft geclommen baven alle choren der engelen" (But on the third day, says the holy Carthusian Peter of Leyden, she was assumed into heaven and was raised above all the choirs of angels).[65] The adjective "holy" is problematic since it would normally imply that Blomevenna had died and been canonized, but it is possible that Blomevenna reached an extraordinarily high stature during his lifetime, earning him this reverential epithet.

THE *ARNHEM MYSTICAL SERMONS*

The Manuscript and Its Content

The codex from the Saint Agnes Convent with the *Arnhem Mystical Sermons* is currently kept in the Royal Library in The Hague. It contains 162 sermons, written on 381 paper leaves, making it the largest known collection of Middle Dutch sermons.[66] The collection is made up of 128 sermons for the cycle of seasons, the temporale, and 34 for the cycle of saints, the sanctorale.

The codex boasts some rather crude drawings, probably done by the scribe. The sermons for the main feast days have historiated initials, and the same decoration type is used in some border designs (fig. 3.3). The most remarkable decorations consist of curling

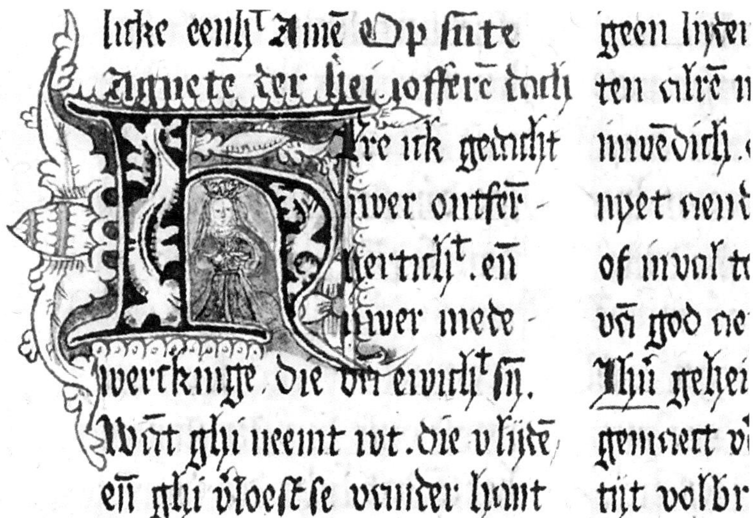

Fig. 3.3. Initial with the Sermon for Saint Agnes's day (Serm. 136, fol. 302v). Image copyright © The Hague, Royal Library, 133 H 21.

banderoles along the side of or beneath a column. The banderoles have Latin texts—in one case Dutch—that are mostly taken from the office of the liturgical feast of that particular day. For example, with the sermon that precedes the three sermons for the three Masses of Christmas, the text in the banderole is: "Puer natus est nobis, et filius datus est nobis."[67] Clearly, the artist-scribe does not really know Latin since she makes several mistakes.[68]

The texts are written in a distinctly eastern Middle Dutch dialect, consistent with Arnhem. Watermark evidence suggests that the codex was written as late as ca. 1575.[69] There are some scribal errors that can only be explained as reading mistakes. Therefore an earlier written version of the sermons must have existed. The sermons could, on principle, go back to a date before the sixteenth century. That this is not the case could also recently be established.[70]

The script gets somewhat unsteady toward the end, suggesting that the codex was written by an older, possibly very old nun. There is even reason to believe that old age or death prevented her from finishing the codex. The sermons in the Proper of the Saints are strictly organized according to the liturgical year of the Utrecht calendar. However, the Proper of the Saints suddenly breaks off in the month of September, and sermons for the occasions in October and November are lacking. What is more, the final sermon is incomplete; it breaks off in the middle of a paragraph, and the final page is written in a markedly wobbly script. The last sentence is a naïve addition by another person.

The codex provides no clues as to its ownership or provenance. As noted before, the codex could be attributed to Saint Agnes on the basis of the script. The manuscript is written by a scribe who wrote part of another manuscript that was written by several nuns from Saint Agnes.[71] Initially I chose to cautiously refer to the sermons as the *Guelders Mystical Sermons*. Since nothing was known with any certainty about the ultimate origin of the sermons, it seemed best to use this rather unspecific designation. Of late, however, we may call them the *Arnhem Mystical Sermons*, now that it is certain that some of the occasions are connected with specific local devotions in Arnhem.[72] It would be useful to know the exact date the texts were originally written. Unfortunately, the date of origin can only be approximated. A *terminus post quem* has been deduced—ca. 1525—and the *terminus ante quem* is provided by the codex itself: because of the paper used, the sermons must predate ca. 1575.[73]

Female Authorship

No collection comparable to the *Arnhem Mystical Sermons* exists in Middle Dutch. It is the only one of a mystical nature among many instructive and moralistic ones. The *Sermons* being anonymous, and originating from a convent, it would seem most likely that they were produced by the priest of the Saint Agnes Convent. He would have been the sisters' guide in the mystical life. Recently, however, the hypothesis of a female author has come to be seen as more plausible. I thus hereafter refer to the author as "she."

Some phrases in the sermons make their use within the context of an audience of cloistered sisters likely. The intended audience unequivocally consists of cloistered sisters: "Ten lesten gaet voert in die strate uwer geloften, van dat doepsel aen tot uwer professien toe" (Finally go down the street of your vows, from baptism up to your profession).[74] They therefore follow the monastic rhythm: "ter myddernacht, of daer om trynt, in die yerste wake; 78rb: Ter sester uren; alsmen te myssen luyt" (At around midnight, during the first wake / at the sixth hour, when it rings for Mass).[75] The sisters, more specifically, follow the Augustinian Rule. In the sermon for the feast of Augustine, it says: "du, die ons . . . een regel des geestelicken levens gegeven ende naegelaten hebt" (You, who has . . . given and left us a rule for the spiritual life).[76] Both author and audience are included in the same group of religious people: "O wij, alle religioese menschen" (O we, who are religious people).[77] Perhaps most intriguing are the phrases that suggest that the author stands outside of the immediate relation between priest and sisters, but seems to prepare them for the liturgical occasions in which they will meet: "Als ghi dan voer den priester coemt" (When you come before the priest);[78] "wanneer hi mit oetmoediger herten die penitentie vanden priester ontfanget" (when he [the sinner] receives with a humble heart the penance from the priest);[79] "wanneer dan die ingeslaten ziel . . . enen wyndt hoert ruysschen uut des priesters mont" (when the introverted soul . . . hears a wind rustle from the mouth of the priest).[80] Further, the implication of some phrases seems to be that the author is a woman. For example when it is said that the sacramental offer "nyet geoffert werden dan vanden gewijden mans persoenen" (cannot be sacrificed unless by an ordained male person).[81] The author, however, encourages the sisters to aspire to the spiritual priesthood (which in some ways is even preferable): "o du ynnige ziel, hebt nu, mit allen heiligen, reynen priesteren u lenden der synlicker begeerten omgort" (O you inner soul, you must now have the loins of your sensuous desires girded, together with all the holy and pure priests).[82] Mary is presented at several occasions (in line with medieval tradition, but forbidden by the Catholic Church in the twentieth century)[83] as first priest and role model at the same time: "Maria, die . . . hoechste ende yerste priester des nijen verbonts" (Mary, . . . the highest and first priest of the new covenant)[84] / "Maria, die waerachtichste yerste priester" (Mary, the most truly, first priest).[85] The author speaks on behalf of the individual members of the community she addresses, as she uses the female form for "sinner": "God, weest my sundersche genadich" (God, have mercy on the sinner that I am).[86]

Attributing the sermons to a woman author dramatically changes our perception of them. One very clear consequence is that the sermons would not have been written with male, clerical authority, and so would necessarily be "extra-liturgical." Another consequence is that the author would for some reason have borrowed the genre-specific textual characteristics of the sermon to clothe her message in. Our idea of the setting has to change as well: with the priest as author one might think of the para-liturgical setting of a *collatio*, a well-known format for instruction in the *Devotio Moderna*.[87] With female authorship, however, there can hardly have been a formal setting for the sermons to have been read or discussed. It also becomes unlikely that all the sisters in the convent were involved in this mystical culture. Since it is impossible to reach any certainty about the practical use of the sermons, imagining a subgroup of sisters united in mystical aspirations emerges as a valid but inevitably hypothetical conjecture.[88]

The Use of Allegory

Being styled as sermons, these texts are both unique and exemplary at the same time. Even though the formal characteristics of the sermons are only borrowed, these texts still—just as traditional sermons—provide an immediate entry into the spiritual core of the community's religious life. The aim of the sermons is to address and express the central spiritual needs and aspirations shared by the members of the group. The author—whom we can now envision as a "spiritual priest"—speaks the group's language. In phrasing the sermons she uses terminology and concepts that the members of the audience use and understand. As a consequence, this sermon collection is arguably as uniquely representative of the spiritual life within the group as any other collection.

The most conspicuous stylistic feature of the sermons is the continuous allegorization of all concepts, substantives, and actions as found in the text of the biblical theme or the pericope.[89] This systematic allegorization is expressed in its purest and simplest form when the mentioning of a substantive or phrase from the pericope is immediately followed by the Middle Dutch words *dat is* (that is), accompanied by the given allegorical meaning. Some examples are: "the daughter of Zion, that is, the faithful soul"; "Mary, that is, the mind"; "the Son of man will be seen coming on the clouds, that is, in the frailty of our flesh"; "There must be signs in the sun, that is, in our mind, in the moon, that is, in our soul, and in the stars, that is, in our humanity." The basis for the quality of the *Mystical Sermons* lies in the ability of the author to devise allegorizations for every single element of a pericope, and that those allegorizations are always connected to a coherent and meaningful mystical doctrine that the author wishes to expound. Not only does the author possess this "technical" quality, but she, moreover, has the ability to phrase the most complex of mystical concepts, such as the interconnection of intra-Trinitarian processes with mental processes in the uppermost part of the human spirit, in terms taken from the relevant pericope from the Gospel or epistle.

In the introduction to the translation of a selection of the *Arnhem Mystical Sermons* in the Classics of Western Spirituality series, I described them as follows: "The sermons are plain yet profound, simple yet sophisticated. Practically no authorities are cited—a lone reference to Augustine left aside. It is as if all authorities pale and become superfluous in comparison to the 'authorities' mentioned numerous times on every page: God and Christ. The allegorizations seem to sprout fresh and new from the mystically imbued mind of the author, who appears to tread in nobody's footsteps. The sermons are among the best products of Dutch literature."[90]

The Mysticism of the *Arnhem Mystical Sermons*

The codex that looks rather unremarkable from the outside has turned out to be of major importance because of the exceptional sermon collection it contains. The sermons convey a specific type of mysticism, which is still in the process of being discovered.

The *Arnhem Mystical Sermons* take us to a place that might seem wholly inaccessible: the place where the true life of the mystical members of the community is lived, the innermost part of their hearts and minds. The spirituality of the Saint Agnes Convent might be introverted and conservative, but the quest for invigorated Catholic interiority, paradoxically, gives birth to a peculiar new type of mysticism in which different currents of mystical life have merged.

The mystical culture of the Saint Agnes sisters is founded on a conviction concerning the faculties of the mind. The accepted premise is that God is not just perceptible in the material world through his works, but that he can also be attained and experienced in his essential being in the innermost part of the spirit. This conviction was arrived at and underpinned philosophically in earlier times, and now it had become, by the sixteenth century, standard opinion. The Christian mystical tradition holds that the highest part of the spirit has the potential to perceive God's eternal transcendence. At this highest level the faculties are united in what is called the essence of man. Here the encounter with the divine is possible, because the essence of man comes forth from and is connected with its origin in God. This highest union of the mind is called by different names, the "essence of man" by Ruysbroeck, the "fünkelin der seele" by Eckhart, the "grunt der seele" by Tauler. The mystic encounters the essence of God in and through the highest faculties that originate from and are permanently connected with their divine origin. The contemplative's objective is to ascend to this highest part of the human essence. He or she longs to live from the experience of the presence of God in this essence, not out of a selfish desire, but based on the conviction that living from God is the most profound reality. To make this optimal mode of being possible, the contemplative strives to have the highest faculties restored to their original purity.

Single-Minded Mystical Desire

Bernard McGinn has argued that if the term "mystical literature" covered only those texts in which personal experiences of mystical union are articulated, there would be few mystical texts.[91] Far more numerous are those texts that express mystical desire or describe the path to a mystical life. The *Mystical Sermons* certainly belong to the category of texts expressing the passionate longing for the experienced presence of God. The single-minded longing for mystical union might well be an introverted response to the turbulent world outside of the convent walls. The sermons have no apparent social, political, doctrinal, or intellectual implications or objectives. The sole aspiration of the members of the group is to be conscious of and ideally experience the presence of God. An important metaphor in this context is the "temple of the soul," referring to the place where the sisters desire the mystical liturgy to take place.[92] The desire for mystical union is formulated at the end of nearly every sermon in an optative sentence, as in the following examples, which are just three out of many:

> Op dat wij nu mit Maria een geestelicke, weerde moeder gods moegen werden, dat Christum Jhesus van ons gebaren mach werden inden duysteren, onbekenden nacht onser nyetheit, dat verleen ons God. Amen.
>
> ———
>
> That we may, with Mary, become a worthy, spiritual mother of God, so that Christ Jesus may be born from us in the dark, unknown night of our nothingness; may God grant us this. Amen.[93]

> dat wij baven die gelicheit in sijn weselicke eenheit coemen, dat verleen ons god. Amen.
>
> ———
>
> That we may rise above similarity with God into his essential unity. Amen.[94]

> Dat wij stadelick onsen gantsen wil alsoe inden wil gods storten moeten, dat wij aldus een in god werden moegen ende sijn, dat verleen ons god. Amen.
>
> ———
>
> That we may continually sink our entire will into God's will, so we might become and be one in God; may God grant us this. Amen.[95]

The sermons express an awareness of the necessity of radical interiority as part of the monastic life. Without the total introversion into one's spiritual depth the mystical life is impossible:

> moeten dan alle die synlicke neygingen, die eygensuekingen, die eygen willen ende die synlicke mynnen af mit al des werlts mynne ende der creatueren. Soe lange deser een noch inden mensche leeft, soe en heeft hi die werlt noch nyet verlaten. Al waer hi oeck bynnen tien mueren geslaten ende al is hi naeden licham uut die werlt, nochtans heeft hi die werlt te mael in hem ende is mittter herten ende der natueren te mael in hoer.
>
> ———
>
> As long as one of these tendencies [i.e., sensuous inclination, selfishness, self-will, love for the world, and createdness] still lives in a person, he (or she) has not really left the world. Even if this person were locked within ten walls and were physically removed from the world, he still carries the world in himself and he is with his heart and nature completely in her.[96]

Influence of Mystical Classics: Synthesis of Two Mystical Currents

At some point during the past century the term "Rhine-Flemish mysticism" has become standard, probably merely due to the fact that it has been used frequently. More common is the French term "la mystique rhéno-flamande."[97] Recently this term has been criticized for lumping together two distinct mystical traditions.[98] Apart from the fact that the supposedly Flemish mystics Hadewijch and Ruysbroeck are in fact from Brabant, the term also ignores the fact that the differences between Rhineland mysticism and Brabant mysticism outweigh the similarities. A Brabantine-Flemish tradition does exist, and Ruysbroeck is its pinnacle; and a Rhineland mysticism, "la mystique rhenane," exists likewise, and Eckhart's sermons are its crowning achievement. However, these are two mutually independent traditions, following separate trajectories of development. The mysticism that comes to a climax in Ruysbroeck is love mysticism, bridal mysticism,

Trinitarian mysticism, for which the foundations were laid by Saint Bernard, William of Saint-Thierry, and the Victorines. Rhineland mysticism, on the other hand, peaks in Eckhart. This is speculative mysticism, carefully executing a balancing act on the dividing line between Christian mysticism and philosophical Neoplatonism.

One of the identifying characteristics of the *Arnhem Mystical Sermons* is that they manifest knowledge and understanding of both traditions, and bring about a synthesis of these two schools of mysticism. The *Sermons* look back to the fourteenth century, but in integrating two revitalized schools of mystical thought, they actually innovate. And the resulting new form of mystical life becomes a new current of mysticism that goes on to influence early modern spirituality and mysticism.

The Saint Agnes Convent owned good copies of key texts from the fourteenth-century masters of mysticism. The sisters had access to texts by Ruysbroeck, Tauler, and Eckhart, to name the most influential.[99] The author of the sermons was clearly immersed in the fourteenth-century mystical classics, as she shows a command of their concepts and terminology. In order for the group members to have been a receptive audience, they must have shared a similar mastery.

Three examples, one concerning Ruysbroeck, one Eckhart, and one Tauler, illustrate the prominence of these mystics. One of the sermons is based on paraphrases of excerpts from John of Ruysbroeck's main work *The Spiritual Espousals*.[100] No other Arnhem sermon is so clearly based on borrowings from another text. This particular sermon is about the gifts of the Holy Spirit, and Ruysbroeck interprets them as ways in which God makes himself increasingly known to the mystic. The author integrates her paraphrases of Ruysbroeck's text into her own literary structure, in such a way that the text becomes more group-oriented.

The sermon for the feast of Paulus Conversio is modeled on Eckhart's German sermon 37.[101] The source text discusses the very Eckhartian notion that "God is nothing." Eckhart expresses his ontological and speculative insights in provocative and paradoxical statements. However, rather than being scared off, the Arnhem preacher embraces this radical position and places it within a moral framework of mystical asceticism. She turns Eckhart's phrase "God is nothing" into an insight that functions as a guide for the aspiring mystic, putting her on a course of self-annihilation and radical introversion. Ultimately the subject's nothingness should be laid bare in order to enable the encounter with the divine nothingness.

In many sermons we hear echoes of Tauler. He was called the *Lebemeister* for combining Eckhart's lofty, speculative insights with his own down-to-earth pastoral approach. Similarly, in the Arnhem sermons the heritage of radical ontological notions is placed in a context of mystical asceticism, whereby the original speculative objective is lost. Key aspects of Tauler's mystical anthropology—especially the notion of *Gemut*—are adopted in the Arnhem sermons.[102]

Christocentrism and Imitatio Christi

In the Saint Agnes variant of Christocentrism, the reflection on and the imitation of the life of Christ are of great importance in the aspired cleansing of the inner faculties of the subject. If this purgative phase is necessary to make the divine encounter possible, then the question is how this can best be accomplished. The sisters chose a radical path. Their life was a continuous, uninterrupted *imitatio Christi*. Christ is the perfect mystical model because he came forth from God to whom he returned. The sisters' life is thus an *imitatio Christi* in a mystical sense. Like Christ they hope to return to God—and "return" does indeed mean to go back to where one came from. Unlike Christ, they would find union with God not by nature but by grace, as adopted children.[103]

Spirituality in Arnhem is characterized by self-abnegation and imitation of Christ, and both objectives are practiced methodically to some extent. The sisters apply themselves to absolute detachment from the lure of the world, through self-annihilation and *Abgeschiedenheit*, as the German mystics call it. The purpose of this radical undoing of oneself, this emptying of the self, is to create the conditions necessary for being engulfed by God. For as water cannot keep itself from filling up an empty vessel, similarly, God cannot keep himself from filling the emptied self with himself. The way to achieve the desired self-annihilation and self-abnegation is through the constant and intensely lived *imitatio Christi.* This imitation must be radical to the extent that the self ceases to exist and the person of Christ takes its place. When that happens, the mystic becomes a daughter or son of God through Christ and participates in God's essential being. The contemplative is then infused with strength, wisdom, and love. These are words that the Arnhem preacher repeats tirelessly. And even though the sisters are not always aware of this divine presence and do not always experience his working in them, still, by constantly striving toward God in conformity with Christ, they in effect live a mystical life.

Living the Liturgy

Another prominent characteristic of the *Sermons* is that the *imitatio Christi* is inseparably connected with living the liturgy. The members of the community strive to attain unity with God by trying to relive the life of Jesus through a spiritualization of his life's events. The *Sermons* advocate not just meditation on Jesus' life, but rather a spiritual reliving of it in connection with the liturgical feasts. The members of the mystical community experience the events of the liturgical year as if they occurred spiritually in their own lives. This reliving takes place in the "temple of our soul," to which the author of the *Mystical Sermons* devotes some of her finest pages in a sermon on the dedication of church.[104]

An example of the most radical spiritual appropriation of the life of Christ is a short meditation on the moment when Christ in the garden of Gethsemane realizes his imminent suffering. Instead of meditating on what Christ must have felt at that moment, the sisters identify spiritually so strongly with Christ that they contemplate together with him their relation to God the Father:[105] "O, alle ynnige menschen, verheft u gemoede in die hoecheit gods, mit een grondeloes ontsyncken uwes selves in ewiger mynnen, ende verblijt u in dat tegenwoerdige nu,[106] ende segt in Christo Jhesu: Vader, die ure is gecoemen, verclaer nu dijn soen. Averformt nu mit dijn claerheit al mijn geschapenheit in di, op dat dijn soen, dats mijn substantie ende wesen dat van di, nae di ende in di gebeelt is, di verclaer,[107] daerom du my geschapen hebste gelick di" (O, all you inner persons, raise your spirit into God's height, through a bottomless sinking away from yourself in eternal love, and rejoice in the present now, and say in Christ Jesus: Father, the time has come. Glorify your Son. Now transform with your clarity all my createdness into you, that your Son, that is, my substance and essence that was modeled by you, after you and in you, may glorify you, for which you have created me like you).[108] This example makes abundantly clear what is *expressis verbis* declared in another sermon, namely that the liturgical feasts in essence take place in the mind or spirit.[109] "Mer wanneer se den mensche inbrengen die festen ende hoechtijden der kercken, ende die ziel hoer daer mede of daer doer bloet tot god inden geest keert daer alle hoechtijden van god waerlick in vernyet ende begaen worden, soe sijn die synnen ende verbeeldingen tot dier stont toe noetdorftich ende guet, soe veer si die ziel leyden ende wijsen tot die waerheit der hoechtijden inden geest" (But when they [i.e., the senses and conceptions] bring to mind the celebrations and high feasts of the church, and the soul with them and through them turns toward God in the spirit, where all the high feasts are truly renewed and celebrated by God, then the senses and conceptions are necessary and good in as much as they lead and direct the soul to the truth of the high feasts in the spirit).[110]

The centrality of radical interiority and of the mind-spirit as *locus liturgicus* is the concept explained in the sermon for the yearly feast of *dedicatio ecclesiae*. The sermon interprets the dedication rite as an event that takes places in the individual mind, in the "temple of the soul," to use the terms of the sermon. "Opten hoegen kerwijngen dach soe sal een getrouwe, ynnige ziel neernstelick in hoer selven gaen ende besien den tempel hoere zielen aen" (On the solemn day of the dedication of church the faithful, interior soul shall attentively go into herself and consider the temple of her soul).[111] The dedication rite is performed only at the actual dedication of the church, and that specific day is kept as a solemnity in that church. It is, however, important to note that the dedication rite is not repeated each year. The office of the dedication recalls and remembers this initial dedication, but without the actual rite. From this fact it becomes even more clear that for the Arnhem sisters the mystical understanding of the rite, being the dedication of the temple of the soul, is key. This is where they live their mystical life.

In the sermon the dedication rite is applied in all its aspects to the temple of the soul. The rite starts with the cleansing of the building from the outside inward and this is understood to mean the cleansing of the senses and the removal of sins. The subject must be purged from all its selfish and worldly desires. In the next phase of the rite the priest anoints twelve crosses on the interior walls. These crosses are taken to signify twelve faculties and affections. The inherent mystical anthropology closely resembles that of *The Evangelical Pearl* and *The Temple of Our Soul*, the two other main texts of Arnhem mysticism. These faculties and affections have been sullied by neglect and sin and they must be lighted by the twelve candles over the crosses. These are again understood symbolically: the candles represent the same twelve faculties and affections but having the perfection that is only found in Christ. To have Christ's perfection light up the darkness of the soul implies that a mystical *imitatio Christi* must take place. Now the priest and the mystical subject enter the third phase of the rite, in which the altar is prepared. Flowers and incense must be used to adorn it. When that is done, the sermon says: "Wat is hier dan te doen in desen tempel? Niet dan die orgelen te spoelen, die zuete stemmen te clyncken, te offeren ende God te dancken ende te laven" (What else is there to do in this temple? Nothing except to play the organ, have sweet voices resound, make offerings, thank and praise God).[112] In the final phase of both the actual and mystical rites the first Mass is celebrated. In the mystical life this means that the soul offers itself in Christ to God. In the cleansed and enlightened innermost depth of the spirit there is a moment of blissful serenity, in which the soul is lifted up by God to be united with him in joy and fruition. The text ends with extensive consolation for those who do not experience this union themselves. They should know this union occurs in every person, albeit that it might happen unnoticed in the dark.

Mystical Birth of God

Since every liturgical event takes place in essence in the spirit—referred to as the temple of the soul—this is also true for Christmas. The feast celebrates the birth of the historical Christ, but for the Arnhem sisters the birth of Christ also takes place in the spirit. In their mystical understanding the soul is spiritually equal to Mary, and it is the desire of each sister to have Christ born in her own soul. The spiritual event is presented as analogous in every way to the historical event, and thus there is a mystical parallel not only to the conception of Christ in Mary but also to the birth of Christ from Mary. Analogously God is born in and from the mind. The theme of the divine birth in and from man is in fact key to the entire collection of sermons. It is already announced on the very first page of the codex in the rubric with the first sermon: "Vander Advent. Hoe een ynnige ziel nyet alleen god ynnichlick ontfangen sal, mer sal mit Maria wesen een ynnige, reyne, goddragende joffer, ende bereyden hoer mit onse lieve vrouwe dat god uut hoer gebaren mach werden" (On the Advent. How an interior soul should not only receive God interiorly, but should be with Mary an interior, pure, God-bearing young woman, and prepare herself with our dear Lady, so that God may be born from her).[113]

It is thus not surprising to find that the entire Advent cycle of eight sermons is concerned with the advent of the divine birth understood in its mystical sense. The Advent cycle is followed by the Christmas cycle, comprising five sermons. The rubric to its first sermon—sermon 9 of the collection—reads: "Opten hoegen kerstnacht, van drie geestelicke gebuerten" (In the solemn Christmas night, on three types of spiritual birth).[114] They are called "spiritual births," as opposed to the physical birth of Christ, because God is born spiritually in man in three different ways. This means that "divine birth in man" is explicitly the predominant theme in the first thirteen sermons.

Sermon 9 introduces these three types of divine birth in each individual person. The birth of Christ is interpreted allegorically as representing each divine birth in each person. First, God is born in the essence of each God-loving spirit; second, God is born in the soul; third, God is born in the entire person. This threefold birth reflects the mystical anthropology that is a frequent subject in the *Arnhem Mystical Sermons*.

The three divine births are discussed separately and extensively in sermons 10 to 12. The rubric to sermon 10 is again very explicit: "Hoe dese drie gebuerten begaen werden in dese drie myssen van huden. Die yerste mysse opten kerstnacht" (How these three births are celebrated in today's three Masses. The first Mass on Christmas Eve).[115] This Mass is celebrated in the dark of the night since it represents the darkness of the spirit that is enlightened by the birth of Christ in it. Sermon 11 discusses the birth in the soul. In the Arnhem anthropology the soul is subordinate to the spirit. The spirit is the center in which the higher faculties of memory, intellect, and will are united; the soul is the center that unites a host of lower faculties. This Mass is celebrated in the morning since while the mind is fully enlightened by God, the soul remains partly "in the dark" about God. Sermon 12 finally deals with the birth of God in the entire person, the person that is physical and active in her or his personal life. This means that the birth of God descends from the highest level in the spirit-mind down to the physical body. It is the ultimate goal for the Arnhem sisters to live in and from this union with God, which means that God has to be born in them.

Conclusion

The *Arnhem Mystical Sermons*, and Arnhem mysticism in general, are the products of the convergence of extraordinary circumstances, the most fundamental of which is likely the rare gathering of remarkable women. The individuals who produced the mystical texts,were exceptionally talented. They most probably came from the highest social classes, which might well have contributed to their self-confidence and the daring self-shaping of their lives. They likely received spiritual support from the Cologne Carthusians. From near and far, from both their spiritual and secular environments, they received unusual attention. This also resulted in the availability of inspirational texts.

Perhaps the presumable lack of formal training was a positive aspect, as it was compensated with inner knowledge, experience, and fervor. The fact, also, that this period was sufficiently distant from previous periods of mystical life—the Brabant monasteries, the Rhineland mystics—and that there had been an interlude of more austere devotional life, saved the Arnhem women from being shackled by established patterns of existing traditions. Finally, the external circumstances of turmoil and reform inevitably elicited some kind of answer from these women. The Arnhem mysticism was their response.

None of the individual characteristics of the mysticism lived by the Arnhem sisters are new; it is the combination of elements that gives their mysticism an innovative quality. Most elements derive from fourteenth-century mystical literature; emphases are in accordance with contemporaneous trends. All the described aspects can be assembled in a summary definition of Arnhem mysticism: a contemplative group united in mystical longing, each sister aspiring to have God born in the depths of her soul. Somewhat methodically the sisters engage in a spiritual *imitatio Christi*, characterized by self-annihilation, and this *imitatio Christi* is practiced in a yearly cycle through a mystical understanding of the liturgy.

NOTES

This article is a reworking of my presentation "The Mystical Sermons from the Arnhem St.-Agnes Convent: Continuity and Change in the Mystical Renaissance" held at the conference "Mysticism, Reform and the Formation of Modernity," Princeton University, February 21–23, 2008. Since almost no English-language literature exists on the subject, most notes inevitably refer to Dutch-language studies.

1. I subscribe to the thesis of Gérald Chaix and others that a period of "Réforme catholique" antedates the "Contre-réforme" (Counter-Reformation), being the organized ecclesiastical response to the Reformation; G. Chaix, *Réforme et contre-réforme catholiques. Recherches sur la chartreuse de Cologne du XVIe siècle*, 3 vols., Analecta Cartusiana 80 (Salzburg: Institut für Anglistik und Amerikanistik, Universität Salzburg, 1981). The demonstrable renewal of religious life that Chaix finds with the Cologne Carthusians well before 1545—and that we also witness in Arnhem—is proof for this thesis. One review of

Chaix's work concludes: "This well-written, exhaustively researched study of the Carthusian monastery of Sainte-Barbe in Cologne during the period from 1507 to 1622 is a valuable contribution to the thesis that a Catholic reform antedated the Counter-Reformation." F. Ellen Weaver, *Church History* 52 (1983): 535. See also Larissa Juliet Taylor, *Heresy and Orthodoxy in Sixteenth-Century Paris: Francois Le Picart and the Beginnings of the Catholic Reformation*, Studies in Medieval and Reformation Thought 77 (Leiden: Brill, 1999), particularly the chapter "Catholic Reform," 151–87 (on the French situation).

2. Kirsten M. Christensen, "Maria van Hout and her Carthusian Editor," *Ons Geestelijk Erf* 72 (1998): 105–21.

3. The Hague, Royal Library, ms. 133 H 13. Some sermons have been published in translation: Kees Schepers, trans., "Mystical Sermons," in *Late-Medieval Mysticism of the Low Countries*, ed. Rik Van Nieuwenhove, Rob Faesen, and Helen Rolfson (Mahwah, N.J.: Paulist, 2008), 349–64.

4. Hans Kienhorst, "Meer mystiek uit het Arnhemse Agnietenklooster. De handschriften Den Haag, Koninklijke Bibliotheek, 71 H 51 en 133 H 13," in *Manuscripten en miniaturen, studies aangeboden aan Anne S. Korteweg bij haar afscheid van de Koninklijke Bibliotheek*, Bijdragen tot de geschiedenis van de Nederlandse boekhandel, New Series, vol. 8, ed. Jos Biemans, Klaas van der Hoek, Kathryn M. Ruday, and Ed van der Vlist (Zutphen: Walburg Pers, 2007), 201–15.

5. Eusebius (August 25), a Roman martyr whose main relics were acquired by Arnhem in the fifteenth century. The feast of Lamentatio Mariae was celebrated on the Thursday of the third week after Easter throughout the Utrecht diocese. Cf. Kees Schepers, "De historische verankering van het *Sanctorale* in de *Arnhemse mystieke preken*," *Ons Geestelijk Erf* 81 (2010): 65–100.

6. Hopefully, it will be possible to explore the complex relations between these texts in the Ph.D. research project by Renske van Nie (of which I am supervisor), which recently started at the Ruusbroec Institute: "Authorship, composition and textual interconnectedness of three 16th-century mystical texts: *Die evangelische peerle*, *Vanden tempel onser sielen*, the *Arnhem mystical sermons*. A stylometric approach."

7. This survey of the history of the convent is based on a slightly more extensive account in Kees Schepers, "Het verborgen leven van de zusters Agnieten. Mystieke cultuur te Arnhem in de zestiende eeuw," *Ons Geestelijk Erf* 79 (2008): 285–316.

8. Koen Goudriaan, "Het Sint-Agnesklooster en de Moderne Devotie," *Ons Geestelijk Erf* 81 (2010): 17–37.

9. The sisters of aristocratic descent, recognizable by their family names, are all from the sixteenth century. In total, some thirty sisters are known from Saint Agnes (mostly noble, mostly sixteenth-century). They are listed in

P. J. Begheyn, "De handschriften van het St.-Agnietenklooster te Arnhem," *Ons Geestelijk Erf* 45 (1971): 3–44, here 43–44, and P. J. Begheyn, "Nieuwe gegevens betreffende de *Evangelische Peerle*," *Ons Geestelijk Erf* 58 (1984): 30–40, here 32.

10. "dat id vurseide convent zeer menichfoldich van gheestelicken jonfferen und religieusen van gueden und treffelicken adel soewel als anderer gueder luijden kynder vervult is." Edition in J. S. van Veen, "Een los blaadje uit de geschiedenis van het St.-Agnietenklooster te Arnhem," *Archief voor de Geschiedenis van het Aartsbisdom Utrecht* 48 (1923): 237–39.

11. On Charles's efforts, see Schepers, "De historische verankering."

12. J. A. F. Kronenburg, *Maria's Heerlijkheid in Nederland. Geschiedkundige schets etc.*, 8 vols. (Amsterdam: Bekker, 1903), 1:1, 223.

13. The following bibliographical data are derived from M. E. Kronenberg, "Contacten van Karel van Gelder met de drukpers en de wetenschappelijke wereld," *Het Boek* 37 (1965–66): 1–10, here 6 and 7.

14. *D. Dionysii Carthusiani, in omnes beati Pauli epistolas* (Cologne: Petrus Quentell, 1533).

15. Johannes van Lochem, *Chronicon Albergense*, in *Albergensia. Stukken betrekkelijk het klooster Albergen*, Vereeniging tot Beoefening van Overijsselsch Regt en Geschiedenis (Zwolle: De erven J. J. Tijl, 1878). Translation into Dutch in J. B. Schildkamp, B. H. J. Lenferink, and W. J. Tops, eds., *1520–1525: de kroniek van Johannes van Lochem, prior te Albergen: vertaling en toelichting* (Albergen: Stichting Heemkunde Albergen, 1995).

16. "Veniens de capitulo Nucie tunc celebrato, ad Arnheijm properavi ubi tunc domum sororum visitare decreveram siquidem iam annus cum dimidio fere a visitatione ultimam domus illius effluxerat et novus illic rector anno uno iam resederat. Verum consulebant nonnulli non tutum esse visitationem longius differre maxime quod sub novo rectore solent nonnunquam nova aliqua emergere quibus oporteat remedio congruo obviare cet. Igitur priusquam actum visitationis inchoarem, prius secrete singulas sorores ad me venire feci, eo ordine quo confessionem facture venire solent. Cumque super statu domus deque communi pace et disciplina singulas requisissem, inveni (gratias deo) domus illius statum talem qualem eum semper invenire optarem optimeque cum suo rectore se contentas profitebantur. Quapropter superfluum ratus plus illic temporis expendere aut certe priorem aliquem ad mecum visitandum convocare, solus quod inchoaveram terminavi, saltem hoc in communi admonens illas quatenus in tali simplicitate et sinceritate perpetuo perseverare vellent cet. Sicque negotio visitationis iuxta antiquam domus illius consuetudinem simpliciter executo salutatisque illis ad domum redi ubi interim Gelrenses fuerant dampnaque (uti praefatum est) ingencia intulerant" (*Chronicon*, 239–40; cf. *Kroniek*, 400).

17. *Chronicon*, 90; *Kroniek*, 283.

18. Van Lochem also mentions a fire raging in the center of Arnhem. Just as the fire approached the convent building, the wind changed and the convent was saved. *Chronicon*, 213; *Kroniek*, 381.

19. The Guelders wars were a series of conflicts from 1492 to 1543 between the house of Habsburg and some regions in the northern part of the Netherlands led by Charles, Duke of Guelders.

20. None of the art from the convent, which must have been plentiful, has survived.

21. Flyleaf of ms. The Hague, Royal Library, 135 E 3: "Iste liber pertinet ad sanctam Agnetem in Arnhem monialium sub custodia sorori Aelberte de Myddachten" (This book belongs to the sisters of Saint Agnes in Arnhem, under the care of sister Alberta de Myddachten). For more on the Middachten family, see W. Wijnaendts van Resandt, *Geschiedenis en genealogie van het geslacht van Middachten 1190–1901* ('s-Gravenhage: W. P. van Stockum & Zoon N.V, 1913).

22. Ms. *olim* Bonn, Universitätsbibliothek, hs. 315, fol. 2r: "Dit boeck hoert tot sancte Agneten bynnen Arnhem by die beste boecke."

23. Begheyn, "De handschriften van het St.-Agnietenklooster," 3–44.

24. *Het Gaesdonckse-traktatenhandschrift*. Olim *hs. Gaesdonck, Collegium Augustinianum*, ms. 16, Middeleeuwse Verzamelhandschriften uit de Middeleeuwen 9, ed. M. K. A. van den Berg et al. (Hilversum: Verloren, 2005).

25. Rudolf Th. M. van Dijk, "Mystiek in het Gaesdonckse-traktatenhandschrift," in *Dit mateloze verlangen*, Pareltjes van Nederlandse en Rijnlandse Mystiek 3, ed. R. Th. M. van Dijk, K. Meyers, and P. Nijs (Leuven: Peeters, 2005), 133–44, 98–105.

26. Kienhorst, "Meer mystiek," 201–15.

27. For Albert Ampe the attribution would have been of great significance. He devoted a significant part of his academic career to *The Evangelical Pearl*. His earliest article dates from 1951 and his publications on the subject continued into the 1990s.

28. *Des erleuchten D. Johannis Tauleri, von eym waren Evangelischen leben, Götlich Predig, Leren, Epistolen, Cantilenen, Prophetien* (Cologne: Jaspar von Gennep, 1543).

29. *Insinuationum divinae pietatis libri v* (Cologne: Novesianus, 1536).

30. Cf. Chaix, *Réforme et contre-réforme catholiques*, 1:293–95.

31. *Hortulus devotionis, variis orationum et exercitiorum piorum, quae mentem in Dei amorem rapiunt . . .* (Cologne: Jaspar von Gennep, 1514).

32. The manuscript was destroyed during World War II; cf. Kienhorst, "Meer mystiek," 210; M. Costard, *Spätmittelalterliche Frauenfrömmigkeit am Niederrhein. Studien zu Geschichte, Spiritualität und Handschriften der Schwesternhäuser in Geldern und Sonsbeck* (Tübingen: Mohr Siebeck, 2011), 509–10. For a

partial edition, see F. Jostes, "Beiträge zur Kenntniss der niederdeutschen Mystik," *Germania: Vierteljahrsschrift für deutsche Altertumskunde* 31, New Series 19 (1886): 1–41, 164–204.

33. *Theologia mystica cum speculativa, tum praecipue affectiva, quae non tam lectione iuvatur quam exercitio obtinetur amoris tribus libris luculentissime tradita* (Cologne: Melchior Novesianus, 1538).

34. *Margarita Evangelica. Een devoet boecxken geheeten Die Evangelische Peerle* (Utrecht: Jan Berntsen, 1535).

35. After the first edition in 1535 many others soon followed. The Latin translation of the *Pearl* was published in 1545 and provided an entry for the text into other parts of Europe. In 1602 the French translation was printed, in 1676 a German one by Angelus Silesius. In 1697 Heribertus Hobusch again translated the text into German. Eventually there were nineteen different editions.

36. J. Huyben, "Aux sources de la spiritualité française du XVIIe siècle," *Supplément à la "Vie spirituelle"* 25 (1930): 113–39; 26 (1931): 17–46, 75–111; 27 (1931): 20–42, 94–122; P. Mommaers, "Internationale uitstraling van de Nederlandse mystieke literatuur," in *Nederlands in culturele context*, Handelingen Colloquium Neerlandicum, Woubrugge 12, ed. Th. A. J. M. Mommaers et al. (Antwerpen: Internationale Vereniging voor Neerlandistiek, 1995), 133–51.

37. Benoît de Canfield, *La Règle de Perfection, The Rule of Perfection*, Bibliothèque de l'École des Hautes Études, Section des Sciences Religieuses 83, ed. Jean Orcibal (Paris: Presses Universitaires de France, 1982).

38. Begheyn argued strongly for Reinalda van Eymeren, great-aunt of Peter Canisius, but the identification was not accepted by Kurt Ruh and Bernard McGinn. P. J. Begheyn, "Is Reinalda van Eymeren, zuster in het St. Agnietenklooster te Arnhem, en oud-tante van Petrus Canisius, de schrijfster der *Evangelische peerle*?" *Ons Geestelijk Erf* 45 (1971): 339–75; Kurt Ruh, *Die niederländische Mystik des 14. bis 16. Jahrhunderts*, Geschichte der abendländischen Mystik 4 (Munich: Beck, 1999), 290–312, here 291–92; Bernard McGinn, "*The Evangelical Pearl*," in *The Presence of God*, vol. 5, *Varieties of Vernacular Mysticism (1350–1550)* (New York: Crossroad, 2012), 143–59.

39. *Die grote evangelische peerle* (Antwerp: Vorsterman, 1542).

40. This has been confirmed by Rob Faesen in "The Three Births of Christ and the Christmas Liturgy in *The Temple of Our Soul*, *The Evangelical Pearl*, and the *Arnhem Mystical Sermons*," *Ons Geestelijk Erf* 81 (2010): 121–37.

41. *Die grote evangelische peerle vol devoter gebeden, godlijcker oeffeninghen, ende geesteliker leeringhen, hoe dat wij dat hoochste goet (dat God is) in onser sielen sullen soecken ende vinden . . . Nu eerstwerf in dye druck gebracht door die Cathuser tot Cuelen* (Antwerp: Henric Peetersen van Middelburch, 1537– 38).

42. Partial translation of "The Great Pearl": Helen Rolfson, trans., "The Evangelical Pearl, part III," in *Late-Medieval Mysticism*, 215–322.

43. A. Ampe prepared a critical edition of *The Evangelical Pearl* that was never published. He had tried to reconstruct the "original version" on the basis of the two printed, widely divergent versions. Ampe finally doubted the premise for his own reconstruction. The sole copy of this unpublished but extremely useful edition is kept in the Library of the Ruusbroecgenootschap in Antwerp.

44. The text is discussed in Ruh, *Die niederländische Mystik*, 299–312; see also McGinn, "Forgotten Classic."

45. McGinn, "Forgotten Classic."

46. Ruh, *Die niederländische Mystik*, 305–6.

47. Partial translation of "The Temple": Rob Faesen, trans., "The Temple of Our Soul (extracts)," in *Late-Medieval Mysticism*, 323–438.

48. *Vanden tempel onser sielen: devote oeffeningen. Hoe wi dyen sullen bereyden ende alle hoochtiden des iaers gheestelick daer in begaen, alsoe dat God altijt in ons woonen mach. Ghemaect door eenen religiosen ende verlichten mensche die de Evangelische Peerle oock ghemaect heeft* (Antwerp: Symon Cock, 1543). Edition in A. Ampe, *Den Tempel onser sielen. Door de schrijfster der Evangelische Peerle*, Studiën en Tekstuitgaven van Ons Geestelijk Erf 18 (Antwerp: Ruusbroecgenootschap, 1968).

49. Edition Ampe, *Den tempel*, 281.

50. See chapter 4 in this volume.

51. http://www.bautz.de/bbkl/l/loher.shtml.

52. http://www.bautz.de/bbkl/k/Kalckbrenner.shtml.

53. *Margarita Evangelica* (Utrecht: Berntsen, 1535), fol. 2r.

54. "Unter Peter Blomevennas Leitung begann die Kölner Kartause die Bahnen zu beschreiten, die sie in den kommenden Zeiten der Gegenreformation gehen sollte. Die Kölner Kartause, die bisher meist im Verborgenen gewirkt hatte, trat an die Öffentlichkeit . . . durch Schriften, in denen sie für den alten Glauben eintraten," in Christel Schneider, *Die Kölner Kartause von ihrer Gründung bis zum Ausgang des Mittelalters*, Veröffentlichungen des Historischen Museums der Stadt Köln, 2 (Bonn: P. Hanstein, 1932), 43.

55. Chaix, *Réforme et contre-réforme catholiques*, 1:95.

56. Chaix, *Réforme et contre-réforme catholiques*, 1:33.

57. H. J. J. Scholtens, "De litteraire nalatenschap van de Kartuizers in de Nederlanden," *Ons Geestelijk Erf* 25 (1951): 9–43, here 30.

58. Chaix, *Réforme et contre-réforme catholiques*, 1:211–19.

59. Christensen, "Maria van Hout and her Carthusian Editor."

60. Gérald Chaix, "L'Édition de 1522 et la réception de Ruusbroec au XVIe siècle," in *Jan van Ruusbroec. The Sources, Content and Sequels of His Mysticism*, Mediaevalia Lovaniensia, series I, Studia 12, ed. P. Mommaers and N. De Paepe (Leuven: Leuven University Press, 1984), 142–52.

61. *D. Ioannis Rusbrochii summi atque sanctiss. Viri, quem insignis quidam theologus alterum Dionysium Areopagitam appellat, Opera omnia* (Cologne: Quentell,

1552); *D. Joannis Thauleri praeclarissimi, sublimisque theologi, tam de tempore quam de sanctis conciones plane piissimae, caeteraque . . . opera omnia . . . nunc primum ex Germanico idiomate in Latinum transfusa sermonem . . . interprete Laurentio Surio Lubecensi . . .* (Cologne: Quentell, 1548); *D. Henrici Susonis, viri sanctitate, eruditione et miraculis clari, Opera (quae quidem haberi potuerunt) omnia . . . Latine translata per F. Laurentium Surium Carthusianum . . .* (Cologne: Quentell, 1555).

62. His works (and subsequent translations from them) are listed in Chaix, *Réforme et contre-réforme catholiques*, 2:635–94.

63. *Margarita Evangelica incomparabilis thesaurus divinae sapientiae, in III Libros divisus . . .* (Cologne: Melchior Novesianus, 1545).

64. http://www.bautz.de/bbkl/b/blomeveen_p.shtml.

65. Serm. 154, fol. 353vb.

66. The sermons are listed with their incipit and explicit in Maria Sherwood-Smith and Patricia Stoop, *Repertorium van Middelnederlandse preken in handschriften tot en met 1550 / Repertorium of Middle Dutch Sermons preserved in manuscripts from before 1550*, 3 vols., Miscellanea Neerlandica 29 (Leuven: Peeters, 2003), 2:1079–1157.

67. The Introit of the third Mass of Christmas Day.

68. For example, *Pasca nostra immalatus es Christus* (instead of *Pascha nostrum immolatus est Christus*); *hec dies que fecit* (instead of *hec dies quam fecit*).

69. One of the sorts of paper used has the watermark Briquet 2220, attested in 1575; cf. C. M. Briquet, *Les filigranes: dictionnaire historique des marques du papier dès leur apparition vers 1282 jusqu'en 1600*. A facsimile of the 1907 edition with supplementary material contributed by a number of scholars, 4 vols., ed. A. Stevenson (Amsterdam: Paper Publications Society, 1968).

70. Cf. Schepers, "Historische verankering."

71. Kienhorst, "Meer mystiek," 214.

72. Preek 144: *Maria, corona spinarum* (S34, 4 mei); Preek 156: Eusebius (August 25).

73. Cf. Schepers, "Historische verankering."

74. Serm. 8, fol. 12vb.

75. Serm. 34, fol. 77ra.

76. Serm. 157, fol. 362ra.

77. Serm. 110, fol. 248ra.

78. Serm. 13, fol. 26rb.

79. Serm. 69, fol. 136va.

80. Serm. 99, fol. 217ra: "wanneer dan die ingeslaten ziel . . . enen wyndt hoert ruysschen uut des priesters mont."

81. Serm. 131, fol. 294ra.

82. Serm. 131, fol. 294rb.

83. In 1913 the Holy Office forbade depiction of Mary as priest. In 1923 it determined that the devotion to Mary as priest was unauthorized.

84. Serm. 138, fol. 306rb.

85. Serm. 144, fol. 328ra.

86. Serm. 115, fol. 261rb.

87. Thom Mertens, "Collatio und Codex im Bereich der Devotio moderna," in *Der Codex im Gebrauch*, Münstersche Mittelalter-Schriften, 70, ed. Christel Meier, Dagmar Hüpper, and Hagen Keller (Munich: Wilhelm Fink, 1996), 163–82.

88. McGinn, "A Forgotten Classic," states in a footnote about the Arnhem sermons: "While the manuscript gives no indication of whether the author was male or female, female authorship is more likely in light of the theological attainment of Maria (van Hout) and the *Pearl* author."

89. Cf. Kees Schepers, "Predigten für den Tempel der Seele. Metaphorik in den Arnheimer mystischen Predigten," in *Die Predigt im Mittelalter zwischen Mündlichkeit, Bildlichkeit und Schriftlichkeit*, Medienwandel—Medienwechsel—Medienwissen, Band 13, ed. R. Wetzel and F. Flückiger (Zürich: Chronos Verlag, 2010), 375–410.

90. Schepers, "Mystical Sermons," 353.

91. McGinn, *Foundations of Mysticism*, xvi.

92. Ruth Horie, *Perceptions of Ecclesia: Church and Soul in Medieval Dedication Sermons*, Sermo: Studies on Patristic, Medieval, and Reformation Sermons and Preaching 2 (Turnhout: Brepols, 2006).

93. Serm. 7, fol. 11vb.

94. Serm. 66, fol. 124ra.

95. Serm. 30, fol. 69rb.

96. Serm. 15, fol. 30va–b.

97. Cf. Louis Cognet, *Introduction aux mystiques rhéno-flamands* (Paris: Desclée, 1968).

98. Paul Verdeyen, S.J., "Une remise en cause de la notion de 'mystique rhéno-flamande,'" in *Maître Eckhart et Jan van Ruusbroec. Études sur la mystique rhéno-flamande (XIIIe–XIVe siècle)*, ed. Alain Dierkens and Benoît Beyer De Ryke (Brussels: Editions de l'Université de Bruxelles, 2004), 207–10.

99. Begheyn, "De handschriften van het St.-Agnietenklooster te Arnhem."

100. Ineke Cornet, "The Incorporation of Ruusbroec's Spiritual Espousals into the Sixteenth-Century Arnhem Mystical Sermons: A Comparative Textual Analysis," in *Church History and Religious Culture* 90 (2010): 547–78.

101. Serm. 37: *Surrexit autem Saulus de terra apertisque oculis nihil videbat*. Cf. J. Quint, ed., *Meister Eckhart. Deutsche Predigten und Traktate* (Munich: C. Hanser, 1955), 327–34.

102. Kees Schepers, "The Foundations of Mystical Consciousness in the *Arnhem Mystical Sermons*," in *Annua Nuntia Lovaniensia* 66 (Louvain: Peeters, 2012), 129–57.

103. Cf. Rom. 8:15, 23; Eph. 1:5.

104. Serm. 128, fols. 286r–291r.

105. Serm. 77: *Opten palmavon*t (Saturday, sixth week, Lent).

106. *dat tegenwoerdige nu*, a clearly Eckhartian notion: *das gegenwärtige Nun*, cf. Eckhart, DW, 1:166, 5.

107. John 17:1, the theme of the sermon taken from the Gospel of the day.

108. Fol. 145rb–va.

109. The Middle Dutch word *gheest* has the ambiguity, lacking in English, of meaning both mind (as a faculty) and spirit (soul, psyche as opposed to body).

110. Serm. 85, fol. 177rb–va.

111. Serm. 128, fol. 286r.

112. Fol. 289rb.

113. Serm. 1, fols. 1r–2v.

114. Serm. 9, fols. 13v–17r.

115. Serm. 10, fols. 17r–20r.

4

"From the very hour that I desire him"

Refiguring Spiritual Communion in Writings by Maria van Hout (d. 1547) and the Sisters of Saint Agnes in Arnhem

Kirsten M. Christensen

> Ich en weisz geyn dynk dair myn geist meer nae verlangt, dann mynen here tzo untfangen, und ich byn ouch van gantzem hertzen wail tzo freden als ich syner usz lieffden moisz untberen.
>
> ———
>
> I know of nothing for which my spirit longs more than to receive my Lord. And I am also completely satisfied if I must, out of love, do without him.
>
> —*Maria van Hout*

This paradoxical declaration of Eucharistic devotion—of an all-consuming desire for a sacrament that is simultaneously utterly dispensable—appears in a letter written by Maria van Hout, also known as Maria van Oisterwijk, in early 1531, to her unnamed confessor.[1] Maria, a beguine who led a small community of similarly devout women in Oisterwijk in the duchy of Brabant, is identified in numerous sources as the author of *Der rechte wech zo der evangelischen volkomenheit* (*The Right Path to Evangelical Perfection*), in which this letter appears.[2] In the collection of treatises included in *The Right Path*, Maria expounds on the mystical potential of the church's most fundamental texts and teachings: the Apostles' Creed, the Lord's Prayer, and the imitation of the Virgin and of Christ. In her letters, Maria emerges as a powerful mother-teacher and exemplar to her own and other communities of sisters, as well as to her Carthusian supporters.

Of particular interest in the present context are the letters to her confessor, in which Maria articulates her tortured theology of suffering and obedience—one that appears to have developed in a distinctly Eucharistic crucible, characterized by a conflict with her confessor over the frequency of communion.[3] I argue that this conflict informed a later treatise she wrote, entitled "Wie men dat heilige sacrament geistlich untfangen sal soe duck als men wilt" (How one can spiritually receive the sacrament as often as one wants)[4] which appears in *Dat Paradijs lieffhavender sielen* (*The Paradise of Loving Souls*), published anonymously in 1532 in Low German in Cologne, and again in den Bosch in Middle Dutch in 1535. Both editions were edited by the Cologne Carthusians.

Maria's treatise in *Paradise* claims that for those who have reached mystical union, the Eucharistic presence of the Lord is constantly available and is accessible outside Mass and without priestly mediation. This claim connects Maria to the long tradition of spiritual communion, the practice of inviting the Lord's presence and seeking union with him even when not partaking of, and especially in preparation for partaking of the physical elements of the sacrament.[5] Indeed, the publication and reception of Maria's work indicates that this and other writings were seen as orthodox and broadly applicable. Yet, I believe that viewing Maria's appropriation of the tradition of spiritual communion as a response to her heavy-handed confessor, in particular to his restrictions on her frequency of communion, illuminates her reformist potential. Specifically, I argue that Maria's treatise on spiritual communion functioned as a gentle corrective to her confessor and like-minded clergy who hampered progress toward mystical union by overregulating devotional practice, in particular access to the Eucharist.

As we will also see, spiritual communion had special resonance for the nuns of the Saint Agnes Convent in Arnhem, a community of sisters who, like Maria, strove for a deep interiority. I suggest that a devotional exercise on the "spiritual sacrament" in a manuscript from Saint Agnes, nearly contemporary with *Paradise*, could well have been inspired by Maria's Eucharist treatise and at the least shows that these Augustinian sisters shared Maria's commitment to spiritual communion as a strengthener of the interior life.

I further contend that the enthusiastic reception and dissemination of Maria's writings, including her Eucharistic teachings, by the Cologne Carthusians, means that we must understand these works as particularly relevant for the confessional strife of their day. The Carthusians promoted Maria and the sisters of the Arnhem community as models of interiority and sanctity for a church that needed, most of all, to turn inward if it was to survive.

Maria van Hout, Her Confessor, and the Eucharist

We have only Maria's half of the correspondence with her confessor, but her letters allow the general contours of their conflict to take shape, including the role the Eucharist played in it. It appears that, similar to the situations of a number of medieval mystics, the confessor was not pleased with Maria's bold tongue and pen.[6] Maria wrote rather voluminously and is known to have advised other religious and even townspeople. This independent spiritual outreach must have been a particular thorn in her confessor's side, whose distance from her made it impossible for him to keep her reined in, as it seems he would have preferred. His identity is not known with certainty, but we know that he was far enough away to require letters, through which he clearly made his displeasure known. Maria writes: "Idt duet mir leider dan alle ander lyden dat got so vill uneren dur mich geschuit, dat die lude an mich geergert werden, und bins wail gewoen niet vyll suesser ansichten of worden van mynen oversten tzo haven alle myn leefdage . . . Ach vader nu vallen ich uch tzo voessen mit gevalden henden, und mit bitteren traenen, [dat] yr idt mar vergeven wilt, dat ich ye aventurlich gedain off geschreven hayn. Ich will mich besseren in allet dat in myner macht is" (I am more sorry for this than for anything else that so much dishonor comes to God through me and that people are offended by me. My whole life I have certainly been accustomed to not having favorable [lit. sweet] opinions or words from my superiors. . . . Oh, father, I now fall at your feet with folded hands and bitter tears, that you might forgive me anything I have ever spoken or written too boldly. I want to improve in all ways that are within my power).[7] She does not admit to having erred. She asks for forgiveness not for any clear misstep, but appears concerned, instead, that her God-given gifts have been misunderstood by and thus inadvertently offended her confessor and others.

In a letter to a sister in another community she similarly laments any offense she causes others by the things she says. In this case, however, although her language is disturbing for its masochistic overtones, the submissiveness and ambiguity on display in the letter to her confessor are nonetheless entirely absent, replaced by clear deference to God alone:[8] "Dan idt doet mir alszo wee van binnen, als ich hoeren dat yemantz durch mich untsagt oder scandaliziert wurt in worden off in einige ander wyse; weirt myr muglich ich screyde myn ougen usz, so soild icht got clagen dat he mich doch anders machen woulde . . . ich byn die bereit tzo lyden, koem allet wat lyden mag; myn her myn got isses mir allet wail wert, und hei hait allein macht over mich. Ich vorchte gein creatuir merr" (For it pains me so greatly internally when I hear that someone is unsettled or scandalized by me in words or in any other manner. If it were possible, I would scratch my eyes out and thus lament to God that he might make me different . . . I am ready to suffer whatever may come; my Lord my God is worth all of it to me, and he alone has power over me. I no longer fear any created being).[9]

Maria is willing to suffer, she makes clear, because God is the revealer and she merely the vessel for his revelations. Such self-presentation was, of course, by Maria's day, a well-established and necessary trope for women mystics, who often put themselves at great risk by speaking or writing.[10] Maria's letters highlight the very real "possibility of peril" in her own case as well as the broader fact, identified by Nicky Hallett, that "letters come out of, and into, anxiety," and, indeed, that anxiety is at "the very heart of the epistolary genre."[11] And in the following statement in another letter to her confessor, Maria's repeated self-identification as vessel seems intended to blunt that anxiety: "Als id got belieﬀt dat ich iemantz wat sagen off scryven sall, dan brengt myr der Heer so vil vur [und niet meer] als he wilt dat ich up die tzyt offenbaren sall, und tzohantz byn ichs al weder quyt" (If it pleases God that I should say or write something to someone, then the Lord makes just enough known to me [and no more] as he desires that I reveal at that time, and then I am immediately empty of it again).[12] Here she states unequivocally that God speaks through her, with an almost audible subtext that her confessor should take it up with the source if he is concerned. But she is also ever aware of her confessor's power over her, tortured by the realization that not only is the world a cross she must bear, as it is for all mystics, but that she herself is a cross the world must bear.[13] Her letters are fraught with a constant tension between a clear sense of her mission and the constant reminder that many around her, including her confessor, to her dismay, may hinder her performance of it.

These tensions are uniquely accentuated by the very fact that they are contained in letters, as opposed to, say, in her treatises, since "the state of the reader . . . however carefully the letter is composed, cannot be ultimately arranged." Indeed, "the writer and reader [of any letter] . . .are effectively in parallel temporal universes."[14] These tensions inherent to the epistolary genre also mean that Maria's confidence in her role as messenger is perpetually tempered by apologies for offense and willing acceptance of punishment. Indeed, the previous quote appears in the same letter as this request: "Ich bidt uch umb die liefde gotz schrief ich yet off hoirt ir iet van mich dat uch myszhaget, dat ir mich vry straiffen willet" (I ask you, for the love of

God, if I have written anything, or if you have heard anything of me that displeases you, that you freely punish me).[15]

Maria's confessor took her up on the invitation. For her unwillingness to curtail her activities (which, it is worth noting, she describes to her sister in the quote above as an *inability*), he appears to have forbidden her to take communion for a time. "If you want me to go to the Holy Sacrament," she implores, "then write to me, for my spirit needs to be free, and as long as you have any opposition to it, my spirit cannot overcome that, for I am far too committed to [my vow of] obedience to do so."[16] Her repeated requests for restored privileges went unanswered for some time.[17] Her confessor appears to have acquiesced later, for she indicates in a subsequent letter that he has allowed her to go to communion.[18] But even after allowing this, lest Maria should grow complacent, he added new restrictions: first, a cessation of "secret acts of penance"; second, silence; and third, a requirement that she say prayers "for the pope, emperor, and all those of high station, and in general for all sinful people."[19] It is also clear from this letter that she is writing during Lent and that he had previously required her both to refrain from communion and to fast to an extent that her health is endangered; she speaks of debilitating headaches from the fasting, for example. Her request for permission to eat an evening meal again were ignored even after he granted a return to communion, causing her to state bluntly, "Hedde ich na uch moissen beiden er ir mit [mir, *sic*] schrieft, ich hedde er doet moegen bliven" (If I had waited for you to write me, I would likely have died).[20] Instead of starving, however, God leaves her strengthened with a heavenly fragrance that has the helpful effect of making all food abhorrent to her[21]—all food, that is, except the Host, which also has strengthening powers, as she informs him in a later letter.[22]

Yet even when her infirmities make fasting difficult for her, Maria's Eucharistic devotion remains firm. She explains: "Ich kan niet waill gefasten umb des willen dat ich mynnen heer und got in dem heilgen Sacrament moisz derven" (I can't fast well because it requires that I do without my Lord and God in the Holy Sacrament).[23] Fasting and Eucharistic devotion were almost never separated for medieval holy women and had, according to Caroline Bynum, become a downright expectation of them by the later Middle Ages.[24] Thus Maria's self-castigation that her inability to fast and her dependence on communion makes her "no better than the beasts who feed off the ground" is not surprising.[25] But the sentence that follows this one, which appears as the epigraph to this essay, seems to reveal a certainty that her confessor's withholding of sacramental communion cannot keep Christ himself from her: "Ich en weisz geyn dynk dair myn geist meer nae verlangt, dann mynen here tzo untfangen, und ich byn ouch van gantzem hertzen wail tzo freden als ich syner usz lieffden moisz untberen" (I know of nothing for which my spirit longs more than to receive my Lord. And I am also completely satisfied if I must, out of love, do without him).[26] This assertion that she desires the physical elements of communion but is "equally satisfied" whether she is able to partake of them or not suggests a reading of her self-deprecation as at least partially a performance for her confessor.

The real tension here appears to be between Maria's and her confessor's interpretation of spiritual communion, a tenet central to Eucharistic devotions by Maria's day, but one that was nonetheless variously understood. Although we cannot know for sure, the confessor appears to hold the well-established view that spiritual communion—interior connection to God—was a required precursor to sacramental communion. Partaking of the body of Christ without such preparation was generally understood to mean that one was not worthy and was thus at risk of eating and drinking "damnation to [one]self" (1 Cor. 11:29). For Maria, spiritual communion appears to be not only the foundation for effective sacramental communion, but, indeed, a replication of it. In this way she channels Augustine, for whom spiritual communion was always gustatory. In Heinz Schlette's formulation, "kann kein Zweifel daran bestehen, dass Augustinus den liebeerfüllten Glauben als ein 'Essen' Christi versteht" (there can be no doubt that Augustine understands love-filled faith as the "eating" of Christ).[27] But Miri Rubin's reading of the risks of spiritual communion for various groups suggests that Maria's status as a beguine and thus her connection to a tradition of women who "question[ed] priestly authority in other ways" probably meant that her practice of spiritual communion might have been "particularly suspect."[28]

Maria's confessor and the local priest whom she of necessity sought out more frequently apparently shared suspicions and a desire to keep her under control, for she indicates that this local cleric, too, kept her busy doing penance. He prescribed acts, she writes to her confessor, "dat im duichde dat mir meist tzo weder was" (that he thought would be the most distasteful to me).[29] But in yet another clear message that God alone is her master, she declares that "unde mit der penitentien so kierden ich min hertz ernstlich tzo got, und en lies niet aff mit bidden die nacht of den dach dat ich bekentnisz van got moechte krigen wat got dae mit meinde . . . Also hait Got duck so wunderlich tuschenn uns beiden gewirckt" (And with these acts of penance I turned my heart earnestly to God and did not cease to pray night or day that I might receive knowledge from God regarding what God meant by it . . . and in this way God has often functioned marvelously between the two of us).[30] It is striking that she repeats the word "God" here, rather than using the pronoun "he," lest there should be any confusion regarding whose answer mattered to her most. She both owns and circumvents the limitations these two clerics impose on her. While not denying their control, or even the frustrations it imposes, she finds a way at every turn to remind her confessor that he cannot impede her access to the divine.

Maria van Hout and *The Paradise of Loving Souls*

This conflict between Maria van Hout and her confessor, particularly its Eucharistic component, suggests that Maria was the author not only of *The Right Path*, but also of *The Paradise of Loving Souls.* Although *Paradise* is attributed to Maria in two sixteenth-century sources, her authorship has remained in question in the limited contemporary scholarship.[31] I explore the details of the attribution of *Paradise* in a forthcoming article and argue that it can indeed be attributed to Maria.[32] For the purposes of this essay, I proceed on this basis and focus specifically on the Eucharist treatise I mention above, which appears in the third of the book's three sections. A treatise on the same theme from Arnhem highlights a shared devotional emphasis between

Maria and the sisters of Saint Agnes and clarifies that both found meaning in an approach to the Eucharist that viewed it as an inherently mystical experience with a crucial sensual component, accessible both as part of and outside of Mass. Both treatises reconnect to the physicality and visuality central to medieval Eucharistic cults that urged the faithful to "imagine Christ's suffering body" in the elevation of the Host and thus to view Mass "as a direct *physical* encounter with Christ" (emphasis added).[33]

The first two-thirds of *Paradise* focuses on the life of Christ and the Virgin Mary and also includes a book of hours. The Carthusian foreword to *Paradise*, written by Gerhard Kalckbrenner, procurator of the Cologne Charterhouse and special "spiritual son" to Maria, describes its structure as follows: "Im eirsten und tzweiden deil diß buechlins wirt eyn goet mensch gedreven syne eigen sunden und gebrechen tzo bekennen und aefftzolagen und dat reine leven und den suessen wandel uns heren Jesu Christi in duechden nae tzo volgen . . . Im lesten deil . . . streckt sich de lieffhavende siele voert an umb sich selffs . . . in got tzo verliessen . . . Und begert yren allerliefsten tzo umbfangen tzo beholden in got tzo smeltzen und vereynicht tzo bliven" (In the first and second parts of this little book, the good person is encouraged to confess and let go of his sins and weaknesses and to follow in virtue the pure life and sweet path of our Lord Jesus Christ . . . In the last part . . . the loving soul reaches continually on to . . . let go. And [she] desires to embrace and behold her most beloved and to melt into God and remain united with him).[34]

The structure of the first two sections is distinctly linear and unified, mirroring the stages of *purgatio*, *illuminatio*, and *unio* in the mystical progression. Thus, "vam nedersten graide der penitencien an tzo fangen" (beginning with the lowest degree of penance), these sections lead the reader to the final treatises and "bys tzom hoichsten stande der volkomenheit (dae alle bilde und formen in aiffalen und die liefhavende siele mit lieflicher verynunge in got over gesat wirt)" (to the highest level of perfection [where all images and forms fall away and the loving soul is transformed in loving union with God]).[35] The first two sections are richly illustrated with woodcuts from the life and passion of Christ, but in a useful conflation of content and form, the illustrations "fall away" in the third section, just as they are intended to do in the soul.

By the end of the second section the soul is led, in increasingly ecstatic language, to forgetting, to annihilation,[36] and ultimately to union with the bridegroom. But union is not the climax. The erotically charged narrative directs the bride to be prepared to go constantly out and in, a description reminiscent of the cyclical, revolving-door nature of the sixth and seventh stages in Marguerite Porete's *Mirror of Simple Souls*. But in contrast to Porete and earlier mystics, and, I might argue, in apparent awareness of the dangerous times in which she lived and wrote, union for Maria van Hout is "sacramental," rooted in the church while occurring in the soul. The "inward soul" throws off her "created essence" not independent of church, but indeed out of "obedience to God *and* her confessor." She continues: "O eyn volkomen bruyt Christi hait so stille heisse begeirten gefundeirt in so groisser vrolicheit wurt dissent kyndde dat heilige sacrament geboden off verboiden des isset gelychen waill zo vreden want id is vol goitz willen und syns biechtvaders" (Oh, a perfected bride of Christ has established such silent, burning desire in such great joy that whether she is commanded to take the Holy Sacrament or forbidden it she is equally satisfied, for she is full of the will of God and her confessor).[37] Echoes of Maria's conflict with her confessor are plainly audible here. Indeed, in her correspondence she tells him: "wie der her und ir mit mich doet . . . is myr dat hoichste unnd dat lieffste" (whatever you and the Lord do with me . . . is the highest and dearest thing to me).[38] *Paradise* thus comprises mystical teachings that are shaped by Maria's biography, which reflect the richness of the nuptial mystical traditions from which they sprang, and which also seem to acknowledge the pressing need for loyalty in the tense reality of the church in her day.

The Eucharistic treatise in the third section of *Paradise* entitled "Wie men dat heilige sacrament geistlich untfangen sal soe duck als men wilt" (How one can spiritually receive the Holy Sacrament as often as one wants),[39] takes on particular significance in light of Maria's troubled relationship with her confessor. The treatise harnesses the long tradition of spiritual communion and links it to the multi-tiered mystical pursuit. While Maria describes the desire for the (physical) Eucharist as characteristic of those with the lowest levels of strength, in contrast, she declares exuberantly that a perfected bride of Christ is "equally satisfied" (gelychen waill zo vreden) whether the (actual) Eucharist is offered or denied. In what might seem to be a contradiction, Maria explains that "we" desire the holy sacrament because of the joy it brings to both body and soul and yet in this same moment, she claims that "for this reason" (hie umb) no one can take God from "us": "ich hain ym altzyt in mich" (I have him always in me).[40] Joy of past communions produces desire for more at the same time as it obviates the need for it since God is always in her.

Perhaps anticipating the difficulty of this concept for others, Maria elaborates. Desire for "dat glorificeirde licham uns heren" (the glorified body of our Lord) is crucial, she argues.[41] But "good people,"[42] those who are "anhevend, sinnlich" (beginning and sensual) and have just commenced on their path toward union will view the transubstantiated bread as the only access to that body. Such a person, if communion "ym dan verboiden wurt so is he swarmuedich und unrustich van herzen" (is forbidden him, . . . is melancholy and restless at heart).[43] But if one can bear this restlessness, "sonder murmuren tzer stunt is he dan bi uns mit allet datt syn menscheitt vermaich. Daeumb datt he mynsche is gewoirden all wer dat dusent werf in eynen dage. Also en maich he uns ouch sacramentelich niet genomen warden, want van stunt an als ich ym begeir soe koempt dae bloit Christi und weschet mich und syn gloriose liecham erlucht mich syn heilige siele umb helset mich mit yren overvluedigen duechden . . . Also weirden wyr alle ougenblick heiliger und noch heiligerr" (without murmuring, in that very hour he is with us with all that his humanity allows . . . , even if it is a dozen times in a day. And he cannot be taken from us sacramentally, for from the very hour that I desire him, the blood of Christ comes and washes me, and his glorious body enlightens me, his holy soul encompasses me with his overflowing virtue . . . Thus we become each moment holier and holier).[44]

What emerges is a somewhat paradoxical "counter-chronological" impulse in Maria's grip on communion.[45] For those who, like her, crave the Eucharistic experience that is anchored in real time in the Mass but cannot control their own access to it, she co-opts the long tradition of spiritual communion by unmooring it—and the "*jouissance* of spiritual favors" it can create—from liturgical time.[46] By showing that reception of the Lord is "beyond chronology's container," she links herself to the powerful tradition of many mystics before her.[47] Throughout the treatise her description of such communion, though, is replete with time references. Thus it cannot fully relieve the "constant tension" that arises when "pious progression is marked by the human clock" (including clerically controlled moments), but when an individual also experiences "fragments of beyond-body temporal transgression."[48]

Maria concludes the treatise by arguing for what we might think of as mystical feast days that are not dependent on the liturgical year: "Spreicht der priester niet ee he dat broitt in die hant nempt: Erghesteren is Christus gestorven recht off id dan Paesdaich weer . . . Got is eyn vry heer. He koempt tzo der sielen als ym dat belief . . . und en hait sich nie van mich gekeirt inwendich noch ußwendig" (Does the priest not say before he takes the bread in his hand: "Christ died yesterday," as if it were Easter . . . God is a free lord. He comes to the soul when he wishes . . . and he has never turned from me, internally nor externally).[49] Note that although she begins with a general statement of Eucharistic theology, writing in the third person, she ends it, almost in a grammatical slip, with a first-person testimonial of its relevance to her: "[the Lord] has never turned from *me*" (emphasis added). Yet she also speaks beyond her personal defiance by declaring that God's access to the soul knows no calendar, perhaps a pushback against the general restriction of communion to the faithful only on certain feast days, including the annual requirement of sacramental communion on Easter.

Charles Caspers argues that the sixteenth century generally saw an increase in calls for more frequent communion, but that "geistliche Autoren sowohl aus den Nord- als auch aus den Südniederlanden zugunsten der geistlichen Kommunion dieser Neigung gegenüber auffallend abgeneigt waren" (religious authors in both the north and south Low Countries remained noticeably averse to this innovation, in favor of spiritual communion).[50] A notable exception to this assessment were authors from the *Devotio Moderna* movement. Maria seems to have straddled these opposing trends. Her treatise echoes the broader Netherlandic emphasis in her day on spiritual communion as the preferred approach to the Eucharist, though she does not seem to share the sense of fear of unworthy participation generally associated with such a leaning. On the contrary, and in line with the sense within the *Devotio Moderna* that love was a better motivator than fear, she longs for the physical elements and declares that such a longing is a necessary part of the mystical pursuit.[51] She also requests more opportunities for sacramental communion. When this is not possible, however, spiritual communion serves not merely as the safer alternative, but as its own deeply fulfilling, indeed visceral experience.[52]

Maria's beguine status likely plays a role here. Caspers argues that the later Middle Ages saw distinct differences in expectations surrounding the role of communion between "Kleriker, Ordensfrauen, und 'betrachtende' Laien" (clerics, women in orders, and "notable" laypeople) and "'gewöhnlichen' Gläubigen" (the "common" faithful).[53] For the former, communion was a vehicle for individual spiritual renewal not solely dependent on the intercessory role of the priest. Devotional writings of the period articulate a much more mediated access to communion for the common faithful. Although Maria was not in an order, for her Carthusian, Jesuit, and local contemporaries, she would surely have counted as a "notable" layperson. Her confessor, in contrast, seems to have considered her simply one of the many, whose access was necessarily restricted and more highly mediated than for ordered religious.

Yet Maria's spiritual communion evokes and thereby claims the physicality of sacramental communion even when she (or anyone else) could not actually participate. And while we might be tempted to argue that Maria's language of consuming should be understood, as Ruysbroeck's was, as "a metaphorical challenge, not a theological assertion,"[54] her letters make clear that she desired to devour God in the Host as well as in spirit.

But we miss a major contribution of this treatise if we view it only as an end run around her confessor, as an opportunistic or shrewd response to the restrictions he placed on her. Rather, this treatise has unique value if understood as what we might refer to as an applied interiority. While the first two sections of *Paradise* have a speculative focus in their depiction of the road to *unio mystica*, this Eucharist treatise takes union as its foundation as it moves out of the speculative and into and then beyond a lived liturgical moment. In other words, union with the divine is the starting point, the *sine qua non* and the essence of true communion.

Maria's willingness to commit her teachings on spiritual communion to writing, the Carthusians' willingness to disseminate them, and the theological ground they share with the sisters in Arnhem, which I describe below, reveal a resonance beyond her relationship with her confessor and beyond a repetition of a long established practice. In their introductory paragraph to the final section of *Paradise*, which contains the treatise on the Eucharist, Maria's Carthusian spiritual son and editor Kalckbrenner presents it as "fuirige worde [die] daemit leeren altzyt mit got redden und got heilich werden" (fiery words [that will] teach one at all times to speak with God and become sanctified in God).[55]

It is thus clear that although informed by a personal crisis, Maria's Eucharistic teachings struck a chord among the reform-minded Cologne Carthusians and other religious in the sprawling archdiocese of Cologne, including the sisters of Saint Agnes in Arnhem. This previously unstudied reception of Maria's work by the sisters of Saint Agnes, who also associated with the Carthusians, offers a much more expansive view of the intellectual and spiritual commerce in the region, allowing us to link Brabant (where Maria van Hout and her community lived), Arnhem (the sisters of Saint Agnes), and Cologne (the Carthusians). The communities and individuals in these three centers shared a fervent belief that the mystical pursuit could revive the spiritual life of the church by reforming the interior life of its adherents.

The Spiritual Eucharist and the Sisters of Saint Agnes

Arnhem's sisters of Saint Agnes have been the subject of increasing interest in the past decade, as the convent's manuscript treasures, which have languished for centuries in several archives, have gradually come to light through the dedicated work of Kees Schepers, Hans Kienhorst, and others.[56] Their work has revealed a community that fostered an intense mystical life, characterized by "een spiritueel klimaat waarin mystieke teksten gerecipieerd en gekopieerd werden" (a spiritual climate in which mystical texts were received and copied).[57] Schepers believes that the literary record of Saint Agnes brings to light a fierce commitment to the interior life in the region that he characterizes as a veritable "mystical renaissance."[58] He argues further that these writings allow a glimpse through the doors of history, of the convent, and into the very "hearts and minds of the sisters of St. Agnes," revealing "their inner . . . , most essential life, one that was wholly spiritual."[59]

Although the Arnhem sisters in this period do not appear to have had a troubled relationship with their confessors or other male leaders like Maria did (on the contrary, they appear to have enjoyed great clerical support),[60] their interpretation of spiritual communion nonetheless shows many shared themes with Maria. The treatise I discuss, "Hoemen dat heilige sacrament geestelick sal ontfangen" (How one should spiritually receive the holy sacrament), is included in a manuscript identified as having been produced by the sisters of Saint Agnes, now held in the Bibliothèque Royale in Brussels, ms. 14716. It is bound with a collection of other spiritual texts and comprises the second of three codicological units in the book. Hans Kienhorst dates this manuscript ca. 1540.[61] Its production would thus postdate the publication of both editions of *Paradise* (1532 and 1535), allowing us to understand it as perhaps having been influenced by Maria van Hout's Eucharist treatise.

Although we have no irrefutable proof that the Saint Agnes sisters owned a copy of *Paradise*, one piece of evidence strongly points in this direction. First, we know that a copy of the 1532 edition was associated with a devout woman from Arnhem. The title page of one copy of the 1532 edition of *Paradise*, now housed in the library of the archdiocese of Cologne, contains a carefully handwritten note indicating that the book was "made in Arnhem" (presumably selected for binding and owned) by a "godly friend in Arnhem named Lijesken

Burcharß."[62] Although the identity of Lijesken Burcharß remains a mystery (she cannot be linked with certainty to Saint Agnes, for example), it seems plausible that she was at least associated with the sisters of Saint Agnes, if she was not in fact one of them, and thus would have shared *Paradise* with them (or perhaps they with her).[63]

One other piece of evidence suggests a possible link between *Paradise* and Arnhem. Hans Kienhorst considers it possible, although he has not yet been able to confirm it, that a copy of the 1535 Middle Dutch edition of *Paradise*, also currently housed in Brussels, may well have belonged to the sisters of Saint Agnes. This copy, it turns out, was not procured from the printer, but is rather a meticulously *handwritten* copy of the 1535 print.[64] That is, a sister (or sisters), at Saint Agnes or perhaps another convent, went to the trouble of copying every word of *Paradise*, including the errata, for the convent library. According to Alexandra Walsham and Julia Crick, even after the advent of printing, "script was the choice of writers who sought to communicate with an exclusive circle of readers or retain a reserved status for the knowledge they conveyed: it flattered patrons, concealed secrets, and surrounded religious revelations with an aura of sacredness."[65] The scribes may thus have viewed their painstaking, intimate engagement with each letter of the text as a physical manifestation of its sacredness. Working their way through the text would also have been a fitting metaphor for the mystical progress it describes.

The Arnhem Eucharist Manuscript

Although the sisters in Arnhem, as members of the Augustinian Order, were arguably more structurally bound to the church than Maria and her independent beguines, they shared a desire for mystical union and an understanding of spiritual communion as an avenue to it. The Arnhem manuscript differs in several significant ways from Maria's text, most notably in that it is structured as a devotional exercise in which readers are instructed first to contemplate the body, then the blood, then the spirit, soul, and divinity of Christ, each of which must be spiritually received in turn. The treatise devotes a distinct section to each of these elements, which creates a layered, repetitive, almost pulsating text that lends it a distinctly percussive and thus meditative quality as it builds toward its thematic crescendo, which clearly echoes the sentiments from Maria's text discussed above: "Dar umb begeiren wyr dat heilige sacrament up dat siele und licham beide vreude havenn und spyse . . . O suesse Got koem und versadige mich . . . mucht ich Christum mynen suessen brudegom inlaissen ach dat wulde ich so gerne doin. Alsus behaldt die reyne siele allet dat sy begeren maich und gott is altzyt in sy. O heilige geloeve du maiches den menschen gesunt. Siet Jesum an" (Therefore we desire the holy sacrament so that both soul and body have joy and nourishment . . . O sweet God, come and satisfy me . . . if I might let Christ my sweet bridegroom in, how gladly would I do it. Thus the pure soul retains everything that she might desire, and God is always in her. O holy faith, you make people healthy! Behold Jesus!).[66] The melding of nuptial mysticism with the sacramental, of the interior with the liturgical, which defines the entire treatise is particularly prominent in this passage, not least in the imperative to "Behold Jesus!"—a clear allusion to the elevation of the Host.

In contrast to the somewhat shorter and more speculative *Paradise* treatise, the Arnhem manuscript also firmly grounds this Eucharistic exercise within the context of the Mass: "Meijn begeerte [sal] nu in deser missen vervult werden" (My desire will now be fulfilled in this Mass).[67] In a litany of quite typical late medieval emphases, it highlights the roles of the priest and the real presence and focuses repeatedly on the "worthiness" of the participant and the "merits" of Christ's sacrifice. Yet as it does so, it argues over and over that even the "sacramental" Eucharist will not be efficacious if the worshiper is not prepared for the "spiritual" Eucharist—the receipt of Christ into the soul.[68]

As with Maria van Hout, the Arnhem author also unequivocally couples the experience of the Eucharist with mystical union using nuptial vocabulary, thus moving the Eucharist beyond the Mass: "O zuete god coem en versadige my want my gheen dinck versadigen en mach dan du alleen. Dan o myn ziel trecket Ihm aen dat is dat roede clede des lydens alsoe duck als du begeres enn willes bruloft holden dat is di mit god te vereinigen" (O sweet God, come and satisfy me, for nothing can satisfy me but you alone. Then, O my soul, put on the red cloak of suffering as often as you desire. And keep your marriage, that is, unite yourself with God). Although the phrase "as often as one wants" is not part of the title of the Arnhem manuscript treatise, as it is in *Paradise*, the word "often" nonetheless occurs in the main text, as in this passage, further emphasizing the extra-liturgical possibilities of spiritual communion.[69] Even in this brief description, the parallels in these two treatises are clear.

The Treatises in the Context of Late Medieval Eucharistic Devotions and the Reformation

The interpretations of the Eucharist in these two texts are surely enabled, at least in part, by the shift, widely evident by the thirteenth century, and described by Bynum and many others, "from communion to consecration as the focal point of [Eucharistic] devotion."[70] But what we see in these texts is not merely ocular communion *as* spiritual communion—the move away from *consumption* of the Host toward the *raising and seeing* of it as the most sacred moment of communion.[71] We see not just "a fervent viewing, even without tasting, of Christ"[72] but a call to see the Host with the soul's "inner eye," so to speak.

For Maria van Hout, the Eucharistic supplicant herself owns the entire ocular experience as both presenter and beholder since the context of the Mass is noticeably absent in her text. That a woman could elevate the Host (in her own mind) by envisioning it is striking for what it suggests about the dispensability of the actual Host—not to mention of the priest—a potentially slippery slope, especially for an unprotected beguine like Maria. She is, of course, not the first to have a vision of the Mass (cf. Mechthild von Magdeburg's *Flowing Light*, book II, chapter 4),[73] but advocating communion outside of the Mass in the sixteenth century is potentially more problematic precisely because of the more volatile confessional situation of the region.

In the Arnhem manuscript, Mass is central for its value as a catalyst *in and past* the liturgical moment to real communion, whereas in the *Paradise* treatise one need not be at Mass to receive the spiritual Eucharist.[74] For Maria, transubstantiation is assumed, as it had been for several centuries by that point, but simultaneously irrelevant.[75] "Der nu hait eyn vast gelove und begeirt syn lichamliche tgegenwoirdicheit der vercryget dat alle in den heiligen sacrament. Want eyn glorificyrt licham is in eyn ougenblick durch hemel und eerde iae durch eyn muoer all weer sy hunder dusennt mylen dick alsoe en is got niet geslossen in yemantz hende" (Those who have a firm faith and desire his bodily presence will receive all of that in the Holy Sacrament. For, in a moment, a glorified body penetrates heaven and earth, indeed through a wall, even if it were a hundred thousand miles thick. Thus, God is not locked in anyone's hands).[76] The message could hardly be more overt: although priestly hands are authorized to elevate the Host, they do not confine the presence of God. These texts present both the transubstantiation of wafer to flesh and wine to blood and of desire to divine presence. There is a subtle shift here from other understandings of spiritual communion. Whereas presence of the body of Christ in the Host in late medieval Mass was supposed to waken the desire of the faithful to be unified with him, Maria argues conversely that desire conjures his presence.

Bynum speaks of an "asymmetry between the body and blood symbols" in certain late medieval Eucharistic accounts that was, in part, the fruit of an intentional liturgical focus on the Host and consequent downplaying of the blood or wine.[77] The Eucharistic treatises in both *Paradise* and the Arnhem manuscript re-establish that symmetry by emphasizing the central importance of both blood and body. Moreover, in a powerful semantic turn, both texts spiritually "flesh out" the body and blood by including God's spirit, soul, and divinity among the elements of the Eucharist.

These texts in *Paradise* and the Arnhem manuscript seem to underscore Miri Rubin's understanding of the sacrament as a devotional element whose symbolism was available for diverse interpretation, not just by theologians, but perhaps especially by the faithful.

"[The Eucharist]," Rubin claims, "was a prime marker which people wore with pride, rejected with passion, and claimed with invention and even audacity."[78] Maria van Hout's response to her confessor's restrictions certainly highlights the audacious potential of the Eucharist. But it also evokes Bynum's sensitive reading of the Eucharist as having unique meaning for and requiring particular creativity of women.[79]

Rubin has further argued that the Eucharist—more specifically, defining Eucharistic purity—was at the center of many "processes of refiguration" in the fourteenth and fifteenth centuries and ultimately in Reformation and Counter-Reformation efforts.[80] Maria van Hout and the Arnhem sisters "refigure" mystical union by anchoring it in established Eucharistic piety, and by asserting their own and others' worthiness to take part in communion. They eschew any debate about *signum* versus *res*, or about form, ritual, substance, usury, or desecration. Instead, they focus, like all good mystics, on the interior—in this case on the Eucharist as offered and received in the heart of the believer. There is a unique confidence in their willingness to move communion outside liturgical time and space, based not only on tradition but also on their presentation of the mystic as one who is "intently poised in a devotional present."[81]

And although these two treatises never refer overtly to the confessional upheaval that characterized the church in their day, they are nonetheless linked to it through their associations to the Cologne Carthusians. Other scholars and I have written extensively of the Carthusians' zealous efforts to promote mysticism as a source of spiritual power for the church, even in the decades before it was embattled by the Lutheran onslaught.[82] Their efforts included tireless copying and publication of the church's great mystical works, ardent support for Maria van Hout and her sister beguines, and promotion of Maria's writings and those of spiritual women in Arnhem. Their interest in the Eucharistic texts I have discussed here powerfully underscores an understanding they shared with these women authors that effective spiritual reform must anchor the life of the church in an abiding interiority best accessed through the mystical pursuit.

Notes

1. *Der rechte wech zo der evangelischen volkomenheit* (*The Right Path to Evangelical Perfection*), letter 8. I refer to the letters from this text hereafter as *The Right Path*, with the letter number. Excerpts from the original text are from J.-M. Willeumier-Schalij's edition of the letters, with facing Dutch translation: *De Brieven uit 'Der rechte wech' van de Oisterwijkse Begijn en Mystica Maria van Hout (†Keulen, 1547)* (Louvain: Peeters, 1993), which I hereafter abbreviate as *De Brieven*, with page numbers. Excerpt here from *De Brieven*, 96. All translations from *The Right Path* are mine.

2. Rob Faesen's recently published translation of two letters from *The Right Path* translates *recht* as "straight." Although I choose to stay with the English rendering of "right" that I have used for many years, I acknowledge the conundrum of translating a word with many nuances. While "right" establishes what I believe to be Maria's sense that the path she articulates comes from God and is thus "right" in the sense of correct, "straight" is also a useful rendering since it suggests progression, a central concept in many mystical writings, including Maria's. See Rob Faesen, "Maria van Hout: Two Letters," in *Late Medieval Mysticism of the Low Countries*, ed. Rik van Nieuwenhove, Robert Faesen, S.J., and Helen Rolfsen (New York: Paulist, 2008), 365.

3. A number of studies have explored Maria's relationship to her confessor in depth, especially her understanding of obedience. See J.-M. Willeumier-Schalij, "Maria van Houts gehoorzame ongehoorsaamheid," *Ons Geestelijk Erf* 66 (1992): 134–44, and *De Brieven*, esp. 52–65. See also the work of Ulrike Wiethaus: "'If I Had an Iron Body': Femininity and Religion in the Letters of Maria de Hout," in *Dear Sister: Medieval Women and the Epistolary Genre*, ed. Karen Cherewatuk and Ulrike Wiethaus (Philadelphia: University of Pennsylvania Press, 1993), 171–91, as well as idem, "'For this I Ask you, Punish me': Norms of Spiritual Orthopraxis in the Work of Maria van Hout (d. 1547)," *Ons Geestelijk Erf* 68 (1994): 253–70. In addition, see my previous work: "Mapping Mysticism onto Confessional Cologne," in *Topographies of the Early Modern City*, ed. Arthur Groos, Hans-Jochen Schiewer, and Markus Stock (Göttingen: Vandenhoek and Ruprecht, 2008), 109–27; "The Gender of Epistemology in Confessional Europe: The Reception of Maria van Hout's Ways of Knowing," in *Seeing and Knowing: Women and Learning in Medieval Europe*, ed. Anneke Mulder-Bakker (Turnhout: Brepols, 2004), 97–120; and "Maria van Hout and her Carthusian Editor," *Ons Geestelijk Erf* 72, no. 1 (1998): 105–21.

4. *Dat paradijs der lieffhavender sielen* (Cologne: Johann Soter, 1532) and (den Bosch, 1535). Text referred to throughout as *Paradise*. All excerpts here are from the 1532 edition, and all translations are mine.

5. For foundational work on this tradition, see Caroline Walker Bynum, "Women Mystics and Eucharistic Devotion in the Thirteenth Century,"

Women's Studies 11 (1984): 179–214; and idem, *Holy Feast and Holy Fast: The Religious Significance of Food to Medieval Women* (Berkeley: University of California Press, 1987).

6. A conflicted yet productive relationship with a confessor or priest acting as spiritual guide and advisor was by the fifteenth century something of a commonplace in mystical literature. One thinks of Mechthild of Magdeburg's *Flowing Light of the Godhead* (thirteenth century), for example, in which certain chapters begin with a response to the confessor's critique. Mechthild of Magdeburg, *The Flowing Light of the Godhead*, ed. and trans. Frank Tobin (New York: Paulist, 1998), for example, book V, chapter 12; or Margaret Ebner's revelations written during a period of correspondence with her spiritual advisor, Heinrich von Nördlingen (fourteenth century). See Philipp Strauch, ed., *Margaretha Ebner und Heinrich von Nördlingen: Ein Beitrag zur Geschichte der deutschen Mystik (1882)* (Amsterdam: P. Shippers N.V., 1966). Probably the most well-known example of this relationship (also fourteenth century) is documented in *The Book of Margery Kempe*, TEAMS Middle English Texts series, ed. Lynn Staley (Kalamazoo, Mich.: Medieval Institute Publications, 1996). For a popular dialogue demonstrating the workings of the confessor-religious woman relationship that also circulated in Low German- and Dutch-speaking regions, see the fourteenth-century anonymous texts "Sister Catherine and the Twenty-One Year Old Woman," in *Ladies, Whores, and Holy Women*, Medieval German Texts in Bilingual Editions V, ed. Ann Marie Rasmussen and Sarah Westphal-Wihl (Kalamazoo, Mich.: Medieval Institute Publications, 2010), 47–95; and on the significance of these texts within the tradition, see Sara S. Poor, "Women Teaching Men in the Medieval Devotional Imagination," in *Partners in Spirit: Men, Women, and Religious Life in Germany, 1100–1500*, Medieval Women in Texts and Contexts 24, ed. Fiona J. Griffiths and Julie Hotchin (Turnhout: Brepols, 2014), 339–65.

7. *The Right Path*, letter 10; *De Brieven*, 102.

8. See Wiethaus's extended discussion of the shift in tone between her letters to her sisters and those to her male supporters in "'If I had an Iron Body,'" esp. 179–81.

9. *The Right Path*, letter 4; *De Brieven*, 82–83.

10. Hildegard of Bingen, the twelfth-century abbess of her own convent, is likely the most prominent woman to use this trope. For a good introduction to Hildegard studies, see Barbara Newman, ed., *Voice of the Living Light: Hildegard of Bingen and Her World* (Berkeley: University of California Press, 1998).

11. Nicky Hallett, "Introduction 2: 'Anxiously yours': The Epistolary Self and the Culture of Concern," *Journal of European Studies* 32 (2002): 107–18, here 107–8.

12. *The Right Path*, letter 11; *De Brieven*, 108.

13. "Die werelt ys mir ein swair cruitz, unnd ich bin ir einn cruitz" (The world is a heavy cross to me, and I am a cross to it). *The Right Path*, letter 11; *De Brieven*, 108.

14. Hallett, "Introduction 2," 109–10.

15. *The Right Path*, letter 11; *De Brieven*, 104.

16. *The Right Path*, letter 10; *De Brieven*, 100.

17. *The Right Path*, letter 11; *De Brieven*, 104.

18. *The Right Path*, letter 9; *De Brieven*, 98. Gerhard Kalckbrenner, the Carthusian who edited Maria's letters for publication, grouped them by addressee, rather than chronologically. I concur with Willeumier-Schalij and the much earlier work by Kettenmeyer that the likely chronological order of Maria's first four letters to her confessor is 10, 11, 8, and 9. See Willeumier-Schalij, *De Brieven*, 52; see also J. B. Kettenmeyer, "Uit de Briefwisseling van eene Brabantsche Mystieke uit de 16e Eeuw," *Ons Geestelijk Erf* 3 (1927): 280 ff.

19. "Also hait ir myr verboden dat ich gein heimliche penitentie soiled doyn, und dat ich swygen solde, und yr laist mich tzom hilgen sacrament gain, so duc alst mir mit vreden werden mag, und yr hait mir tzo penitentie gesat dat ich solde bidden vur Paesz, Keiser und alle staden, und vor int gemein vur al sundige menschen." *The Right Path*, letter 9; *De Brieven*, 98. The "secret acts of penance" she alludes to appear to have been various mortifications of the flesh. "Ich denck duck als ich tzo dem hilgen Sacrament gain, idt is wunder dat got mich nit en liest versyncken, kunde ich mich selver verslynden und tzo niet gewerden, ich woulde gern wer idt Gotz wille mich selver tzo pulver vermalen. Ach wie guyt is Got der myr durch uch hait penitentie laissen verbieden, want mucht ich gewerden na miner begerten, och wie strackelich suldt ich mich selver kastyen" (I often think when I go to the Holy Sacrament that it is a wonder that God does not cause me to sink into the earth. If I could consume and annihilate myself—if it were God's will—I would gladly grind myself to dust. Oh, how good is God that he, through you, has forbidden me to do penance. For if I acted according to my desires, oh, how severely would I chasten myself!) *The Right Path*, letter 9; *De Brieven*, 98.

20. It seems quite clear that her editor and supporter Kalckbrenner knew of and was dismayed by these clerics' obstructive behavior to someone as mystically gifted as Maria. In the introduction to a Latin translation of one of Maria's letters, which Kalckbrenner published in 1532 and thus is not included in *The Right Path*, he claims that she had been persecuted by those in high position, an almost certain allusion to her struggles with her confessor. See *Frater Gerardus ab Hamont procurator Carthusiensium in Colonia pio lectori gratiam et pacem a domino nostro Jesu Christo* (Cologne: n.p., 1532), located in the Universitätsbibliothek Basel, D. A., VI 19, Nr. B13.

21. *The Right Path*, letter 10; *De Brieven*, 104.

22. "Ich hain den dag geleefft dat myr die erdtsche spyse tgegenn walchde, und ich sy niet en mucht, und leefde gentzlich by der spysen des hilgen sacramentz, und ich was vil starcker dan nu" (There was a time in my life when I gagged on earthly food and could not eat it, and I lived solely by the food of the Holy Sacrament, and I was much stronger than now). *The Right Path*, letter 8; *De Brieven*, 96.

23. *The Right Path*, letter 8; *De Brieven*, 96.

24. Bynum, *Holy Feast and Holy Fast*, 83.

25. "Ich [byn] mit den beesten suygende in der erden." *The Right Path*, letter 8; *De Brieven*, 96.

26. *The Right Path*, letter 8; *De Brieven*, 96.

27. Heinz Robert Schlette, *Kommunikation und Sakrament: Theologische Deutung der geistlichen Kommunion* (Freiburg im Breisgau: Herder, 1959), 15.

28. Miri Rubin, *Corpus Christi: The Eucharist in Late Medieval Culture* (Cambridge: Cambridge University Press, 1991), 150.

29. *The Right Path*, letter 11; *De Brieven*, 106.

30. *The Right Path*, letter 11; *De Brieven*, 106.

31. See brief discussion of the attributions in J. B. Kettenmeyer, "Maria van Hout (†1547) und die Kölner Kartause," *Annalen des historischen Vereins für den Niederrhein* 144 (1929): 1–33.

32. Kirsten M. Christensen, "The Case for Maria van Hout as Author of *Dat paradijs lieffhavender sielen*, 1532" (in progress).

33. Jennifer Garrison, "Mediated Piety: Eucharistic Theology and Lay Devotion in Robert Mannyng's *Handlyng Synne*," *Speculum* 85, no. 4 (2010): 53 and 52.

34. *Paradise*, fol. A2v.

35. *Paradise*, fol. A2r.

36. zo niet worden, *Paradise*, fol. R6r.

37. *Paradise*, fol. V7v.

38. *The Right Path*, letter 8, *De Brieven*, 96.

39. *Paradise*, fol. V6v.

40. *Paradise*, fols. V7v–V8r.

41. *Paradise*, fols. V6v–V7r.

42. *Paradise*, fol. V7v.

43. *Paradise*, fol. V7v.

44. *Paradise*, fol. V7r.

45. Nicky Hallett, "'So short a space of time': Early Modern Convent Chronology and Carmelite Spirituality," *Journal of Medieval and Early Modern Studies* 42, no. 3 (2012): 539–66, here 540.

46. Hallett, "'So short a space of time,'" 540.

47. Hallett, "'So short a space of time,'" 539. Hallett's essay focuses specifically on Carmelite writings but provides powerful insights of broad import on understanding of time in spiritual and mystical self-writing. Of special interest are her explorations of mystics' perceptions of time while enraptured and of the ways in which quotidian aspects of convent life "gain[ed] meaning and form by claims of boundlessness" associated with the sisters' mystical experience (541).

48. Hallett, "'So short a space of time,'" 551.

49. *Paradise*, fols. V8v–X1r.

50. Caspers, "Magister consensus: Wessel Gansfort (1419–1489) und die geistliche Kommunion," in *Northern Humanism in European Context, 1469–1625: From the 'Advert Academy' to Ubbo Emmius*, ed. F. Akkermann et al. (Leiden: Brill, 1999), 94.

51. See Maximilian von Habsburg's succinct overview of the history of spiritual communion and his discussion of Thomas à Kempis's treatment of it and its place in the *Devotio Moderna* in *Catholic and Protestant Interpretations of the "Imitatio Christi," 1425–1650: From Late Medieval Classic to Early Modern Bestseller* (Burlington, Vt.: Ashgate, 2011), esp. 28–29.

52. "Aber dat glorificeirde licham uns heren mois men begeiren und als uns dan dat niet gebueuren maich und wye dan dae van bangicheit haven . . . tzer stunt is he dan bi uns mit allet datt syn menscheitt vermaich" (But one must desire the glorified body of our Lord. And if that is not permitted and we are afraid because of it, . . . in that hour he is with us with all that his humanity is capable of). *Paradise*, fols. V6v–V7r.

53. Caspers, *Magister consensus*, 87.

54. Brian Patrick McGuire, *Jean Gerson and the Last Medieval Reformation* (University Park: Penn State University Press, 2005), 11.

55. *Paradise*, fol. O7v.

56. See Kees Schepers's contribution to this volume. See also the issue of *Ons Geestelijk Erf* 81, no. 1 (2010), which is dedicated entirely to manuscripts from Saint Agnes and neighboring convents. Although a number of manuscripts have been identified, interpretive work to date has focused almost exclusively on the *Arnhem Mystical Sermons* (The Hague, Royal Library, ms. 133 H 13).

57. Hans Kienhorst, "Meer mystiek uit het Arnhemse Agnietenklooster: De Handschriften den Haag, Koninklijke Bibliotheek, 71 H 51 en 133 H 13," in *Manuscripten en miniaturen: Studies aangeboden aan Anne S. Korteweg bij haar afscheid van de Koninklijke Bibliotheek*, ed. Jos Biemans, Klaas van der Hoek, Kathryn M. Rudy, and Ed van der Vlist (Zutphen: Walburg Pers, 2007), 210.

58. "Toch kan de opvallende mystiek-religieuze opleving in het tweede en derde kwart van de zestiende eeuw met recht een renaissance worden genoemd" (Indeed, the striking mystical-religious revival in the second and third

quarters of the sixteenth century can rightly be called a renaissance). See Kees Schepers, "Het verborgen leven van de zusters Agnieten. Mystieke cultuur te Arnhem in de zestiende eeuw," *Ons Geestelijk Erf* 79 (2008): 285. He uses the actual term "mystieke renaissance" in the discussion that follows on 286. See also Schepers's contribution to this volume.

59. "We moeten de deur openen naar het hart en de geest van de zusters Agnieten"; "hun innerlijke . . . , meest wezenlijke leven, dat volledige spiritueel was." Schepers, "Het verborgen leven van de zusters Agnieten," 286.

60. Schepers discusses the intriguing account of Jan van Lochem, prior of a convent in Albergen, who was asked to pay a visit to the Arnhem sisters in 1523, two years after they had been appointed a new prior. Apparently concerned that the presence of a new prior might have caused some upheaval among the sisters, Lochem interviewed sisters individually to best determine the state of affairs. His account describes "[een] gemeenschap [dat] . . . in perfecte harmonie aan het religieuze leven was toegewijd" (a community that . . . was dedicated to the religious life in perfect harmony). See Schepers, "Het verborgen leven," 291–92.

61. See Kienhorst, "Mystiek op schrift in vrouwenkloosters uit de traditie van de Moderne Devotie. Een oriënterende vergelijking van drie collecties: Arnhem, Geldern en Maaseik," *Ons geestelijk erf* 81, no. 1 (2010): notes 10 and 11.

62. "Dyt buechlin ist gemaecht zo Arnhem dur ein gotliche Frundyn genant lijesken burcharß." *Paradise*, fol. A1r.

63. I discuss the Burcharß link in detail in a forthcoming study exploring the authorship of *Paradise* ("The Case for Maria van Hout as Author of *Dat paradijs lieffhavender sielen*, 1532").

64. Brussels, Bibliothèque Nationale, ms. 3004. Several other manuscript copies of printed texts associated with the Carthusians are also connected with Saint Agnes, thus rendering conceivable the possibility that ms. 3004 also stemmed from the sisters there.

65. *The Uses of Script and Print, 1300–1700*, ed. Alexandra Walsham and Julia Crick (Cambridge: Cambridge University Press, 2004), 8.

66. *Paradise*, fols. V8r–V8v.

67. Brussels ms. 14716, fols. 222r–222v.

68. Brussels ms. 14716, fol. 223v.

69. Brussels ms. 14716, fol. 228v.

70. Bynum, *Holy Feast and Holy Fast*, 54.

71. See Bynum, "The Blood of Christ in the Later Middle Ages," *Church History* 71, no. 4 (2002): 686, who uses the German term *Augenkommunion*.

72. Rubin, *Corpus Christi*, 64.

73. On this vision of Mechthild, see Sara S. Poor, "Cloaking the Body in Text: Mechthild von Magdeburg and the Question of Female Authorship," *Exemplaria* 12, no. 2 (2000): 417–53.

74. Certainly Jesus himself had initiated an understanding of the elements of the sacrament as a catalyst for mystical union with him: "He that eateth my flesh, and drinketh my blood, dwelleth in me, and I in him" (John 6:57).

75. See Bynum, *Holy Feast and Holy Fast*, 55.

76. *Paradise*, fols. V3r–V3v.

77. See Bynum, "Blood of Christ," 687–88.

78. Miri Rubin, "Whose Eucharist? Eucharistic Identity as Historical Subject," *Modern Theology* 15, no. 2 (1999): 199.

79. See Bynum, *Holy Feast and Holy Fast*, esp. 76 ff.

80. Rubin, "Whose Eucharist?" 202.

81. Hallett, "'So short a space of time,'" 554.

82. See my study "Mapping Mysticism," as well as Sigrun Haude's important essay: "The Silent Monks Speak Up: The Changing Identity of the Carthusians in the Fifteenth and Sixteenth Centuries," *Archiv für Reformationsgeschichte* 86 (1995): 124–40. See also Joachim Vennebusch's highly readable essay on the library of the Cologne Charterhouse: "Die Bücher der Kölner Kartäuser: Zur Geschichte der Klosterbibliothek (1451–1794)," in *Die Kartause in Köln. Festschrift der evangelischen Gemeinde Köln zum 50. Jahrestag der Einweihung der Kartäuserkirche in Köln zur evangelischen Kirche am 16. September 1978*, ed. Rainer Sommer (Cologne: Gebrüder Friedrichs, 1978), 77–104. The following also contribute significantly to our understanding of the Carthusians' promotion of mysticism: Gérald Chaix, "Les Traductions de la Chartreuse de Cologne au XVIè Siecle," in *Kartäusermystik und -mystiker: Dritter Internationaler Kongress über die Kartäusergeschichte und –spiritualität*, vol. 5, Analecta Cartusiana 55, ed. James Hogg (Salzburg: Universität Salzburg Institut für Anglistik und Amerikanistik, Universität Salzburg, 1982), 67–78; and Marion Grams-Thieme, "Die Kölner Kartause und ihre Beziehungen zu den Niederlanden," in *Die Kölner Kartause um 1500*, ed. Werner Schäfke (Cologne: Kölnisches Stadtmuseum, 1991), 359–72.

5

Saintly Idiocy and Contemplative Empowerment

The Example of Dame Gertrude More

ARTHUR F. MAROTTI

In using the term "idiocy" in my title, I am not signaling that I am interested in "mysticism for dummies," but rather I refer to the literal meaning of "idiot" as "unlearned,"[1] the sense of the term used in the titles of two works associated with the seventeenth-century Benedictine nun Dame Gertrude More: *The Holy Practises of a Devine Lover or The Sainctly Ideots Deuotions* (Paris, 1657) and *The Spiritual Exercises of the Most Vertvous and Religious D. Gertrvde More of the holy Order of S. Bennet and English Congregation of our Ladies of Comfort in Cambray, she called them . . . An[d] Ideots Deuotions. Her only Spiritual Father and Directour the Ven. Fa. Baker stiled them . . . A Louers Confessions* (Paris, 1658).[2] Both comprise material compiled by that seventeenth-century English lawyer-priest-mystic Dom Augustine Baker, O.S.B. The first is a collection of exemplary devotional exercises assembled by Baker and probably used by More to develop her own method of prayer.[3] The second work, the *Spiritual Exercises*, is a gathering of manuscript devotional and other writing left behind by More at her death.

"Sainctly Ideot" and "spiritual director" are textually inseparable, especially so in a third text, Baker's manuscript life of Dame Gertrude More, which includes excerpts from More's poetry and prose.[4] In order to examine this seventeenth-century nun as a post-Reformation Catholic mystic, I focus on her *Spiritual Exercises*, using as a framework for the discussion Baker's biography of her (mostly an overblown exposition of the contemplative methods he taught his followers).[5]

We might begin with a few biographical facts, viewed through the lens of Baker's non-hagiographic *Life* of More, a work in which he insists on presenting her flaws as well as her virtues. Born in 1606 in Essex, Helen More, the daughter of Cresacre More and the great-great-granddaughter of Sir (or Saint) Thomas More, lost her mother at the age of five, and was raised by her father, who, in the More tradition, provided his two daughters with an intellectually substantial education that included the learning of Latin, a language in which she became proficient. At sixteen, she indicated her aversion to marriage and was later persuaded by a priest who was her spiritual guide, Dom Benet Jones, to go to the Continent to live the life of a nun, a plan that involved her father's providing the financial backing for the establishment of a new Benedictine convent at Cambrai in the Spanish Netherlands. She left England at the age of eighteen with eight other young women, took the habit of the Benedictine Order, and went to the new Monastery of Our Lady of Comfort in Cambrai, taking the name of Gertrude, after a saint to whose life she was attracted and whose writings she consumed.[6] Unhappy in her new religious life for the first year-and-a-half or two years in the convent, she nevertheless made her profession as a nun in January 1625, but with many misgivings. During the period of her discontent she changed, as Baker observes, "from an humble, simple, obedient, gentle, quiet, and tractable nature" to one who was "factious, craftie or wilie, willful stobborne and disobedient," living in a state he characterized as one of "spiritual confusion" (*Life*, 3), supposedly because she had not yet found a method of prayer suitable for her. Gertrude More portrays the early years of her convent life as one of suffering because she had not found a productive spiritual direction:

> I had suffered so much before *God* did bestow his fauour vpon me of being put into a course that was proper for me, and this for nearly fiue years after my coming over . . . though I made a shift a days to sett a good face on it, yet in the night I bewailed my miseries with more than ordinary Teares, of which *God* and our blessed Lady were Witnesses of, though few others on earth. And I did rowse vp all the books in the howse, and whatsoever I found that any had done to please *God* I took notes of it, and did it as I could. And this course I always held since I came into Religion: as also to consult with al the men that any had found good by in the howse, and yet al this would do me no good. And me thought I Was as great a stranger to *Almighty God* as I was in England, when I scarce thought (as to any good I did) whether there were a *God* or no. And, being thus perplexed and tossed with a thowsand imaginations, and ouerwhelmed with miseries, yea almost desperate through the feare, and consideration of my sins; my Mistress aduised me to go to Father Baker . . . a very grave man, and one that was much respected in the Congregation . . . I in my nature being not very hard to be ruled (though I remember I had no great mind to it of my-self) did as she bid me which being done I found myself in fifteen days so quiet that I wondered at myself: the which was so soone as I had receiued from him some general instructions *As that I must giue al to God without any reseruation, wittingly, and willingly, of any inordinate affection to any creature*: the which I found my-self willing to do. *And that I must vse prayer twise a day*, which I found my-self capable of; and though I found little of that which is called sensible deuotion, yet I found that with a little industry, I was able to vse it with much profit, and that it did make any thing very tollerable which happened to me. Yea, and it made me capable of vnderstanding any thing that was necessary for me in a spiritual life, and it discouereth daily to me that which is an impediment between *God* and my soul. (*Spiritual Exercises*, A90–92)[7]

In the fall of 1624, she had been advised by her friend Catherine Gascoigne (who later became abbess) to seek the counsel of Baker, the convent's newly appointed spiritual director, but she initially resisted his spiritual direction, even mocking him to others. However, as she wrote, she later sought him out and, with his help, had a conversion experience. As he was reading to her a discussion of spiritual desolation from Constantine Barbanson's *The Secret Paths of Divine Love*, she exclaimed, with regard to that writer's contemplative practice, "'Oh! Oh! That must be my way'"[8] and wholeheartedly accepted the kind of prayer Baker was recommending to her.

In Baker's division of More's convent life into four "stations," or stages, this discovery of contemplative prayer initiated the second stage of six years in which "she founde the meanes and waie to becomme recollected, and to leade an internall life" (*Life*, 6). The third stage of her convent life, however, was characterized by "great and extraordinarie affliction and probation in soule" (*Life*, 6), mainly because the convent's new confessor, Father Francis Hull, opposed Baker's teachings and the form of contemplative prayer practiced by him and his followers. This created for More and others a crisis of obedience and authority. The final stage Baker defines is that of the final eighteen or nineteen days of More's life, in which she was ill from smallpox, finally dying on August 17, 1633, at the age of twenty-seven. At the end of his discussion of Gertrude More and of her contemplative practices, Baker adds material from other sources, including the account by a fellow nun who was close to her of More's life and behavior (*Life*, 327–46). In just a few pages, we get a much livelier sense of More's personality, feelings, and social functioning than we do in Baker's rambling, abstract prose. More confided to this nun that "she camme to Religion much against her will, and in a maner forced by him, whome she had not power to resist, by reason of the great affection she bore unto him" (*Life*, 328). Originally, "she camme and receaved the habit with no desire or intention at all to professe" (*Life*, 328–29).

> she past over the most parte of her Novitiate . . . with small confort or satisfaction to herself . . . Yet when the time of Profession drew neere, I am sure she was wonderfullie irresolute and much troubled about it. . . .

> But after her profession made, then did she live in greater miserie then ever before, discontented in minde and wonderfullie unsatisfied, sorrie for having taken the course uppon her, greeved at all those who had furthered her anie waie, or ben an occasion of bringing her into such slaverie and servitude, as she esteemed her life to be, which seemed most bitter and tedious to her; and especiallie she was most of all offended with her Ghostlie Father of England for having brought her to so great miserie, that she was scarse able to endure to heare his name without vexing and chafing in her minde against him. (*Life*, 329–30).

The difference in her behavior before and after finding her congenial way of prayer with Baker's help was striking: "whereas before she had writte to Father President divers letters of complaints of her Superior and other difficulties, she now turned the leafe, and writte to him letters of recantation, and retracted all her former complaints and misbehavior of hers towards her Superior or otherwise either by workes or writings, and humbly besought him to pardon what was past" (*Life*, 333). She became, however, not a meek and passive nun, but rather "the ringleader" (*Life*, 333) of the nuns following Baker's methods of prayer and "by her example and wordes she was able to animate the weak and faint hearted" (*Life*, 333). Her fellow nun acknowledges More's leadership role in the convent:

> God Allmightie had chosen her for a foundresse and leader of this little flock gathered together in his name and for his service. By her temporall meanes we had our beginnings, but much more was she enriched with gifts and spirituall graces, sufficient not onlie for herself, but allso to helpe and beare up the communitie in greate part in all belonging to our state and profession; I meane for manadging the temporal affaires of it and promoting of the spirituallitie of it with as great zeale as can be imagined. Hetherto she hath ben the cheifest piller and upholder of the house. . . .
>
> She was indeed for her yeares of birth one of the yongest in the house; but for her discretion and other vertues of the maturest and

> eldest. And though she was verie zelous, yet was she withall as carefull as she could not to proceed in such maner, as might justly geve occasion of offence. Notwithstanding . . . her doengs and proceedings were by some others misunderstoodde and misinterpreted, and her wordes taken in a quite contrarie sense to her meaning and intention. (*Life*, 337–38)

More is compared in this account to Saint Teresa: "her example and wordes were so moving and so effacacious, and proceeding from a heart so enflamed with divin love and zelous of God Allmighties honor, that if a soule were even so much dejected, as that she was readie to fall or faint, they were of force to raise her up againe and move her to confidence and couradge" (*Life*, 338).

Actively recusant Catholics in the Elizabethan and early Stuart periods had two choices: living a hazardous life in England as part of a repressed minority trying to survive as a community or fleeing to continental exile—either to schools, seminaries, and convents or to politically alienated and active exile groups. Dame Gertrude's father, Cresacre More, first chose to study abroad for the priesthood. Had he persevered, his career might have been either that of a member of a continental religious or educational community or that of a missionary returning to England. When it was clear, however, that his branch of the More family needed him to produce children, he agreed to leave his studies and marry.[9] One can look on his decision to encourage two of his daughters to live their lives in a continental convent he helped to establish as his way of actually and vicariously living out both of the recusant Catholic options. Each path was, in effect, one of political resistance. Although Gertrude More was a member of a religious establishment that had political significance in relation to her home country, for her the micro-political context of the convent loomed larger than the macro-political one of international Catholicism's relationship to English Protestant nationalism. The issue of resistance, however, was present in both the small and large worlds. The very existence of an exile Catholic community—in convents, seminaries, or continental refuges used by laypersons—was a threat to English national self-definition, a contesting of the association of the home country with Protestantism. Of course, all the continental exile communities, especially the religious ones, fostered and maintained their connections with the recusant Catholic networks in England, Wales, Scotland, and Ireland, relying on them for financial support, students to be educated (in places such as the school at Saint Omer's), and future nuns and missionary priests.[10]

Were we to stay within the terminology of Augustine Baker's and Gertrude More's devotional and contemplative practices, or even within the local political struggles of the Cambrai convent, we would not acknowledge some of the theoretical and practical political implications of Gertrude More's beliefs and behavior. With regard to the question of authority and obedience, she argues for an interesting sort of personal autonomy that threatens the structure of subordination that was built not only into the church and the rules of religious orders, but also into the hierarchical, monarchical state. She herself defines three kinds of relationship to authority: the first one, unproblematic, is that of obedience to superiors who responsibly and discreetly exercise their power; the second is the obedience to an arbitrary and unjust superior of the enlightened practitioner of contemplative prayer, who has discovered a divinely infused inner liberty, a submission accepted as a providential affliction meant to improve the spiritual condition of the subordinate; the third is that of resistance by the enlightened contemplative to a superior trying to force on her uncongenial and ineffective practices counter to the ones by which she felt empowered. This last is the religious equivalent of civil disobedience. If we think of the achievement of contemplative enlightenment as one way of expressing the religious or political subject's freedom and autonomy, we can see how More's ideas and behavior question the legitimacy of any constituted authority and put the decision for obedience in the hands of the subordinate. Just as early Stuart Parliamentarians could use the ideology of the "ancient constitution" to delimit the power of a monarch who wished to exercise top-down authority under the aegis of divine-right kingship,[11] so too More used mysticism's divine sanction of the individual contemplative to exercise a kind of political freedom within the convent structure that appeared to her opponents as a form of rebellion.

It is interesting to note that Baker was a friend of Sir Robert Cotton, whose medieval research was aimed at identifying Parliamentary rights against a contemporary assertion of royal absolutism, and Cotton provided him with some manuscripts of the writings of medieval mystics that Baker used to develop his own system of contemplative prayer.[12] More hedged her bets by repeatedly insisting that, out of her love for God and his general injunction that subordinates obey regularly constituted (lay or religious) authority,[13] she willingly subordinated herself under most circumstances to her superiors, but she uses two metaphors that betray her real attitudes. Several times she says she would obey a dog or a worm if they were in positions of authority above her.[14] The condition for this obedience, however, is her freedom to follow the spiritual course she has chosen. In the "Apology" she wrote to defend Augustine Baker and the methods of prayer and contemplation followed by those he instructed, Gertrude More defines obedience as flowing out of the practice of contemplation. Without the freedom to pursue this spiritual course, obedience is impossible and resistance inevitable. She argues that, if a superior hinders the prayer of a contemplative in the house, "he wil also incurre an inconveniency, though not so great as hers. Which is that she who would (by prosecuting discreatly a course of *Mental prayer*) haue become subiect if it were necessary euen to a very dogg; becometh for want of that strength, and helpe which therein shee got, to be almost impossible to be ruled by the wisest man in the world" (*Spiritual Exercises*, A13).[15]

At stake in the conflicts of Father Francis Hull with Baker and his disciples was Hull's authority to impose Jesuit meditative discipline on all the nuns at Cambrai and Baker's teaching an alternate method of prayer—one that rejects the use of sensuous imagery and discursive reasoning. More discusses the Jesuits' practices of spiritual direction and mental prayer in several ways, stating that they are suitable to that order's commitment to the active life in the world and unsuitable to cloistered nuns.[16] She objects to the behavior of all Jesuits who take charge of establishments belonging to other orders:

> they . . . vphold the same forme, and grow in al too hard for al other orders; they being al in a manner diuided amongst themselves, and

> these of al nations standing against al the world for themselues. Besides the subordination is also much strengthened with the feare they haue, who desire to make any resistance how litle soeuer of being put out of their order to their perpetual infamy and shame, and want with al of that which is necessary: which they are incident to who leaue this order. (*Spiritual Exercises*, A62–63)

She notes that the founder of the Jesuits, Saint Ignatius, "absolutly forbad them the care, and gouernment of Religious women" and she wishes "he had so prouided that they indeed had neuer medled, or vndertaken in this kind" (*Spiritual Exercises*, A64).[17]

More suggests that the order declined from the idealistic goals set by Saint Ignatius and became known as practitioners of Machiavellian "policy": "though they haue a great advantage by their vniformity in exercises, and their agreement among themselues, yet this being generally accounted to proceed, and to be vpheld by policy; it worketh no great effect for the most part, further then by it with al others, and against al others to serue their own turn" (*Spiritual Exercises*, A65). Although her main focus is the problem of imposing Jesuit methods of meditation and prayer on her and on others whose real aptitude is for a kind of contemplative prayer that is not based, like the Jesuit spiritual exercises, on the senses and imagination, sometimes her remarks on the Jesuits reproduce the anti-Jesuit codes found both among Protestant polemicists and among rival clerical groups within Catholicism: "It will neuer go wel, and peaceably in the world as long as they are only imployed, and haue the spiritual government of souls, who take policy for their cheif ground next to Faith" (*Spiritual Exercises*, A71). She suggests, in fact, that the Jesuits' polemical aggression is a less productive way of winning back apostates and converting Protestants than is the more pacific and edifying practice of contemplation. Idealizing early monasticism, she points to contemporary conflicts among the various orders as a scandal that needs to be done away with by the practice of prayerful contemplation:

> O *Lord, my God*, if this *Spirit* [of early monasticism] might be reuiued againe, how much would my soul rejoice? If Saint Benets his,

> S. Francis his, S. Ignatius his, *&c.* children were perfectly, as this life wil permit, vnited together, and with one hart, and consent did seek and labour to aduance *thy* honour and praise, as our founders do in Heauen, which if we did then would the *Spirit* of the primitiue Church flourish, and *thy* torn and mangled members be healed and perfectly set againe together; Then heretiks and sinners would easily be conuerted by them to thee. (*Spiritual Exercises*, B249–50)

Gender politics were implicit in the situation Gertrude More faced. She accuses her main oppressor, Father Hull, of bullying women in his illegitimate exercise of authority:

> these spiritual men . . . would be so absolute that there is no power left in the soul thus vnder such to haue relation, or confidence in *God*, whereby those for the most part vnder them, if they be poor, simple women, or how good *spirits* soeuer, liue miserable, deiected liues: for it is their only way to bring their politicke, and absolute gouernment about. And ordinarily, vnder this pretense they do it; saying that there is no way to make this, or that soul humble, but to bring them into such feare, that they neither dare speak, think, or do any thing without their approbation. (*Spiritual Exercises*, A56–57)

Baker himself referred to Hull's authoritarianism when he warned "what mischief will arise by his monarchical Authoritie and government!"[18] The tightening of spiritual authority that came with the Counter-Reformation and the development of Catholic political resistance theory are contexts for this attitude.[19]

Baker thought women were "naturally . . . devouter . . . then . . . men, and more seeke after Perfection, then do men" (*Life*, 189). The practice of contemplative prayer by More and other nuns gave them "more then womanly fortitude and couradge" (*Life*, 168). He wrote in his *Life* of More, "women of their owne natures are over fearfull and verie amorous. And for thes reasons the passions of Love (speaking generallie of women) should be promoted in them, and the other of feare rather mortified and abated then increased" (*Life*, 243). Thus he objected to over-frequent confession and over-scrupulous self-examination because he thought daily self-examinations and an emphasis on one's personal unworthiness could be an impediment to the business of contemplation, where the total focus is on God. More herself criticized confessors who used fear to intimidate those, especially those women, who came to them for spiritual guidance.[20]

More was attracted to the radical form of self-denial intrinsic to Baker's mystical practices. Self-abnegation, mortification, and, as an extreme, self-annihilation occasionally take extreme forms in Gertrude More's confessions. Baker noted in his biography of her that her greatest affliction was the "temptation about iterating of Confessions of her former life" (*Life*, 117; cf. 132). She cries out in one of her prayers: "O *when* shal I be by profound *Humility* reduced to the *nothing*, which alone makes a soul capable of *thee*, *who* art al *good* things, who art that simple *good*, in which nothing is wanting?" (*Spiritual Exercises*, B266). She exaggerates her own sinfulness in an almost boastful way: "Is there any sin that I haue not committed, at least by my wil? . . . I neuer read, or heard of any, whose sinnes (for one reason, or other) could be compared to mine" (*Spiritual Exercises*, B156). Without God she is "a sack full of filth, and the map of all misery" (*Spiritual Exercises*, B219). In *The Sainctly Ideots Devotions*, Baker enacts, through a series of "Acts of Resignation," a process of self-abjection that is astoundingly particularized, including not only a long list of physical and mental diseases and disabilities, but also social disgraces and humiliations. At one point, he expresses a desire for his dead body to be made "a prey and food for beasts, and fowles: as hath beene, and often is the case of Martyrs" (165); at another, he wishes that, after his death, he be "esteemed to have killed, or destroyed my self and thereuppon to be according to the custome of our countrey pearsed through the midst of my Bodye with a stake, and buried in the high way; and every one that passeth by, to cast a stone on my Grave in detestation of mee to the unspeakable shame, confusion, and damnation of my owne fame, and to the fowle Aspersion of my Familye" (173). With regard to his intellectual abilities, he says: "For the love of *God* I resigne my selfe to be by all that doe know, or heereafter shall know mee esteemed the most abject, unworthy, base, ignorant, foolish, witlesse, and most contemptible of all humayne creatures: And therefore not only incapable of all Office, and imployment; but alsoe vnworthy to be admitted into the company, or conuersation of any Others though of neuer soe meane condition" (199). He competitively strives for the *ne plus ultra* of abjection.

Paradoxically, More found in this extreme form of self-denial a form of personal empowerment that both fostered her spiritual development and gave her the courage to oppose within the micro-politics of the convent the coercion of unsympathetic superiors. She constantly appealed to divine authority to undermine or limit the spiritual authority of superiors. In her most argumentative piece of writing, the "Apology for Herself and her Spiritual Guide and Director, Venerable Augustine Baker," a piece she wrote shortly before her death to be used in his defense against charges brought against him within the order of practicing a dangerous form of devotion[21] and of encouraging insubordination, she argues that "the warrant & security of *God* which a true internal liuer findeth from *God* is far beyond the warrant of a mortal man" (*Spiritual Exercises*, A53). A nun who was with her at her death reported that More would often say:

> *it is not a pretended obedience nor the applause and warrant of anie man, nor of all the men in the worlde, that will serve to excuse us in conscience before God, when he himself doth so plainly and manifestly shew us his will: and that it was nothing to undergoe the hard opinion and censures of men, nor all the difficulties, that they were able by anie meanes to procure, so that a soule might enjoye the divin light and conduct of his heavenlie grace, in comparison of which all aggreevances, afflictions and miseries are easie and tolerable: for nothing is miserie to a soule but to be deprived thereof.* (*Life*, 339)

She concedes the need to use confessors "for confession of mortal sins" and for helping to settle "true doubt," but once a nun's observations of the Rule of the Benedictines "and other obligations of Religion" are performed "out of Obedience to *God*, and superiors," "what warrant . . . will she need (after her conscience is once wel settled) from confessor or Superior?" The unmediated presence of the God within has priority over mediated, inconsistent, and potentially arbitrary authority without: “For to-day I haue a Confessor which wil warrant me, and to morrow another who wil doubt of my case” (*Spiritual Exercises*, A53–54). Her bottom-up model of authority consists of “the Superior accommodating him-self to the *interior diuine cal* of his subject” (*Spiritual Exercises*, A106).

Gertrude More’s “Apology” ends with a strong statement of confidence in her own empowerment as a contemplative certain about the course of her inner life and outer behavior:

> if a soul be a capable soul of contemplatiue instructions, and be wel grounded in them by help of one who is experienced, and walk the way of *entire abnegation*, seeking *God*, and not *his* guifts, and be diligent in obseruing what *God* wil do by himself in her soul, and wherin *he* referreth her to others, and walk with that *indifferency* that it is al one to her which way, or by whom *God* wil manifest *his wil* to her: she shal as easily see what, and how to do in al things to please *God* best, as she may discerne the Sun from the Moon. And this is *to giue to God what is Gods and that to Cesar that is Cæsars*. (*Spiritual Exercises*, A112)[22]

Elsewhere she refers to a “*humble* confidence” gained from practicing contemplation and to her taking charge of the management of her own spiritual life as seeming “to some a great presumption” (*Spiritual Exercises*, A18). Baker was so useful to her as a spiritual director because, she claimed, he gave her a set of general guidelines and suggestions, rather than a rigid scheme of devotional practice, and let her follow what he and she termed her “Divine call” or inner light:

> But going to Father Baker, almost in a desperate case: He told me my way must be by *Prayer*, for which he gaue me some instructions according as he deliuereth them in his *Ideots Deuotion*, and referred me for the rest in that point to *God*. Which he doing, and giuing al other instructions for other things sutable: I found presently that course of *loue* which I so much desired. And though I went so simply to work that I desired to know nothing, (for curiosity in reading those things which help to this course is very dangerous though in

> themselues they seeme but simple,) yet *God* did make al things to me so plain that was necessary for me to know, that I wondered to see such alteration in my soul. (*Spiritual Exercises*, A32)

The judgment, or "discretion," she exercised in deciding her devotional path, then, trumped the authority of any confessor or would-be spiritual guide. She confidently criticized those who were unsympathetic to her contemplative and mystical way:

> *The obseruing of the divine cal*, which indeed should be, and is the very life of a spiritual life, Is by most spiritual Maisters now a days turned into a scorn, or scoff. And therefor no mervail that true spirituality should in these dayes be so rare, and almost vnknown. Nay if a soul but giue her-self to prayer she shal haue an hundred enemies one obiecting against one point, another against another of her proceedings.
>
> Euery one (according to their spirit, and humour) desiring to reforme her in they know not what themselues; which if she be moued with, no other effect is like to come of it, then happened to the Painter who altered his work so long, and often that at last it had neither forme nor fashion; And al other that had procured this alteration in the picture (which at first was a very good one) called the workman fool for his labour. (*Spiritual Exercises*, A37–38)

More uses a paradoxical concept of "liberty" to describe the total self-abjection and liberating mystical union she experienced in contemplation, an experience in which she was "drowned and swallowed vp in that . . . *Diuine love*" (*Spiritual Exercises*, B126), or one in which she was "wholy transformed into the *Diuine loue*" (*Spiritual Exercises*, B183).[23] She speaks of "loosing of our selues" as a "sweet and happy exchange" providing "the greatest *liberty* in this world" (*Spiritual Exercises*, B2–3), a "happy liberty" (*Spiritual Exercises*, B28) consisting of conforming to God's will.[24] Disengaging from distracting affections to creatures and concentrating on the Creator freed the soul—though others might perceive such a withdrawal of what Freud called "cathexes" from the world as a hostile or antisocial act.[25] It is this liberty that grounds the self-confidence of the contemplative, grants her the "*Discretion*" or divinely sent enlightenment, "which iudgeth between custome and true reason; between opinion and . . . true Iustice" (*Spiritual Exercises*, B236), empowering her as an individual to decide what is the best course for her to follow, even in the face of opposition by superiors.

This independence was perceived as a threat by her rigid and coercive confessor, Father Francis Hull:

> *he* pretended that contemplatiue instructions were in no way proper for me, and that I took too much liberty by them, they being proper for those of more tender and fearful consciences than I was. And, in fine gave it me vnder his hand very resolutely, as a determination from my Gostly Father, as in the place of *God Almighty*, that those that gaue me contemplatiue instructions, and applyed the liberty that was necessary for contemplatiue souls (of which he saith there are not two in al the howse), *might give me peace, but never true peace in God.* (*Spiritual Exercises*, A90)

She resisted Hull's coercion with a confidence in her own enlightened judgment: "if I had thus put my-self on him, I had done great wrong to *God*: and I might haue bid farewel to al true peace hereafter: but standing to my former warrant, and giuing him the respect was due to him, and being reserued towards him, I haue hitherto *God* be praised kept my-self out of his fingers" (*Spiritual Exercises*, A55–56).

In both Augustine Baker's and Gertrude More's writings, contemplation and mystical experience are topics resisting definition. Since the experiences are extra-rational, akin, as Baker asserts, to the direct intuition enjoyed by angels (toward which humans imperfectly aspire), there is a discomforting lack of specificity to Baker's and More's discourse—whether they are writing in a devotional, prayerful mode or in a more rationally expository manner. In *Sancta Sophia*, Baker defines mystic contemplation as an experience "by which a soule without discoursings & curious speculations, without any perceptible vse of the Internall sences or sensible Images, by a pure, simple, & reposefull operation of the mind, in *the obscurity of Faith*, simply regards

God as Infinite & Incomprehensible Verity, and with the whole bent of the will rests in him as (her) *Infinite, Vniversal, and Incomprehensible good*" (2:241).[26] Progress in mystical contemplation is one in which "the soul comes to operate more and more abstracted from sense, and more elevated above the corporal organs and faculties, so drawing nearer to the resemblance of the operations of an *Angell or* separated spirit" (*Sancta Sophia*, 2:244–45). And so, there is not only an abandonment of the "sensible," but also of the rational and deliberative powers in a process that reduces the self to a calm, stress-free, simple "nothing" in which a union with God dissolves individuality.

As is typical of mystics, Baker asserts: "*God is nothing of all that I can say or thinke, but a Being infinitly beyond it, & absolutely incomprehensible by created Vnderstanding*" (*Sancta Sophia*, 2:253). Dealing with the inability of the sensible imagination and the understanding to produce an adequate image of God, he says with regard to the latter:

> wheras it [the understanding] was before all bepainted with Images of Creatures: yea when it regarded God, it saw him by an Image of its owne creating: Now the soule looses all remembrance of it selfe and of all created things: And all that she retains of God is a remembrance that he cannot be seene nor comprehended. All creatures, therefore, being remoued, and no particular distinct Image of God admitted, there remains in the soule and mind as it were *a Nothing* and mere *emptines*: The which *Nothing* is more worth than all Creatures: for it is all that we can know of God in this life: This *Nothing* is the rich inheritance of Perfect soules, who perceiue clearly that God is nothing of all that may be comprehended by our senses or Vnderstanding. The state, therefore, of such soules, for as much as concernes knowledge, is worthily called *The Clowd of vnknowing*, and *The clowd of forgetting*, by the *Authour* of that *Sublime Treatise* so called. And this is the perfectest and most *Angelical knowing* that a soule is capable of in this life. . . . This *knowledge of nothing* is by *F. Benet Canfield* called an *Active annihilation*. (*Sancta Sophia*, 2:262–63)[27]

In the writings of Dionysus the Pseudo-Areopagite, the fifth-century monk who was, for one thousand years, confused with the Dionysius converted by Saint Paul, we read: "in speaking about God we should declare the Truth, not with enticing words of man's wisdom, but in demonstration of the power which the Spirit stirred up in the Sacred Writers, whereby, in a manner surpassing speech and knowledge, we embrace those truths which, in like manner, surpass them, in that Union which exceeds our faculty, and exercise of discursive, and of intuitive reason."[28] In following, as do other mystical writers, the *via negativa*, Dionysus wrote: "Unto this Darkness which is beyond Light we pray that we may come, and may attain unto vision through the loss of sight and knowledge, and that in ceasing thus to see or to know we may learn to know that which is beyond all perception and understanding (for this emptying of our faculties is true sight and knowledge)."[29]

In *Sancta Sophia*, Baker states that it is necessary for the will of the contemplative

> to vntwine & withdraw its adhesion from creatures, that it may eleuate it selfe & be firmely fixed to this her only *Good*: And at last . . . the Obiect begins to appear in its owne perfect light, and the affections to flow freely, but yet with a wonderfull stillnes, to it; And then such soules are sayd to be arriued to *Perfect Mystical Vnion* or *Contemplation*.
>
> This is properly the *Exercise of Angells*: for their knowledge is not by discourse, but by *one simple intuition* all Obiects are represented to their view at once, with all the natures, qualities, relations, dependencies, & effects. But *Man*, that receiues all his knowledge first from his senses [the Aristotelian maxim], can only by effects & outward appearances with the labour of Reasoning collect the nature of Obiects, & this but imperfectly. But his reasoning being ended, then he can at once *Contemplate* all that is known vnto him in the Obiect. (*Sancta Sophia*, 2:241–42)

In the *Life*, he writes of More: "as to her knowledge of God she had it in her in that sorte, which all Divins doe saie to be the truest knowledge that is of him in this life, and that is by waie of negation, which is that God is none of all things that we can imagin or conceave with our understanding" (228). Gertrude More refers to the "*diuine* tranquillity" that is experienced in mystical union with God as a state that "cannot be expressed by any pen" (*Spiritual Exercises*, B64).

Nevertheless, Gertrude More both read and wrote. As a well-educated scion of the More family, she loved reading and consumed virtually all the writing in manuscript and print available to her in the convent. In addition to "the whole English Bible" (*Life*, 22), she read not only Augustine Baker's manuscript works, but also devotional and mystical texts of Saint Augustine, Thomas à Kempis, Ludovicus Blosius, Johannes Tauler, Saint Teresa of Avila, and others. She also read "the saiengs and doengs of Philosophers and other wise men, and secular stories judiciouslie written. . . . She was much delighted with such of them, as were Historicall; and more in bookes, that were written in good verse and rime, then in prose" (*Life*, 87). Baker mentions her reading of Tacitus (*Life*, 100) and of Sylvester's translation of Du Bartas (*Life*, 87). But she consistently denigrated worldly knowledge and what passed for worldly wisdom. More kept extensive notes on her devotional reading and composed her own devotional prose, explaining in her own writing that this was done to aid her memory and enable further devotional acts. In her *Spiritual Exercises* she addressed her God: "one learneth more in *Prayer* of *thee* in one hower, then all creatures in the world could teach one in fifty years; for that which *thou* teachest is sound, solid, and secure; because it tends to nothing but to *loue thee*, & neglect it selfe" (*Spiritual Exercises*, B10). In his *Saintly Ideots Devotions*, Baker rejects all things other than what is "absolutelie necessary to salvation . . . especiallye . . . all curiosities and impertinencies" (177).[30]

Occasionally More expressed herself in verse, but in an anti-imaginative and unpoetic idiom consistent with her practice of contemplation. More's *Spiritual Exercises* contains poems expressing her devotional longings and contemplative experiences. Baker's *Life* also has several of her poems. Isolated from the framework of her discursive account and from the contemplative system within which she operated, this poetry looks spare and cliché-ridden, a kind of devotional doggerel. It avoids linguistic virtuosity, metaphoric innovativeness, and prosodic complexity, utilizing a plain-speaking idiom that foregrounds a didactic message. Written in ballad-meter (4/3/4/3), or "fourteeners" broken into four line units, it versifies her prose exposition of her devotional and contemplative experiences. She has, for example, a thirty-two-line poem "To ovr Blessed Lady, the Aduocate of Sinners" (*Spiritual Exercises*, B279–80), a twelve-line poem to Saint Augustine (*Spiritual Exercises*, B13), and, in the long seventh confession of her *Spiritual Exercises*, a poem that relates to her conflict with her coercive confessor, a 162-line piece that translates a passage from Thomas à Kempis's *Imitatio Christi* (*Spiritual Exercises*, B46–52).[31]

Gertrude More was intelligent, strong-willed, and sociable, a leader in her religious community from the start.[32] It might seem strange to us, then, that she turned inward to practices of contemplative prayer that abstracted her from her immediate environment, broke her affective ties to friends and family, and emptied her mind of its intellectual and imaginative content. Whether we view her path as one of holy masochism, passive aggression, or depressive withdrawal, on the one hand, or as a discovery of a form of personal empowerment within the severe constraints in which she functioned on the other, depends on our own view of the psychology of mysticism, of gender politics, and of the complex functions and negotiations of post-Reformation religious culture.[33] Had Gertrude More lived the long life her friend Catherine Gascoigne did we probably would have had a much richer archive of her writings, but also a different narrative of her experiences.

Notes

1. The *Oxford English Dictionary* has several definitions of "idiot" that are relevant: "1.a. A person without learning; an ignorant, uneducated person; a simple or ordinary person . . . 1.b (a) A person without professional training or skill (*obs.*); (b) a private (as opposed to a public) person, an inward-looking person (now rare)." The last of these certainly applies to Dame Gertrude's devotional practices. The medieval mystic Julian of Norwich had described herself as "a simple creature unletterde" (*The Writings of Julian of Norwich:* A Vision Showed to a Devout Woman *and* A Revelation of Love, ed. Nicholas Watson and Jacqueline Jenkins [University Park: Penn State University Press, 2005], ix). The use of the term "idiot" may also suggest the idea, in Dionysius the Pseudo-Areopagite and Nicolas of Cusa, of *docta ignorantia*, a state sought by mystics.

2. I cite the former in the text as *Saintly Ideots Devotions* and the latter as *Spiritual Exercises*. The second volume separately paginates the long letter serving as an "Advertisement to the Reader," which contains Dame Gertrude's "Apology for herself, and her spiritual Guide, and Director the V. F. Augustin Baker" (I preface the page numbers with "A") and the "Confessiones Amantis" and additional material (before whose page numbers I put a "B"). A modern edition of the work is found in *The Writings of Dame Gertrude More*, ed. Dom Benedict Weld-Blundell (London: R. & T. Washbourne, 1910), but, since it not only changes spelling, punctuation, paragraphing, and syntax, but also many words and phrases of the original, as well as the order of the work, I cite instead the 1658 edition. See the text of this work reproduced in *Gertrude More*, Selected and Introduced by Arthur F. Marotti, in *The Early Modern Englishwoman: A Facsimile Library of Essential Works*, ed. Betty S. Travitsky and Anne Lake Prescott, Series II: Printed Writings, 1641–1700: part 4, vol. 3 (Farnham, Surrey: Ashgate, 2009). I use some of the material from the "Introductory Note" (ix–xxiv) in this essay. More apparently entitled her work *Ideots Devotions*, but, as Marion Norman, I. B. V. M., "Dame Gertrude More and the English Mystical Tradition," *Recusant History* 13, no. 3 (April 1976): 203, points out, Baker retitled it so it would not be confused with his own work. Nancy Bradley Warren, *The Embodied Word: Female Spiritualities, Contested Orthodoxies, and English Religious Cultures, 1350–1700* (Notre Dame, Ind.: University of Notre Dame Press, 2010), 281n5, suggests that the title of More's devotional work, *Spiritual Exercises*, "is itself a politicized choice. Given the conflict that raged in English female religious communities in exile in the early modern period concerning the place of Jesuit spirituality in the devotional lives of nuns, that Baker would assign a title to Gertrude's text clearly resonant of the Jesuit text par excellence, the *Spiritual Exercises*, stakes a claim for the primacy of his/her form of devotion as the proper one for Benedictine women religious to adopt. In other words, the choice of the title positions Gertrude's spiritual exercises as the *true* spiritual exercises." In *Saintly Ideots Devotions*, 24, Baker explains that he calls the work "Ideots Deuotions, because they are for such as feruently and simply with all their affections, desire to *aspire* after *God* in the *Clowd of faith and feelings of Love* without troubleing themselues with busye and impertinent operations of the vnderstandinge, commonly called Meditations or discourses of the understandinge." In my citations the italicized words are found in the original texts.

3. After some preliminaries, it is divided into six main sections: (1) "Holy Exercises or Sainctly Ideots Devotions. The Poenitent" (39–111, twenty-one exercises concentrating on one's sins, corresponding, perhaps, to the traditional purgative stage of contemplative practice); (2) "Certayne Amorovs speeches of the soule to her selfe in Prayer" (112–23), four exercises, followed by "An example of Acts, which a Soule maye Exercisee towards God as absent from Her" (123–24) and "An example of speakinges supposed to be made by God to the

soule" (124); (3) "Acts of Love, and wellwishinge towards God" (125–57), four exercises plus "Certaine Amorovs Aspirations, to be vsed accordinge to the Directions, and the Disposition of the soule" (137–57), the latter consisting of 180 "aspirations"; (4) "Acts of Resignation to be vsed accordinge to the Directions: Acts of Resignation in things concerninge the Body" (158–218), consisting of fourteen exercises plus "An Exercise of Deuotion to our Blissed Lady Mother of God" (219–20), "An Exercise to the Holy Angells, and especiallye the Angell Guardian" (221–23), and "An Exercise of Deuotion. Towards our Holy Father, and Religious founder S. Bennet" (224–29); (5) "Hayle Iesus. Or Acts uppon the life, and Passion of our Sauuiour Iesus-Christ" (229–90), twenty-one exercises following a rough chronology of Christ's life, concentrating on the passion, and concluding with the resurrection and ascension, the section ending with a twenty-line poem in fourteeners, "A Dittie to the same subiect" (289–90); (6) "The Topp of the Heavenlie Ladder or The Highest Steppe of Prayer, and Perfection. And the Progress, and complement of the foresaid Practises, and Deuotions" (291–329), which concentrates on the kind of contemplative prayer that represents the height of perfection of the practice. The volume concludes with two items: first, an address to the reader, offering not a list of printed errata, but an invitation to find and correct any mistakes that have been made (330) and, second, a dedication to the abbess at Cambrai, Catherine Gascoigne (331–33). Baker writes, late in the work, "These Exercises, and All Others may, and ought to be enlarged, and dilated accordinge to euerie ones Grace, and Guift: which is the only infallible Guide, and rule of our Prayer, and noe sett, written, or printed forme whatsoeuer; as the directions particularly, and pertinently teach us" (288–89). Augustine Baker, O. S. B., *The Life and Death of Dame Gertrude More*, Analecta Carthusiana 119:19, ed. Ben Wekking (Salzburg: Institüt für Anglistik und Amerikanistik Universität Salzburg, 2002), "Introduction," lxxxi, claims that some of Dame Gertrude's own writings appear in this text. Dorothy Latz, ed., *Neglected English Literature: Recusant Writings of the 16th–17th Centuries* (Salzburg: Institut für Anglistik und Amerikanistik Universität Salzburg, 1997), claims that Dom Serenus Cressy, who edited many of Baker's writings in *Sancta Sophia* (Paris, 1657 [two volumes in one separately paginated]), 15, edited the collected papers of Gertrude More for both these works.

4. For this work, I have used Wekking's edition, cited in the text as *Life*.

5. Augustine Baker needed an editor. His biography of Gertrude More is an astonishingly repetitive, vertiginous exposition that could easily be cut down to one-fifth of its original length. On the other hand, Baker's method is, as it were, incantatory: he musically arranges an ongoing set of concepts and terms, many of which seem idiosyncratically jargonistic ("propension," "elongation," "tendance," "intellective soul," "divine call," "Supernatural inaction," "impulsion," "tracts," etc.), in a kind of verbal fugue that attempts to induce a kind

of devotional spell, much like that expected of the inspired pupil of his spiritual direction. There is something poetic about this most unpoetic and anti-imaginative writer. Baker, *Life*, 5, apologizes for his "tediousness in expressments" and his "iterations in divers places . . . of one and the self same thing."

6. Kitty Scoular Datta, "Women, Authority and Mysticism: The Case of Dame Gertrude More (1606–33)," in *Literature and Gender: Essays for Jasodhara Bagchi*, ed. Supriya Chaudhuri and Sanji Mukherji (Hyderabad, India: Orient Longman, 2002), 53, notes that her works were translated (into French) and published in 1536, with many more editions following.

7. Norman, "Dame Gertrude More," 198, notes that some two hundred volumes of devotional and mystical writing were in the Cambrai library.

8. Wekking, "Introduction," xiii.

9. Wekking, "Introduction," ix.

10. For a recent study that recognizes the political importance of early modern English nuns, see Claire Walker, *Gender and Politics in Early Modern Europe: English Convents in France and the Low Countries* (Basingstoke, U. K.: Palgrave, 2003).

11. See J. G. A. Pocock, *The Ancient Constitution and the Feudal Law: English Historical Thought in the Seventeenth Century* (1957; New York: Norton, 1967).

12. Norman, "Dame Gertrude More," 197, cites the letter Baker wrote to Cotton from Cambrai requesting " 'such bookes as you please, either manuscript or printed, being in English, containing contemplation, saints' lives, or other devotions' " in order to provide reading material for the nuns he was counseling. For example, Watson and Jenkins, eds., *Writings of Julian of Norwich*, 14, note that Baker, in his *Life and Death of Dame Margaret Gascoigne*, mentions that the nuns at Cambrai had an "old manuscript book of [Julian's] Revelations." Wekking, "Introduction," xxi, notes also Baker's associations with John Selden; William Camden; Sir Henry Spelman; and Francis Godwin, Bishop of Hereford.

13. She uses the scriptural command to "render unto Caesar the things that are Caesar's" to apply both to the situation in the convent and to the larger world outside.

14. The mad King Lear's exclamation "a dog's obey'd in office" (4.6.159) reappears in an interesting new context as what the play calls "a great image of authority." More discusses submission to appointed authority with unflattering metaphors: "if a worm, or any creature were ordained by *God* to rule ouer them, they would see, and embrace *with* al their hearts *his wil* by them, for without this total subiection to *God* it is impossible to become truly *spiritual*: for if we resist *his wil* in our Superiors in vain do we pretend to please *him*" (*Spiritual Exercises*, A69–70). Datta, "Women, Authority and Mysticism," 63, claims the worm metaphor comes from Meister Eckhart.

15. For a discussion of the multiple functions of contemplation and mysticism in the life of female religious, see Walker, *Gender and Politics in Early Modern Europe*, 130–72.

16. In *Saintly Ideots Devotions*, 37, Augustine Baker, after a short bibliography of recommended devotional and mystical reading, says: "never looke to finde any Booke for thy turne in this way written by any of the Societie of Jesus, whose genius is the active way, and in that they are excellent, and very commendable, but in this contemplatiue way few or none hath appeared euer since their first institute above these hundred yeares."

17. See the discussion of "discretion" in *Sancta Sophia*, 2:213–23.

18. Appendix to *Life*, 369.

19. For a discussion of Catholic resistance theory, see Peter Holmes, *Resistance and Compromise: The Political Thought of the Elizabethan Catholics* (Cambridge: Cambridge University Press, 1982), 147–60. After the Council of Trent, which tightened the control of spiritual directors and confessors over those in their charge, especially nuns, the issue of insubordination was a sensitive one. See Patricia Ranft, "A Key to Counter Reformation Women's Activism: The Confessor-Spiritual Director," *Journal of Feminist Studies in Religion* 10 (1994): 7–26.

20. See the letter More wrote to him (*Life*, 244) in which she chooses love over fear as the means by which she could thrive spiritually. Datta, "Women, Authority and Mysticism," 60, says of Baker: "He recognized . . . how 'the sensible devotion of a contemplative' operated as a defence against the negative fear-bound examination of conscience demanded by her confessor." In "Did Father Baker Compile the First Constitutions of the English Benedictine Nuns at Cambrai?" in *Dom Augustine Baker 1575–1641*, ed. Geoffrey Scott (Leominster, U.K.: Gracewing, 2012), 38, Margaret Truran states: "As a confessor, Baker had discovered that scrupulosity, particularly about making confession, was one of the besetting temptations at Cambrai. He had given detailed guidance in the *Treatise on Confession* (approved 1629) and also dealt with the subject in *A Secure Stay in all Temptations* (1629)."

21. Wekking, "Introduction," xiii, notes that Hull "went so far as to advise [those practicing the methods of prayer taught by Baker] to stop following Baker's doctrine as it was allegedly anti-authoritarian and contained elements of Illuminism." He further notes: "By 1632 the conflict had reached such a point that the president of the Congregation invited both Baker and Hull to present their views at the General Chapter in 1633. Furthermore, Baker's whole spiritual doctrine was to be thoroughly examined and Dame Catherine and Dame Gertrude were each required to write an account of their personal prayer. Gertrude once more took upon herself the role of a leader, this time of the pro-Baker party. The upshot was that at the General Chapter in Douai Baker's teaching was cleared of the slightest suspicion of unorthodoxy" (ix).

Norman, "Dame Gertrude More," 206–7, argues that More's English quality of moderation and her "acceptance of life ran directly counter to the inertia and rejection of life of the Illuminists and Quietists" condemned as heretics by the Spanish Inquisition. Datta, "Women, Authority and Mysticism," 52, states: "A reason for suspicion of negative theology . . . from the thirteenth century to the seventeenth was the implicit suggestion that outward observances were less important than inner devotion and contemplation and the worship of the divine beyond images—teaching which ran against the grain of an ecclesiastic structure based on external ritualized good works, though not against the monastic ethos."

22. In the account of a fellow nun of More's life in the convent, More's friend quotes her saying "the assurance and securitie which the soule receaveth immediately from God himself, O how farre different is it from that which man is able to geve. For man cannot make a fearfull weake soule to goe to God with confidence, nor is she able to do anie thing longer then he is present with her to warrant her" (*Life*, 345).

23. Datta, "Women, Authority and Mysticism," 63, observes: "Dame Gertrude's view of spiritual discipline involved self-abnegation, detachment, and 'annihilation' of personal desires in terms which a Buddhist would recognize, but which derive from her reading of Ruisbroec and Harphius, writing in the Flemish and Rhineland tradition indebted to the women mystics, Hadewijch, Mechtild of Magdeburg and Beatrijs of Nazareth, who had expressed a similar passion for self-surrender, engulfment and the ineffable."

24. In her seventeenth confession she exclaims: "no *liberty* is to be compared to the *happines* of depending of *thee*" (*Spiritual Exercises*, B101). Elsewhere she says there is a "freedom and liberty, which was got by suppressing of natural passions" (*Spiritual Exercises*, B309).

25. See Baker's *Sancta Sophia*, Treatise II, sect. I, chapter 6, "Of abstraction of life, and solitude" (I cite the 1657 edition of this work in the text). This turning away from social ties involves giving up "*all vnnecessary conuersations* & correspondencies, Complementall visits &c., but likewise all engagement of affections in *particular friendships*. This last is necessary in Religious communities, because from such frendships proceed Partialities, factions, murmurings & most dangerous Distractions & multiplicity" (1:286).

26. Baker distinguishes between two kinds of mystic contemplation or union: "1. *Actiue* and ordinary: being indeed an habituall state of perfect soules by which they are enabled, whensoeuer fit occasion shall be, to vnite themselues actiuely and actually to God by efficacious, feruent, amorous, and constant, yet withall silent & quiet, eleuations of the Spirit" and "2. *Passiue* & extraordinary: the which is not a state but an *actuall Grace* & favour from God, by which he is pleased at certaine times, according to his free Good pleasure to

communicate a glimpse of his Maiesty to the spirits of his seruants, after a secret & wonderfull manner" (*Sancta Sophia*, 2:243).

27. *The Cloud of Unknowing* is the anonymous late fourteenth-century work of mysticism. The Capuchin friar Benet of Canfield (William Fitch) (1562–1610) wrote *The Rule of Perfection* (first printed ed., 1609); see Kent Emery Jr., *Renaissance Dialectic and Renaissance Piety : Benet of Canfield's Rule of Perfection: A Translation and Study* (Binghamton, N.Y.: Medieval & Renaissance Texts & Studies, 1987).

28. Dionysius, *The Divine Names*, in *Dionysius the Areopagite on The Divine Names and The Mystical Theology*, ed. C. E. Rolt (1920; New York: Macmillan, 1940), 51.

29. Dionysius, *The Mystical Theology*, in Rolt, ed., *Dionysius the Areopagite*, 194. For a discussion of Baker's adherence to the late medieval tradition of "affective Dionysianism," see Peter Tyler, "Mystical Writing as *Theologia Mystica*," in *Dom Augustine Baker 1575–1641*, ed. Geoffrey Scott (Leominster, U.K.: Gracewing, 2012), 51–63. Tyler states that "Within Dionysius' mystical game the strategy of deconstruction is complemented by the strategy of embodied, erotic affectivity" (61).

30. Drawing on the tradition of certain knowledge as either morally useless or forbidden, John Milton's Raphael makes the same point to Adam in *Paradise Lost* (VIII.66–187), when the latter starts to ask abstruse astronomical questions. In *Sainctly Ideots Devotions*, Baker states: "inward affection to curiosity of knowledge is perhaps . . . more prejudicial to contemplation, and produces effects more hurtful to the soul, because more deeply rooted in the spirit itself than some sensual affections" (194).

31. The poem that is found in most copies of *Spiritual Exercises* in the book's preliminaries opposite the engraving of Dame Gertrude (beginning "Renowned, *More* whose bloody Fate"), addressed to Dame Gertrude's ancestor, Thomas More, refers to her in the third person, portrays her, like Saint Teresa, with "a broken Hart, / Wounded with a Seraphick Dart" (ll. 7–8), and uses visual imagery that is out of line with her typical poetic style. It was almost certainly written by someone else. Geoffrey Scott, "The Image of Augustine Baker," in *The Mysterious Man: Essays on Augustine Baker*, Analecta Carthusiana 119:15, ed. Michael Woodward (Salzbürg: Institut für Anglistik und Amerikanistik Universität Saltzburg, 2001), 106–7, claims it was composed by Dom Leander Normanton. I am grateful to Warren, *Embodied Word*, 99, for this reference.

32. Wekking, "Introduction," xiii, notes that she was a "steward" or "chief celleraria" in charge of lay sisters who did many of the necessary practical tasks in the convent. During the internal conflict in the convent between Baker and Father Francis Hull, who was installed in the convent as vicar by

the General Chapter of the Benedictines, she was a leader of the group defending Baker.

33. For a discussion of the way mysticism was interpreted by French feminism and Lacan, see Amy Hollywood, *Sensible Ecstasy: Mysticism, Sexual Difference, and the Demands of History* (Chicago: University of Chicago Press, 2002). For a recent collection of essays on mysticism, several of which use postmodern theology to interpret mystical experiences, see *Mystics: Presence and Aporia*, ed. Michael Kessler and Christian Sheppard (Chicago: University of Chicago Press, 2003).

6

Quaker Mysticism as the Return of the Medieval Repressed

English Women Prophets before and after the Reformation

Genelle C. Gertz

Midway into the seventeenth century, England witnessed an outpouring of women's prophetic speech. Around three hundred women prophets were active, publishing a total of seventy-two titles between 1640 and 1660.[1] Emerging out of the social turbulence of the Civil Wars, the breakdown of press censorship, and theological interest in apocalypticism, radical Protestant women appeared in unprecedented numbers.[2] Many spoke to gathered congregations and also wrote of their experiences, either through amanuenses or in their own hands. Among the women prophets, the millenarian Eleanor Davies (1590–1652), the Fifth Monarchist Anna Trapnel (fl. 1642–60), the Baptist Elizabeth Poole (ca. 1622–ca. 1668), the Behmenist Jane Lead (1624–1704), and many Quaker women, including Anne Audland Camm (1627–1705), Esther Biddle (1629/30–97), and Elizabeth Hooten (d. 1672), published accounts of their visions.[3] England had never seen this many women prophesying at one time, although as a phenomenon, the meteoric rise of women's visionary writing and experience had happened once before, in medieval Europe.

The twelfth to the fifteenth centuries saw "the flowering of women's visionary writing" in Europe, under which authors such as Hildegard of Bingen (d. 1179), Marie d'Oignies (d. 1213), the three Helfta nuns (1282–1302), Angela of Foligno (d. 1309), Bridget of Sweden (d. 1371), and Margery Kempe (d. after 1438), were widely read by churchmen and the laity.[4] After this moment, and in spite of increased literacy as well as cheap book production, women prophets did not enjoy popularity within the English church. The Reformation played a major role in eradicating conditions for women's prophecy by de-emphasizing revelatory experience and destroying the cult of the saints, several of whom were women visionaries. It is this historically repressive element of the Reformation to which my title refers. The Reformation ended, or repressed, medieval women's prophetic speech while social conditions as well as theological innovations in the seventeenth century contributed to its re-emergence. It is therefore surprising that it was out of Protestantism in England, and not out of Catholicism, that so many numbers of women prophets arose in the seventeenth century. There were, however, smaller numbers of Catholic women in the seventeenth century who took on the role of the visionary in convents abroad.[5]

This essay compares the conditions for women's prophecy in the late medieval era with that of mid-seventeenth-century England, explaining that a different set of church-historical conditions made each prophetic movement possible.[6] In spite of these differences, both historical periods saw major theological emphases on the importance of revelation, and this contributed to the rise of women's prophecy. Particularly the early Quakers, through their reinvention of the role of the Holy Spirit, cultivated a religious atmosphere in which it was possible for most members of the community—not just a select few—to experience revelation. Revelation, or the visionary, was itself mystical; it uncovered what was previously "hidden" (the Greek sense of "mystical") from Christians and not ascertainable from reading scripture or knowing history.

Quaker mystical knowledge hearkened back to medieval mysticism through its emphasis on personal vision. Bernard McGinn, in *The Essential Writings of Christian Mysticism*, groups George Fox with Hildegard of Bingen, Hugh of Saint Victor, and Richard Rolle. According to McGinn, both Fox and the medieval mystics privilege the visionary state of perception where "the contemplative vision of God (*theôria theou*)" is associated with "extraordinary states of consciousness, periods of being 'snatched away, or raptured (*raptus*),' or 'standing outside oneself' (*ecstasies*)."[7] Fox's *Journal* uses language of rapture to describe the accession of visionary wisdom: "One day when I had been walking solitary abroad and was come home, I was taken up in the love of God, so that I could not but admire the greatness of his love; and while I was in that condition, it was opened unto me by the eternal Light and power, and I therein clearly saw."[8] Quaker mystical knowledge displaces the person from the landscape ("takes" one "up") and gives the believer a divine perspective, a "clear" vision.

Crucially, Quaker mysticism reopened access to visionary experience that had been limited during the Reformation to scripture alone. Fox taught that mystical knowledge lay outside texts and human authorities: "Zeal in the pure knowledge of God, and of Christ alone, without the help of any man, book or writing" led to revelation. Fox therefore reckoned, "though I read the scriptures that spake of Christ, and of God; yet I knew him not, [except] by revelation . . . And then the Lord did . . . let me see his love which . . . surpasseth all the knowledge that men have in the natural state, or can get by history, or books."[9] Fox's codified knowledge—history, books, and especially scripture—cannot access divine illumination; instead, mystical vision is granted only through a divine gift as well as "zeal" for godly understanding. Ultimately, I argue in this chapter that the Quakers returned to the medieval mystical repressed precisely because it had been so long removed from Protestantism. Out of the Reformation's denial of revelatory experience, and out of Protestantism's emphasis on scripture alone, prophetic experience was reborn.

Medieval Women Visionaries

Comparatively, but over a much longer period of time, medieval women prophets experienced the same unexpected flourishing as did Protestant women in seventeenth-century England. Medieval women visionaries prospered in the greatest numbers in the high and late Middle Ages, while before this moment there was very little visionary writing by women.[10] The late medieval period, especially, saw the greatest numbers of devout women living beyond the convent (either in a lay or tertiary capacity) who experienced visions and acted on them. How was this possible? Just how was it that late medieval Europe got a Catherine of Siena, a Bridget of Sweden, *and* a Joan of Arc? Why did so many women prophets arise at this time, and why did clerics and political figures pay attention to them? Such questions have generated a fascinating body of work on medieval visionary women and their remarkable presence in history.[11]

On the one hand, increased theological interest in apocalypticism ensured that reformist church leaders would be looking for prophets. In the thirteenth and fourteenth centuries European apocalyptic writers began "to understand history in terms of its eventual end by prophesying a complex pattern of events which [would] occur before—often long before—The End of the World."[12] Reading their own time as ripe for renewal, and as an age leading to the End, apocalyptic writers sought "new readings of biblical texts or earlier writers, or . . . visions and revelations, or . . . inspired interpretations of current history."[13] Hildegard of Bingen, as Kathryn Kerby-Fulton has written, issued many prophecies and visions about the state of the church in relation to end times. In the *Scivias* Ecclesia herself gives birth to a monstrously bloody, dung-ridden Antichrist.[14] Such a negative view of the church assumes the great need for reform, and a quick one at that, in order to change the course of events leading to the end.

Besides the effect of apocalyptic thinking on visionary writers in medieval Europe, changes in religious office affected the kind of spiritual vocations women could assume. A decided reduction in ecclesiastical, and especially monastic, roles left medieval women with fewer avenues for religious leadership. And it was out of this loss of agency, as Caroline Bynum has shown, that women visionaries emerged: "From the thirteenth century on, we find religious women losing roles that paralleled or aped male clerical leadership but gaining both the possibility of shaping their own religious experiences in lay communities and a clear alternative—the prophetic alternative—to the male role based on the power of office."[15] At once Bynum explains what women lose—authority over houses and other administrative duties in monasteries. Yet the alternative in some ways builds on this banishment from monastic leadership. The new environment for leadership is the lay environment: living in community to minister to the urban poor (beguines); traveling on pilgrimage, and in this way, reaching lay audiences (Bridget of Sweden; Margery Kempe); speaking or corresponding with political and military leaders (Bridget; Catherine; Joan of Arc).

Even within this lay environment, however, clerical authorization proved necessary to survival. Especially, clerics determined the authenticity of a woman prophet's revelation and set out both to advertise and defend her work to the church. As Rosalynn Voaden has shown, a widely accepted standard for determining the truth of a vision was the *discretio spirituum*, or discernment of spirits. Jean Gerson, chancellor of the University of Paris from 1392 to 1429, codified this rigorous method of testing visions, which thereby increased the power of spiritual directors, especially in the case of women visionaries. In Gerson's analysis, according to Voaden, "[T]he spiritual director is the instrument by which the visionary can be both counseled and controlled. His function is to examine the spiritual life of the visionary and to assess the nature and content of vision and revelation according to the principles of *discretio spirituum*."[16]

Thus, the most successful women visionaries had spiritual directors who authenticated their visions and promoted their cause.[17] *Discretio spirituum* made it possible for clerics to believe in the authority of women's visions, and to believe that God spoke to women for the purpose of delivering that message to others. At the same time, *discretio spirituum* bolstered the role of the male cleric; he became the guarantor of God's voice and the necessary link to ensuring a visionary's acceptance by the ecclesiastical hierarchy. Alfonso of Jaén achieved this for Bridget of Sweden; Jacques de Vitry for Marie d'Oignies, whose *vita* he wrote; Raymond of Capua for Catherine of Siena; Fra Arnaldo for Angela of Foligno. The hope that the female visionary might one day be canonized, as were Bridget and Catherine, certainly influenced the promotion that male clerics made of women.

Of course, we have to remember that medieval women prophets were championed as lay voices—still in that "alternative" category to church office—but championed they were, at least by male confessor-biographers who hoped to promote their penitents' sanctity. Beyond the existence of individual clerics who copied down the sayings and lives of women, the Franciscans generally encouraged lay devotion that imagined personal contact with the divine. That is, as Margery Kempe does, readers or listening audiences were authorized to imagine themselves present at the scene of the crucifixion, at the nativity, and during the early years of Christ's life. For someone mystically inclined, like Margery Kempe, this method of contemplation invited personal experience of divine events that included Margery's dialogue with Christ and his mother.[18] Franciscan meditation, however, did not recruit women for careers as mystics or prophets. It merely supplied a devotional technique amenable to affective mystical visions.

In late medieval England, a growing manuscript, and later, print culture encouraging devotion on the life of Christ, and on the lives of the saints, reinforced lay access to divine content.[19] Stories about Mary Magdalene, who led preaching missions in France, and Katherine of Alexandria, who debated with philosophers and converted kings, were familiar not just in sermons, but in devotional reading and parish iconography.[20] Margery Kempe, we know, was also aware of contemporary holy women since she mentions both Bridget of Sweden and Catherine of Siena. Among political elites as well, the revelatory writings of Bridget and Catherine "had an established place in the libraries of the politically influential in fifteenth-century England."[21] The lives and writings of contemporary holy women provided some cultural models for women's prophecy, even though priests who told their stories were careful to distinguish between the everyday, ordinary, lay folk and the inspired saints.

The Reformation in England

When the Reformation appeared in England, in the 1520s and 1530s, it singled out faith as crucial to religious experience, even of salvation. Noted reformed preachers like Edward Crome, William Garrett, Robert Barnes, and Robert Wisdom passionately argued that the Christian faith was "only belief, only, only, nothing else."[22] Each individual now *had* to believe—to come to some kind of position about God while denying the efficacy of certain rites (especially confession, pilgrimage, and prayers for the dead) and the priests who officiated them. With *sola fide* came *sola scriptura*: those facing the pressure to have faith, or believe, beyond the traditional forms of church custom and creeds, came to rely on the Bible as a way of giving shape and substance to their belief.

Thus begins a period in English history that profoundly shapes lay religious expression. In some sense, the Reformation's emphasis on access to scripture, and the need for every person to know it, merely continues the trajectory of late medieval religious devotion. The growing availability during the Reformation of the Bible in English, and of devotional writing based on scripture, and of sermons, builds on the vernacular devotional momentum of the fifteenth century (of course, the English Bible was not legal in late medieval England, but biblical stories were known through sermons and devotional texts).

In one sense, then, it would seem that reformed emphasis on biblical knowledge and salvation by faith would encourage the prophetic alternative. The Bible in English was now the literal revelation of God; to speak it aloud was to take on the prophet's role: delivering God's word to others. This is at least a way of understanding what happens to the prophetic impulse in the Reformed context; Bible reading becomes a form of divine communication in a way that, for many lay readers, was not previously possible.

The prophetic nature of Bible reading is evident in the lay group of "Bible Brabblers," or reformed lay men and women during the 1530s and 1540s who took to reading the English Bible in public places.[23] Their Bible reading, though it did not contain extra-biblical visions from God, involved interpretation. And this interpretation had a prophetic element to it, as the people who spoke it were not licensed to preach and, moreover, believed that their biblical interpretations were inspired directly by God. The Protestant martyrologist John Foxe tells of one John Porter, a lay preacher of the Bible at St. Paul's in London, who read frequently from one or more of the six chained Bibles standing on pillars throughout the building. (An injunction from 1538 had demanded that every parish acquire an English Bible.) Porter, "because hee coulde read well and had an audible voyce," drew "multitudes" of people to hear him. In 1541 he was called before Bishop Bonner and imprisoned for making "expositions vppon the texte, and gather[ing] great multitudes about him to make tumults."[24] At the same time that Bonner investigated Porter, he questioned a woman reader of scripture, Mrs. Castell, of St. Nicholas in the Flesh Shambles. According to Foxe, Castell was brought before Bonner "for beyng a medler and a reader of the Scripture in the Churche."[25]

The Bible even inspired spontaneous preaching in the streets of London. One of the most famous lay preachers was John Harrydaunce, an illiterate bricklayer who variously used the tree in his garden and the window of his house as pulpits. He was so confident in his preaching skills that when the mayor of London brought him to court and accused him of illegal preaching he responded by using the opening words of a sermon. As the mayor reported to Cromwell, "he began his sermon before us "*In nomine Patris et Filius et Spiritus Sanctus Amen*," and declared some part of it. He hath the New Testament ever about him."[26]

"Bible Brabblers," such as Harrydaunce, Mrs. Castell, and John Porter, bear a resemblance to some of the seventeenth-century prophets in England, as well as medieval visionary women, in so far as they embrace an apostolic mission of preaching. The Bible inspires their voices, calling them to testify to others. Some telling passages in the Henrician martyr Anne Askew's examinations reflect explicitly on the Bible as God's literal voice spoken to her. She writes, "Loke what he hath layed unto me with hys owne mouthe, in hys holye

Gospell, that have I with Gods grace, closed up in my harte."[27] Or again, she entreats her audience to "loke what God hath charged me with hys mouthe, that have I shutte up in my harte."[28] The metaphor of enclosing God's word within the heart derives from Psalm 119:11 ("Thy word I have treasured in my heart"), yet it is somewhat misleading in Askew's case, for the shutting was actually memorization and exposition—an internalization that led to external delivery through her reading of the Bible aloud and her teaching of others.[29]

Equally significant, Askew couches Bible reading in auditory rather than visual terms. The metaphor of God's mouth directly conveying truth to her emphasizes a conversational intimacy with the divine. In this respect Askew's understanding of what it means to read scripture follows directly in the tradition of medieval women's visionary literature. For Askew, the scripture is no less powerful or immediate than the celestial conversations Margery Kempe enjoys with Christ, or the scenes of Christ's passion that Julian of Norwich witnesses on her presumed deathbed.[30] The intimacy Kempe and Julian find in God's visionary communication exists to the same degree, for Askew, in the words of the text.

But Askew was, after all, burned at the stake. Ample evidence in Foxe shows that she was admired by later Protestants, especially under Mary. But prominent lay ministers in the underground Henrician and Marian churches defended their own right to preach while denying that this option was available to women. Edmund Allin, a miller from Kent, stood trial for illegal preaching in 1557. Instead of denying that he preached, he defended his right to do so by reference to Paul's first epistle to the Corinthians. Yet at the same time that he authorized his own preaching he denied women's capacity to preach, arguing "Doth not S. Paul forbid any mans spirite to be quenched? Doth he prohibite any man that hath any of these giftes, which he repeateth. 1. Cor. 14. to practise the same? Only he forbiddeth wome(n), but no ma(n)."[31] When Elizabeth restored Protestantism as the official religion of England, the option of prophecy through scripture disappeared altogether. Elizabeth ended the "prophesyings," or debates after sermons, conducted by Grindal's clergy with their lay audiences.[32]

So, although it is indeed true that the Reformation enabled every voice that chose to read the Bible aloud, it eventually silenced, or repressed, the lay preacher's voice. With this, the Reformation's attachment to *sola scriptura* eradicated the late medieval privilege of extra-biblical revelation. Just as there was no official possibility of venerating them, there was now, within the Church of England, no possibility of hearing from Mary, Saint Katherine, or Saint Michael. The last Catholic visionaries were either punished or forgotten. Henry VIII executed Elizabeth Barton, a nun from Kent whose prophecies denounced the king's divorce from Queen Catherine. Thomas More mentions a gentleman's daughter who received visions but, on her entrance to a convent, recorded nothing more.[33]

Looking back on visionary women of the late medieval period (and it was mostly women who were visionaries), what becomes clear is that the visionary-confessor relationship achieves a kind of protection, as well as patronage, for the visionary. Under Protestantism's revision of a priest's role, and especially, its elimination of confession, there is no mechanism for "discovering" a woman visionary and bringing her to the attention of the ecclesiastical hierarchy. Magisterial Protestantism's understanding of apocalypticism, moreover, was not millenarian. It looked backward rather than forward when interpreting the ages described in the book of Revelation. Thus John Bale and John Foxe read the apocalypse as a history of the Protestant church leading to the reign of Elizabeth, and not beyond it. Visionary voices were not sought after in the present day since the necessary reform, in their eyes, had already occurred.[34] Additionally, without belief in extra-biblical revelation (including, of course, the whole process of discerning spirits), Protestants had no reason to look for writers who experienced visions. When Reformed visionaries such as Askew did arise, there were no Reformed clergy presiding in the Church of England who could benefit from her inspired career. Exiled reformers did promote it, as John Bale quickly published her text and distributed it to the Protestant community. But undoubtedly he, and later Foxe, did this because Askew was a martyr and not because she was a brilliant preacher or potential saint.

The Reformation's emphasis on individual faith and interpretation of scripture, without the mediation of a priest, thus carried radical implications; but after a brief historical moment they disappeared. Biblical learning did inspire women's writing, but not prophecy, preaching, or vision. As detailed in both formative and recent studies of Protestant women writers, the kind of women's writing that Elizabethan and Jacobean Protestantism developed involved translation (Anne Vaughan Lock; Mary Sidney), debate (Rachel Speght), autobiography (Grace Mildmay and Elizabeth Isham), and instruction, especially that of households and children (Elizabeth Jocelin; Margaret Hoby).[35] These genres suited the roles that women played within Protestantism's spiritualized household.

Especially, women's responsibility to educate children and other household members in religious matters gave them spiritual authority.[36] So the Puritan gentlewoman Margaret Hoby (1570/1–1633) became a kind of spiritual supervisor for her household by overseeing the catechizing of servants, including hearing their repetitions of Sunday sermons and reading them works of Puritan divines. Within the Puritan community, women like Hoby or her contemporary Jane Ratcliffe (d. 1640) achieved status as noted exegetes. In a published funeral sermon for Ratcliffe, as Peter Lake has discussed, the minister John Ley admitted that he so admired Ratcliffe's interpretation of scripture that he "seriously desired her to write down her observations on the bible as she read it in her constant course."[37]

Thus, though somewhat plentiful in numbers, Protestant women's writings never developed a purely prophetic textual authority. The poet Aemelia Lanyer, in her *Salve Deus*, for instance, boldly reinterprets Eve's motives in the garden, as well as her culpability for the fall. Nancy Bradley Warren details how Lanyer even takes up medieval mystical themes such as the suffering body of Christ and mystical marriage.[38] But Lanyer pursues these readings in the role of the poet seeking patronage, not as a chosen vessel who gives voice to divine thought. And the distinction between these roles is very important. An author's claim to direct, divine inspiration (not the standard invocation of the Muses) greatly increases the authority quotient of a text, putting it on a plane equivalent to the pulpit or the Bible itself.

Why, then, does the female prophetic voice emerge again in England in the 1640s, and is it any different from before?[39] There are some obvious historical answers as to why it emerges. The dissolution of the national church and the rise of Presbyterianism and Independent churches changed the way the church was run as well as how it could define its membership. Any church with a sectarian leaning placed emphasis on a person's standing in the congregation itself, and thus, privileged the voice of each member. The Independent congregations headed by John Rogers, for instance, made testimony before the congregation central to membership, and based all decisions on the assent of the community.[40] Besides changes in church government, the breakdown of press censorship enabled the printing of greater numbers and varieties of texts.

But also, a fundamental shift occurred in Protestantism with regard to biblical interpretation. Though admittedly a small portion of the Protestant community in seventeenth-century England, the Quakers made an important innovation on biblical hermeneutics that substantially increased the possibilities for prophetic discourse. This involved the new presence of the Inner Light, which gave biblical and personal revelation the same authoritative weight, sometimes privileging individual revelation over written tradition. As Geoffrey Nuttall remarks, within Protestant circles before the rise of Quakerism "God's Word in Scripture [had] been treated as the criterion by which to test faith and experience. Now, [among Quakers] the Holy Spirit [was] introduced as the touchstone by which all else [was] to be tried, including the Bible itself." Nuttall further clarifies that "Quakers tend[ed] to contrast and . . . even to oppose the Spirit in themselves to the Spirit in the Word, and to treat the former, not the latter, as the criterion."[41] Thus the Quaker Katherine Evans proclaims early in her tract relating her imprisonment in the Roman Inquisition, even though she has used biblical language, she has "written the things which [she] did hear, see, tasted and handled of the good Word of God."[42] In the text, the first person "I" is italicized, emphasizing Katherine's personal and individual experience of God, which she perceives comprehensively through auditory, visual, gustatory, and tactile senses.

Sarah Cheevers, missionary companion to Katherine Evans, described the prophetic experience in a letter to Friends at the Bull and Mouth meeting (separate from letters collected in Baker's editions) this way: "we cannot hold our peace; the God . . . of glory doth open our mouth, and we speak to his praise, and utter his voice . . . my heart, soul and spirit that is wholly joined to the Lord, stream[s] forth to you."[43] Operating both externally and internally, the divine compels Sarah to speak, opening her mouth, but it also originates from within her, flowing out of her "heart, soul and spirit."[44]

The prominent London preacher Rebecca Travers spoke about prophecy in theological terms, likening the Inner Light to a New Covenant. Just as Christ's teachings superseded the Jewish law, so Quaker prophesying supersedes scripture and other religious teaching. Travers identifies "the new Covenant written in the heart, put in the inner parts" that directly conveys knowledge. The people who experience or "come to [the New Covenant], need not any to teach [them], but are all taught of God from the least to the greatest, knowing the pouring forth of the spirit upon sons and daughters, whereby [Quakers] prophesy."[45] Thus, the inner Covenant bypasses the teaching of clergy, and, presumably, scripture. The living language of God exists within Quakers, who prophesy to all, and those who hear this prophecy understand it.

What made Quaker prophecy understandable, according to Esther Biddle, was precisely the fact that it was spoken by contemporaries. Quaker prophets were the most relevant translators or embodiment of God's voice. She writes, "the Lord doth not speak unto us in an unknown Tongue, but in our own Language . . . we hear him perfectly, whose voice is better than life." Prophecy thus becomes the most immediate idiom and more effectual than previous religious writing. For Biddle, prophecy explains more than the teachings of priests, and even scripture: "we are not like the World, who must have a Priest to Interpret Scriptures to them, and when he is removed, they . . . know not what to do; but my friends, we witness the Scriptures fulfil'd, who hath said in the latter days, *He would pour out his Spirit upon Sons and Daughters*, and *they should Prophesie*."[46] Quaker prophecy not only stands in place of the missing priest, but also, takes the place of scripture itself. Biddle's reference to the fulfillment of scripture here suggests, on the one hand, that prophecy partakes in the same spirit as scripture itself; and on the other it suggests the idea that Quaker prophecy supersedes scriptural teaching.

As Biddle's writing also makes clear, prophecy goes hand in hand with the expectation of Christ's second coming, and thus, the belief that the "latter days" foretold in scripture have now arrived. Millenarianism was prevalent among the radical Protestant sects forming in the 1640s and 1650s and thus links this time period back to the high and late Middle Ages by virtue of its interest in apocalyptic thought. What millenarianism authorizes, again shown by Biddle, is the new voice, just as the coming of the Antichrist encouraged Hildegard and her contemporaries to speak out against injustices in the church.

What seems different to me about Quaker prophecy in contrast to the medieval prophetic alternative is Quakerism's assumption about who has access to the spirit. The Quakers believed in the general pouring out of the spirit in the latter days, which qualified everyone in the community to be a prophet. It was not a question of being especially pious or holy, though presumably one's involvement with Friends would lead to pious behavior. Instead, it was a matter of recognizing one's own capacity for vision. Margaret Fell reports that the message of access to divine prophecy was even what convinced her of the truth of Quakerism. When George Fox preached, "You will say, Christ saith this, and the apostles say this; but what canst *thou* say?" she was moved to accept the truth of Quakerism.[47] The legitimization of her own expression here is crucial, as is the idea that prophecy itself is constitutive of Quaker belief and practice. Not surprisingly then, it is Quakerism that develops the first defense of women's right to preach outside exceptional circumstances.[48]

What Quaker women writers did not have, however, was a wide readership. Medieval mystics could be assured of readers and promoters of their visions within the church at large. There was always the possibility that women mystics would be authorized by priests and bishops, and sometimes, as their confessors hoped, canonized after death. The larger church structure therefore was open to their visions, or the possibility of their having visions, as long as they were authorized. By contrast, Quaker women visionary-preachers never made it into the mainstream religious culture, and therefore had no recorders or promoters except within their own congregations. This is why no one beyond their sect read them for the purpose of edification, and again, this contrast shows how crucial the recognition of women mystics in the medieval church was. Yet, at the same time, women's preaching, and therefore, women's visionary writing and prophecy, was automatically accepted within Quakerism rather than being tested for authenticity or outright rejected. This made the difference between the reputation of an Anne Askew (who had to die to be remembered) and that of a Quaker like Elizabeth Hooten, who simply had to preach to be remembered.

Within sectarian congregations, though women were authorized to speak, the publication of their writing was sometimes promoted by male supporters as well. The words of women prophets such as Anna Trapnel and Jane Hawkins were recorded by prominent men in their congregations. A printing of Trapnel's text may have been used as a Bible for the Fifth Monarchists.[49] In this sense, sectarian male coreligionists in the seventeenth century played a role similar to that of the priests of the medieval era who authorized a female visionary's text.

But beyond understanding the social institutions that either supported or blocked women's visionary writing in both the Middle Ages and the seventeenth century, we can still ask whether the same spirit exists in both eras. To the extent that Quakerism emphasized the uncontainable nature of the spirit—the uninhibited pouring forth of God's voice on the individual so that she has no choice but to speak—this can be traced back to late medieval holy women and the uncontrollable roaring of Margery Kempe or the plentiful tears of Marie d'Oignies. Kempe's bodily performance of the divine presence usually takes place in public settings—in church, during pilgrimage, in a town street. So too, Quakers experience the tremulous power of the divine and must speak in spite of themselves in church, or shake before one another in meetings. The same charismatic spirit exists in both ages, with the difference being that Quaker men experience mystical revelations and bodily signs of the spirit just like the women, while male clerics of the medieval period eschewed charism and saw themselves as categorically different from the women they confessed and promoted.[50]

As the title to this essay suggests, I think we can finally say that Quakerism is the return of the medieval repressed precisely because it responds to the deadening effects of the Reformation's emphasis on *sola scriptura*. Fox recognized that the Bible alone can become a deadening letter, and needs to be tested against what God might reveal in the present and in other inspired individuals. As the Quaker maid Isabel put it while debating Baptists in their church in Fen Stanton, "the Scriptures" should be tried "by the Spirit, and not the Spirit by the Scriptures."[51]

Notes

1. Patricia Crawford, *Women and Religion in England, 1500–1720* (London: Routledge, 1996), 106; Phyllis Mack, "Women as Prophets during the English Civil War," *Feminist Studies* 8 (1982): 24.

2. Women's prophetic texts spiked during the Interregnum period, totaling about seventy-two titles in a total of ninety-two titles for the entire century. Yet the total numbers of women involved in the radical religious movement were small, as the majority of women at the time were Anglican or underground Catholics. The radicals comprised about 5 percent of the population. See Crawford, *Women and Religion in England*, 107, 130.

3. A full list of seventeenth-century visionary women and their writings appears in the appendixes of Phyllis Mack's *Visionary Women: Ecstatic Prophecy in Seventeenth-Century England* (Berkeley: University of California Press, 1994).

4. Rosalynn Voaden, *God's Words, Women's Voices: The Discernment of Spirits in the Writing of Late Medieval Women Visionaries* (Woodbridge: York Medieval Press, 2000), 17.

5. See Arthur F. Marotti's essay in this volume on Gertrude More. Catholic women visionaries in the seventeenth century were not as plentiful as the sectarians, but when they pursued vocations in convents abroad, such as More did, they seem to have been nurtured and promoted by male clerics in the same way that medieval women were. See also Claire Walker, "Recusants, Daughters and Sisters in Christ: English Nuns and their Communities in the Seventeenth Century," in *Women, Identities and Political Cultures in Early Modern Europe*, ed. Susan Broomhall and Stephanie Tarbin (Aldershot: Ashgate, 2008), 61–76; "'Spiritual Property': The English Benedictine Nuns of Cam-

brai and the Dispute over the Baker Manuscripts," in *Women, Property, and the Letters of the Law in Early Modern England*, ed. N. Wright, M. Ferguson, and A. R. Buck (Toronto: University of Toronto Press, 2004), 237–55; and Heather Wolfe, "Dame Barbara Constable: Catholic Antiquarian, Advisor, and Closet Missionary," in *Catholic Culture in Early Modern England*, ed. Christopher Highley and Arthur F. Marotti (Notre Dame, Ind.: University of Notre Dame Press, 2007), 158–88.

6. I have explored this topic differently, and in shorter form, in the conclusion to *Heresy Trials and English Women Writers, 1400–1670* (Cambridge: Cambridge University Press, 2012), 174–80.

7. Bernard McGinn, *The Essential Writings of Christian Mysticism* (New York: The Modern Library, 2006), 310.

8. George Fox, *The Journal*, ed. Nigel Smith (London: Penguin, 1998), 16.

9. Fox, *Journal*, 14.

10. Bernard McGinn, "'To the Scandal of Men, Women Are Prophesying': Female Seers of the High Middle Ages," in *Fearful Hope: Approaching the New Millennium*, ed. Christopher Kleinhenz and Fannie J. Le Moine (Madison: University of Wisconsin Press, 1999), 59–85.

11. Elizabeth Petroff, *Medieval Women's Visionary Literature* (Oxford: Oxford University Press, 1986); idem, *Body and Soul: Essays on Medieval Women and Mysticism* (New York: Oxford University Press, 1994); Caroline Walker Bynum, *Holy Feast and Holy Fast: The Religious Significance of Food to Medieval Women* (Berkeley: University of California Press, 1987); Diane Watt, *Secretaries of God: Women Prophets in Late Medieval and Early Modern England* (Woodbridge: Boydell and Brewer, 1997); Barbara Newman, *From Virile Woman to WomanChrist* (Philadelphia: University of Pennsylvania Press, 1995); Voaden, *God's Words, Women's Voices*; Maud McInerney, ed., *Eloquent Virgins From Thecla to Joan of Arc* (New York: Palgrave Macmillan, 2003); Dyan Elliott, *Proving Woman: Female Spirituality and Inquisitional Culture in the Later Middle Ages* (Princeton, N.J.: Princeton University Press, 2004); Kathryn Kerby-Fulton, "When Women Preached: An Introduction to Female Homiletic, Sacramental, and Liturgical Roles in the Later Middle Ages," in *Voices in Dialogue: Reading Women in the Middle Ages*, ed. Linda Olson and Kathryn Kerby-Fulton (Notre Dame, Ind.: University of Notre Dame Press, 2005), 31–55; Nancy Bradley Warren, *The Embodied Word: Female Spiritualities, Contested Orthodoxies, and English Religious Cultures, 1350–1700* (Notre Dame, Ind.: University of Notre Dame Press, 2010).

12. Kathryn Kerby-Fulton, *Reformist Apocalypticism and* Piers Plowman (Cambridge: Cambridge University Press, 1990), 4.

13. Kerby-Fulton, *Reformist Apocalypticism*, 4.

14. Kerby-Fulton, *Reformist Apocalypticism*, 32.

15. Bynum, *Holy Feast and Holy Fast*, 22.

16. Voaden, *God's Words, Women's Voices*, 57.

17. On this phenomenon, see John Wayland Coakley, *Women, Men and Spiritual Power: Female Saints and their Male Collaborators* (New York: Columbia University Press, 2006).

18. See, for instance, *The Book of Margery Kempe*'s description of the Franciscans' leading of devotions during Margery's pilgrimage in Jerusalem, chapters 28–30. The meditations on Christ's suffering invite "ghostly sight" (gostly sygth) and penitential weeping that the *Book* links to the tears of other women mystics, such as Elizabeth of Hungary and Marie d'Oignies. See *The Book of Margery Kempe*, EETS, o.s., 212, ed. S. B. Meech and H. E. Allen (London: Oxford University Press, 1940), 68. Appropriately, Christ speaks to Margery on the day she visits the location of Pentecost (chapter 29). For an understanding of how Margery's devotion to Christ embodies trends in late medieval parish piety, see Christine Peters, *Patterns of Piety: Women, Gender and Religion in Late Medieval and Reformation England* (Cambridge: Cambridge University Press, 2003), 89–93.

19. Vincent Gillespie, "Vernacular Books of Religion," in *Book Production and Book Publishing in Britain, 1375–1475*, ed. Jeremy Griffiths and Derek Pearsall (Cambridge: Cambridge University Press, 1989), 317–44; Eamon Duffy, *The Stripping of the Altars: Traditional Religion in England 1400–1580* (New Haven, Conn.: Yale University Press, 1992), 53–87.

20. See Osbern Bokenham, *Legendys of Hooly Wummen*, EETS, o.s. 206, ed. Mary S. Serjeantson (London: Oxford University Press, 1938); Karen A. Winstead, ed., *Chaste Passions: Medieval English Virgin Martyr Legends* (Ithaca, N.Y.: Cornell University Press, 2000), 115–63, 184–201. On parish iconography, see Peters, *Patterns of Piety*, 97–129.

21. Warren, *Embodied Word*, 22.

22. Quoted in Susan Bridgen, *London and the Reformation* (New York: Oxford University Press, 1989), 265.

23. The term "Bible Brabbler" or "babbler" was used by ecclesiastics to mock laypersons for having a passing knowledge of scripture but no understanding of either the original languages in which the Bible was written, or of church doctrines and commentary on them by the fathers. Interestingly, no educated reformer who quoted liberally from the Bible—no Tyndale, Barnes, or Bradford—was ever called a babbler. For a fuller account of the babblers, see Gertz, *Heresy Trials*, 80–86.

24. John Foxe, *The Unabridged Acts and Monuments Online* or *TAMO* (Sheffield: HRI Online Publications, 2011). Available from www.johnfoxe.org (accessed January 20, 2012). See the 1570 edition, 1420. Subsequent quotations are from this edition.

25. Foxe, *Unabridged Acts*, 1416. See also Susan Wabuda, "The Controversy on Women and Bible Reading," in *Belief and Practice in Reformation England: A Tribute to Patrick Collinson from his Students* (Aldershot: Ashgate, 1998), 54.

26. *Letters and Papers Foreign and Domestic, of the Reign of Henry VIII*, vol. XII/ii. 624, ed. J. Gairdner and R. Brodie (London, 1898–1910), September 1, 1537.

27. Anne Askew, *The Examinations of Anne Askew*, ed. Elaine V. Beilin (Oxford: Oxford University Press, 1996), 143.

28. Askew, *Examinations of Anne Askew*, 118.

29. On Askew's preaching, see Gertz, *Heresy Trials*, 86–97. For a similar interpretation of Askew as preacher, see David Lowenstein, "Writing and the Persecution of Heretics in Henry VIII's England: *The Examinations of Anne Askew*," in *Heresy, Literature, and Politics in Early Modern English Culture* (Cambridge: Cambridge University Press, 2006), 11–39.

30. *Book of Margery Kempe*, 16–18; *The Showings of Julian of Norwich*, ed. Denise Baker (New York: W. W. Norton, 2005), 3–37.

31. John Foxe, *Acts and Monuments* (London, 1570), 2206.

32. On the widespread practice of prophesying, see Patrick Collinson, John Craig, and Brett Usher, eds., *Conferences and Combination Lectures in the Elizabethan Church, 1582–1590* (Woodbridge, Suffolk: Boydell, 2003), xxvi–xxxiii.

33. Crawford, *Women and Religion in England*, 28–29, 107–8.

34. Katherine Firth, *The Apocalyptic Tradition in Reformation Britain, 1530–1645* (Oxford: Oxford University Press, 1979); Paul Christianson, *Reformers and Babylon: English Apocalyptic Visions from the Reformation to the Eve of the Civil War* (Toronto: University of Toronto Press, 1978); Jane Facey, "John Foxe and the Defense of the English Church," in *Protestantism and the National Church in the Sixteenth Century*, ed. Peter Lake and Maria Dowling (London: Croom Helm, 1987).

35. Elaine Beilin's seminal work, *Redeeming Eve: Women Writers of the English Renaissance* (Princeton, N.J.: Princeton University Press, 1987), first brought attention to Rachel Speght, Amelia Lanyer, and Anne Dowriche, among others. Margaret Hannay's *Silent But for the Word* (Kent, Ohio: Kent State University Press, 1985), initiated analysis of women's religious writing. Later studies by Erica Longfellow, Kimberly Coles, and, most recently, two essay collections edited by Micheline White and Johanna Harris and Elizabeth Scott-Baumann, greatly expand our understanding of the religious cultures, both theological and material, which informed Protestant women's writing. See Longfellow, *Women and Religious Writing in Early Modern England* (Cambridge: Cambridge University Press, 2004); Coles, *Religion, Reform and Women's Writing in Early Modern England* (Cambridge: Cambridge University

Press, 2008); White, ed., *English Women, Religion, and Textual Production, 1500–1625* (Farnham, Surrey: Ashgate, 2011); and Harris and Scott-Baumann, eds., *The Intellectual Culture of Puritan Women, 1558–1680* (Houndmills, Basingstoke, Hampshire: Palgrave, 2011).

36. Margo Todd, "Humanists, Puritans and the Spiritualized Household," *Church History* 49 (1980): 25. Peters, *Patterns of Piety*, 201–2, emphasizes Protestant stereotypes of women's roles as more spiritual and connected with ritual observance, both of which were associated with the household.

37. Peter Lake, "Feminine Piety and Personal Potency: The 'Emancipation' of Mrs Jane Ratcliffe," *The Seventeenth Century* 2 (1987): 149. On Hoby's reading of scripture and her conversations with her chaplain, Mr. Rhodes, see Joanna Moody, ed., *The Private Life of an Elizabethan Lady: The Diary of Lady Margaret Hoby, 1599–1605* (Thrupp, Stroud, Gloucestershire: Sutton, 1998), 110–12, 144–45.

38. Warren, *Embodied Word*, 47–51. On Lanyer, see also Coles, *Religion, Reform and Women's Writing*, 149–86.

39. Some of the earliest cases are the 1620s (Eleanor Davis and Jane Hawkins), but I use this date because it is the time in which a marked increase in prophecy occurs.

40. Longfellow, *Women and Religious Writing*, 160–61; Kathleen Lynch, *Spiritual Experience: Protestant Autobiography in the Seventeenth-Century Anglophone World* (Oxford: Oxford University Press, 2012), 121–78; Crawford, *Women and Religion in England*, 143–44.

41. Geoffrey Nuttall, *The Holy Spirit in Puritan Faith and Experience* (Chicago: University of Chicago Press, 1992), 28, 30.

42. Katherine Evans and Sarah Cheevers, *A True Account of the Great Tryals and Cruel Sufferings undergone by those two faithful servants of God, Katherine Evans and Sarah Cheevers* (London, 1663), 25.

43. "Sarah Chevers Epistle to Friends to read at Bull and Mouth," Friends House Library Portfolio Manuscripts, 31/60. Quoted in Mack, *Visionary Women*, 136.

44. "Sarah Chevers Epistle to Friends to read at Bull and Mouth." Quoted in Mack, *Visionary Women*, 136.

45. Rebecca Travers, *For those that meet to worship at the steeplehouse, called John Evangelist* (London, 1659), 32. On Travers and the role of God's word, see Catie Gill, *Women in the Seventeenth-Century Quaker Community* (Aldershot: Ashgate, 2005), 128.

46. Esther Biddle, *The Trumpet of the Lord Sounded forth unto these Three Nations* (London, 1662), 11.

47. Nuttall, *Holy Spirit*, 26 (emphasis added).

48. Though many years earlier the Lollard Walter Brut had argued in his heresy trials that women could preach, Quakers were the first to write treatises

expounding and defending women's right to preach. For one of the earliest defenses of women's preaching, see Richard Farnsworth, *A Woman forbidden to speak in the Church: The grounds examined, the Mystery opened, the Truth cleared, and the ignorance both of Priests and Peeple discovered* (London, 1654). See also Elaine Hobby, "'Come to live a Preaching Life": Female Community in Seventeenth-Century Radical Sects," in *Female Communities, 1600–1800: Literary Visions and Cultural Realities*, ed. Rebecca D'Monte and Nicole Pohl (London: Macmillan, 1999), 76–92.

49. Longfellow, *Women and Religious Writing*, 155, 171.

50. See John Coakley, for instance, on the ways Raymond of Capua represented his relationship with Catherine of Siena. According to Coakley, "Raymond pictures himself prominently as a party to interactions with Catherine in which she has access to the divine in a way that he does not and that, as he would have it, supply deficiencies in himself." See *Women, Men, and Spiritual Power*, 218.

51. Quoted in Nuttall, *Holy Spirit*, 30.

7

"Between the Rational and the Mystical"

The Inner Life and the Early English Enlightenment

Sarah Apetrei

One of the central themes of the early English Enlightenment, particularly in the years following the Glorious Revolution, was the disavowal of the mysterious and obscure points in the Christian religion. Defenses of the "Reasonableness of Christianity," and cries of "Christianity not Mysterious," expressed this discomfort with doctrines and practices that seemed not only to be counterintuitive, but to require that universal reason be subordinated to particular revelation, tradition, or, what was worse, extraordinary illuminations. It is frequently remarked that the rationalist thinkers of this period—Deists, Lockeans, and Latitudinarians—were enemies of enthusiasm and "mysticism." In recent scholarship of the eighteenth-century church, particularly Brian Young's study of *Religion and Enlightenment in Eighteenth-Century England*, there has been a renewed focus on mysticism as a Counter-Enlightenment phenomenon: a repudiation of precisely this demystifying tendency and the new hegemony of natural philosophy.[1] However, this may be putting the cart before the horse, and the extent to which rationalizing forces were *reactions* as well as stimulants to mystical currents has not been explored. The Enlightenment obsession with "mystery" and "enthusiasm," with all its obvious evocation of popish superstition and sectarian disorder, has rarely been linked to the existence of both Protestant and Counter-Reformation mystical traditions in English writing after the Restoration, and to an enduring controversy over the catholicity and authority of what was known disparagingly as "mystical divinity." This essay aims to recover those traditions and the debates they inspired, and make some suggestions about the formative significance—both positive and negative—of mystical theology in the Long Reformation and early Enlightenment.

As early as 1655, mystical theology and enthusiasm were linked in English print, in Meric Casaubon's *Treatise Concerning Enthusiasme*, which set out to demonstrate that "*Mystical Theology*, highly commended by some Christians as the most perfect way," was nothing more than "the invention of Heathen Philosophers."[2] He discredited the classic mystic formulations of Dionysius the Areopagite as the work of a fraud, and identified the ecstasies of mystics with the bodily distempers and delusions of contemporary sectarian visionaries. The abridged spiritual writings of the Benedictine Augustine Baker appeared in 1657, as *Sancta Sophia, or Directions for the Prayer of Contemplation* (edited by another Benedictine, Serenus Cressy, a former Great Tew intellectual), and apparently became quite popular as well as thoroughly contested in certain circles: it would become a classic text of Western mysticism.[3] This textbook of apophatic spirituality was certainly something of a bogey for Anglican detractors of "enthusiasm." During the period after the Restoration, the establishment's horror of both popery and sectarian inspiration helped to sharpen the anti-mystical polemic. Edward Stillingfleet influentially turned his guns on "Mystical Divinity," and especially the "way of unknowing" and self-annihilation recommended in *Sancta Sophia* by Baker and Cressy, in *A Discourse Concerning the Idolatry Practised in the Church of Rome* (1671). He warned against the twin anti-intellectual dangers of superstition and enthusiasm, prescribing as an antidote for both "the true understanding of the nature and reasonableness of the *Christian Religion*, which fills our minds with a true sense of *God* and *goodness*, and so arms us against *superstition*, and withall acquaints us that the conduct of the *Spirit* of *God* is in the use of the greatest reason and prudence, and so prevents the follies of *Enthusiasme*." Stillingfleet, recently made Royal Chaplain, ridiculed "abstractedness of life, mental prayer, passive unions, a Deiform fund of the soul, a state of introversion, divine inspirations" described by Serenus Cressy, which, as he put it "must either end in *Enthusiasme* or madness."[4]

Largely thanks to Stillingfleet, any association with "mystical divinity" was generally to be avoided by those concerned with intellectual respectability. Gilbert Burnet complained in 1696 of being charged with "loving an *Ascetical life*, and *Mystical Divinity*" and, concomitantly, of being represented as "an *Enthusiast*."[5] Mysticism was coterminous with obscurity, or popish obfuscation: "jargon, or nonsense," in the words of one nonconformist minister.[6] Henry Wharton's hostile biography of Saint Ignatius of Loyola published on the eve of the Revolution scoffed at the "foolish Canting" of his "Mystical Divinity," which "talks much of the love of Christ in a most unintelligible manner" and "is commonly too mysterious for Learned men." With half an eye on the English sects, he commented accusingly that many popish doctrines "derive their original from Enthusiastick Visions and Revelations."[7] Samuel Wesley remarked somewhat more sympathetically on "the so much talk'd of *mystical Divinity*" in 1693, that it "seems indeed no more than an affectation of hard Words to express or rather conceal such Truths as are plain and easie."[8]

The apparent synergies between papist and enthusiast doctrines only deepened the suspicions of "moderate" commentators about mystical religion. The Quakers, in particular, were linked to this new mysticism. One anti-Quaker polemicist, having summarized the main principles of that "popish fanatick" Serenus Cressy as expressed in his prefaces to *Sancta Sophia* and Julian of Norwich's Revelations, concluded: "Is not this the very frame and mould of our *Quakers*?"[9] The Earl of Clarendon, perhaps unfairly synonymous with Anglican persecution after the Restoration, observed in a 1673 controversy with Cressy, that

> Men are not to be blamed, and it may be less in our Country, which hath and doth still suffer by men and women too of *disturbed fancies*, who pretend to *Revelations and Illuminations* and such *Enthusiasms*, not only to introduce many *extravagant opinions* in *Religion*, but to warrant and justifie *unquiet* and *seditious actions* in the *State*, from some *light within*, . . . and therefore when they meet with this spirit revived again in the writings of some *modern Catholicks* . . . it cannot be wondred at, that men are not willing to give any countenance to those *infusions* which have so often been discovered to be mere *delusions*, or that many who have read all *Mother Teresa*'s *visions* and *ecstasies*, and accidentally meet with some *well exercised Quakers*, are apt to think their stile very like.[10]

At a time when the church was deemed to be in danger on two fronts and the Declaration of Indulgence had so recently shocked British Protestants and especially royalist Anglicans to their core by legalizing private Catholic worship, the shared illuminism of the Counter- and Radical Reformations was particularly threatening.[11] Quakers were, indeed, co-opting the language of mysticism and apophatic thought, as their theologians identified their principles and practice with a universal "Mystick" heritage, in which Baker and the Benedictines were equally involved. In 1678 Robert Barclay wrote that the spiritual worship of the Quakers had

> been testified of, commended, and practised by the most Pious of all sorts, in all ages, by many evident Testimonies might be proved, so that from the professing and practicing thereof the name of *Mysticks* hath arisen, as of a certain Sect generally commended by all, whose Writings are full both of the explanation and of the commendation of this sort of worship, where they plentifully assert this *inward introversion*, and *abstraction of the mind*, as they call it, *from all Images and Thoughts*, and the *prayer of the will*, yea they look upon this as *the height of Christian perfection*, so that some of them, though professed Papists, do not doubt to affirm, that such as have attained this method of Worship, or are aiming at it, (as in a Book, called *Sancta Sophia*, put out by the English Benedictines, Printed at *Doway*, anno. 1657).[12]

Omnivorous Quaker readers were also encountering the mystical writings of Hendrik Niclaes, and translations of Johannes Tauler, the *Theologia deutsch*, and the spiritualist reformers Hans Denck and Sebastian Franck by the antinomian divine John Everard.[13]

The historiography of English religion in the seventeenth century is full of "isms": Puritanism, Arminianism, Latitudinarianism, Quakerism. Mysticism has not traditionally been an organizing category for our thinking about religious life in this period, except perhaps to refer obliquely to Laudian reform, the metaphysical poets, or the spiritual sects. Historians writing in the early to mid-twentieth century were far more comfortable than their successors in designating the Quakers and experimental Puritans as "mystics," and some traced an English mystical tradition via Donne, Traherne and Crashaw, and Baker and the Cambridge Platonists.[14] More recently, studies of the structure of radical religious discourse and confessional histories of the Quaker tradition have acknowledged the importance of a mystical heritage.[15] However, few have dreamed of claiming for England that which has been claimed for France: that the seventeenth century was *le grand siècle* for mysticism.[16] Certainly Restoration England—characterized by an aggressive Anglican establishment, anti-Catholicism, and rational religion—is not often associated with mystical tendencies. However, it may be the case that our preoccupation with the politics of early modern religion has prevented us from seeing how trends in the discourse of spirituality can also have historical agency. The Anglican polemics of Stillingfleet, Hyde, and Wharton suggest that the discrediting of mystical divinity formed part of a two-pronged attack on Catholicism and dissenting enthusiasm. Yet there were also those who earnestly appealed to mystical religion as a panacea for Europe's post-Reformation troubles, and it is my argument that the turn to mysticism was part of the same movement that led to a radical critique of Christian orthodoxy: the repulsion from propositional religion and scholastic forms of theology, skepticism about biblical supremacy, an indifference to forms, and the questing toward an infallible supply of religious knowledge on which Christian unity might safely rest. The universal, inward principles of reason on the one hand and mystical experience on the other both seemed to provide solutions to the problems of authority and catholicity in Western Christendom. The mystics of seventeenth-century England promoted inward ascent, visionary illumination, and apophatic theology as a foil to the irreconcilable controversies of the age, just as the exponents of discursive reason and advocates for the separation of philosophy and theology attempted to safeguard intellectual and political stability from bitter religious passions.

As a starting point for exploring this claim that mysticism should be rehabilitated as an important theme in the scholarship of early modern English religion, I offer two attempts to delineate a genealogy of seventeenth-century English mystics. In the late 1690s two Anglican clergymen, prominent in the London Societies for the Reformation of Manners, separately identified themselves with an "Inward Mystical Way in England," which they believed had been revived over the past half-century.[17] This movement linked them not only to Platonist divines and the spiritual radicals of the 1640s and 1650s, but also to English Catholicism and more deeply to a late medieval heritage. One of these men was Richard Roach, an accomplished musician and hymn-writer, fellow of St John's College, Oxford, and rector of St. Augustine, Hackney, a sinecure living in which he had very little obvious interest. Instead, Roach was a founding member of a religious movement, the Philadelphian Society, which met in Hoxton in the city of London, for charismatic meetings. The Philadelphians were disciples of the German theosopher Jakob Böhme, and envisioned the healing of breaches in the Christian world, in a dawning Age of the Spirit that would defeat all ungodliness. They later supposed that this era had opened on August 23, 1697, in fulfillment of the contemporary calculations of the millenarian Thomas Beverley, when Roach appeared to defend the activities of the Philadelphian Society before Archbishop Tenison and other (unnamed) bishops at Lambeth Palace.[18] In his address, or "Testimony of ye Rising Powers of ye Spirit" as he called it, Roach confessed that

> He has long been Inclin'd to Believe a more Glorious State of ye Church to be Promised & set forth in ye Scripture than has ever yet been; not finding it any way Inconsistent with ye *Principles* of ye Church of *England* but rather *Conformable* to her Doctrine of Receiving whatever appears to have been ye Doctrine of ye Three First Centuries of Christianity . . . About two years since & a half having for some time applied himself more diligently & strictly than before to ye service of God, & earnest Prayer for ye Propagation of the Gospel, & Increase of Piety; he had many things *Extraordinary* Opend in himself, partly by *Vision*, partly by a soft Inspeaking Voice, but chiefly by a clear *Irradiation* of ye Intellectual Faculty & Powerful *Impressions* of some Truths upon his mind; & some things yt God would bring to pass: & this so forcibly yt he could not wthhold his Assent tho he strove much agt it. That all Antichristianism, & whatever is contrary to ye truth & Holiness of Christ, was to be Destroy'd by ye *Breath* of his Holy Spirit, & yt there was to be even a Revelation of ye Lord Jesus from Heaven, in ye Power & Majesty of ye Father, to possess & *Rule* ye Utmost Ends of ye Earth, as his Heritage.[19]

Roach was also a great advocate of women's ministry, and on November 2, 1697, at a second meeting with Tenison, he prophesied that this new spiritual epoch would see "ye Restoration & Advancement of ye Female Sex to ye same Freedom & Dignity with ye Male."[20]

As a prelude to the apocalyptic moment, Roach supposed that the late seventeenth century had seen an outpouring of spiritual gifts in a series of prophetic figures, in whom Christ was revealing his new, inward communion with humanity. These included mystics like Antoinette Bourignon, Madame Guyon, and the Pietist Rosamunde Juliane von der Asseburg (significantly all female), but also a line of English *illuminati* originating with Mary Pordage, the wife of a notorious Berkshire clergyman and one of those known as Seekers, who was tried by the county commissioners for blasphemy in 1654 for preaching that God was manifest in the flesh of his saints. These prophetic vessels were distinguished not only by "ye general Qualification of Mystical Knowledg & Experiences," but also by having "been Actuated by a fresh Rising Gale of Extraordinary Power, about ye middle of ye last Century. Wch opend first upon Mrs Pordage & then upon Dr Pordage her Husband Mr Bromly & several others, thro whom it was Propagated."[21] After the Restoration, John Pordage's community had survived underground and relocated to London, where his son served as court physician under Charles II and where he developed a spiritual community with female visionaries such as Jane Lead and Anne Bathurst, who formed the core of the Philadelphian Society of the 1690s. It is my view that the Pordage and Philadelphian circle probably had roots in the elusive Family of Love, not least because Bathurst's "seraphick" mystical writings contain references to her experience of being "Goded with God," an "Old, and indeed Odd Expression" defended by Richard Roach from the charge of blasphemy in a later apocalyptic treatise.[22] Bathurst herself may well have been the "Anne Jurien," a member of the Dutch Church in London (originally from Woudrichem), who married John Bathurst in 1681 and with him hosted the Behmenist mystic and poet Quirinus Kuhlmann at their home.[23] Probably supported by his London friends, Kuhlmann embarked on a self-ruinous missionary project to promote his own vision of universal renewal, which ended with his execution in Moscow in 1689 for promoting rebellion.[24]

However, Roach's canon was not restricted to the wild fringes of Protestant radicalism. As well as the medieval mystics, Thomas à Kempis, Tauler, and the *Theologia deutsch*, he also wrote of "many Authors, or Writings, more truly of a *Middle* Nature, between the Rational and the Mystical," among them Saint Augustine, but more recently the Cambridge Platonists John Smith, Henry More, and Peter Sterry; the great jurist Sir Matthew Hale; the Oxford philosopher John Norris; the Aberdeen scholar Henry Scougal; and Robert Boyle.[25] In 1703 the Philadelphian Francis Lee, a London physician and nonjuror,[26] also drafted proposals "for the raising a STOCK to print BOOKS of MYSTICAL DIVINITY, PHILOSOPHY and HISTORY. In order to the advancement of the most ancient and universal religion, as professed by Christ and his apostles, and of the most curious and solid learning, throughout all the ages and parts of the world." This work of propagation would include new editions of the desert fathers, the "heathen mystics" or Neoplatonists, as well as an anthology of mystical texts by recent authors, "Catholic and Protestant."[27] The Philadelphians also nurtured a fascination for the Eastern churches. In 1698 Lee wrote a series of "Proposals given to Peter the Great" produced "at his own request," indicating that they had become acquainted during Peter's brief visit to Oxford in that year. Eulogizing "the most glorious *Greek* Church" (by which he presumably implied all churches of the Orthodox East), Lee made practical suggestions for improvements to all aspects of public life in Muscovy, including the establishment of seven "Committees or Colleges" devoted to public reform, among them a college for the Reformation of Manners and schools of prophets erected in every diocese as compulsory seminaries for bishops and senior clergy.[28] The Philadelphians' vision for a universal spiritual reformation, leading the true church out of the wilderness into triumph and glory, involved the whole of Christendom and beyond, as they also revered "the Antient *Mystick Knowledge* of the *Eastern* [i.e., non-Christian] *Nations*, which we do esteem no contemtible Key, towards Right and Fundamental Understanding of great Part of the *Sacred Writings*."[29]

For Roach and Lee, the defining characteristic of authentic mysticism was the spirit of charity, which transcended forms and party politics. This was the third dispensation of the Spirit, after the dispensations of law and gospel, and in their founding documents the Philadelphians pronounced that just as "this Spirit is Catholick: . . . thence the Church must be also Catholick; according to the most strict sense of the Word, in an universal Latitude of Love, without any Narrowness, Partiality, or Particularity of Spirit."[30] In his private papers, Richard Roach wrote that the mystical voices throughout history, and especially in recent British history, reflected the reality of an invisible, "Philadelphian" church: "ye Church Mystick & Catholick wherever Dispersd throughout ye Christian World, whose Bond of Union & Communion in its Wilderness state is ye Life & Power of ye Holy Ghost felt & witnessd among em & ye cement of Brotherly Love wch their Name imports." He went on to reflect that

> As there was among ye Jews a sort of people called ye Essenes, who lived a more speculative & Abstracted Life; & were more conversant with ye Mysteries of Religion & thereby better Prepard to receive Christ as it is said these generally did; so in ye Christian Church there has been a People also, thus Inclin'd; & looking beyond ye rest yt keep in Vulgar Truck of Opinions & Traditions of ye Age wherin they Live; & Endeavour to Cultivate ye True & Primitive Christianity; & ye Inward work of Regeneration; & to Revive & Partake of ye Primitive Power & Spirit of Religion; & Attain a real Communion & Conversation wth God. Such have been ye Mysticks, in all Parts & of all Denominations; who have overlookd & shot beyond ye Particularities of their own Church or Party as in an Outward Visible Form, & kept to ys Interior or Spiritual Way; in wch there may be Offerd as Great a Harmony & Unity even among those of Externally Different denominations, as there is among those in the Outward Way, & forms a Disunity & Disharmony.[31]

This irenic spiritualism, shooting beyond particularities and visible forms, betrays the influence of Radical Reformation sensibilities that seem to have shaped the Interregnum sects, through the writings of Böhme and Niclaes, as well as John Everard's translations.[32]

However, the supreme principle of charity above doctrine and party was by no means exclusively anti-formalist and sectarian. Writing at much the same time as Roach, the Aberdeenshire Episcopalian George Garden, a Jacobite sympathizer but also disciple of Antoinette Bourignon, wrote in a letter to a patron that

> Since God is the incomprehensible Truth, & Wisdom, as unsearchable in his ways as in his Essence, so that we cannot penetrate them with our Understanding, we ought humbly to accept of all the Manifestations he has made by his Spirit in all the fullness of the sense & meaning intended by the Divine Spirit without cleaving so to One Meaning or one way as if it were the only meaning or only way of the Spirit, & all others were false. And God being *Love*, & all he doth & saith tending to *Love*; that sense & way that Leads us effectually to

> the *Love* of God is good & saving to us, & instead of a solid Truth, whether it be true in it self or not.[33]

In this way, the mystical emphasis on the *Deus absconditus*, disavowing all scholastic assertions and insisting instead on an experimental knowledge of divine love, is linked intimately to irenicism and antidogmatism. This is a catholicity of love, intellectually self-denying, and inhering in a common experience of union with God attested to by Christians of all ages and in all conditions. For Garden, this ecumenical spirit was not in conflict with a commitment to episcopal and liturgical forms, nor with his partisan loyalty to James VII. In fact, it raises the possibility that for some, James Stuart was regarded as a prophetic figure, standing for mystical catholicity in his vision of universal toleration, but also as a forsaken father, representing a traumatic breach of Christian charity.

This odd interplay between Philadelphian enthusiasm and the spirituality of the nonjurors and Jacobites found its most memorable expression in the person of William Law, who was deeply conscious of his debt to earlier Behmenists such as Lead and Pordage, as well as to the English Platonists and High Church saints.[34] While the leading nonjuring bishop George Hickes may have been partly responsible for making "enthusiasm" a fashionably pejorative label for charismatic and mystical movements, the nonjurors themselves were not immune to mystical and prophetic currents, in which they were immersed both locally and internationally.[35] Christopher Walton's nineteenth-century *Notes and Materials* for a biography of William Law reads like a who's who not only of English Behmenism (Thomas Bromley, Dionysius Freher, Jane Lead, Francis Lee, and John Pordage), but also of the nonjuror party (Henry Dodwell, George Hickes, and Robert Nelson).[36] Böhme's complex exposition of the sacramental mysteries undoubtedly struck a chord with High Church spirituality; it was also the reason why he was eventually disavowed by the Quakers.[37] But there were also more contemporary mystical heroes and heroines, among them, the suffering Quietists in Louis XIV's France.[38] The nonjuror bishop George Hickes was Archbishop Fénelon's translator; he also recommended warmly the second edition of George Stanhope's

Imitatio Christi.[39] In George Garden's Scotland, a large and influential circle of Episcopalian, Jacobite mystics corresponded prolifically with the French Quietists, London Philadelphians, and Dutch followers of Antoinette Bourignon, and certainly regarded these four movements as being part of the same mystical revival.[40] The physician James Keith moved readily between the London and Aberdeenshire circles. Anne Bathurst's extempore hymns, and substantial extracts from her visionary diaries, can be found among the papers of the Ogilvy family, members of the Scottish peerage. They appear alongside volumes containing portions of Madame Guyon's *Short and Easy Method of Prayer* and correspondence with Archbishop Fénelon, Bourignon's foremost disciple Pierre Poiret, and the colorful Jacobite Andrew Ramsay, so instrumental in the development of French Freemasonry.[41]

However, there was also a great deal of intersection between Behmenism and the English Platonists, usually associated with "Latitudinarian" and Whig parties in Anglicanism and, in some cases, Protestant Dissent. Despite Henry More's resistance to Behmenist doctrine, his disciple Lady Anne Conway and her companion Elizabeth Foxcroft were fascinated by Böhme, whose writings may have been partly responsible for the former's eventual conversion to Quakerism.[42] Conway's *Principles of the most Antient and Modern Philosophy* (1692) was also one of the publications advertised in the Philadelphian Society's *Theosophical Transactions*.[43] William Law includes in his "Catalogue of all the Eminent Spiritual or Mystic Writers" Peter Sterry, formerly Cromwell's chaplain and an Independent preacher after the Restoration, and the only Cambridge Platonist to have responded favorably to Böhme.[44] Sterry and his friend Jeremiah White, who can also be numbered among the nonconformist Platonists, were described by Francis Lee as "old Friends" of the Behmenist visionary Jane Lead, and she requested that White give her funeral sermon.[45] The redoubtable Tory Platonist Mary Astell wrote approvingly of the archbishop of Cambrai, expressing her appreciation for the "Noble Simplicity" of his piety, which "consists in a perfect disengagem^t^ from ourselves, as well as from ye World, & a concern to approve ourselves to GOD only."[46] Astell's critic and an intimate of John Locke, Damaris Masham, also wrestled with the mysticism of the Quietists and Baker's *Sanca Sophia*, rejecting the "inward way, or Life of Contemplation," as a blasphemous and inhumane disavowal of reason and the created world. She concluded with Bishop Stillingfleet that "If once an unintelligible Way of Practical Religion become the Standard of Devotion, no Men of Sense and Reason will ever set themselves about it; but leave it to be understood by mad Men, and practis'd by Fools." Crucially, she identified the continental mystics with English Platonism, represented by Mary Astell and John Norris, the main targets of her *Discourse Concerning the Love of God*.[47]

The general appetite for mysticism should be set against the wider context of Protestant renewal, which drew on the inspiration of both ancient and contemporary spiritual writers. High Church reformers in particular looked for a primitive Christianity that was both practical and liturgical: they found it in the Neoplatonic mysticism of Eastern patristics, in the late medieval *Devotio Moderna*, and in Counter-Reformation and Pietist spirituality. Anglicans were not only nourished by spiritual resources in contemporary Western religion. Their fascination with the wisdom of the Eastern church was also a symptom of this ambition to form part of a truly "catholic," living spiritual tradition that cut across the confessional disputes tearing Western Christians apart.

The second of our mystic historiographers was a High-Church man, Edward Stephens, a trained lawyer, and the son-in-law of Judge Matthew Hale. He apparently became a nonjuror late in life. Stephens was an ecumenist in the tradition of James I, and envisioned the healing of the breaches in Christendom, primarily through (in his words) "the Restitution of Catholick Communion between the Greek Churches and the Church of England." Like Francis Lee, he was an enthusiast of Orthodox traditions and boasted of having been admitted to the Greek communion in 1701. The failed attempt to establish a Greek College at Oxford between 1698 and 1705 (recently commemorated at Worcester College) had much to do with Stephens's advocacy, and he was appalled by the shabby treatment of the young monks who had traveled across Europe from Smyrna and Constantinople, only "to be so ill accommodated, both for their Studies and other Necessaries, that some of them staid not many Months."[48] Stephens was also an energetic and eccentric campaigner for the Reformation of Manners, claiming to be its principal instigator, and was responsible for a number of initiatives, including a Religious Society for Single Women and the revival of daily Eucharistic observance in a Gloucester parish.[49]

In his *Theologia Mystica*, published in 1697, Stephens attempted to demonstrate "the Antiquity, Tradition, and Succession, of Mystical Divinity."[50] The essence of this branch of divinity, according to Stephens, was the "experience" of the "Divine Conduct" that guided individual souls by the promptings of conscience and divine love in the same way as the Shekinah led the Israelites through the wilderness into the Promised Land. The goal of the spiritual life was, significantly, the "Acquisition of . . . Love, and not of *Knowledge*."[51] Although Stephens despaired of his generation, apostate as it was in its pursuit of empty rationalism, he noted that

> in this degenerate Age God hath not left himself without Witness, but rais'd up some of a more generous Spirit; such as *Mr. Smith* of Cambridge, the late profound *Dr. Cradoc*, whom I much esteemed for his Generosity, as well as Judgment, in preaching up this Doctrine, who told me, he had Preached 20 or 30 Sermons upon it; and that if we deny that, we may burn our Bibles; for he knew not (he said) what Religion would signifie without it; and the Learned Mr. *Matthew Scrivener*, who hath left us a Discourse concerning Mystical Divinity, Intituled, The Method and Means to a true Spiritual Life, and others; to say nothing of some I know now Living.[52]

It is striking that among these Protestant writers Stephens should list the Welsh Independent Walter Cradock, preacher to the Barebones Parliament and associate of radical ministers including Fifth Monarchists. Cradock's aura of dangerous enthusiasm survived into the eighteenth century, when the first Methodists in Wales were labeled "Cradockites."[53] However, Stephens reserved his greatest warmth for

Catholic mystics, among them Augustine Baker and Serenus Cressy, and the controversialist Abraham Woodhead. Between them, these men were responsible for translating into contemporary English editions of many classic texts of medieval and Counter-Reformation mysticism from the 1660s to the 1680s, among them, Saint Teresa, Julian of Norwich, and the *Cloud of Unknowing*.[54]

The keynotes of Stephens's mysticism, unlike that of the Philadelphians, were obedience, order, sacramental devotion, and the authority of tradition. As he put it:

> Here are no new Speculative Verities or Revelations of Mysteries pretended; no private new-found-out Interpretations of Scripture bragg'd of . . . Here the Established Order of God's Church, and the Unity essential thereto is not prejudiced. Yea, the Inspirations expected and obtained by Pure Internal Prayer do more firmly and unalterably fix Souls under this Obedience, and to this Order and Unity.[55]

External forms were not marginalized by Stephens's mysticism. Indeed, the daily observance of the Eucharist was essential to this spiritual catholicity, not only as a vital link to the worship of the greater part of the Christian world, but also as the act that most purely expressed the mutual love between God in Christ and saved humanity. Stephens believed that the "Neglect of the *daily Sacrifice*" in the Reformed churches, "so manifestly contrary to the Practice of the Catholick Church," had been a diabolical deviation in the Reformation and had brought judgment on the English Church in the form of multiplying divisions and sectarian dissent.[56] By diminishing the highest symbol and vehicle of divine charity, the priority of loving communion had been visibly compromised. The strategic and dramatic solution he proposed was a reunion with the Eastern churches, revising the Anglican liturgy in line with ancient catholic practices (he recommended the 1637 Scottish Prayer Book as the best recent model). According to Stephens, who claimed to have corresponded directly with the ecumenical patriarch, once this was achieved "the Recovery of Cath. Communion with the Greeks would be very easy."[57] The political and apocalyptic significance of such a momentous event in Christian history was not lost on this canny lawyer. "The Restitution of such a Communion," he wrote,

> between the *Greek* Churches (a Communion of themselves of larger Extent than that of the Roman) and the Church of *England*, may by the good Providence of God, prove an Occasion to bring off *our Confederates* from the *Roman* to this, being truly Catholick; which cannot otherwise be expected; and so break the Papal Faction (and without hands) and bring in such a *Universal Reformation*, as has been long since foretold by some, and is much expected by many about this time, and much to be desir'd by all sincere Christians.[58]

In a related spirit of catholicity, a later generation of nonjurors would go on to make unsuccessful overtures to the Eastern patriarchs, through Peter I, between 1712 and 1725.[59]

It is tempting to distinguish between two discrete mystical milieus in English religion on the basis of these two case studies: the first belonging to the world of Catholic and High Church reform, its distinctive emphases being Eucharistic catholicity and conformity; the second, radically anti-formalist, prophetic, and essentially Protestant. Michel de Certeau regards early modern mysticism as a response to cultural bereavement, the traumatic relocation of the sacred from sacraments, scripture, and ecclesial structures to a wholly inward spirituality. In the context of late seventeenth-century Anglicanism, however, there was a synchronism between this anti-institutional mysticism and the kind of sacramental mysticism that flourished in Orthodox, medieval, and Counter-Reformation piety. I consider them as part of the same process by which certain Anglicans responded to apparently fatal divisions in religion, and sought to reinstate charity as the essence of Christian experience. In this limited sense, the rationalist critics of mystical divinity were right to link enthusiasm and popery, but only because Protestant and Catholic mystics collaboratively sought an alternative, inspired pathway in the Enlightenment quest for peace and piety in Christendom.

Notes

1. B.W. Young, "The Way to Divine Knowledge: The Mystical Critique of Rational Religion," in *Religion and Enlightenment in Eighteenth-Century England: Theological Debate from Locke to Burke* (Oxford: Oxford University Press, 1998), 120–66. See also Clarke Garrett, "Swedenborg and the Mystical Enlightenment in Late Eighteenth-Century England," *Journal of the History of Ideas* 45 (1984): 67–68; C. D. A. Leighton, "William Law, Behmenism, and Counter Enlightenment," *Harvard Theological Review* 91 (1998): 301–20.

2. Meric Casaubon, *A treatise concerning enthusiasme, as it is an effect of nature, but is mistaken by many for either divine inspiration, or diabolical possession* (London: Roger Daniel, 1655), chapter III, "Of Contemplative and Philosophicall Enthusiasme."

3. Some examples of the broad and enduring reception of Baker's work among Quakers, Cambridge Platonists, and nonjuror mystics are given in David Lunn, "Augustine Baker (1575–1641) and the English Mystical Tradition," *Journal of Ecclesiastical History* 26, no. 3 (1975): 269–70.

4. Edward Stillingfleet, *A Discourse Concerning the Idolatry Practised in the Church of Rome* (London: Robert White, 1671), 326–28.

5. Gilbert Burnet, *Reflections upon a pamphlet entituled, Some discourses upon Dr. Burnet and Dr. Tillotson* (London: Richard Chiswell, 1697), 86.

6. Abraham Clifford, *Methodus Evangelica, or, The gospel method of Gods saving sinners by Jesus Christ practically explained in XII propositions* (London: for Brabazon Aylmer, 1676), 174.

7. Henry Wharton, *The enthusiasm of the church of Rome demonstrated in some observations upon the life of Ignatius Loyola* (London: Richard Chiswell, 1688), 17, 70.

8. Samuel Wesley, *The life of our blessed Lord & Saviour, Jesus Christ, an heroic poem* (London: Benjamin Motte and Charles Harper, 1693), 70.

9. John Brown, *Quakerisme the path-way to paganisme* (London: for John Cairns, 1678), 430.

10. Edward Hyde, *Animadversions upon a Book, intituled Fanaticism Fanatically Imputed to the Catholic Church, by Dr Stillingfleet* (London: for Richard Royston, 1673), 230–31.

11. On the enduring dynamics of Reformation politics in England, see Jonathan Scott, *England's Troubles: Seventeenth-century English Political Instability in European Context* (Cambridge: Cambridge University Press, 2000).

12. Robert Barclay, *An apology for the true Christian divinity, as the same is held forth, and preached by the people, called, in scorn, Quakers being a full explanation and vindication of their principles and doctrines* (London, 1678), 256.

13. See Henry J. Cadbury, "An Obscure Chapter of Quaker History," *Journal of Religion* 24, no. 3 (1944): 201–13, 203; idem, "Early Quakerism and Uncanonical Lore," *Harvard Theological Review* 40 (1947): 177–205, 193.

14. See, for example, W. K. Jordan, "Sectarian Thought and its Relation to the Development of Religious Toleration, 1640–1660: Part I: 'The Mystics and Enthusiasts,'" *Huntington Library Quarterly* 3, no. 2 (January 1940): 197–223; Jerald C. Brauer, "Puritan Mysticism and the Development of Liberalism," *Church History* 19, no. 3 (September 1950): 151–70; David Knowles, *The English Mystical Tradition* (New York: Harper & Brothers, 1961); Geoffrey F. Nuttall, "Puritan and Quaker Mysticism," *Theology* 78 (October 1975): 519–31.

15. See Nigel Smith, *Perfection Proclaimed: Language and Literature in the English Revolution* (Oxford: Oxford University Press, 1989); Carole Dale Spencer, *Holiness: The Soul of Quakerism; An Historical Analysis of the Theology of Holiness in the Quaker Tradition* (Milton Keynes: Paternoster, 2007).

16. See Kent Emery Jr., "Mysticism and the Coincidence of Opposites in Sixteenth- and Seventeenth-Century France," *Journal of the History of Ideas* 45 (1984): 3–23, 3.

17. Richard Roach, "An Acct of ye Rise & Progress of the Philadelphian Society," in Bod. ms. Rawl. D. 833 (Papers of Richard Roach), fol. 63v.

18. On the fulfillment of Beverley's prophecies, see "An Account of ye Philadelphian Society in England" in Bod. ms. Rawl. D. 833, fols. 83r–v: "There had been a Great Alarm in this Nation; & an Expectation raisd in many, of some Appearance more than Ordinary of ye Power of Christs Kingdom, to be manifested in ye year of our Lord 1697, by ye writings of Mr Tho. Beverly, who had pointed out that year, & even a particular Day in that year viz. ye 23 of August to be signalizd by some Manifestation of ye Power of ye Kingdom . . . Accordingly in a Providential Juncture he unexpectedly was calld out, & an offer made him of Introduction to ye Archbishop of Canterbury . . . This offer was accepted, & ye Person that made it appointed ye Day, wch prov'd to be ye 23 of August, & yt wthout any Design of either of ye Persons concern therein, as has been solemnly declar'd."

19. "An Address and Declaration in Testimony of ye Rising Powers of ye Spirit & Kingdom of Christ offerd to his Grace ye Archbishop of Canterbury & others, Bishops & Clergy of this Land, on ye Twenty third of August in ye year 1697. By R. Roach B. D. in way of Apology to the Church of England, for His Late Proceeding wth ye Philadelphian Society others in Proclamation of the Kingdom of Christ," in Bod. ms. Rawl. D. 833, fols. 6v–7r.

20. Lambeth Palace Library, Gibson ms. 942/141, 12; on Roach's hymn-writing, see, for example, his diary entries for 1706–7, in Bod. ms. Rawl. D. 1152, 1, 30, 89, and *Lyra Davidica or, A Collection of Divine Songs and Hymns, Partly New Composed, partly Translated from the High-German, and Latin Hymns*

(London: for John Walsh, 1708); also Tom Dixon, "Love and Music in Augustan London: The 'Enthusiasms' of Richard Roach," *Eighteenth-Century Music* 4 (2007): 191–209.

21. "Wt are the Philadelphians & wt is ye Ground of their Society?" Bod. ms. Rawl. D. 832, fol. 54v.

22. "December 25 1692," in a volume of "Mrs Ann Bathurst's Writings," Bod. ms. Rawl D. 1263, 525; Richard Roach, *The Great Crisis: or the Mystery of the Times and Seasons Unfolded* (London, 1725), 115.

23. See Robert L. Beare, "Quirinus Kuhlmann: Where and When?" *Modern Language Notes* 77 (1962): 379–97, esp. 380–82.

24. On Kuhlmann, see Klaus Vondung, *The Apocalypse in Germany* (Columbia: University of Missouri Press, 2000), 99; Walter Dietze, *Quirinus Kuhlmann: Ketzer und Poet* (Berlin: Rutten & Loening, 1963).

25. Roach, *Great Crisis*, 106–8. On the Platonists, see C. A. Patrides, *The Cambridge Platonists* (Cambridge: Cambridge University Press, 1969); on Hale, see Alan Cromartie, *Sir Matthew Hale, 1609–1676: Law, Religion and Natural Philosophy* (Cambridge: Cambridge University Press, 1995); on Norris, see W. J. Mander, *The Philosophy of John Norris* (Oxford: Oxford University Press, 2008); on Scougal, see Isabel Rivers, "Scougal's *The Life of God in the Soul of Man:* The Fortunes of a Book, 1676–1830," in *Philosophy and Religion in Enlightenment Britain*, ed. Ruth Savage (Oxford: Oxford University Press, 2012), chapter 2; on Boyle, see Michael Hunter, *Robert Boyle Reconsidered* (Cambridge: Cambridge University Press, 2003).

26. That is, one of those clergymen or office-holders who refused to swear the Oath of Allegiance to William III and Mary II, believing that they were still bound in fealty to the exiled James II.

27. "From the Papers of Francis Lee, 1703," in Christopher Walton, *Notes and Materials for an Adequate Biography of The Celebrated Divine and Theosopher, William Law* (London, 1854), 237–38.

28. Francis Lee, "Proposals Given to Peter the Great, Czar of Muscovy, Anno M. DC. XCVIII," in *Apoleipomena: or, Dissertations Theological, Mathematical and Physical*, I (London, 1752), 1–2, 8–9.

29. Francis Lee and Richard Roach, *Theosophical Transactions by the Philadelphian Society: Consisting of Memoirs, Conferences, Letters, Dissertations & c. For the Advancement of PIETY, and DIVINE PHILOSOPHY* (London, March 1697), 1–2.

30. "Propositions Extracted from the Reasons for the Foundation and Promotion of a *Philadelphian Society*, Which were Read at the First Meeting of the same in *Westmorland* House, *London*," Lambeth Palace Library ms. 942/129, fol. 5.

31. Bod. ms. Rawl. D. 833, fols. 54r–v, 63v.

32. On mystical influences on the Interregnum sects, see Smith, *Perfection Proclaimed*, pt. II.

33. "Copy letter from Dr G[eorge] G[arden] to James Cunningham of Barns, 2 Dec 1709," National Archives of Scotland, GD 248/570/4 .

34. See Walton, *Notes and Materials*.

35. George Hickes, *The Spirit of Enthusiasm Exorcised* (London: for Walter Kettilby, 1680); see Ronald A. Knox, *Enthusiasm: A Chapter in the History of Religion* (Oxford: Clarendon, 1950), 1–8.

36. B. J. Gibbons, *Gender in Mystical and Occult Thought: Behmenism and its Development in England* (Cambridge: Cambridge University Press, 1996), 10, comments that "many Behmenists were Nonjuring and Jacobite in sympathy: Francis Lee, George Cheyne, John Byrom and William Law are all examples." G. H. Henderson, in *Religious Life in Seventeenth Century Scotland* (Cambridge: Cambridge University Press, 1931), 229, also notes that Scottish followers of Antoinette Bourignon tended to be Jacobites. See also John Hoyles, *The Edges of Augustanism: The Aesthetics of Spirituality in Thomas Ken, John Byrom and William Law* (The Hague: Martinus Nijhoff, 1972).

37. Andrew Weeks, *Boehme: An Intellectual Biography of the Seventeenth Century Philosopher and Mystic* (New York: State University of New York Press, 1991), explains how Luther's sacramental theology informed Böhme's system. See esp. 35–60. On Böhme and the Quakers, see Ariel Hessayon, "Jacob Boehme and the Early Quakers," *Journal of the Friends Historical Society* 60 (2005): 191–223.

38. On British links with the Quietists, see G. H. Henderson, *Mystics of the North-East* (Aberdeen: Spalding Club, 1934). Recent scholarship on the Quietist controversy and its reception in Europe includes Ronney Mourad and Dianne Guenin-Lelle, *The Prison Narratives of Jeanne Guyon* (Oxford: Oxford University Press, 2012); and Richard Parish, *Catholic Particularity in Seventeenth-Century French Writing* (Oxford: Oxford University Press, 2011), chapter 7.

39. Thomas à Kempis, *The Christian's Pattern: or the Imitation of Christ*, 2nd ed., book II, trans. George Stanhope (London: William Redmayne and Samuel Keble, 1710), "The Epistle Dedicatory." See Walton, *Notes and Materials*, 238.

40. See Henderson, *Mystics of the North-East*.

41. National Archives of Scotland, Seafield papers, GD 248/563; CH 12/20. For Bathurst's hymns and visions, see CH 12/20/9.

42. See Sarah Hutton, *Anne Conway: A Woman Philosopher* (Cambridge: Cambridge University Press, 2004), 65–66. Elizabeth Foxcroft was the sister of the leading Cambridge Platonist, Benjamin Whichcote.

43. See Paula McDowell, "Enlightenment Enthusiasms and the Spectacular Failure of the Philadelphian Society," *Eighteenth Century Studies* 35, no. 24 (2002): 515–33, at 531.

44. See N. I. Matar, "Peter Sterry and Jacob Boehme," *Notes and Queries* 231 (1986): 33–36; Emmanuel College, Sterry ms. I. fol. 385. Law was ambivalent about Henry More's mystical credentials, however, and is reported to have commented that "Many good things may be said of Dr More, as a pious christian, and of great abilities. But he was a *Babylonian philosopher* and divine, a bigot to the Cartesian system, knew nothing deeper than an hypothesis, nor truer of the nature of the soul than that which he has said of its pre-existence, which is little better than that foolish brat descended from it, the transmigration of souls. I know no other name for his 'Divine Dialogues', than a jumble of learned rant, heathenish babble, and gibberish, dashed or heated here and there with flashes of piety. His after sentiments of J[acob]. B[oehme]. are in his 'Philosophiae Teutonicae Censura', both in the preface and the tract. I never read it in his works, but only as recited in a German editor of J. B. . . . What you have seen of his severity against the light within, (which is, in other words, *God within*,) is sufficient to determine his character with you." Walton, *Notes and Materials*, 162.

45. See Letters of Francis Lee, Lambeth Palace Library ms. 1559, fol. 24. White had also preached at Ann Bathurst's funeral.

46. "Letter XXX: To Lady Ann Coventry, 1/8/1720," "Mary Astell's Letters, 1693–1730," in *The Celebrated Mary Astell: An Early English Feminist*, ed. Ruth Perry (Chicago: University of Chicago Press, 1986), 389.

47. James G. Buickerood, ed., *The Philosophical Writings of Damaris Masham* (Bristol: Thoemmes, 2004), 1–7, 120–26.

48. Edward Stephens, "A Good and Necessary Proposal for the Restitution of Catholick Communion between the Greek Churches and the Church of England," 1705, in Lambeth Palace Library mss. 935/30 and 938/13. See Peter M. Doll, ed., *Anglicanism and Orthodoxy: 300 Years after the 'Greek College' in Oxford* (Oxford: Oxford University Press, 2006), esp. appendix F, 513–26; see also Nicholas Keene, "John Earnest Grabe, Biblical Learning and Religious Controversy in Early Eighteenth-Century England," *Journal of Ecclesiastical History* 58 (2007): 656–74.

49. Edward Stephens, *The More Excellent Way: Or, a Proposal of a Compleat Work of Charity* (London, 1696), 1; see also *A Letter to a Lady, Concerning the Due Improvement of her Advantages of Celibacie, Portion, and Maturity of Age and Judgement* (London: for the Religious Society of Single Women, 1695).

50. Edward Stephens, *Theologica Mystica: Two Discourses concerning Divine Communications to Souls Duly Disposed* (London: for the author, 1697), 1.

51. Stephens, *Theologica Mystica*, preface and 56.

52. Stephens, *Theologica Mystica*, preface.

53. See Geraint H. Jenkins, *The Foundations of Modern Wales, 1642–1780* (Oxford: Oxford University Press, 1993).

54. See, for instance, Abraham Woodhead, *The Life of the Holy Mother St. Teresa, Foundress of the Reformation of the Discalced Carmelites According to the Primitive Rule* (London, 1671); Serenus Cressy, *XVI Revelations of Divine Love, Shewed to a Devout Servant of God, called Mother Julian* (London, 1670); Justin McCann, ed., *The Cloud of Unknowing and Other Treatises*, with preface by Augustine Baker (London: Burns and Oates, 1947).

55. Stephens, *Theologica Mystica*, 30–31.

56. Stephens, *Questions Concerning the Proper and Peculiar Christian Worship*, Lambeth Palace Library ms. 938/2, 1–4.

57. Stephens, letter to Convocation dated December 12, 1705, Lambeth Palace Library ms. 929/131, fol. 2v.

58. Stephens, "Good and Necessary Proposal," 2.

59. See Judith Pinnington, *Anglicans and Orthodox: Unity and Subversion 1559–1725* (Herefordshire: Gracewing, 2003), 156–97.

8

Seraphic Discourse, Mystical Bodies

John Austin's Original Psalms

Alison Shell

Heightened religious experiences may be personal, but they need not happen in private. William James's famous definition of religion as "the feelings, acts, and experiences of individual men in their solitude, so far as they apprehend themselves to stand in relation to whatever they may consider the divine" bears qualification on many fronts, particularly, perhaps, the large-scale communal ecstatic experiences that have characterized much Christian worship and so often heralded religious revival.[1] From Pentecost onwards, religious ecstasy has also occurred within small and select groups of Christian worshipers; this essay gives an account of an early modern Catholic liturgist, John Austin (1613–69), whose aim was to evoke mystical sensation in this context, especially through the use of original psalms.[2]

Austin's *Devotions in the Ancient Way of Offices* (1st ed., 1668) was a liturgical compilation inspired—as the title indicates—by the Daily Office, but freely adapted for the use of devout laymen and laywomen.[3] Within the book, Matins, Lauds, Vespers, and Compline are given for all days of the week and for various festivals. Each service, like its monastic model, is made up of versicles and responses, Bible readings, metrical hymns, prayers, and psalms; the latter, significantly, are not taken from the book of Psalms but are original compilations.[4] Compiled in the first instance for limited use among Austin's Catholic associates, the *Devotions* circulated widely in manuscript, then ran through several editions from Catholic presses. When reformed twice for a Protestant readership in the late seventeenth century, it achieved even greater popularity. Its various Protestant editors were strikingly diverse in sympathy: Theophilus Dorrington, who issued the *Reformed Devotions* in 1686, was an Anglican clergyman; Susanna Hopton, who worked on a more lightly edited version of the *Devotions*, was an Anglican who converted briefly to Catholicism; while George Hickes, who saw Hopton's revised edition through to publication, was a nonjuror.[5] If the book had a similarly broad appeal to other readers, this would help to explain why the *Devotions* sold well throughout much of the eighteenth century.

Well-affected worshipers working through the book would have participated in a sequence of intimate, confessional occasions that, at many points, referred directly to the privations experienced by Catholics in seventeenth-century England; they would also have aspired toward a shared mystical experience that owed much to contemporary ideals of spiritual affinity, particularly through the original psalms that form the main focus of this essay. These contain a performative evocation of transcendental experience, the effect of which is heightened by the breaking of metrical bounds in a manner that pastiches Old Testament psalmody, but also looks forward to free verse.

Original Psalms

The phrase "original psalm" has two possible meanings: religious verse that pastiches the unrhymed, parallelistic effect of biblical psalms, using nothing but rearranged texts from the book of Psalms or from elsewhere in scripture, or verse of a similar kind that intermingles portions of scripture and biblical reference with original reflection.[6] Also known as "private psalms," the latter had been composed from the early days of Christianity; ironically in view of the genre's later importance within recusant writing, the Catholic Church tended to be wary of them because they were often associated with heretical groups, but occasional examples, like *Gloria in excelsis Deo* (Glory be to God on high) found a place in mainstream worship.[7] Psalms drawn exclusively from the Bible were a fairly common form of devotional literature in sixteenth- and seventeenth-century England, private psalms less so; both cross over with the genre of meditation, though could also be seen as bypassing it. Austin's contemporary Gertrude More, whose devotional exercises are parallelistic in the manner of original psalms, believed that these "Ideots Devotions" offered a more direct route to God than other kinds of prayer, "for such as fervently and simply with all their affections, desire to aspire after God in the Cloud of faith and feelings of Love without troubleinge themselves with busye and impertinent operations of the understandinge, commonly called Meditatio[n]s or discourses of the understandinge, to move and excite the will; which in the case of these devine & Seraphicke Ideots, are superfluous, they beinge alreadye sufficiently, yea aboundantly excited and bent to love God."[8]

Psalm-texts have, of course, been widely deployed within Judeo-Christian writing at all dates, and Austin's era was no exception to this. Helen C. White summarizes the use of psalms in early modern devotional literature as follows: "Like their predecessors in antiquity and the Middle Ages the devotional writers of the 16th century began to make their selections from the Psalms and to arrange and re-arrange them in new contexts and compositions. So again the text of Scripture became the springboard for fresh devotional creation. And the themes and the phrases of the Psalms were handled with increasing freedom until they came to furnish not so much the source as the very language and idiom of fresh creation."[9] As she also remarks, the freer compositions in this idiom "have a way of glancing on and off the text of the Bible that is endlessly teasing . . . the fruit of a tradition so pervasive as to constitute almost a language rather than a source."[10] Nevertheless, Austin's contributions to the genre are distinctive for several reasons. First, they were explicitly intended for shared worship rather than private prayer—something in which Austin may have been anticipated by a co-religionist, Ralph Buckland, whose work he probably knew.[11] Second, while the *Devotions* does quote heavily from the book of Psalms and other biblical texts, it frequently veers from scriptural precedent in the interests of pursuing contemporary relevance: one example among many of post-Reformation English Catholics' ability to innovate under constraint.[12] Lastly, the psalms' tone is unique: fervently moralistic, permanently reflexive, as intimate and ardent as any contemporary love-poem, and surely giving us an insight into how Austin himself wished to appear before God.

Philip H. Pfatteicher, one of the few scholars to have studied Austin, has noted the way in which his psalms follow homiletic norms, progressing from general statement to an exposition of the meaning, and lastly to personal application. This trajectory connects the psalms set for each part of the Daily Office, and can be observed within individual psalms. Put another way, the psalms direct the congregation to recite a biblical text, then articulate the orthodox response to it, and finally adjure the reader to mean what they have just said; in this, they manifest a sophisticated understanding of what, following the example of Austin's namesake, our own age terms "performativity."[13] The following quotation, taken from "Compline for our B[lessed] Saviour," gives a flavor of this:

> My God, when I remember those words of Thine *Repent, for the Kingdom of Heav'n is at hand*:
> When I consider they were the first thou speakest in publick; the chosen text of the Eternal Wisdom:
> Instantly I'm struck with the importance of the duty; and deeply affected with the power of the motive.
> If what this last line says be not wholly true; but repeated in course, as a form of devotion:
> Forgive, dear Lord, the deceitfulnes of my heart; and make me think as well as say my Prayers.
> Make me apply those searching words to my self, and bind them fast on my own soul,
> Repent, O my soul, for the Kingdom of Heav'n is at hand; repent, for the Kingdom of Heav'n depends on thy repentance.[14]

This is designed to foment a heightened, reflexive self-awareness extending even to the details of one's physical carriage and breathing, and indeed the psalm for Monday Matins warns the speakers to be mindful of their deportment and concentration:

> While we are alone, He minds our contrivings; and the ends we aim at in all our Studies:
> When we converse with others, He observes our deportment; and the good or ill we do them, or our selves;
> In our devotions he notes our carriage; and regards with what attention we recite our pray'rs.
> . . . Thou appear'st still ready to punish our sins; that the shake of thy Rod may prevent our miseries.
> Sure, O my God, thy favours must needs be sweet; since even thy threatnings have so much mercy. (59–60)

Part of Austin's audacity is to point out the disadvantages of set prayers; the psalms quoted above have a disconcertingly mind-reading quality in the way they call a wandering mind back to its orisons. Another original psalm, from the "Compline for our Blessed Saviour," gently but unmistakably curbs the natural tendency when reciting an office to measure with one's eye how far one has got, and how much there is to come; Austin asks his audience how they can begrudge any apportionment of their time, where divine wisdom is in question:

> Hark but this one word more, and you'l stay too; if any sense of your eternal good can hold you.
> Hark how he kindly tels us this new and glorious Secret: *We shall be hereafter like the Angels in Heav'n.*
> O sweet and precious word to them that relish it, and thoroughly digest its strong nourishment.
> To them that feed on't often as their daily bread; *We shall be hereafter like the Angels in Heav'n.* (337)

In one of the original psalms set for Monday Matins, the problem is addressed most directly of all, ending in a re-endorsement of the Daily Office as a quotidian means of keeping oneself up to the mark:

> But, O improvident we! how unwilling to pray * are most of us always, and all of us sometimes.[15]
> How do our little Offices seem long and tedious, and half an hour quite tire our Patience!
> How are we slow to begin, and swift to make an end; how heavy while they are saying, and glad when they are said! . . .
> Often, O dreadful Lord! when we speak to Thee, we do not so much as hear ourselvs:
> Often we pursue impertinent objects; and our careless thoughts contradict our words.
> But, O thou blessed End of all our labors, and only Center of all our wishes!
> Do thou reclaim our wandring fancies; and guide and fix them to attend thy service.
> Night and Day let us call on Thee; and never cease knocking at the Doors of thy Palace. (62)

This finds a different experiential focus in one of the original psalms set for Tuesday Matins. The familiar cycle of text repetition and spiritual reflection, here with a constellation of references to the beginnings of psalms—Psalm 69, 115, and 127—is used to figure the suppliant's dependence on God; just as the breath-control of the congregation members depends entirely on God's goodwill, so they live entirely through the spiritual breath of life imparted by the scriptures:

> Not unto us, O Lord, not unto us; but to thine own blest Name give all the glory.[1]
> When we have apply'd our utmost cares, and us'd all the diligence that lies in our power:
> What can we do, but look up to Thee; and second our endeavours with pray'rs for thy blessing? . . .
> We know, and Thou thy self has taught us; unless Thou defend'st the City, the Guard watches in vain.[2]
> We know, and our own experience tells us; unless thou reach forth thy hand, we are presently in danger of sinking.[3]

> Every moment of our day subsists by Thee; and every step we take moves by thy strength.
> Even the line we now repeat, must beg its breath of Thee; and stop if thou deny'st it. (93–94)[16]

In their consciousness of the process of reading, of both acceptable and unacceptable modes of worship, and of the physical conditions under which Daily Offices are recited, these texts manifest an extraordinary degree of performative sophistication, and would surely have encouraged a high degree of intimacy among their users. Here, Austin is surely feeding off the notion of Neoplatonic spiritualized friendship.[17] While this had many outworkings in the religious literature of seventeenth-century England, it was especially associated in Austin's time with Robert Boyle's *Some Motives of the Love of God, better known as Seraphic Love*. Composed in the 1640s and printed in 1659, this work urges its readers to convert human passion into religious devotion, and as Frances Harris has commented in her study of the spiritual friendship between John Evelyn and Margaret Godolphin, it popularized the term "seraphic love" as a way to describe spiritual intimacy between individuals.[18] The *Devotions* is predicated on personal closeness to such an extent that the term seems appropriate for it too; its emphasis on shared confessional disclosure, and more generally the quasi-monastic bonding experience of saying the Offices at all, would have exquisitely fomented the kind of passionate religious friendship that the word "seraphic" connotes.

Religious intimacy between two individuals is, though, only one connotation of "seraphic." While the concept would have sanctified special friendships of a kind perhaps more possible to laymen than to members of a religious order, the celibate Gertrude More uses the term simply to denote those who love God.[19] As a description of ardent, refined, spiritualized earthly love that seemed to offer a glimpse of heaven, the word had a long pedigree within Christian devotion, often as part of the phrase "seraphic fire," signifying the ardent worship of the seraphim.[20] The way in which seraphs could model the devout believer's ideal response to God can be seen in a passage from Saint Francis de Sales's devotional writing:

> And here, the soule ravished with admiration, sings the song of sacred silence. *Unto thy peerlesse worth / Silence doth sing, / Th'Hymne of Admiration / O Sion's Kinge*. For so Isaie his Seraphins, adoring and praising God, vayled their faces and feete, confessing therein theire want of sufficiencie, sufficiently to contemplate or serve him: for our feete, whereon we goe, signifies service. Howbeit they flie with two wings in the continuall motion of Complacence and Benevolence, their Love resting in that delightfull unrest.[21]

The early modern examples of "seraphic" given in the *Oxford English Dictionary* confirm that the word was most often used as a technical term denoting heightened religious ecstasy, a state which, for all its exemplary power, often made contemporary commentators nervous. Austin's editor George Hickes describes Austin's work as combining "the highest flights of Devotion, with Liturgical Gravity, in a seraphick, but sober Style" (fol. a2b); his qualification indicates how the term could have pejorative connotations among those whose preference was for orderliness in worship.[22] This wariness could be denominationally inflected too. Non-Catholics, even where they were sympathetic to Catholicism, would have associated Catholics with some level of indiscriminate devotion, and notions of unbounded worship, however enticing, would have had to be checked accordingly. Anglican anxieties are, for instance, clearly to the fore in Susanna Hopton's revision of the *Devotions*, of which Nathaniel Spinckes wrote that:

> the Divine Temper of her Soul . . . led her to make Choice of a Book of such unusual Flights of Devotion, such rapturous Fancy, and such highly affecting Expressions, as are rarely, if ever, to be met with in any work of merely humane Composure. It was no little Time and Pains that she laid out, in correcting these seraphick Offices, purging out what was offensive in their original Draught, and fitting them for the use of all well-disposed Members of the Church of England, whereby to elevate their Souls to God.[23]

Hopton's manuscript annotations to the 1672 edition of the *Devotions* survive, and together with the printed revisions, illustrate precisely how high one High-Church woman felt she could go. For instance, as part of a general drive to eliminate allusions to the active mediation of saints and the Virgin Mary's intercession, she cuts the following reference to virgin saints: "Praise [God] in the Angelical purity of Virgins, whose hearts he enflam'd with his divine charity. / That they might kindle ours with the same chast fire; the same fervent love to the Spouse of our souls."[24]

Though the *Devotions* clearly had a robust life above and beyond its original users, it may be relevant to consider Austin's known friendship patterns here. On a memorial plaque in Holy Trinity Church, Baswich, put up by William Fowler in 1700 to commemorate his family, Austin is described as buried near one Walter Fowler—a funerary practice commonly used to indicate special friendship or sworn brotherhood between two men.[25] If the *Devotions* was ever said at the now demolished Fowler family home at St Thomas's Priory, "a part-medieval and part-Tudor complex of buildings" built, as the name suggests, on the site of a former Augustinian priory, this would only have heightened its quasi-monastic flavor.[26] Moreover, the writer of the preface to the *Devotions* envisages use by a pair of worshipers; Alan Bray has remarked on how sharing the Eucharist was often the sign of special friendship between two individuals, and in the same spirit, it is easy to imagine the fervent dual experience of the *Devotions* as repeatedly consecrating an attachment.[27] No proof has yet been found that Austin's friendship with Fowler inspired the *Devotions*, but the possibility is an intriguing one.

If there seems a contradiction between the idea of seraphic worship and the set nature of the *Devotions*, this may be because we underestimate the feelings that liturgical recitation and singing could excite. Certainly, contemporary writing on the topic of coterie worship does encourage a quest for the affective extremities of religious devotion. Josiah Woodward, for instance, wrote in his study of religious societies: "Let us therefore now strain up our Affections to the highest pitch; and so sing the Praises of God in Heart and Spirit, . . . that Angels and Saints may join with us now, and we with them for evermore."[28] Suggestively, Woodward is speaking about the correct way to approach psalm-singing. On the one hand—as I argue below—the free style of psalms lent itself well to evoking religious unboundedness, while on the other, their scriptural source and their liturgical deployment legitimized the sensation. Austin veered away from scriptural authority in writing his own psalms, yet to his admirers, his raptures remained allowable, a circumstance that surely validates the liturgical nature of his endeavor.

Liturgy is generally taken to be a means of containing and controlling worship, not of breaking bounds, but a compelling quality of the *Devotions* is its sustained tension between private ecstasy and communal decorum. Again this is well illustrated by Spinckes, who quotes with approval the sentiment that Austin's work was designed "not only to excite, but to govern and regulate Devotion; not only raising the Dull, quickening the Sluggish, and warming the Frozen Spirits, but tempering the Fervour of over hot Votaries, and securing them with great Art against the Enthusiasm of their Tempers, and from running into the Reveries, and rapturous Excesses of mystical Devotion."[29] Mysticism and enthusiasm, both opprobrious terms here, are seen as predisposing a worshiper to private "Reveries" which, it is implied, the set words and liturgical framing do much to "govern and regulate"; the comment may also acknowledge the checks imposed by the patternings of parallelism.[30]

The divergent implications of parallelism and rhyme can be seen in the marked—if not invariable—difference of subject-matter and tone between hymns and psalms in the *Devotions*. In general, the former have a moralistic quality, and deal with quotidian Christian experience. The psalms, on the other hand, strive for a seraphic effect; God's glory and man's inability to express it are emphasized, and spiritual ecstasy is invoked via notions of intimacy between God and mankind. The "Compline for the Blessed Virgin," for instance, portrays Mary as a lover pining for her beloved:

> Often she thought of her treasure in Heav'n, and silently longed to go and enjoy it.
> Often she counted the tedious minutes of her stay, and with an amorous Impatience chid their slownes:
> Which kept her on the rack of delayed hope; her and her lov'd Son still asunder:

> Till all on fire with love, and wrought up to desires, * too strong to be longer imprisoned in Clay:
> Like an active spark from fiercest flames, she broak out from her flesh to shine with God for ever. (423)

In the context of Catholic worship, the metaphor of the rack would have had a particular charge, something that is also illustrated in a passage from the Matins for the Holy Ghost, which imparts a blatantly recusant agenda to the apostles' evangelical activity after Pentecost:

> They, who thorough fear forsook their Lord! and fled all away from the danger of being his,
> Now rejoyce in suffering for his Name; and neither life nor death can forbid them to confess him . . .
> They, who, even after our Saviour's Resurrection, shut fast the dores for fear of the Jews;
> Now, in the open streets and publick Synagogues, confidently proclaim the Name of JESUS.
> These were new Bottles fill'd with new wine; that made them quite forget their former selvs.
> Wine that exalted them into a generous Spirit * of despising all things for love of JESUS.
> Wine that, in the midst of Racks and Prisons, made them often break forth into that sweet extasy,
> No joy like the pain of suff'ring for JESUS, no life like the death indur'd for his love.
> O were there now such tongues of fire, to kindle in the world those divine flames!
> O were there now such hearts in the world; to receive the holy sparks that fall from Heav'n! (349–50)

In this passage, Austin may be referring back to the work of Ralph Buckland, whose original psalms were printed around 1604 under the title *Seaven Sparkes of the Enkindled Soule*. The book's epigraph, "In my meditation breaketh out fire," is taken from the book of Psalms and heralds frequent incendiary metaphors within Buckland's own work, such as the declaration that God "will come as a flame: that bursteth out beyond the fornace" (33).[31] According to Anthony Wood, these inspired James Ussher to claim that Buckland had prior knowledge of the Gunpowder Plot; but a less paranoid explanation is that both Buckland and Austin were exploiting the linkage of the psalm genre with fiery seraphic devotion.[32]

Psalms were associated with the heights, extremes, and limits of religious language because they were thought of as qualitatively different from, and more exalted than, other kinds of sacred verse. Humphrey Sydenham, for instance, equates psalmody with spiritual ambitiousness, following Saint Augustine, who separated the commands *cantate* and *psallite* in Psalm 104: "hee sings to God that barely professes him, he Psalmes it that obeys him; the one is but Religion voyc'd, the other done."[33] Though the distinction here is between degrees of fervor rather than between the psalm and other sorts of spiritual song, it has obvious generic implications. As Stella Revard has remarked, the Psalms were often seen by early modern literary critics as the church's equivalent to Pindar's odes; a vatic authority was ascribed to both Pindar and David, thanks to their combination of divine subject matter with a free style of versification.[34] Other scriptural matter could be seen in this light too: describing the Benedicite, Francis de Sales praised its "glorious Psalmist, [who], wholy moved by a holily irregular passion to praise God, goes without order leaping from heaven to earth, from thence to heaven againe, invoking pel-mel, Angels, fishes, mountaines, Waters, Dragons, Birdes, Serpents, Fire, Haile, Fogges, assembling by his desires all creaturs" and visualized the devout soul as imitating David: "who having environed, and as it were in Spirite runne over the wo[n]ders of the divine goodnesse, sacrificed upon the Altar of his heart the mysticall Hoste of the out-cryes thereof in Canticles and Psalmes of admiration and Benediction."[35] Here, Christians are invited to stretch their devotion to the limits by using the rhapsodical freedoms of scripture.

But as Austin seems to have been well aware, irregularity without scriptural warrant was a more dangerous thing. There is a crucial distinction between the sensations that he invites worshipers to experience and the relative flatness of what he actually puts on the page; one could argue that this is due to his limitations as a writer, but given his overall affective sophistication, it seems plausible that these are limitations consciously upheld. His is a didactic route to ecstasy: instructing, not showing, in a way that present-day literary scholars have been trained not to value, but appropriate to the liturgical occasion of which the psalms form part. Indeed, given how far Austin went, it was probably wise of him not to go further. His work would not have been so widely adopted if, like that of his more radical Protestant contemporaries, it had mimicked the wilder flights of religious ecstasy, rather than merely summoning them and giving them space to act.[36]

The sense that Austin is "seraphic but sober," to be praised as much for his restraint as for his ardor, illustrates a nervousness, common at this date, about where mystical experience might lead. Sometimes this was articulated even by those who, like Austin's Catholic contemporaries, would have enthusiastically endorsed the contemplative life as practiced by those in religious orders under appropriate spiritual direction. Certainly, the experimental spiritualities of 1650s England appear to have alarmed the Benedictine Serenus Cressy. Introducing a treatise by another member of his order, the mystical writer Augustine Baker, he reflects how the "frantick Spirits of this Age doe falsely make *pretended Inspirations* the cause and ground of all the miseries and mischeifes of late hapning in our Nation."[37] This is echoed by a third Benedictine, Leander Norminton, in verses prefixed to the frontispiece portrait of Baker:

> [S]ome have falsely thought his sober flame
> With those Wild-fires that haunt our Isle, the same[.]
> So Idolls to Church-pictures like may be,
> And fondest love resemble Charity.[38]

Baker did much to preserve and recast medieval mystical writing, and Austin is, like him, an assiduous updater of the Catholic heritage with a pronounced interest in mystical experience; it is no coincidence that both are praised for sobriety by their contemporary admirers, as a way of distancing them from the era's wilder religious experiments.

Despite Austin's real originality, this is probably what he would have wished too. Pastiches of psalms and canticles could inspire poetic indecorum, as Christopher Smart—not coincidentally, a poet much inflected by the radical religionists of Austin's time—was to prove in the next century; his long ecstatic hymn *Jubilate Agno* practices parallelism, has the Benedicite as a constant point of reference, and could certainly, to recall Car's translation of de Sales, be described as "moved by a holily irregular passion."[39] Critics still debate about whether Smart's poetry is to be seen as that of madman, or as feigning mad utterance, or as consciously experimental: a writer who was, like Austin, more interested in conveying ecstatic opportunities to others than in expressing his own sensations of God could not have risked such ambiguity.

Imaginative praxis often runs ahead of critical theory, and Austin can be added to the list of writers who discovered, through pastiche and devotional creativity, something of the governing principle behind biblical parallelism well before Robert Lowth gave definitive shape to it in the late eighteenth century.[40] As has been well documented, Lowth's treatise *De sacra poesi Hebraeorum* (1753) was highly influential, not only on Smart but on later notions of sublimity current among Romantic writers.[41] The figure of the poet as prophet is central to Romantic poetry, and poets of that era are just as preoccupied as mystics with the limits of language and experience. Nevertheless, there is a broadly secularizing agenda to the opinions shared by so many poets of the period: a tendency toward universalism, a suspicion of ecclesiastical in-fighting, a quasi-sacred view of the poetic vocation.[42] Austin was neither a priest nor a member of a religious order, and the *Devotions*, designed for the use of other laymen, strongly implies that he believed mystical experience too good to be left to the professionals; yet this laicization of ecstasy went well beyond what he would have approved.[43] Still, it was the way ahead, and can be seen as reaching its logical conclusion in modernist writing: the period when the poet, if not altogether replacing the priest in practice, is widely perceived as having done so, and when, after a series of false starts, free verse becomes mainstream.

If the book of Psalms suggested the possibility of verse that used neither rhyme nor classically inspired quantitative meter, and if original psalms made visible the option of original composition in a free, accentual, and parallelistic mode, then Austin, who pushed the genre to its limits, is a figure of real significance in the prehistory of free verse.[44] Even while making this claim, one must not exaggerate it; Austin's work is still circumscribed by grammar on the one hand, and the requirements of antiphonal delivery on the other. More important still, a writer who sank into obscurity from the late eighteenth century on is unlikely to have had any direct influence on modernist metrical experimentation, and there is no reason to believe that he did.[45] Yet the use made of biblical verse by, for instance, Walt Whitman and the Imagist proponents of *vers libre* gives us fascinating analogies to Austin's poetic practice. As a recent commentator has put it, Whitman's *Leaves of Grass* exploits "a kind of experimental verse cast in unrhymed long lines with no identifiable metre, the voice an uncanny combination of oratory, journalism and the Bible"; F. S. Flint, describing the genesis of the Imagist movement, remarked on how poets associated with the movement believed poetics could be revivified by imitating "poems in a sacred Hebrew form."[46] Like Austin, these early practitioners of free verse used biblical poetics for countercultural ends; like him, they aspired toward truth and transcendence through stretching and abandoning conventional meter. The *Devotions*, in sum, is an extraordinarily diachronic literary event—a quintessentially medieval form of worship remodeled for the use of post-Reformation English Catholics, in a way that anticipates the metrical and mental unshacklings of modernism.

Notes

I am grateful to the following people for help with this essay: Alan Ford, Helen Hackett, Arnold Hunt, Elisabeth Leedham-Green, Arthur Marotti, and the editors of this volume.

1. William James, *The Varieties of Religious Experience*, ed. Martin E. Marty (1982; New York: Penguin, 1985), 31. See also Gretchen L. Finney, "Ecstasy and Music in 17th-Century England," *Journal of the History of Ideas* 8, no. 2 (1947): 153–86.

2. See J. and F. Blom, "Austin, John [*pseud.* William Birchley]," *Oxford Dictionary of National Biography*.

3. On this and similar initiatives, see Philip F. Pfatteicher, "John Austin: A Liturgist Worth Remembering," *Worship* 42, no. 5 (1968): 299–302, drawing on the same author's "The Life and Writings of John Austin, 1613–1669" (Ph.D. diss., University of Pennsylvania, 1966); Edgar Hoskins, *Horae Beatae Mariae Virginis* (London: Longmans, Green, 1901), 309–46; and Joannes Maria Blom, *The Post-Tridentine English Primer* (1979; London: Catholic Record Society, 1982), esp. chapters 6 and 7. Saint Francis de Sales's writing, which explored the ways in which laymen and laywomen could lead a holy life, was influential in mid-seventeenth-century England: see John Spurr, *The Restoration Church of England, 1646–1689* (New Haven, Conn.: Yale University Press, 1991), 372–73. On monastic styles of worship within English Protestantism, see the bibliography to Nicholas Cranfield's *Oxford Dictionary of National Biography* entry for Nicholas Ferrar, founder of the Little Gidding community.

4. On Austin as a pioneering post-Reformation hymnodist, see my "Intimate Worship: John Austin's *Devotions in the Ancient Way of Offices*," chapter 12 in *Private and Domestic Devotion in Early Modern Britain*, ed. Alec Ryrie and Jessica Martin (Farnham, Surrey: Ashgate, 2012).

5. On the Hopton-Hickes adaptation, see Shell, "Intimate Worship," and Julia J. Smith, ed., "Susanna Hopton," in *The Early Modern Englishwoman: A Facsimile Library of Essential Works*, 2 vols., ed. Betty S. Travitsky and Anne Lake Prescott (Aldershot: Ashgate, 2010), 1:xiii–xvi. On the churchmanship of Dorrington, Hopton, and Hickes, see their respective *Oxford Dictionary of National Biography* entries by Jim Spivey, Julia J. Smith, and Theodor Harmsen. On nonjurors' interest in liturgy, see Ruth M. Wilson, *Anglican Chant and Chanting in England, Scotland and America, 1660–1820* (Oxford: Clarendon, 1996), 129.

6. On the related genre of cento, see *Oxford English Dictionary* (first citation dated 1646). On parallelism, see James L. Kugel, *The Idea of Biblical Poetry: Parallelism and its History* (New Haven, Conn.: Yale University Press, 1981), and Adele Berlin, *The Dynamics of Biblical Parallelism* (Bloomington: Indiana University Press, 1985). For Renaissance knowledge of psalm-meter, see Israel Baroway, "The Bible as Poetry in the English Renaissance: An Introduction," *Journal of English and Germanic Philology* 32 (1933): 447–80, and "The Accentual Theory of Hebrew Poetry: A Further Study in Renaissance Interpretation of Biblical Form," *English Literary History* 17, no. 2 (1950): 115–35. For an example of type 1, see "A psalme for a private fast," in Daniel Featley, *Ancilla Pietatis: or, the Hand-Maid to Private Devotion* (1625; London, 1628), 695–99; for an example of type 2, see the meditations in *Eikon Basilike*, long attributed to Charles I: see the edition by Jim Daems and Holly Faith Nelson (Ontario: Broadview, 2006), 17–21 (discussing questions of authorship) and 26 (on the use of the psalms in original meditation). Prayers from *Eikon Basilike* were set to

music by John Wilson: see Kevin Sharpe, "'An Image Doting Rabble': The Failure of Republican Culture in 17th-Century England," in *Refiguring Revolutions: Aesthetics and Politics from the English Revolution to the Romantic Revolution*, ed. Kevin Sharpe and Steven N. Zwicker (Berkeley: University of California Press, 1998), 25–56, at 33.

7. Pierre Battifol, *History of the Roman Breviary*, trans. Atwell M. Y. Baylay (London: Longmans, Green, 1912), 6–7.

8. *The Holy Practises of a Devine Lover or the Sainctly Ideots Devotions* (1657), 24. The title alludes to another term for private psalms, *psalmi idiotici*: see Arthur F. Marotti's essay in this volume. At this date the word "ideot" had several meanings: the pejorative one with which we are still familiar, and a more neutral designation referring to the laity or to the unlearned, used especially by Catholic authors: see my "The 16th- and 17th-Century 'Lives' of Edmund Gennings," *Recusant History* 30, no. 2 (2010): 213–27.

9. *The Tudor Books of Private Devotion* (1951; Westport, Conn.: Greenwood, 1979), 233. The "psalters" attributed to Saint Jerome and Saint Augustine are discussed in chapter 3.

10. *Tudor Books of Private Devotion*, 49.

11. See Josephine Evetts-Secker, "An Elizabethan Experiment in Psalmody: Ralph Buckland's *Seaven Sparkes of the Enkindled Soule*," *Sixteenth Century Journal* 15, no. 3 (1984): 311–26, and "Jerusalem and Albion: Ralph Buckland's *Seaven Sparkes of the Enkindled Soule*," *Recusant History* 20, no. 2 (1990): 149–63. See also further in this essay.

12. See Lisa McClain, *Lest We Be Damned: Practical Innovation and Lived Experience among Catholics in Protestant England, 1559–1642* (New York: Routledge, 2004), and my *Oral Culture and Catholicism in Early Modern England* (Cambridge: Cambridge University Press, 2007), conclusion.

13. J. L. Austin, *How to Do Things with Words: The William James Lectures Delivered at Harvard University in 1955*, ed. J. O. Urmson and Marina Sbisà (Oxford: Oxford University Press, 1976). For a recent introduction to speech-act theory, see James Loxley, *Performativity* (London: Routledge, 2007). On performativity and early modern worship, see Ramie Targoff, *Common Prayer: Models of Public Devotion in Early Modern England* (Chicago: University of Chicago Press, 2001).

14. John Austin, *Devotions in the Ancient Way of Offices*, 3rd ed. (1684), 334–35. All quotations, unless otherwise indicated, are taken from this edition.

15. Throughout the *Devotions*, asterisks are used to indicate caesuras where these are not signaled by a syntactical pause in the text.

16. Numbered references respectively to Ps. 115:1; Ps. 127:1; Ps. 69:1–2, 14–15 (King James Bible).

17. On the Stuart court and Christian Neoplatonism, see Erica Veevers, *Images of Love and Religion: Queen Henrietta Maria and Court Entertain-*

ments (Cambridge: Cambridge University Press, 1989), and Karen Britland, *Drama at the Courts of Queen Henrietta Maria* (Cambridge: Cambridge University Press, 2006). The *topos* of mystical marriage is common within both mainstream and esoteric Christian devotion. See Elizabeth Clarke, *Politics, Religion and the Song of Songs in 17th-Century England* (Basingstoke: Palgrave Macmillan, 2011), and B. J. Gibbons, *Gender in Mystical and Occult Thought: Behmenism and its Development in England* (Cambridge: Cambridge University Press, 1996); the way in which seraphic love both draws on the idea of mystical marriage and proffers an alternative to it would be worth further study.

18. Frances Harris, *Transformations of Love: The Friendship of John Evelyn and Margaret Godolphin* (Oxford: Oxford University Press, 2002), esp. 80 ff. In his biography of Austin, printed in the 1672 edition of the *Devotions*, John Sergeant remarks that they were "long us'd by divers private Friends" (fol. A5a).

19. See Arthur F. Marotti's discussion in this volume.

20. For example, "*Seraphicall*: Inflamed with divine love like a Seraphim." John Bullokar, *An English Expositor* (1616), fol. N7a. The vision of heaven recorded in Isaiah 6 is often alluded to in this context (Boyle, *Some Motives*, 10), and the Trisagion sung by the seraphim ("Holy, holy, holy") is sometimes referred to as the "seraphic hymn."

21. *A Treatise of the Love of God*, trans. Miles Car (*pseud.* Miles Pinkney), 18th ed. (1630), 315. Car does not spell out the reference to Ps. 64:1 in this passage: see instead *The Love of God: A Treatise*, trans. Vincent Kerns (London: Burns & Oates, 1962), 212. See also Terence A. McGoldrick, *The Sweet and Gentle Struggle: Francis de Sales and the Necessity of Spiritual Friendship* (Lanham, Md.: University Press of America, 1996).

22. Quotation taken from the 1700 edition of Hickes's *Devotions*. Cf. the discussion of "enthusiastic" and "mystical" further in this essay. For an example of a Church of England conformist rejecting the adjective in the description "a seraphical zealot for the service-book," see John Ley, *A Debate Concerning the English Liturgy* (1656), esp. fols. B1a–C2a, and the entry for Edward Hyde (1607–59) in the *Oxford Dictionary of National Biography*.

23. *A Collection of Meditations and Devotions* (1717), fol. A4b.

24. Trinity College, Cambridge, C.20.31, 334. On the Hopton-Hickes adaptation, see note 5, above.

25. See Alan Bray, *The Friend* (Chicago: University of Chicago Press, 2003). The relevant portion of the inscription reads: "In Memory likewise of his dearest brother WALTER FOWLER Esq[r] who died at London and lyes buried in Covent Garden church near his vertuous and devout friend Mr IOHN AUSTEN." My thanks to the vicar and churchwardens of Holy Trinity, Baswich, Staffordshire, for granting me access to the church, and allowing me to take a transcription. On Austin's burial place, see my "Intimate Worship,"

272. I am grateful to Cedric Brown for sharing his unpublished research on the Fowlers with me; for the Fowler genealogy, see also Deborah Aldrich-Watson, ed., *The Verse Miscellany of Constance Aston Fowler: A Diplomatic Edition* (Tempe: Renaissance English Text Society / Arizona Center for Medieval and Renaissance Studies, 2000), xvi. The Walter Fowler in question is the youngest of those listed, and Austin might originally have acted as tutor to him (*Oxford Dictionary of National Biography*).

26. Rose Longden, "The Fowlers of St Thomas, near Stafford, 1542–1738," *Staffordshire Studies* 16 (2005): 91–111, here 92. See also Joseph Gillow, *St Thomas's Priory* (London: Burns & Oates, n.d.), and "The Priory of St Thomas near Stafford," in *A History of the County of Stafford*, 20 vols. (London: Institute for Historical Research, 1970), 3:260–67 (also available online: http://www.british-history.ac.uk/report.aspx?compid=37855).

27. Bray, *Friend*, index under "Eucharist." On paired worship, see also my "Intimate Worship," which discusses the preface to the *Devotions*. In his 1672 biography of Austin (see above, note 18) John Sergeant relates that "the Prayers throughout this Book were by his desire writ by a worthy Hand, with whom he joyn'd His in a perfect friendship" (fol. A5b). On the antiphonal worship of the seraphim, see John Donne, "Sermon on Revelation 4:8," preached at St. Dunstan's, Trinity Sunday, 1627, in *The Sermons of John Donne*, ed. George R. Potter and Evelyn M. Simpson (Berkeley: University of California Press, 1953–62), 8:56.

28. *An Account of the Rise and Progress of the Religious Societies*, 2nd ed. (1698), 172; Spurr, *Restoration Church*, 334.

29. *Collection of Meditations and Devotions*, fol. A5a. The "late Dean of Worcester" whose opinion is quoted is probably George Hickes, installed into the office on October 13, 1683 (*Oxford Dictionary of National Biography*).

30. Many early uses of the word "mystical," both pre- and post-Reformation, are pejorative (*Oxford English Dictionary*).

31. Psalm 38 (Douai Bible); cf. Ps. 39:3 (King James Bible).

32. See Anthony Wood, *Athenae Oxonienses*, 4 vols., ed. Philip Bliss (1813–20; New York: Johnson Reprint Corporation, 1967–69), 2: cols. 105–7. Wood gives as his source a sermon preached at St. Mary's, Oxford, in 1640; this has not been traced, but on Ussher's anti-Catholicism, see Alan Ford, *James Ussher: Theology, History and Politics in Early Modern Ireland and England* (Oxford: Oxford University Press, 2007), 3, 59–64, 106, 111–14, 114–18, 272–74.

33. *Sermones Upon Solemne Occasions* (1637), 29. Sydenham was a conformist (*Oxford Dictionary of National Biography*).

34. See *Pindar and the Renaissance Hymn-Ode: 1450–1700* (Tempe: Arizona Center for Medieval and Renaissance Studies, 2001), 3, 12, 14–16, 20–25.

35. Sales, *Treatise*, trans. Car, 300 and 296. The "Benedicite" is the name by which vv. 35–66 in the Song of the Three Children (Apocrypha) is gener-

ally known: it formed part of the service of morning prayer in the Prayer Book from 1549 on (see *The Book of Common Prayer: The Texts of 1549, 1559 and 1662*, ed. Brian Cummings [Oxford: Oxford University Press, 2011], 10–11, 107–8, 244–45).

36. On radical religion in seventeenth-century England, see Nigel Smith, *Perfection Proclaimed: Language and Literature in English Radical Religion, 1640–1660* (Oxford: Clarendon, 1989); David R. Como, *Blown by the Spirit: Puritanism and the Emergence of an Antinomian Underground in Pre-Civil-War England* (Stanford, Calif.: Stanford University Press, 2004).

37. Serenus Cressy, "A Preface to the Reader," in Augustine Baker, *Sancta Sophia: or, directions for the prayer of contemplation*, 2 vols., ed. Serenus Cressy (Douai, 1657), 1:xxi.

38. Augustine Baker, *Sancta Sophia*, 1, fol. † † † 3a and unsigned leaf facing title-page, headed "On the Picture and Writings of the late venerable F. Augustin Baker." The latter leaf is not present in all copies: this transcription is taken from the British Library's copy of the book (G 20024).

39. Clement Hawes, *Mania and Literary Style: From the Ranters to Christopher Smart* (Cambridge: Cambridge University Press, 1996), and idem, ed., *Christopher Smart and the Enlightenment* (New York: St. Martin's, 1999).

40. Cf. Evetts-Secker, "Elizabethan Experiment," on Buckland and contemporary Hebraists.

41. See Brian Hepworth, *Robert Lowth* (Boston: Twayne, 1978); Roberta E. Tovey, "'I speak for all': Smart's Conversion of the Hebrew Psalm," *Philological Quarterly* 62, no. 3 (1983): 315–33; and Daniel J. Ennis, "Christopher Smart's Cat Revisited: *Jubilate Agno* and the Ars Poetica Tradition," *South Atlantic Review* 65, no. 1 (2000): 1–23. Ennis comments on the equation of "an Hebraic verse-form with enthusiastic Anglican religious sentiment" (9; see also 5).

42. Robert Ryan, *The Romantic Reformation: Religious Politics in English Literature, 1789–1824* (Cambridge: Cambridge University Press, 1997).

43. Austin is associated, through his friend John Sergeant (see above, note 18), with the Blackloists, a mid-seventeenth-century group of Catholic radicals who, among much else, stressed the importance of laymen in perpetuating English Catholicism. On them, see Beverley C. Southgate, *Covetous of Truth: The Life and Work of Thomas White, 1593–1676*, International Archives of the History of Ideas 134 (Dordrecht: Kluwer, 1993); Dorothea Krook, *John Sergeant and his Circle: A Study of Three 17th-Century English Aristoteleans*, Brill Studies in Intellectual History 39, ed. and intro. Beverley C. Southgate (Leiden: Brill, 1993); George H. Tavard, *The Seventeenth-Century Tradition: A Study in Recusant Thought*, Studies in the History of Christian Thought 16 (Leiden: Brill, 1978); Jeffrey R. Collins, "Thomas Hobbes and the Blackloist Conspiracy of 1649," *Historical Journal* 45, no. 2 (2002): 305–31; and my *Oral Culture and Catholicism in Early Modern England*, conclusion.

44. On this topic, see H. T. Kirby-Smith, *The Origins of Free Verse* (Ann Arbor: University of Michigan Press, 1996).

45. Austin's work might possibly have been familiar to Gerard Manley Hopkins, Catholic himself and well aware of his recusant forbears: see the notes to "[Margaret Clitheroe]," 125–27 and 346–47 in Katherine Phillips, ed., *Gerard Manley Hopkins: The Major Works* (1986; Oxford: Oxford University Press, 2002).

46. Ed Folsom and Kenneth M. Price, *Re-Scripting Walt Whitman: An Introduction to his Life and Work* (Malden, Mass.: Blackwell, 2005), 42; F. S. Flint, "History of Imagism," *The Egoist*, May 1, 1915: quoted in Peter Jones, ed., *Imagist Poetry* (Harmondsworth: Penguin, 1972), 15. On the interest in biblical parallelism within the Imagist movement, see G. S. Fraser, *Metre, Rhyme and Free Verse* (1970; London: Methuen, 1977), chapter 6. On Smart's afterlife among twentieth-century creative writers, see Karina Williamson, "Surfing the Intertext: Smart Among the Moderns" and "Twentieth-Century Encounters with Christopher Smart," chapters 12 and 14 in *Christopher Smart and the Enlightenment*, ed. Clement Hawes (New York: St. Martin's, 1999).

9

Between the Eucharist and Eroticism

Embodiment in the Poetry of Catherina Regina von Greiffenberg (and an Edition by Johann Reinhard Hedinger from 1702)

Franz M. Eybl

The poetry of Catherina Regina von Greiffenberg[1] focuses on the concept of doxology, on the moment of the encounter with God, and on the motif of the incarnation, exhibiting a radical use of language unmatched in Baroque German literature. During periods of melancholy, the poet upheld the "Deoglori" as a general principle[2] with its solid basis in Lutheran theology, as is evident again and again in the epistolary exchange with her mentor and editor, Sigmund von Birken, in Nuremberg.[3] The moment of the encounter with God was her literary stimulus, which produced the volume of poems called *Geistliche Sonnette, Lieder und Gedichte, zu Gottseligem Zeitvertreib, erfunden und gesetzet* (Nuremberg, 1662, reprint Darmstadt, 1967),[4] in addition to an ever expanding series of meditations. Organized and published not in relation to her biography, but rather according to salvation history, these meditations include *Menschwerdung / Geburt und Jugend JEsu Christi* (1678, SW 3–4), to *Des Allerheiligst- und Allerheilsamsten Leidens und Sterbens Jesu Christi / Zwölf andächtige Betrachtungen der Passion* (1683, SW 9–10),[5] and finally the *Lehren und Wunderwercken*

(1693, SW 5–8). Formally and poetically, they are unique works of both art and edification.[6] The Eucharist as image and mystical phenomenon stands out among the mystical ideas productively circulating in these works. As both a thematization and an interpretation of the incarnation of Christ that is also, of course, religious and indeed, "sacramental,"[7] it calls for the actualization of a physical union. Correspondingly, the poet comprehends the "receipt of communion as an actual 'unio' with the Son of God."[8] The divine body, whether sacramentally represented or in its "real presence" in the sacrament, encounters the human body and unites with it in the act of consumption. I examine this double perspective in three steps. First, I investigate the thoroughly unstable form of representation for divine and erotic bodily processes, as well as its multiple dynamics, which Greiffenberg's lyrical language effectively evokes. Second, I turn briefly to the opposing poles of literary discourse and concepts of the body between which the work oscillates. In what can be described as an artful doubling, Greiffenberg couples descriptions of physical sensations with the potential of poetic language. Taking the measure of the way her poetry plays with both the bodily and the poetic, the specific gendering of the body comes to light. In the *Passionsbetrachtungen* this gendering is revealed as an "inscription and transmutation of gender."[9] Finally, I turn to the edition of a Greiffenberg poem by Hedinger from the year 1702 from which the gendering has been completely excised. Long referred to as marginal and otherwise unexamined, this edition displays what could be described as an act of male erasure. (See Appendix for this poem and Hedinger's edition.)

The goal of the essay is to discuss these individual facets with close attention to only a few examples drawn from the specific thematic context of Christ-centered mysticism. The broader purpose is to make Greiffenberg's poetry productive for comparative studies of the larger tradition of Eucharistic poetry.

Transformations

Greiffenberg's transformations are mostly oriented toward two guiding parameters: toward a tradition of mystical self-transformation and toward a tradition of the Real Presence of Christ that cites the sacrament of the Eucharist in its Lutheran form and thematizes this as representative form of union. Both are staged through concepts of corporeality. An animated, rhythmical effect is created through the construction of points of reversal where artistic mimesis and meditative performance intersect.

The poem "JESU! ich bin voller Flammen" (JESU! I am full of flames), from the ninth meditation in the *Passionsbetrachtungen*,[10] gives poetic form to the theme of self-transformation. Departing from the dominant metaphor of burning, the lyrical-*Ich* (Lynne Tatlock speaks of a "textual persona") describes its own transformation.

1. JESU! ich bin voller Flammen/
JESU! ich bin voller Brand!
Lob und Liebe schlägt zusammen/
setzt mich in entzündten stand.
Deine Brunst verzehrt mich ganz.
Steh in liechten lohe Glanz!
Geist / sinn / seel / hertz und gedanken
werden lauter lobes-fanken!

2. Wann / wie Faros-Fackel / brennet/
all mein Mark und fettigkeit;
Wann mein Hertze sich zertrennet/
wie ein wachs in glut bereit;
Wann ich Troja in dem Brand/
Und den Etna überwand/
weit zuruck Vesuven liesse:
alles doch zu wenig hiesse.

3. Wann ich mich / in heisser Liebe/
auch verfönixt´ alle stund;
wann ich alle Hitzes-triebe/
in den Adern laden kunt;
das Geblüt zu Pulfer macht/
alle meine kraft verkracht/

dir zu ehren / herzen-König!
wär es doch noch viel zu wenig.

4. Wären Adern flamen-Minen
und die Geister Zünde-strick/
giengen an und loß von innen/
sprengten auch im Augenblick
meine Seel in ursprungs-luft
und den Leib in seine Gruff[t]:
wer es zwar die Lieb geübet/
aber noch nicht satt geliebet.

5. Die sonst lang´ und bange Zeiten/
viel zu kurtz mir sind zur Lieb:
ja / mich deucht die Ewigkeiten
auszuüben ihren Trieb/
Und die angenehme Lust/
so sand-mängbar mir bewust/
werden mir darzu nicht klecken/
Liebe will sich weiter strecken.

6. Ach! wär bald der Leib zerrissen!
Ach! wär bald die Seele frey!
meines Liebsten zu geniessen/
und zu sehen / wer der sey/
der so hell im dunkeln ist/
der das bitter so versüst/
der so hertz-ergetzlich liebet/
ja / sich selbst ins Hertze gibet.

7. Hertze! wann mein Hertze weichet.
Seele! die bey meiner Seel
bleibet / wann sie aus mir streichet.
Unerschöpffte Liebes-Quell!
die mich liebt / wann ich mich haß/
nicht verläst / wann ich mich laß:

Bring / wann ich sein´ Huld verschertze/
wieder mich in GOttes Hertze.

———

1. Jesus! I am full of flames! Jesus! I am full of fire! Praise and love smash together, they set me in a state of burning! Your fire consumes me fully. I stand in the brilliance of your bright fire! The mind, the senses, the soul become pure sparks of praise!

2. If like the torch of Pharos, all my marrow and fat burns, or my heart rips itself apart, like wax prepared in a blaze, or I leave Troy behind aflame, or I overcome Etna and leave Vesuvius far behind, that would all mean too little!

3. If I, in hot love, at once died a Phoenix and was reborn, if I could load all the force of heat into my veins, turn the blood to powder, if I could explode all my strength, in order to honor you, King of my heart, it would still be much too little.

4. If my veins were mines of flame, and the spirits were match-cords that would go off and burst from inside; if in an instant they exploded my soul into the air of its origins and the body into its tomb, although this would be done for love, there would not yet have been enough loving!

5. These otherwise long and frightening times are much too short for my love; yea, I think that eternity is best suited to fulfill that desire! And my pleasant desire, to me as infinite as individual grains of sand, will not run out, love will push itself onward!

6. Oh! If only my body were soon torn apart! Oh! If only my soul were soon free! So that I could enjoy my beloved and could see who that is who is so bright in the dark, who sweetens the bitterness, who loves so heartily, who sends himself into the heart!

7. Heart! when my heart vanishes—soul! who stays with my soul when she beams out from me! Unexhaustible well of love! who loves

me when I hate myself, does not leave me when I leave myself! Bring me, should I forfeit his grace, back to God's heart!

If first body and then soul ignite in the first strophe ("Geist / sinn / seel / hertz und gedanken / werden lauter lobes-fanken!") (The mind, the senses, the soul become pure sparks of praise!), then the lyrical dissolution of the body continues in the second strophe through an *enumeratio*, beginning with reminiscence of the biblical context: "[es] brennet / all mein Mark und fettigkeit" (all my marrow and fat burns). The allusion here is to the burnt offerings of the Old Testament,[11] whose ranks the speaker joins. The body is conceived as a sign ("Faros-Fackel") and is inscribed in the referential system of literature and the sciences through the comparison, *a minore ad maius*, with the destruction of Troy through fire, as well as with the two "classical" volcanoes, Aetna and Vesuvius.[12] Neither the perpetuation of self-destruction in the form of the phoenix (str. 3), nor even the forced rupture of soul and body (str. 4) here are worthy of God.

Following the introductory scalar comparison ("doch zu wenig," str. 2; "viel zu wenig," str. 3), the middle strophe goes on to unite thoughts of dissolution with notions of temporality, for the second half of the poem takes as its theme the "zu wenig" (too little), that is to say, the brevity of time at the speaker's disposal: "Die sonst lang´ und bange Zeiten / viel zu kurtz mir sind zur Lieb" (the otherwise long and frightening times are much too short for my love) (str. 5). One lifetime should pass quickly so as to allow its fulfillment in the knowledge of the beloved ("meines Liebsten," str. 6), and this reunion means the homecoming of the soul in death. The "processuality" of self-dissolution is inserted into a temporal model informed by salvation history, whereby the art of divine reversal ("Göttliche Verkehrungs-Kunst") consists in transforming the hardships of earthly existence into the exultation of heavenly reward.[13]

Two models of the protean and the transformative are developed in the poem. It shows the dissolution of the speaker through a gradual process of fiery liquefaction, as well as a quicker process of exploding like fireworks. The elements of disintegration are fluidity and fire. These elements are inscribed in a long tradition of the mystical language of flames and heat, which is already prefigured in the Song of Songs. There one finds descriptions of the fusion brought on by the heat of love, as the speaker in 5:6 relates in the words of the Vulgate: "anima mea liquefacta est, ut dilectus locutus est" (My soul melted when my beloved spoke). The formulation is significant because its phrasing issues a double appeal: to the effects of the heat in an argument *a causis* and to a concept of corporeality *ab effectu*. The ambiguity here, verging on the bodily, appears to have affected the German transmission of the verse, for in Luther's translation and its subsequent editions there is astonishing timidity in the description of female desire as conveyed in the Latin rendition of the Song of Songs. The German editors express the verse in various translations: "und mein Inneres ward seinetwegen erregt" (and my inside was excited because of him) (Elberfelder, 1905), for example, or even "da geriet mein Herz in Wallung seinetwegen" (then my heart went into palpitations because of him) (Schlachter, 1951). Martin Opitz remained closer to the Latin corpus in his translation from 1624: "Mir zittert meines Hertzens grundt" (the center of my heart trembled).[14] Luther's translation strays farthest from the female body, in his reinterpretation of physical arousal as a search for words: "Da gieng meine Seele [h]er aus nach seinem wort" (then my soul went out searching for his word), as it appears in the 1545 edition,[15] and again word for word in a Bible from the year 1665 (and thus closer to the age of Greiffenberg): "Da gieng meine Seele herauß nach seinem Wort / ich suchte ihn / aber ich fand ihn nicht" (then my soul went out searching for his word, I searched for him, but I could not find him).[16] It is not until a 1912 edition of the Luther Bible that the female voice is permitted to say: "Meine Seele war außer sich, als er redete" (my soul was beside itself as he spoke). In opposition to this evasion, the Catholic tradition stayed close to the express corporeality in the Vulgate. On the basis of the Catholic translation of Johann Dietenberger and Caspar Ulenberg, Thomas Aquinas Erhard translated the verse in question in the year 1723 as follows: "Mein Seel ist zerschmoltzen, da er redete" (my soul melted as he spoke).[17] Such excitement or ecstasy only enters the tradition of German-speaking Lutheran translations several centuries later—before that the liquefaction of the female soul remains absent.

The meditational literature of the seventeenth century offers one tradition that talks of precisely this type of melting during the poet's lifetime, in works such as Hermann Hugo's *Pia Desideria*, first published in 1624. Here it is possible to trace the medieval tradition of exegesis whose metaphorical material leads directly to the formulations of Greiffenberg, cited according to the first German edition of 1669:

> Gleich wie das Wachs fleust von dem Feuer / also ist die Seel angezünt von seinem Angesicht: Mein Seel ist zerschmoltzen / da mein Geliebter redete. O wie eine süsse Stunde / in der die Seel zerschmoltzen / un[d] mit diesem feurigen Bach vermischet wird: wie subtil ist sie in jenem Augenblick! wie ausgemergelt! wie beweglich! Aldann ist kein Faulkeit in ihr / nichts hartes übrig / keine rauhe / sondern alles ist warm und schmeltzend. Das zerschmeltzende und warme seynd untereinander verwand: In diesen zweyen stehet der Gebrauch der Bechsauung [*recte* Beschauung].
>
> O mein wunderbare und sehr feurige Krafft deß Worts / sie entzündet das Hertz / verändert die Nieren / machet das Gemüth zu nichten in ihrem Aufschauen und Bedencken ihres Gottes: Macht von ihr selber zerschmeltzen / und ohnmächtig zu werden / also / daß jetzunder die Seel nicht bey dir sey.[18]

———

> Just as wax melts from fire, the soul is set aflame by his visage. My soul melted when my beloved spoke. Oh what a sweet hour in which my soul melts and is mixed with this fiery stream! How subtle it [the soul] is in that instant, how emaciated! How agile! Then there is no decay in it [the soul], nothing hard remains, nothing rough; rather everything is warm and melting. The melting and the warm parts are related to one another: in these two things lies the practice of viewing [God] (*Beschauung*).
>
> O my wonderful and very fiery strength of the Word! It sets my heart on fire, changes my kidneys, turns my mind into nothing as it views and meditates on God: It spontaneously melts and becomes unconscious, so that the soul is no longer in you.

Until well into the eighteenth century, images of the melting woman accompany the Song of Songs in emblem form, from the first edition of Hugo Hermann's *Pia Desideria* in 1624 until the final edition of its reworking by Johann Christoph Hainzmann (*Himmlische Nachtigall*, Frankfurt am Main, 1730, 1st ed., 1684), as well as even later German-language editions of the *Pia Desideria*. Hermann had a direct impact on the female mystic from Seisenegg, as has been determined on the basis of other shared imagery, such that Greiffenberg can be considered "als eine direkte Rezipientin des Antwerpener Emblembuches" (as a direct recipient of the Antwerp emblem book), as Cristina M. Pumplun writes.[19] Her poetry thus invokes a larger mystical tradition, as I argue, within the framework of contemporary concepts of corporeality that were coded as female. The images considered here are to be found in the climax of the meditations, in the ninth reflection ("sie kreuzigten ihn"), ushered in by a call to prayer: "Laß deine Liebe das einige seyn / wornach ich ziele / zische / flische [sic] / flamme und fliege. Laß alle andere Begierden in mir zu Eise / diese aber zu einem eisen-schmeltzenden Blähaus werden / [NB: a furnace, as Greiffenberg's comments make clear] daß ich / mit höchster Warheit / singen und sagen möge: 1. JESU! ich bin voller Flammen/" (Let your love be the only thing that I strive for, crackle, flow, burn, and fly. Let all other desires in me become ice; but let those first ones become a furnace that melts the iron, so that I can sing and say with the greatest truth: 1. Jesus! I am full of flames!) (SW 10, 602). The lyrics then find their release following a short transition from the next: "Ach ja! laß in dieser Brunst mich immer höher kommen / daß es bey mir heisse: / 1. ACh JEsu! ich bin ganz entglüht" (Oh yes! Let me come ever higher in this blaze, so that it will be said of me: 1. Oh Jesus! I am completely ablaze!) (SW 10, 604). Where other poems pause in the moment of mystical union, however, the poem in question closes with an appeal to the *vita activa* (str. 7): it is a plea for the forgiveness of sins, thus providing for a (theologically correct) period of earthly probation. A transformation has already taken place, for it is the heart and soul of Christ that have become the "better" self of the lyrical-*Ich*. Christ's heart and soul remain after "mein Hertze" (my heart) and "meine Seel" (my soul) depart in death, and they can also reconcile the two antithetical halves of the disintegrated speaker: “die mich liebt / wann ich mich haß / nicht verläst / wann ich mich laß” (that loves me when I hate myself and does not abandon me when I abandon myself). The conciliatory figure of self-transformation cannot endure as an end in itself though; instead, it must always begin and continue anew. It thus remains in the realm of exercitation, such that it should not be considered an outcome, but rather an ongoing meditative practice—with its respective successful poetic formulation.

The poem “Vom H. Nachtmahl” (On the Last Supper) in the second *Passionsbetrachtung* leads not only to dissolution, but also to union, depicting the reception of Holy Communion in a progression of images over the course of twenty-two strophes.[20] Beginning with its own reconfiguration, the text gives rise to a series of transformations commonly found in the dogma and rhetoric of the Eucharistic sacrament.[21] An introductory strophe is followed by four strophes of unspecified chronology, which traverse an otherwise general meditation in the comparative style of *a minore ad maius*. The sixth strophe is similarly followed by four further strophes, the latter differentiated from the initial four strophes through their heightened stylistic quality and distinctly more grandiose forms of expression. In this second group of strophes, the poet suggests that communion has just commenced, so that the entire arrangement appears as a progression from expectation to fulfillment. In the first group—after its introductory second-person apostrophe “O Liebe!”—there remains a great distance between the person and the divinity present in the Eucharist, for these two entities appear collective and indefinite; this distance is expressed in the paronomasia of the sinner (“dem / der dich hat betrübet” [of him who has saddened you]), with the deictic *allhier* or the personal pronoun *uns*, whereas the second passage incorporates personal pronouns such as *du*, *ich*, and *wir*, such that even the syntax works to assimilate the actors. This finally culminates in an appellation to the self in the middle strophe of the poem, forming the *jetzt* (now) of the actual communion event:

11. Mein Herze! herz dein Herz im innern Grunde.
Ach küß und iß ihn ganz / vor Lieb / mein Munde!

Ach Seel und kehl! zugleich mit innern springen
solt ihr den Geist der Wollust jezt verschlingen.[22]

---

11. My heart! Hearten your heart to its very bottom. Oh kiss and eat him all for love, my mouth! Oh soul and throat! Immediately, with inner dancing, you should swallow the spirit of lust.

At this point, the second half of the poem, which has itself been subject to numerous interpretations in Greiffenberg and Baroque scholarship, deserves brief consideration. It looks back to the received communion and reasons via anaphora, as its chain of interlocking strophes invokes the immediate *hier* (here) of the present to describe the effects of the communion (str. 13–16). The strophe then develops the imagery of heavenly radiance, and finally lapses into silence, a lapse to which I return in the final section.

A fulcrum of sorts, the sixth strophe combines the two scenes of transformation—and thus, representation—as parallel processes on multiple levels of image and meaning:

6. O Himmel-mahl! O Geist- und Weißheit Weitzen!
O mache mich den Hertzen-Ofen heitzen.
Ach backe dich mit meinen Liebes-Kohlen/
der du uns wirst / wie wir nur selber wollen.

---

6. O heavenly supper! O wheat of spirit and wisdom! Oh cause me to fire the oven of my heart. Oh bake me with your coals of love, so that we become yours, which is our only wish.

Greiffenberg often couples levels of image and meaning by means of compound neologisms.[23] Whereas "Himmelmahl" (heavenly supper) or "Geist- und Weisheitweizen" (wheat of spirit- and wisdom) designate the Godhead and his representation (not, however, metaphorically, but rather via synecdoche), the terms "Hertzens-Ofen" (oven of my heart) and "Liebes-Kohlen" (coals of love) refer to the speaker-figuration of the *anima* through the use of personal and possessive pronouns.[24] The threefold anaphoric exclamation "O" leads to the sigh "Ach" and finally to the mystical paradox, in which the interconnection of God and the self in the mutually desired conversion ("der du uns wirst") attains to representation. The doubling appears as a transformation and, in increasing complexity, as an inversion at the same time within the represented processes: wheat becomes bread as the speaker becomes an oven. In an inversion then, as is evident in the parallel internal rhymes of the imperatives "mache mich"—"backe dich" (make me—bake you), it is the bread that warms the oven and bakes itself. The fact that Greiffenberg's imagery on the preparation of food alludes to an Easter hymn by Luther provides a slightly firmer theological footing for the otherwise genuinely lyrical complexity of the represented events,[25] though, as I show, the allusion is not enough.

Compared to the miracle of transubstantiation, the transformation of writing, which stands metonymically for Greiffenberg's own poetry, into flames would be no miracle at all. To describe a poetry here that "permanently oscillates between the literal and the figurative"[26] does not go far enough because the figurative itself is set into motion and, moreover, the instruments of language develop not only cascades of meaning but also the sense of being present in space as well as of embodiment. Beyond the moment of bursting into flames, metonymic and metaphorical games are made possible, which allows attention to shift from the burning speaker of the text back to the poet ("die Dinte"), as well as to Christ's transubstantiation under the conditions of the metaphorical heat: the Lamb of Heaven is roasted through "Glut und Kohlen" (embers and coals) and prepared for consumption, metonymically through the ink and at last, through poetry itself.

Greiffenberg's emphasis on writing, figuration, and poetry on the one hand corresponds to an emphasis on falling silent on the other. The earlier mystical tradition had long-since emphasized and explored the inadequacy of human speech in the face of God, demanding its silencing. The *topos* of the failure of language turns up frequently in the works examined here, for instance, in the sonnet "JEsu´! Bronne meines Lebens" (*PB*, Siebende Betrachtung, SW 9, 396), in which Greiffenberg writes: "ach! wer kan vor freud die freud / und vor Lust die wollust sagen? / Da / vor ursach-überfluß / ich den haupt-beweiß nicht weiß. / Ich sih nichts vor lauter licht" (Oh! Who can speak of joy while in a state of joy, and who can speak of lust while in a state of desire? Because, due to the sensory overload, I do not know the chief piece of evidence, I see nothing because of too much light).[27] The rhetorical phrase "inopem me copia fecit" (the abundance makes me poor) is carried over into imagery of light and its ability to blind the viewer. In the ninth meditation, the effects of light emerge as the theme of the prose in the central passage "Und sie kreutzigten ihn / an der Städte Golgatha" (SW 10, 549):

> Es thun sich mir ganze Bestürzung- und Preiß-Abgründe auf / daß ich nicht weiß / zu welchem ich schreiten / an welchem ich anheben / oder welchen ich zum höchsten und äussersten treiben soll. Ich werde arm vor Reichthum / stumm vor Preiß-begier / und matt vor überflüßigen Gedanken-schwall / sie auszusinnen. Wie kan ich die Bestürtzung aussprechen / die ich fühle über das Leiden des mit göttlicher Majestät vereinigten / über die Erniedrigung des Allerhöchsten / über das würm-elend der selbsten Himmels-Herrlichkeit? (SW 10, 556f.)
>
> ———
>
> Entire abysses of dismay and of praise open before me, so that I do not know which ones I should approach, which ones I should carry myself over, or which ones I should drive to the highest and furthest away. I become poor in wealth, mute in desire for praise, and feeble from the overwhelming wave of thoughts considering these things. How can I give voice to the dismay that I feel about the suffering of those who are united with the divine majesty, about the humiliation of the highest, about the wormlike misery of the same heavenly glory?

The excess of words that pours forth from an all-too full heart becomes excessive in the silencing of the speaker. The upsurge of language and its subsequent exhaustion through its own inadequacy lead to perpetual movement through its assertion followed by revocation, creating the impression of an interminable pulsation. Thus, in the aforementioned sonnet on the fount of Jesus (SW 9, 396):

> Wann diß ewig Wort mir redet/
> so entlehnt mein herz die zunge / daß ich Antwort geben kan/
> sag so starkes Geistes-Ja / daß mein ganze kraft erblödet/
> in das herz zusammen sinket / geht dann wieder Himmel-an.
>
> ———
>
> When this eternal Word speaks to me, my heart borrows my tongue, so that I can answer, I say such a strong spiritual yes that all my strength turns to nothing and sinks down into my heart, then goes back up to heaven again.

The pulsation is clearly marked as activity: the strength of saying yes requires such great force that it results in a weakening ("mein ganze kraft erblödet") and then compels a period of rest, after which another attempt at speech may be made.[28] Laudation and silence oscillate between the poles of language and text ("so starkes Geistes-Ja") and the languishing body.

Still, the act of falling silent can also be seen to signal an intensification and escalation. In the framework of the poem—more specifically, within the second meditation in the *Passionsbetrachtung* on the verse "Es ist vergossen für viele / zu Vergebung der Sünden" (it is spilled for many for the forgiveness of sins), and in the initial strophe—Greiffenberg stages the Eucharistic transformation in language. The silencing of the meditator leads not to wordless silence, that is to say, a form of interiority preceding language in the sense of a meditative achievement of imagination and emotion, but instead to an escalation of language in poetry. Only the song is allowed to continue: "Ich kan vor lauter Liebe und Bewegung / nicht fortreden / will demnach die Geistes-Kräfte / zu erholen / diese Betrachtung mit Singen unterbrechen" (I cannot, out of pure love and movement, say any more, I want, in order to recover my powers of spirit, to interrupt this meditation with song) (Zweite Betrachtung, SW 9, 43). Here too, there is a pulsation, this time on the level of the text, between speech and song, between narration and meditative reflection.[29]

Transformation and inversion create textures of a back-and-forth motion, a form of performative passing-through, since the situation is no longer linear but rather can be represented and executed only in continuous reversals. With respect to the older *topos* of silence, this pattern is new and a fundamentally modern element in Greiffenberg's poetry, connecting her to Leibniz: Greiffenberg composes calculations that surpass the fundamental operations of arithmetic with respect to the fourfold meaning of scripture and the allegorical potential of alchemy in their dynamics and scope. In her poetics of transformation, she operates with a concept of the infinite, or in the truest sense of the word, with an infinitesimal poetry.

Poetry and the Body

There can be no doubt that Greiffenberg's poetic language and style refer to contemporary poetics and writing practices, especially as found in the artistic center of Nuremberg. Nevertheless, as has occasionally been vehemently argued, the striking sense of physical sensation conveyed by Greiffenberg's poetry can only be productively analyzed in terms of its representation through language,[30] the contours of which become more pronounced with recourse to the poetic techniques of her contemporaries and their conception of the body. The sonnet "Mein Glaube / ist ein Glas" (SW 10, 565) in the ninth *Passionsbetrachtung* is a good example of Greiffenberg's use of these literary techniques:

> Mein Glaube / ist ein Glas / dein Wunden-wundoel fanget
> mit höchster Andacht auf / es an die Sonne setzt
> Der Erz-Gerechtigkeit / die selbst damit ergetzt/
> weil wiederstralung sie aus dessen Glantz erlanget.
> In aller Schmerzen-noht man Linderung empfanget/
> durch dieses edle Oe[l] / sey wie man wo verletzt.
> Wann man ein sprintzlein nur mit diesem Seel-Oel netzt/
> der ganze innre Mensch voll Geist-ausschüttung pranget.
> Es nützet und behagt. Auf heilig fromme Weiß/
> es GOttes Herrlichkeit im Glauben uns vorstellet;
> auf alle Fragen auch aus diesem Blutes-schweiß/
> ein süßes Gnaden-Ja und gute Antwort fället.

> Die flammen-volle Flut / der Lieb-flut überfluß/
> so lieblich labt / daß man vor Lieb [v]erstummen[31] muß.
>
> ———
>
> My faith is a glass that catches the wound-oil of your wounds with the greatest devotion, sets it in the sun of arch-righteousness, which rejoices in it, because its [the oil's] reflected rays reach it [the sun] from its [the oil's] brilliance. In all the affliction of pain, one receives relief from this noble oil, however injured one might be. If one applies but a little drop of this oil of the soul, the entire inner person shines forth from the release of the spirit. It is useful and pleases. In a holy, pious way it presents us with God's glory in faith. In response to all petitions even to this bloody sweat falls a sweet yes of grace and a good answer. The flaming flood, the excess of the flood of love, refreshes so lovingly that one must become mute out of love.

The alliterations of the introductory verse immediately illustrate the poetic technique of allegorical interpretation: the formulations "Mein Glaube / ist ein Glas" (my faith is a glass) and "dein Wunden-Wundöl" (a salve for your wounds) connect the spiritual register of the text to the level of pharmaceutical imagery. The application and heating of oil allude to well-known (and in the everyday culture of the time, female-coded) steps in the preparation of herbal medicines. Johann Schröder's *Medicin-Chymische Apotheke* (Nuremberg, 1685) instructs the reader in the preparation of oils (*Von denen gekochten und infundirten Oelen*) in a method still used today to refine herbs; the reader should place medicinal herbs in pure oil, then "macerirs eine Zeitlang / und stells an die Sonn-Strahlen / oder sonst an einen warmen Ort" (macerate it for a time and then place it in the sun or another warm place).[32] The second and third quatrains describe and interpret the salutary effects on both registers. The fluidity of the oil in the poem, however, ultimately refers back to a central concept for Greiffenberg, that is, the theme of the inner flame (melting) and the deluge through the massive alliterative flood of *f*- and *l*-sounds.

Aside from the preparation of medicinal substances, with its proximity to alchemistic imagery,[33] further transformations and processes appear and move beyond this level of the text. The first quatrain stages a back-and-forth movement between the production of such herbal remedies through the sun and the God's presence in the medicine, for which the speaker in the poem acts as a container. Until its final lapse into silence though, the poem is supercharged with meaning on the level of language and poetry. This extends from the "Geistausschüttung" (release of the spirit) through the motto, to the dialogic structure of the third quatrain with its "Gnaden-Ja" (mercies-yes) and "gute Antwort" (good reply) and finally to the closing rhymed couplet on falling silent. In this, the poet favors the structure of an emblem,[34] whose *pictura* presents the oil flask in the sun, while the *subscriptio* performs that which the speaker envisions ("uns vorstellet"). The motto "Es nützet und behagt" (it is useful and pleases) reveals just how firmly the sonnet is rooted in literary tradition, for this is nothing other than the old Horatian adage, *prodesse* and *delectare*: "aut prodesse volunt aut delectare poetae." Indeed, for Greiffenberg, sacred literature is the literature that emerges victorious. If the passage in Horace reads, "omne tulit punctum, qui miscit utile dulci" (*Ars Poetica*, V. 343) then Greiffenberg responds: "Es nützet und behagt." It is the conjunction "und," joining the two equal terms together, which occupies the position of metrical stress.

Yet a specific form of corporeality accompanies this multifaceted poetic technique, as implied by the imagery of blood and its concomitant staging of the body in language. "Die Greiffenbergschen *Betrachtungen* über das Leben Jesu sind Betrachtungen über das Abendmahlsblut" (Greiffenberg's *Meditations* on the life of Jesus are meditations on the Eucharistic blood). As Ruth Liwerski has argued, they offer "Blutrede" (blood-speech) on every page: "Der Blutgott residiert auf jeder Seite" (the God of blood resides on every page).[35] The poet's so-called *Blutkult* (cult of blood), as Daniel Weidener writes, is also well known.[36] Following the oil allegory, Greiffenberg continues the theme of fluids and fluidity in the sonnet "O Blut / voll glut und gut" (O blood, full of fire and good) (SW 10, 565 f.), separated typographically from the preceding verse only by three asterisks. The first quatrain is devoted to the description of heating the blood, which warms the heart of the lyrical-*Ich* and as such, sets the latter in motion ("in fluß") toward the goal of mystical union ("daß es in deines fließ"), yet it also describes a chemical process of physical separation: that which had once separated the speaker from God melts away.

> O Blut / voll glut und gut / zerschmelzte Lieb im Leiden!
> zerschmelze mir mein Herz und bring es auch in fluß /
> daß es in deines fließ / durch milden tränen-guß.
> Wolst mich von allem / was von dir mich scheidet scheiden.
> Ach! daß ich alles / ja mich selber / könte meiden/
> um ganz in dir zu seyn / du aller Lust-Beschluß!
> mir ist die gantze Welt ein tödlicher Verdruß.
> Nur das wär meine freud / in deinen Rosen weiden.

———

> O blood, full of fire and good, molten love in suffering! Melt my heart and set it in motion, so that it flows into yours through a mild pouring of tears. You heal me from everything, separate everything that separates you from me. Oh! if only I could avoid everything, even myself, in order to be entirely in you, you vessel of all delight! The entire world is a deadly displeasure to me. Only this would be my joy, to graze among your roses.

Hydro-physics and alchemy are here combined with penitential meditation. On the level of the prayer, the "mild" stream of tears stands for the act of flowing together, as found in the historical genre of the *threnae*, or the songs of prayer and lamentation, popular in the seventeenth century.[37] The gesture of lament continues into the second quatrain with the exclamation "Ach!" and the elliptical wish stated in the first relative clause, all underscored by the will to self-abnegation ("ja mich selber / könte meiden") and removal from the world.

The sextet imagines a moment of good fortune, yet its structure hovers between temporal and conditional meaning through the use of the once ambiguous term *wann* in threefold anaphora, thus naming a point in time and a wish simultaneously:

> Beglückter Augenblick! Wann in der Einsamkeit
> ich / kniehend / deine krafft / im Glauben / kan anziehen/
> wann deine Allheit mich einsenkend hertz-erfreut/

> die Allmacht-Blumen mir / in Glaubens-Augen / blühen/
> wann ich / O süßheit-Seel! von dir beperlet bin:
> gäb ich Leib / Leben / Welt und alles / frölich hin.

———

> O blessed instant! If I, in my loneliness, can draw, kneeling, on your strength, in faith, if your everything-ness will make my heart rejoice while I sink down; the flowers of almightiness bloom in the eye of my belief when I, O soul of sweetness, am pearled by you: I would give up my body, life, the world, and everything gladly.

The turning point of the sonnet in terms of both form and content comes in the eighth verse: "Nur das wär meine freud / in deinen Rosen weiden" (Only this would be my joy, to graze among your roses). After its farewell to worldly affairs, the final verse of the octet speaks to the joy at its own exception from the lamentable world in the cautious subjunctive, "Nur das wär meine freud." Thc lyrical-*du*, here Christ, shifts from the metonymic blood to the paronomasia "Lust-Beschluß," or the vessel of all delight, then finally to the counterpart of the roses, which in the iconography of the Song of Songs approaches the lover of the Beloved: "Mein Freund ist mein / vnd ich bin sein / der vnter den Rosen weidet / Bis der tag küle werde / vnd der schatten weiche" (My friend is mine and I am his who grazes among the roses until the day cools and the shadows soften).[38]

At this point in the text, in Greiffenberg style, the allegorical meaning unfolds beside the literal ("krafft / im Glauben") through the use of "allegorical" compounds ("Allmacht-Blumen," "Glaubens-Augen"). The mystical encounter is structured as a play with and within language: the two personal pronouns, *du* and *ich*, circle one another in a series of chiastic and parallel crosses in the dative and accusative cases (emphasis added):

> *ich* / . . . *deine* krafft/
> *deine* Allheit *mich*
> [*deine*] Allmacht-Blumen *mir* /
> *ich* / . . . von *dir* beperlet
> gäb *ich* . . . [*dir*] alles / frölich hin.

Following this interaction, the moment of delight ("beglückte Augenblick") disintegrates into a succession of mystical images, namely into the four moments of investiture, penetration, vision, and moistening. This amounts to (at least) one active and two (or three) passive actions. The poet groups these by anaphora into tercets and augments them by the exclamation "O süßheit-Seel!" (O sweetness-soul!). The passage would appear rather conventional if its elements were not connected in one essential way: everything converges in the reference to the body, which is clothed, penetrated, optically incorporated, and at last wetted. The erotic components at play here are evident and require no further elaboration. In Johann Christian Günther's "Aria. An seine erzürnte Schöne [Louise],"[39] to give another example, the final strophes of the speech alternate suggestively between a love-death, represented here through the metaphor of sinking, and the resurrection:

Sencke meine Schuld der Lüste
    In dein tieff Erbarmen ein!
Laß den Schnee gewölbter B[rüste]
    Meine Todten-Bahre seyn!
Deine L[eibes] rundte E[nge]
    Zeige mir mein Grab-Mahl an,
Daß ich nach beliebter Länge
    Wieder aufferstehen kan.

Sink my guilt of desires into your deep mercy! Let your snow-like breasts be my death bier! Let your body display the round narrowness of my grave, so that I can, after the amount of time that will please you [*beliebter Länge*], rise up again.

What in Greiffenberg's language appears as wetted and pearled, appears as dew or "Wollust-Tau" in the—here, male—gallant poetry, for example in Hoffmannswaldau's "Albanie":[40]

Albanie, weil noch der wollust-thau
Die glieder netzt, und das geblüte springet,
So laß doch zu, daß auff der Venus-au

> Ein brünstger geist dir kniend opffer bringet,
> Daß er vor dir in voller Andacht steh.
> Albanie.

———

> Albania, because the dew of lust still wets the limbs and the blood shoots up, so allow that on the meadow of Venus a blazing spirit on his knees brings you a sacrifice, so that he will stand before you in complete devotion. Albania.

Or in the case of Lohenstein, one finds similar evidence as recorded in the *Deutsches Wörterbuch*: "Cupido leidet durst, die liebe musz verwelken, / samt dir, wenn nicht mein thau beperlet deine nelken" (Cupid suffers thirst, love must wither, together with you, if my dew did not pearl your cloves).[41] In the third meditation of the *Menschwerdungsbetrachtungen* (1678), Greiffenberg invokes the image once again in all its vividness: "Er komme / er komme / ach ja / er komme über mich / der gebenedeite Thau aus der Höhe! Er lasse seine Tröpflein in meinen Schos fallen wie der Thau auf das Fell Gideons" (Let him come, let him come, Oh yes, let him come over me, the blessed dew from on high! Let him allow his little drops to fall into my lap like the dew onto the pelt of Gideon).[42] Her choice of words recalls the double miracle of Gideon: in the course of a single evening, a fleece is drenched in dew, while the rest of the world remains dry; then, on the following night, the fleece remains perfectly dry and the world is filled with dew.[43] The suspension of the laws of physics enters into the semantics of conception; the pictorial world corresponds to the literality of the contemporary notion of procreation.[44]

Recent Greiffenberg scholarship has departed from the insight that bodily presence and the construction of gender in her texts deserve closer inspection.[45] At the same time, following the work of Hans-Georg Kemper, it is clear how closely these lyrical representations in Greiffenberg's poetics of contemplation are connected to a historical, more specifically a *gender*-historical conception of the human body, as Kemper writes: "Die der 'heißen' 'unio'-Sehnsucht zugrundeliegende Vorstellung vom Feuer im Herzen war auch im damaligen wissenschaftlichen Verständnis keineswegs eine Metapher" (the notion of fire in the heart, based on the "hot" desire for "unio," was by no means merely a metaphor even in contemporary scientific understanding); but rather, according to the teachings of Galen, "ließen sich die das 'unio'-Erlebnis offensichtlich begleitenden körperlichen Spannungszustände . . . in der Übereinstimmung mit der subjektiven Körpererfahrung der Mystiker als feurige 'Hitzestriebe' deuten" (the apparent bodily states of stress accompanying the "unio"-experience were allowed . . . to be interpreted as a fiery "heat-drive" in accordance with the subjective bodily experience of mystics).[46] The model for this derived from humoral pathology, with its depiction of the human body as regulated by fluids and temperatures. Its notion of a certain combination of bodily fluids, that is to say, the actual steering mechanisms of human organism, as being responsible for the character of man and his profession, nation, age, and so forth in the form of temperaments—this was but the most general of surface-level information. It was above all the particular admixture of fluids known as melancholy that ennobled poets to their calling, the consequences of which were studied as a valid theory well into the eighteenth century.[47]

Greiffenberg's mystical speech thus draws on the body not only in terms of its imagery,[48] but also with respect to its processes, the acts of heating and liquefaction. She appeals here to a far-less exquisite model of transformation than that of alchemy. Heating and liquefaction were still central elements of early modern conceptions of female anatomy according to the anthropological and medicinal standards of humoral pathology. In the context of its theory of procreation, the female body provided both a metaphor and its representation simultaneously, in the body's purification of blood through heating processes,[49] as well as its circulation of the fluids necessary for conception.[50] The extraordinary discursive engagement with this association may be seen in Gianlorenzo Bernini's representation of the ecstasy of Saint Theresa of Avila (1515–82), perhaps the most famous example of mystical surrender in art.[51]

The discourse around the *unio mystica* could be coded by Greiffenberg as Eucharistic embodiment, as well as by Greiffenberg and Bernini as the physical sex act of intercourse. What distinguishes the poet is her representation of a kind of birth-in-language as the result of the mystical act of procreation. The disjunction of bodily fluids and writing processes, which Albrecht Koschorke sees as developing in the eighteenth century, has not entered Greiffenberg's poetry, but rather is suspended in her portrayal of the female body. "Sein Blut ist Ein Durst- und Dinten-Magnet" (his blood is a thirst- and ink-magnet)[52] she writes to Birken, depicting a hydro-mechanical triangle of desire between Christ (blood), body (thirst), and script, whose power resides in its uncontrollable force of attraction—magnetism. As Kemper notes:

> das psychologisch Frappierende an diesem Bildfeld, dass hier nicht verdrängte Sexualität als Unbewusstes die "compassio" in einen himmlischen "Verkehr" verkehrt, sondern dass der Text diese Konnotationen offenbar bewusst riskiert, ja geradezu braucht und genießt . . . So fließen Opferblut und Samen in *eine* "Tinctur´" zusammen und sind weder zu trennen noch zu verdrängen.[53]
>
> ———
>
> the astonishing thing about this pictorial field from a psychological perspective is not that repressed sexuality in its unconscious form turns "compassion" into a kind of heavenly "intercourse," but rather that the text clearly and knowingly risks such connotations, indeed it needs and enjoys them . . . Thus, the sacrificial blood and semen flow together into one "tincture" and can neither be separated nor repressed.

The so-called tincture is the ink of the writer.

The imprecision of the pictorial fields here touches on an imprecision between formulation and meditation, between expression and assimilation, or on a nondescript difference between verbal representation and meditative-religious performance. It reflects exactly the difference between reading and writing, between poet and recipient. In the writing process, both roles become inextricably commingled, and all the more so in the transcription of mystical observations, with the double necessity of their expression and their generation.[54] Blood and ink flow—indeed, at the very same time—in both directions and the pull of divine presence comes into being through the performative agogic, for Greiffenberg invokes the presentist character of Christ through an appeal to martyrdom, or in the words of Kemper "[einen] realitätsanalogen Mitvollzug des Martyriums" (a concurrence of martyrdom analogous to reality).[55] There is hardly another author (or perhaps even a genre), whose work so perfectly illustrates the interdependence of the construction of meaning and the effect of presence than the one explored here.[56] Her verses oscillate between the embodiment of communion and the expressive potential of poetry: "Den Himmel auf der Zung, im Mund die Sonne" (heaven upon the tongue, the sun in the mouth). They float between a metaphorical reading as a representation of the Savior in the reception of communion (with the presence of Christ in the Host, the faithful receive "den Himmel auf der Zung, im Mund die Sonne") and in a metonymic reading, in which tongue and mouth are understood to be the instruments of poetry: the tongue praises heaven in the present actions of the writing body, as the mouth praises the sun. The chiasmus in this formulation, as part of a further presence effect of the highly poetic language, traces the cross itself.

Erasure

A conception of the body, mystical embodiment, and verbal expression are thus correlated and suggest a very specific form of gendering. It has rightly been observed, as Kemper does, "daß die in Glaubensfragen stets kompromisslos strenge Orthodoxie gegen die geistliche Poesie und erbauliche Schriftstellerei einer zwar gebildeten, aber unstudierten theologischen Laiin mit ihrem mystischen Bekenntnis niemals eingeschritten ist" (that the strict orthodoxy, always without compromise in questions of faith, never intervened in the religious poetry and edifying literature of this sophisticated, yet theologically unstudied layperson and her mystical confessions) and he designates this apparent lack of intervention as noteworthy.[57] Still, such arguments are not entirely correct, for indeed, a number of her poems underwent revision by her contemporaries. Through careful attention to some reception circumstances that have received insufficient treatment in Greiffenberg scholarship,[58] it is possible to study the ways in which a male theological discourse was able to overwrite this so specifically female form of religious and esoteric representation.

The court chaplain, songbook anthologist, and early Pietist Johann Reinhard Hedinger (1664–1704) of Stuttgart published *Zwölf Andächtige Betrachtungen Oder Passions-Spiegel* in 1702, an anthology of remarkable literary quality intended for religious use. Aside from the eponymous twelve meditations on the passion, the anthology contained passion-emblems, numerous song lyrics, and poetry. Just as Hedinger interpolated his "Württembergisches Gesang-Buch" or *Andächtiger Hertzens-Klang* (Stuttgart, 1713) with seven religious songs by Magdalena Sibylla, the Duchess of Württemburg,[59] the *Passions-Spiegel* also contains texts by other authors, and these include a certain "Zugabe Einiger Andachten und Lieder / Welche sich in der gottseligen Frauen Catharinæ Reginæ, Frauen von Greiffenberg / Freyherrin zu Seissenegg / &c. Ann. 1673. zu Nürnberg gedruckten Passions-Betrachtungen befinden" (addition of certain devotions and songs which are found in the *Meditations on the Passion* of the blessed Lady Catharina Regina, Lady of Greiffenberg, Baroness of Seisenegg etc., printed AD 1673 in Nuremberg).[60] Here, Hedinger edited ten songs and "Etliche Geistreiche Sonneten. obgedachter vornehmen Auctorin" (several spiritually edifying sonnets of the aforesaid distinguished author) (1702, 280). The thirteen sonnets (1702, 280–93) derive from Greiffenberg's *Passionsbetrachtungen*, taken and adapted or rather "Hier und da geändert" (changed here and there) from the original, as Hedinger reports in a caption. Compared to Greiffenberg's version from 1683, nearly every instance of mystical representation that had been phrased in terms of clearly female humidity and temperature is rephrased or omitted in Hedinger's edition.

The revisions may be explained through three driving forces. First, the revisions belong to a poetological program: the literary society of the Pegnitzschäfer, whose exponent Sigmund von Birken set the standard for the writings of Greiffenberg, had long been out of fashion by 1700. Her so-called *nürnbergisierenden* style had already elicited ironic commentary from her contemporaries, such as the literary historian Erdmann Neumeister (*De Poetis Germanicis hujus seculi*, 1695).[61] Soon after her death, the literary qualities of her poetry were not as well received as their theological message. Zedler characterized her—not without condescension—as "ein in der Theologie wohlerfahrnes Fräulein" (a young lady well-versed in theology).[62] At the beginning of his short article from 1712, Christian Franz Paullini named only her meditations on the nativity and the passion as poetic works "die sie gar anmuthig heraus gegeben" (that she graciously issued) while her volume of sonnets from 1662 receives no mention. Paullini approvingly cites Wagenseil's remark on the style ("ob des lieblichen Styli") in which she had written so profoundly on "diese heilige und göttliche Sachen" (these holy and godly matters). The article closes with a final comment that despite her midsized stature, her "Geist und Gemüth aber schwung sich immer Sternenwerts" (her spirit and mind, however, always swung toward the stars).[63] Hedinger, well-versed in the literary fashions of the day and oriented toward the gallant ideals of Neumeister, claimed in another caption to have "freed" the poems from their original style: "Vieler Orthen sehr geändert / und von denen gar zu hohen / zum Theil hartlautenden Redens-Arten / der Einfalt zum besten / befreyet" ([I have] in many places changed much and freed them [the poems] from the much too high, in part harsh-sounding manner of speech in favor of simplicity).[64] He frames his revisions as acts of modernization, to aid in the understanding of the text, of course at the expense of its poetic complexity. The work of revision, in line with the *genus medium*, was a success by his criteria: if Greiffenberg's seventeenth strophe exhibits considerable variation on the motif of sweetness, then Hedinger composes his version of strophe 14 according to contemporary literary practice as "Honigseim" (unrefined honey), "Rosen-Düffte" (rose-aromas), and "Feüer-Blick" (fire-gaze). His version disambiguates the paronomasia "der in dem Schoß des Höchsten ist gesessen" (who has sat in the lap of the highest one) (str. 3), reading simply: "Der doch ist GOttes Sohn / und aller Himmel Preiß" (who is the son of God and praise of all heaven). Complex imagery is flattened out, as in the expression "O mache mich den Hertzen-Ofen heitzen. Ach backe dich mit meinen Liebes-Kohlen" (Oh cause me to heat the heart-oven, Oh bake yourself with your coals of love) in the sixth strophe, which becomes "Dring durch das Hertz hinein / und mehre seine Krafft / Die Honig-Speiß allein Muth / Trost und Leben schafft" (pierce through my heart and increase its strength. The food of honey alone gives me courage, comfort, and life). Some revisions go awry in their intent, as in the changes made to Greiffenberg's bold reformulation of the Good Shepherd, who is sheltered in the mouth of the faithful during communion: "Der Sünder Mund zum Schafstall . . . beliebet" (who loves to use the mouth of sinners as a sheep pen) (str. 2); Hedinger maintains the vocalism to confusing effects: "Selbst dieser Sünden-Wurm zum Schaf-Stall dir beliebt" (even this worm of sin is pleasing for you to use as a sheep pen). The original apostrophe "O Liebe! was will man doch mehr verlangen?" (O love! what more can one desire?) (str. 2) loses its meaning through the preservation of the homophone, revised to read "O Liebe! Was soll ich von deinem Meer verlangen?" (O love! What should I desire from your sea?).

Throughout the later edition, the original references to the speaker in first-person personal pronouns are changed and thus objectified to the third-person: "sind Sachen / die im Wunder-Lufft verzucken / und uns / aus uns erstarrend fast verrucken") ([there are] things that cause ecstasy in the miraculous air and nearly bring us outside of ourselves in our petrification) (str. 4) in the original reads in Hedinger's revision as: "Ist ein Geheimnüß / das den schwachen Geist berückt / Und aus Erstarrung ihn zum dritten Himmel rückt" ([there is] a secret that captivates the weak soul and pushes him from his petrification into third Heaven). Petrification and heavenly flight (str. 16) are omitted entirely, while Hedinger cuts all passages that attest to the interior experiences of the speaker, such as the phrase in the seventh strophe: "in dir hab ich all Hertz-Begierd gefunden" (in you I have found all my heart's desire). The same can be said for the emotional register of the text. Greiffenberg's restatement of *Gier* (lust/desire) three times in strophes 8, 9, and 22, as well as a further instance in the aforementioned "Hertz-Begierd" (heart's-desire) are all missing from the revision. In the seventh strophe of Hedinger's edition, the speaker has lost her lust (str. 9), but now evinces a theological impossibility in her ability to taste "aus Christi Brust den Born der Ewigkeit" (the spring of eternity from Christ's breast).

The second aspect necessary to explain Hedinger's revisions then concerns the theological program in the specific medial format of the hymnal. The contents of such a hymnal were not considered lyrical works in their own right, but rather texts open to revision and reformulation.[65] Thus, Hedinger is not alone in his treatment of Greiffenberg's poetry, or in the words of Schöllkopf he shows a "typischen aneignenden Umgang mit der Tradition" (typical appropriative approach to the tradition).[66] He moves from the collective voice ("Wir") of the Reformation to the more personal lyrics ("Ich") of Pietism and uses the same poetic framework to revise Greiffenberg's theological propositions. The later editor redacts the mystical outpourings of the lone poet whose style lingered in the glory days of Birken. Hedinger represents the moderate position of Württemberg Pietism, which was averse to the all-too mystical religiousness as found in the example of Greiffenberg. "Dem nur schwach ausgeprägten Buß- und Sündenbewußtsein der Greiffenberg korrespondiert eine schier unerschütterliche Erwählungsgewißheit" (Greiffenberg's only weakly developed awareness of penance and sin is opposed to a nearly unshakable certainty of election),[67] as Kemper argues, and it is clear that Hedinger intervenes to restore the balance between these two poles. The way in which he changes her passionate mystical address to the Heavenly Groom—whose speaker invites identification with the audience, wards off the fatal "Zauber-Gifft" (magic-poison) of sin, and in the exigency of death, becomes a new person—into a careful church hymn is also clear. Greiffenberg writes enthusiastically in a series of exclamations and apostrophes:

> 13. Hätt ewig doch der Augenblick gewähret!
> ach! wäre mir all Augenblick bescheret
> diß theure Glück! O Jesu! ich wolt sterben/
> auch tausentmahl / könt ich nur dich erwerben.

> 13. If only the instant had lasted forever! Oh! if only this dear happiness were granted to me every instant! O Jesus! I would die a thousand times if only I could win you.

In the rational style of theological reflection, her editor Hedinger replaces the end-rhyme *erwerben* (earn, win) and its promise of hope with fears of ruination:

> 11. Der Sünde Zauber-Gifft kan nimmer mich verderben:
> Jch fange an mit dir gantz süssiglich zu sterben/
> Und diese Sterbens-Noth gebiert was Neus in mir/
> Daß ich / der Boßheit tod / hinkünfftig lebe dir.

———

> 11. The magic poison of sin can never corrupt me: I start to die sweetly with you, and the misery of dying births something new in me, so that I, dead to evil, in the future may live for you.

Greiffenberg's poetic multiplication of God in the tenth strophe ("von GOtt / mit GOtt / durchgöttert" [by God, with God, thoroughly divinized]), along with the disjunctive line on the separation of the Spirit and God, "Es ist der Geist im Himmel / GOtt im Leibe" (it is the Spirit in heaven, God in the body) seem to have motivated Hedinger in his simplification of the eighth strophe:

> Gewünschtes Paradeiß! Du Himmel auf der Erden/
> Kan ich genug durch dich in GOtt verherrlicht werden?
> Weil JEsus in mir wohnt / der Fürst vom Sternen-Kreiß/
> So bleib ich seine Lust / Er aber meine Speiß.

———

> The paradise I desire! You heaven on earth, can I be glorified in God enough through you? Because Jesus lives in me, the prince of the orbit of the stars, so I remain his desire, but he my nourishment.

Against the sensual experience of the *unio* in the fourteenth strophe ("der schmecke hier / und fühl / was man genieße" [let him taste here and feel what one enjoys]), Hedinger asserts the Pauline theology of the cross of the new man in Romans 6:6 (str. 12).

The aforementioned emphasis on the theological dimension over the emotional may be seen in particular in those passages in which

Greiffenberg writes of lust and desire. Ever the man of the institutional church, Hedinger intervenes and replaces these with the more straightforward text: "Wie bin ich aller Lust und ihrer Lockung feind" (how I hate all desire and all temptation) (Hedinger, str. 10). For her part, Greiffenberg has written in the eleventh strophe of a joyful swallowing up of the so-called spirit of lust ("Geist der Wollust"). So too, the same strophe ends with the *adhortatio* "Ach küß und iß ihn ganz / vor Lieb / mein Munde!" (Oh kiss and eat him up out of love, my mouth!) and yet Hedinger replaces this with a far-less erotic variant, the compound adjective in the phrase "Küß und iß ihn gantz mit rein-verliebtem Munde" (kiss and eat him up with a pure, in-love mouth). The eighteenth strophe on the amorous reverberations of the speaker's heart ("das Herz von Liebes-Praßlen hallet" [the heart echoes with the crackling of love]) consequently disappears from the later revision entirely, as well as the explicit twentieth strophe on the Heavenly Groom. The editor accomplished this effective discharge of sensual imagery by charging the text of his revision with religious references: the dewy joyfulness of the cellar ("Keller") yields to the more somber tomb ("Keller-Gruft") (str. 15/13), and similarly, Greiffenberg's orthographically ambiguous verse, "wo ich den Mund zur Himmels-Hölle mache / der nimmer-satt / vor Freuden weinend-lache" (where I make my mouth into a cave (or: a hell) of heaven that is never sated, weeping, I laugh out of joy) (str. 15), now reads: "Vor Freuden weine ich / und jauchze doch dabey: / Ich dencke / daß es schon deß Himmels Vorspiel sey" (out of joy I weep and rejoice nevertheless while I do. I think that it is already the prelude to heaven) (Hedinger, str. 13).

With this register of emotion in mind, the body comes into view as seen from a female perspective—and with it, the third aspect of the revisions considered here, that is, the erasure and reversal of gender marking. The twentieth strophe is erased, along with the gender marking of the (mystical) female union; it is said that "die Hertzens-Lamp´ erglänzt von diesem Oele" (the lamp of the heart, brightened by this oil), whereby the lamp filled with oil is none other than the wise virgins in the parable in Matthew 25:1–13. Strophes 12 through 14 are erased, along with their evident performance of bodily experience, so too the strophes concerning Christ as a man (str. 7) and bridegroom (str. 20). If Greiffenberg apostrophizes the soul and throat, which "zugleich mit inner springen" (at once with inner dancing) and "[den] Geist der Wollust jezt verschlingen" (swallow the spirit of wantonness) (str. 11), then Hedinger takes up the coupling-metaphor, but only at a distance admissible to the institutional church: "Hier Bräutigam und Braut / Als zwey in eins gepaart / auf ewig sind getraut" (here bridegroom and bride, as two paired as one, are forever wedded) (str. 9). All manifestations of the amorous female body—such as lust, the stiffening of the body in ecstasy, or the fireworks of the all-too powerful internal heat that is only accessible to the "cold" female body of humoral pathology in the loving act of copulation or in mysticism—are omitted (str. 8, 16, 18) or changed (see str. 4, 11).

The final strophes exhibit an editorial effort that professes to be a mere revision, yet actually produces a reversal. In this closing phrase, too, Greiffenberg arrives at the *topoi* of falling silent and the inadequacy of speech in light of a plenitude of emotion:

> 21. Was für ein Lob kan man dafür auch geben?
> wann alle Lüft voll Engel wurden schweben/
> noch könten sie kein Wörtlein nicht erreichen.
> Ich werde stumm / weil ichs nicht kan vergleichen.

———

> 21. What sort of praise can one give for it? If all the air would float full of angels, they would not be able to say a single little word. I become mute, because I can compare nothing with it.

Hedinger consequently excises the poetological reference to the Song of Songs, beginning with the initial line that connects the fluid *Dinte* (ink) of the writer back to the traditional allegorical flames of the heart; it can be no surprise that the intricate verse "den Himmel auf der Zung / im Mund die Sonne" (Heaven on the tongue, in the mouth the sun) is also absent from the later edition. At the close of his rendition of the poem, Hedinger now also invokes the *topos* of the inadequacy of language—but while Greiffenberg employs the device as a punch line of sorts at the end of the poem, its lyrical potency proving quite the opposite of silent resignation, her later editor allowed the lyrical-*Ich* to babble without language in sheer wonder when faced with circumstances beyond rational explanation: "Was lall' ich aber viel von unermessnen Dingen / Die durch der Liebe Macht mich zur Verwundrung zwingen" (why do I prattle about unmeasured things that force me, through the force of love, to wonderment). The inability to express oneself under such conditions corresponds to a wealth of emotions, a warming of the soul in love, which is no longer produced by the female partner, but through God as a man and through "seiner Liebe Gluth" (the embers of his love). In plain, theologically sanctioned manner, Hedinger positions the order of the sexes as somewhere between the intellect and sensation. God created "unermessne Dinge" (unmeasured things) which compel the intellect of the speaker into amazement through the performance of divine "Liebe[s] Macht" (power of love). The heat of love and the flash of female ardor appear exclusively as products of the divine agent, God: "Ich fühle JEsu Krafft / und lebe Lieb-erhitzt / Weil seiner Liebe Gluth in meinen Adern blitzt" (I feel the strength of Jesus and live heated by love, because the blaze of his love flashes in my veins). This editorial (yet theologically comprehensible) displacement of activity onto Christ complements the now-passive portrayal of the speaker from the beginning: while Greiffenberg transformed ink into heat that actively roasted the lamb of heaven ("Himmels-Lamm," str. 1), her transformations from breath (*Odem*) into embers (*Glut*), from soul (*Seele*) into fiery coals (*Kohlen-Brand*) through the coming of the Savior are made passive, closed off through the inactive first-person speaker. So too, the final strophe of the original features a lyrical-*Ich* that is at once an active, speaking, feeling, thinking, and meditating first-person narrator:

> Ich sterbe schier / vor Gier / GOtt für zu preisen/
> verzehre mich mit Freuden / diesen Speißen/
> der Erz-Herz-lieb ein wenig nachzudenken.
> Ja / ich erstumm / will ganz mich drein versenken.

———

> I will soon die from my desire to praise God, will devour myself with joys, those foods, in order to consider a little the love of the heart of God. Yes, I go mute, I want to sink myself completely into it.

Hedinger's speaker, by contrast, inserts an act of submission between the active and transitive sinking (*Versenken*) and the passive sinking-in (*Einsinken*) by means of the semantic difference between the initial syllable and the compound verb: "Sey ewig über mich ein ohnumschränckter Meister! / Verschlinge mich in dich; Ich sincke in dich ein" (be ever an unbounded master over me! Swallow me into yourself. I sink into you). Whereas Greiffenberg celebrated her own meditative performance with death, self-consumption, and falling silent, Hedinger's version of the poem culminates in a benedictory apostrophe and a double interjection. The formulation in this version has become so completely passive with respect to God that the speaker wishes to be swallowed up and absorbed into him. The ascription of gender is thus expanded and completed through the additional opposition between active and passive; knowledge and desire are designated as unfathomable and unrealizable respectively, and finally, the latter is even supplemented with a moment of pain along the lines of a theology of the female sex (see Gen. 3:16),[68] exclaiming: "O süsse Liebes Pein" (O sweet pain of love). The metaphor of the active sinking ("Ein*senken*," emphasis mine), which for Greiffenberg and in the gallant tradition of poetics designates physical union from the male perspective, here turns into its opposite. The passive sinking *in* ("Ein*sinken*," emphasis mine) of the female speaker into the master ("Meister") effectively erases the erotic context in its Pietistic reworking and finds itself produced anew in the mystical speech of a male order of the sexes.

Translated by Hannah Hunter-Parker, Sara S. Poor, and Jonathan S. Martin

Appendix

Synopse des Abendmahlslieds Greiffenbergs und der Bearbeitung Hedingers

Catharina Regina von Greiffenberg
Vom H. Nachtmahl.

1. KEin Wunder wär/ die Dinte würd zu Flammen/
wann sie vormahlt des Erz-Verliebten Namen.
Jezt muß sie gar zu Glut und Kohlen werden/
indem sie brätt das Himmels-Lamm auf Erden.

2. O Liebe! was will man doch mehr verlangen?
du gibst nicht nur dich in das Fleisch gefangen:
Der Sünder Mund zum Schafstall dir beliebet.
Du wirst zur Speiß/ dem/ der dich hat betrübet.

3. Ein grosses war/ ein Mensch vor Menschen werden;
ein grössers noch/ ein Lämmlein vor die Herden;
das gröste doch/ den geben selbst zu essen/
der in dem Schoß des Höchsten ist gesessen.

4. Der Süßheit Marck/ vor bittre Gallen/ geben;
mit Heiligkeit/ im Sü[n]den-Schlamme schweben:
sind Sachen/ die im Wunder-Lufft verzucken/
und uns/ aus uns erstarrend fast verrucken.

5. Es will/ in einem Stäublein/ zu dem S[t]aube/
der Höchst´/ auf daß den Hochmuth er betaube.
weil [recte „will“?] daß alhier die Ertz-Krafft aller Kräfften
in Brößlein Brod sich pfleget ein zu häfften.

6[.] O Himmel-mahl! O Geist-und Weißheit Weitzen!
O mache mich den Hertzen-Ofen heitzen.
Ach backe dich mit meinen Liebes-Kohlen/
der du uns wirst/ wie wir nur selber wollen.

7. O Wunder-Mann´ und rechtes Engel-Hönig/
du Purpur[-]Milch aus unserm Herzen-König/
Lieb-flüssigs Gold/ aus seinen Wunder-Wunden!
in dir hab ich all Hertz-Begierd gefunden.

Johann Reinhard Hedinger
Lied/ Von dem H. Abend-und Liebes-Mahl/ welches Christus eingesetzet vor seinem Tod. Mel. Nun dancket alle Gott/ &c.

1.
KEin Wunder wär/ wenn jetzt mein Hertze gieng zu Flammen
Jn rein verbundner Lieb zu JEsu aufzustammen!
Mein Odem würde Gluth/ die Seele Kohlen-Brand!
Der Heyland kommt zu mir von jenem Engel-Land.
2.
O Liebe! Was soll ich von deinem Meer verlangen?
Du gibst dich nicht allein in armes Fleisch gefangen;
Selbst dieser Sünden-Wurm zum Schaf-Stall dir beliebt:
Du wirst zur Seelen[-]Speiß dem der dich hat betrübt.
3.
Ein grosses war´s/ ein Mensch vor blöde Menschen werden:
Ein grössers aber noch/ ein Lämmlein vor die Heerden:
Diß alles übertrifft/ sich geben selbst zur Speiß/
Der doch ist Gottes Sohn/ und aller Himmel Preiß.
4.
Das süsse Lebens-Marck vor bittre Gallen geben;
Mit lauter Heiligkeit im Sünden-Schlamme leben/
Jst ein Geheimnüß/ das den schwachen Geist berückt/
Und aus Erstarrung ihn zum dritten Himmel rückt.
5.
Es kommt der starcke GOtt beym Stäublein einzukehren:
Wer wolte seiner Macht die schlechte Herberg wehren?
Er schleußt sich in das Brod voll Wunder selbsten ein/
Der alle Welt erfüllt; und will die Nahrung seyn.
6.
O! Himmels-Gnaden-Mahl: O Geist-begabter Weitzen/
Du kanst mich durch Genuß zu tieffer Andacht reitzen:
Dring durch das Hertz hinein/ und mehre seine Krafft/
Die Honig-Speiß allein Muth/ Trost und Leben schafft.

8. Ja allem Schmack der Seelen bist du eben/
kanst alles/ ja mehr/ als wir wünschen/ geben/
kanst nicht die Gier nur stillen/ auch vermehren/
und gleichwohl mehr/ als man verlangt/ bescheren.

9[.] O Sättigung! mit einem Meer man stillet
den Durst/ den sonst ein Tröpflein wohl erfüllet:
und pfleget doch die Gier noch fort zu glimmen/
ob wir schon satt im Meer der Süßheit schwimmen.

10[.] O Paradeis[/] O Himmel auf der Erden!
da wir von GOtt/ mit GOtt/ durchgöttert werden[.]
Es ist der Geist im Himmel/ GOtt im Leibe.
JEsu mein Herz! im Herzen ewig bleibe.

11. Mein Herze! herz dein Herz im innern Grunde.
Ach küß und iß ihn ganz/ vor Lieb/ mein Munde!
Ach Seel und kehl! zugleich mit innern springen
solt ihr den Geist der Wollust jezt verschlingen.

12. O Lieblichkeit! O Ausbund aller Wonne!
den Himmel auf der Zung/ im Mund die Sonne/
im Hertzen GOtt/ im Leibe Christum haben/
im Geist den Geist mit tausend-hohen Gaben.

13. Hätt ewig doch der Augenblick gewähret!
ach! wäre mir all Augenblick bescheret
diß theure Glück! O Jesu! ich wolt sterben/
auch tausentmahl/ könt ich nur dich erwerben.

14. Wer in der Schrifft GOtt nicht kan sehn und finden/
der komm hieher: so wird er ihn empfinden.
Wer wissen will ob sey ein GOtt wie süße:
der schmecke hier/ und fühl/ was man genieße.

15. Hier sind die Keller/ wo ich fast versinke/
wo ich mich voll und jauchzend-trunken trincke/
wo ich den Mund zur Himmels-Hölle mache/
der nimmer-satt/ vor Freuden weinend-lache.

7.
O süsse Sättigung! Mit einem Meer man stillet
Den heissen Durst/ den sonst ein Tröpfflein wohl erfüllet:
Hier schwimmt er in dem Strohm der höchsten Lieblichkeit/
Und schmeckt aus Christi Brust den Born der Ewigkeit.
8.
Gewünschtes Paradeiß! Du Himmel auf der Erden/
Kan ich genug durch dich in GOtt verherrlicht werden?
Weil JEsus in mir wohnt/ der Fürst vom Sternen-Kreiß/
So bleib ich seine Lust/ Er aber meine Speiß.
9.
Mein Hertz! So hertze denn dein Hertz im innern Grunde/
Ach! Küß und iß ihn gantz mit rein-verliebtem Munde/
Ein Geist mit Geist zu seyn. Hier Bräutigam und Braut/
Als zwey in eins gepaart/ auf ewig sind getraut.
10.
Ach! Könnt ich selbsten mich in dir/ mein Eins/ verliehren!
Du wilst mich ohnedem aus mir zum Leben führen:
Wie ist mir doch so wohl in dir/ mein Hertzen-Freund!
Wie bin ich aller Lust und ihrer Lockung feind?
11.
Der Sünde Zauber-Gifft kan nimmer mich verderben:
Jch fange an mit dir gantz süßiglich zu sterben/
Und diese Sterbens-Noth gebiert was Neus in mir/
Daß ich/ der Boßheit tod/ hinkünfftig lebe dir.
12.
Wer aber schmecken will die theure Himmels-Gaaben/
Dardurch der Hirte pflegt der Lämmer-Heer zu laben;
Der komm zu diesem Mahl und Christi Wunder-Weyd!
Hier stirbt der alte Mensch/ und mit ihm alles Leyd.
13.
Hier ist die Keller-Grufft/ worinn ich fast versinke/
Und mich in dessen Safft durch Glauben truncken trincke:
Vor Freuden weine ich/ und jauchze doch dabey:
Jch dencke/ daß es schon deß Himmels Vorspiel sey.

16. Hier ist der Saft/ der mich fast ganz versteinet/
daß mein Leib todt vor Kraft und Leben/ scheinet.
Hie ist der Brunn/ der mich in Federn kleidet/
zum Himmel-Flug/ weil er mich him(m)lisch weidet.

17. Verzuckter Zucker/ so die Süßheit führet/
mit Engel-Würtz und Rosen angerühret!
O Marck/ das aus der GOttheit Mittel kommen!
wie süß bist du/ wann dich der Glaub genommen?

18. O Feuerwerck! das in dem Blick angangen/
wann in den Mund den HErren wir empfangen/
da alles kracht/ auffsteiget/ wallt und knallet/
daß fast/ das Herz von Liebes-Praßlen hallet.

19. Die Gnaden-Strahlen alle Luft bedecken.
es schimmert alls vor Lieb in allen Ecken/
es strahlet/ funkert[/] glänzet/ als die Sterne.
Es dunkt der Himmel uns nicht halb so ferne.

20. Man hat den Schöpfer durch sein ertz-erbarmen/
und JEsum Christ/ als Bräutgam/ in den Armen/
den Flammen-Geist und Meister in der Seele.
die Hertzens-Lamp´ erglänzt von diesem Oele.

21. Was für ein Lob kan man dafür auch geben?
wann alle Lüft voll Engel wurden schweben/
noch könten sie kein Wörtlein nicht erreichen.
Ich werde stumm/ weil ichs nicht kan vergleichen.

22. Ich sterbe schier/ vor Gier/ GOtt für zu preisen/
verzehre mich mit Freuden/ diesen Speißen/
der Erz-Herz-lieb ein wenig nachzudenken.
Ja/ ich erstumm/ will ganz mich drein versenken.

14.
Hier ist das Zucker-Rohr/ so nichts als süsses führet/
Dabey man Honigseim und Rosen-Düffte spühret.
Hier ist der Feuer-Blick/ der Marck und Hertz verzehrt/
Und diese bleiben doch im brennen ohnversehrt.

15.
Die Gnaden-Strahlen hier der Seelen Hauß bedecken:
Es schimmert/ gläntzt und prangt das Licht an allen Ecken:
Es glimmt der Liebe Stern im Abgrund/ daß ich meyn´/
Der Himmel müsse mir ums halb-Theil näher seyn.

16.
Was lall´ ich aber viel von unermessnen Dingen/
Die durch der Liebe Macht mich zur Verwundrung zwingen.
Jch fühle JEsu Krafft/ und lebe Lieb-erhitzt/
Weil seiner Liebe Gluth in meinen Adern blitzt.
17.
Ach JEsu bleib bey mir/ du König reiner Geister/
Sey ewig über mich ein ohnumschränckter Meister!
Verschlinge mich in dich; Jch sincke in dich ein/
O! Unergründte Lust/ O süsse Liebes Pein!

On the Lord's Supper
(Translation by Jonathan S. Martin)

1. It would be no wonder if the ink turned to flame, for it grinds the name of the first-beloved. Now it must turn to ashes and coal while it roasts the heavenly Lamb on earth.

2. O love! What else can one desire? You don't just surrender yourself into the flesh as a prisoner. The mouth of sinners is pleasing to you as the stall for the lamb. You turn into food for the one who has saddened you.

3. It would be a great thing to become a man among men, but greater still to become a little lamb among the herds, and yet the greatest thing would be to provide Him as food who has sat in the lap of the Highest one.

4. To give the pulp of sweetness for bitter gall, to wallow with holiness in the slime of sin, these are things that cause ecstasy in the miraculous air and nearly bring us in awe outside of ourselves.

5. The Highest one wants to [come] to the dust in a speck of dust, so that he numbs pride. He wants to cause the ultimate-strength of all strengths to integrate itself with [his] crumbly bread.

6. O heavenly supper! O wheat of soul and wisdom! O cause me to fire the oven of my heart. O bake yourself with my coals of love, so that you will come to us, which is our only wish.

7. O wondrous man, true honey of the Angels! You purple milk from the King of Hearts, gold flowing with love from his wondrous wounds! In you I have found all my heart's desire.

8. Yea, you are equal to every taste of the soul, you can grant everything, yea even more than we wish. You not only quench our desire, you also increase it, and nevertheless grant even more than we ask for.

Song of the Holy Lord's Supper and Meal of Love, which Christ instituted before his death. Melody: *Nun dancket alle Gott* etc.

1.

It would be no wonder if my heart now went up in flames, in order to rise up to Jesus in pure bonded love! My breath would become a blaze, my soul, burning embers! The savior comes to me from that land of angels!

2.

O love! What should I desire from your sea? You don't only render yourself into poor flesh; even this sinful worm would please you as a stall for the lamb. You turn into the food of souls for the one who has saddened you.

3.

It would be a great thing to be a man among feeble men, but greater still to be a little lamb among the herds. All of this is superseded by giving oneself as food -- him who is indeed the Son of God and the praise of all Heaven.

4.

To give the sweet pulp of life for bitter gall, to live in pure holiness in the slime of sin, this is a secret that ambushes the weak soul and pushes him from his awestruck state to the third Heaven.

5.

Strong God comes in the form of a grain of dust: who would want to prevent his might from taking these bad lodgings? He shuts himself up in the bread, full of wonder, he who fills all the world and wants to be its nourishment.

6.

O! Heavenly meal of grace: o wheat graced with spirit! You can stimulate me to deep devotion through your enjoyment. Pierce into my heart and increase its strength. The honeyed food alone gives me courage, comfort, and life.

9. O satiation! With an ocean is quenched that thirst that would otherwise be satisfied with a droplet. And yet desire continues to glow uninterrupted, whether we swim in a sea of sweetness or not.

10. O paradise! O Heaven on earth! For we are thoroughly made God by God with God. The soul is in Heaven, God in the body. Jesus, my heart! Stay in my heart forever!

11. My heart! Hearten your heart to its very core. O kiss and eat him up for love, my mouth! O soul and throat! Immediately, with inner dancing, you should swallow the spirit of lust.

12. O loveliness! O paragon of all joy! To have heaven on the tongue, the sun in the mouth, God in the heart, Christ in the body, the Spirit in the soul with a thousand lofty gifts.

13. If only the instant had lasted forever! o! if only every instant this dear happiness were granted to me! O Jesus! I would like to die even a thousand times if only I could win you.

14. Whoever cannot see or find God in Scripture, let him come here: thus will he feel Him. Whoever wants to know how sweet a God is, let him taste this and feel what one enjoys.

15. Here are the cellars where I almost sink, where I drink myself full and rejoicingly drunk, where I make my mouth into the Hell of Heaven that is never sated and weeping, laugh for joy.

7.

O sweet satiation! One quenches this hot thirst with an ocean that would otherwise be satisfied with a droplet. Here he swims in the current of the highest loveliness and tastes the spring of eternity coming from Christ's chest.

8.

Wished for paradise! You Heaven on earth! Can I be glorified in God enough through you? Because Jesus lives in me, the prince of the orbits of the stars, thus I remain his desire, but he my food.

9.

My heart! Thus hearten your heart at its core! O! Kiss and eat him up with a pure in-love mouth, in order to be a spirit with spirit. Here bridegroom and bride, as two paired as one, are forever wedded .

10.

O! If only I could lose myself in you, my One! You want to lead me out of myself to life regardless. How very comfortable I feel in you, friend of my heart! How greatly do I hate all desire and temptation?

11.

The magic poison of sin can never corrupt me: I begin to die sweetly with you, and the moment of dying gives birth to something new in me, so that I, dead to iniquity, in the future may live for you.

12.

Whoever wants to taste the dear gifts of Heaven through which the Shepherd refreshes his horde of lambs, let him come to this supper and to Christ's wondrous pasture! Here the old person dies, and with him all suffering.

13.

Here is the cellar-tomb, in which I almost sink and drink until I am drunk through faith from its juice. I weep for joy and rejoice as well. I think that this is already the prelude to Heaven.

16. Here is the juice that turns me nearly completely to stone, so that my body seems dead in strength and life. Here is the spring that clothes me in feathers for the flight to heaven, because He grazes on me in heavenly.

17. Rapturous sugar, that contains such sweetness, that is mixed with the herbs of angels and roses! O pulp that comes forth in the transmitter [i.e., the bread?] of divinity! How sweet are you once belief has taken you?

18. O fireworks! that explode in our eyes when we have received the Lord in our mouth, when everything cracks, rises, rolls, and pops, so that the heart almost echoes with the crackling of love.

19. The rays of grace blanket all the air. In every corner, everything glows from love, it shines, sparkles, glows like the stars. Heaven does not seem half as far from us.

20. One holds the creator, through his supreme mercy, and Jesus Christ, as bridegroom in one's arms, the Spirit of flames and master in the soul. The lamp of the heart glows from this oil.

21. What sort of praise can one give for it? If all the air would float full of angels, they would not be able to say a single little word. I become mute, because there is nothing to compare.

22. I will soon die of the desire to praise God, will devour myself with joys, those foods, in order to consider a little the love of the ultimate heart. Yea, I go mute, I want to sink myself completely into it.

14.

Here is the sugarcane that contains nothing but a sweetness in which one tastes honey and the scent of roses. Here is the look of fire which devours marrow and heart, and yet they remain uninjured while they burn.

15.

The rays of grace blanket the house of souls here. The light sparkles, shines, and is resplendent in all corners. The star of love glimmers in the abyss so that I feel like Heaven must be half as close to me.

16.

Why do I prattle on about infinite things that through the power of love compel me to wonderment? I feel Jesus' strength and live heated by love because the blaze of his love sparkles in my veins.

17.

O Jesus, stay with me! You king of pure souls, be ever an unbounded master over me! Swallow me into yourself. I sink into you. O! Unfathomed desire! O sweet pain of love!

Notes

This essay is a translation of Franz M. Eybl, "'Den Himmel auf der Zunge,' im Mund die Sonne: Catharina Regina von Greiffenberg zwischen Eucharistie und Erotik," in *Scharfsinn und Frömmigkeit: Zum Werk von Catharina Regina von Greiffenberg (1633–1694)*, Berliner Beiträge zur Literatur- und Kulturgeschichte 16, ed. Gesa Dane (Frankfurt am Main: Peter Lang, 2013), 39–77; translated and published with permission.

1. Gerhard Dünnhaupt, *Personalbibliographien zu den Drucken des Barock*, 6 vols. (Stuttgart: Anton Hiersemann Verlag, 1991), 3:1752–58. For an introduction, see Louise Gnädinger, "Ister-Clio, Teutsche Uranie, Coris die Tapfere. Catharina Regina von Greiffenberg (1633–1694): Ein Porträt," in *Deutsche Literatur von Frauen*, 2 vols., ed. Gisela Brinker-Gabler (Munich: C. H. Beck, 1988), 1:248–64; see the chapter on Greiffenberg, "Ketzereien aus Rechtgläubigkeit (Greiffenberg)," in Hans-Georg Kemper, *Deutsche Lyrik der frühen Neuzeit*, 6 vols. (Tübingen: Niemeyer, 1988), 3:245–78; Lynne Tatlock, "Catharina Regina von Greiffenberg (1633–1694)," in *Deutsche Frauen der frühen Neuzeit. Dichterinnen, Malerinnen, Mäzeninnen*, ed. Kerstin Merkel and Heide Wunder (Darmstadt: Wiss. Buchgesellschaft, 2000), 93–106; for useful discussions, see the special edition of the *Jahrbuch des Wiener Goethe-Vereins* 100–101 (1996–97), which documents the proceedings and contributions of the 1995 symposium on Greiffenberg; and a report on the state of Greiffenberg scholarship in Werner Wilhelm Schnabel, "Vom Ister an die Pegnitz: Lebenssituationen der Barockdichterin Catharina Regina von Greiffenberg," in *Exulanten aus der niederösterreichischen Eisenwurzen in Franken. Eine familien- und kirchengeschichtliche Untersuchung, bearb. v. Manfred Enzner u. Eberhard Krauß* (Nuremberg: Gesellschaft fur Familienforschung in Franken, 2005), 265–301.

2. On Greiffenberg's theology, see the chapter "Doketische 'Betrachtungen' über den 'Gold-Geist' Christus," in Kemper, *Deutsche Lyrik*, 3:252–59; Dietz-Rüdiger Moser, "Judas die Lippen-Viper, Jesus das auserlesenste Küsse-Ziel: Zu den Passionsbetrachtungen der Catharina Regina von Greiffenberg," *Literatur in Bayern* 38 (1994): 50–57; Jörg Baur, "Jesusfrömmigkeit und Christologie bei Catharina Regina von Greiffenberg (1633–1694)," in *Pietas in der lutherischen Orthodoxie*, ed. Udo Sträter (Wittenberg: Drei-Kastanien-Verlag, 1998), 100–124. For more on the context of theology in Nuremberg, see Johann Anselm Steiger, "'Der Tauben-Fels, ist diese süsse Höle': Die lyrische Verarbeitung eines Topos der Hohelied-Exegese in der Kasuallyrik Sigmund von Birkens," in *Theorie und Praxis der Kasualdichtung in der Frühen Neuzeit*, ed. Andreas Keller, Elke Lösel, Ulrike Wels, and Volkhard Wels (New York: Rodopi, 2010), 343–65; Vanessa Lohse, "Poetische Passionstheologie. Betrachtungen zu Catharina Regina von Greiffenbergs Betrachtungen des Leidens Christi," in *Passion, Affekt und Leidenschaft in der frühen Neuzeit*, 2 vols., ed.

Johann Anselm Steiger (Wiesbaden: Harrassowitz, 2005), 1:289–99, Lohse forgoes a cogent rhetorical analysis in the context of the *sermo-humilis* concept.

3. See the essay by Hartmut Laufhütte, "Passion Christi bei Sigmund von Birken und Catharina Regina von Greiffenberg," in Steiger, *Passion, Affekt und Leidenschaft*, 1:271–87.

4. Catharina Regina von Greiffenberg, *Sämtliche Werke*, 10 vols., ed. Martin Bircher and Friedhelm Kemp (Millwood, N.Y.: Kraus Reprint, 1983), vol. 1. Hereafter, references to the *Sämtliche Werke* will be given as follows: (SW volume number, page numbers).

5. English translations of selections of the meditations are available in Catharina Regina von Greiffenberg, *Meditations on the Incarnation, Passion, and Death of Jesus Christ*, trans. Lynne Tatlock (Chicago: University of Chicago Press, 2009).

6. Tatlock, "Catharina Regina von Greiffenberg," 95.

7. This distinction comes from Stefanie Ertz, Heike Schlie, and Daniel Weidner, eds., *Sakramentale Repräsentation: Substanz, Zeichen und Präsenz in der Frühen Neuzeit* (Munich: Fink, 2012).

8. Kemper, *Barock-Mystik*, 262.

9. "Greiffenberg creates extravagant images of protean and transformative female bodies that suffer as well as alleviate suffering." Lynne Tatlock, "Empathic Suffering: The Inscription and Transmutation of Gender in Catharina Regina von Greiffenberg's Leiden und Sterben Jesu Christi," *Wolfenbütteler Barock-Nachrichten* 34, no. 1 (2007): 27–50, here 44.

10. SW 10, 603 f. The following observations focus on this ninth meditation (SW 10, 520–631), which concerns the crucifixion and thus the culmination of the series.

11. There are more than three dozen references to *Fett* (fat) in the sacrificial context in Luther's translation of the Bible; for the connection with *Mark* (marrow), see Isa. 25:6. For the suggestion of an alchemical transformation through fire (though far less obtrusive in the context of Greiffenberg's lyric, with their firm scriptural basis), see Burkhard Dohm, *Poetische Alchimie: Öffnung zur Sinnlichkeit in der Hohelied- und Bibeldichtung von der protestantischen Barockmystik bis zum Pietismus* (Tübingen: Max Niemeyer, 2000), 75–78.

12. In her study, Vanessa von der Lieth does not move beyond the observation that the comparative and exegetical relationship of the terms "zumeist durch Kontrast und Überbietung gekennzeichnet ist" (is primarily distinguished through contrast and emulation). Vanessa von der Lieth, "Die Rezeption antiker Mythologeme im Betrachtungswerk Catharina Regina von Greiffenbergs," in *Welche Antike? Konkurrierende Rezeptionen des Altertums im Barock*, 2 vols., ed. Ulrich Heinen (Wiesbaden: Harrassowitz, 2011), 2:737–51, here 740.

13. Lehel Sata, "Dichtung als 'Göttliche Verkehrungs-Kunst': Zu Catharina Regina von Greiffenbergs 'Des Allerheiligst- und Allerheilsamsten

JESUS-Leidens / Erster Betrachtung,'" in *'Der Rest ist—Staunen': Literatur und Performativität*, ed. Erika Hammer and Edina Sándorfi (Vienna: Praesens Verlag, 2006), 9–40, here 21–25.

14. Martin Opitz, "Salomons hohes Lied Von Martin Opitzen in Reime gebracht," in *Geistliche Poëmata* (1638), ed. Erich Trunz (Tübingen: Max Niemeyer, 1966), 13–34, here *Das fünffte Lied*, 27.

15. Martin Luther, *Biblia, Das ist die gantze Heilige Schrifft Deutsch auffs new zugericht* (Wittenberg, 1545), 3 vols., ed. Hans Volz (Munich: Deutscher Taschenbuch-Verlag, 1974), 2:1155.

16. Martin Luther, *BIBLIA, Das ist / Die gantze Heilige Schrifft / Alten und Neuen Testaments* (Wittenberg: Wust, 1665) (Kupfertitel: Wittenberg, 1671), available online at http://resolver.staatsbibliothek-berlin.de/SBB000079DC00000000 [22.1.2013], Print:393, digital version, 863.

17. Thomas Aquinas Erhard, *Biblia Sacra Latino-Germanica oder Lateinisch und Teutsche Bibel*, 2nd ed. (Augsburg: Verlag Johann Strotters, 1726), 1:822. In the edition of the Dietenberger Bible, the verse appears as follows: "Mein seel ist zerschmoltzen nachdem der geliebt geredt hat." Johann Dietenberger, *Bibell: Das ist / Alle Bücher Alts vnd News Testaments* (Cologne: Quentel, 1604), 295.

18. Hermann Hugo, *Gottseelige Begierden der Büssenden / Heiligen und in GOTT verliebten Seelen* (Sulzbach: Lichtenthaler, 1669), 370 f., with the following citation: "Guilb. Abb. Ser. 44. in Cant.," available online at http://books.google.de/books?id=nRk9AAAAcAAJ&printsec=frontcover&hl=de&source=gbs_ge_summary_r&cad=0#v=onepage&q&f=false.

19. Cristina M. Pumplun, "Die gottliebende Seele und ihr Wegbereiter: Catharina Regina von Greiffenbergs *Geburtsbetrachtungen* (1678) und der Einfluß der Embleme der *Pia Desideria* Herman Hugos S.J. (1624)," in *Brückenschläge: Eine barocke Festgabe für Ferdinand van Ingen*, ed. Martin Bircher and Guillaume van Gemert (Amsterdam: Rodopi, 1995), 211–31, here 225. For more on an emblem design by Birken in Greiffenberg's *Passionsbetrachtungen*, which also makes reference to the Song of Songs, see Steiger, *Tauben-Fels*, 343 ff.

20. The full text is given in the appendix. Burkhard Dohm provides a detailed analysis of this song in the chapter "Die Liebesalchimie der Abendmahlspoesie" (*Poetische Alchimie*, 86–129), in which he draws in detail on the exegetical and literary tradition. Dohm attempts to bring the thematic references together in line with his initial thesis, which sees alchemistic notions, magical knowledge, and a hermetic doctrine of signs in the examined texts: Greiffenberg is said to present "gerade im vorliegenden Gedicht in besonders reicher Fülle ihre alchimistischen Abendmahlsbilder" (her alchemical visions of the communion in rich abundance, particularly in the poem here) (128). See also Daniel Weidner, "Der Körper des Wortes: Sakrament und Poetik in der geistlichen Lyrik," in Ertz, Schlie, and Weidner, *Sakramentale Repräsentation*, 82–114, here 102 ff.

21. Michael Stolz refers to the "Eucharistie als konstantes Thema und wichtiges Subsystem literarischer Kommunikation im Mittelalter und in der frühen Neuzeit" (Eucharist as a constant theme and important subsystem of literary communication in the Middle Ages and in the early modern period), though he understands the sacrament as the entryway of hermeneutic culture into the cultural formation of presence in the Middle Ages, in Hans-Ulrich Gumbrecht's sense of the term (see note 56 below), and draws on narrative texts. See Michael Stolz, "Kommunion und Kommunikation: Eucharistische Verhandlungen in der Literatur des Mittelalters," in *Literarische und religiöse Kommunikation in Mittelalter und Früher Neuzeit, DFG-Symposion 2006*, ed. Peter Strohschneider (New York: de Gruyter, 2009), 453–505, here 453.

22. See appendix.

23. See the interesting, yet purely linguistic-formalist arguments in the dissertation of Hilke Möller, "Thränen-Samen und Steckdosenschnauze. Linguistische Beschreibung von Neubildungen Catharina Reginas von Greiffenberg und Wolfdietrich Schnurres" (Zürich, 1975).

24. The alchemical association, which hints at a "tiefes Lebensgeheimnis" (deep secret of life) in a wheat stalk by virtue of a hermetic doctrine of signs (and receiving no further mention here, see Dohm, *Poetische Alchimie*, 97), obscures the play on language through metaphors and metonymies, which are of primary concern in this essay.

25. Dohm shows this with respect to the initial strophe; in Luther's Easter hymn, "Christ lag in Todesbanden" (Christ lay in chains of death), the Easter lamb is "ynn heisser lieb gebroten" (roasted in hot love) on the cross. See Dohm, *Poetische Alchimie*, 90.

26. Weidner, "Körper des Wortes," 106.

27. SW 9, 396. The fluency of the related *topos* of blindness through light can be seen also in Milton's *Paradise Lost*, in which God the Father and Christ are said to appear "as from a flaming mount, whose top / Brightness had made invisible" in line 598 f., another cipher for the blind singer of God. For more on the *topos* of the inadequacy of speech and falling silent, see Dohm, *Poetische Alchimie*, 127 ff.

28. Weidner introduces the image of flowing, in order to discuss "permanente Figurierung" (permanent figuration). As such, Greiffenberg's rules of performance and the connections between the action and the (female) body are lost from view: "Eine solche poetologische Selbstreflexion ist typisch für eine geistliche Literatur, die im eigentlichen Sinne über-flüssig ist: Sie vergegenwärtigt das Wort Gottes, das eigentlich einer solchen Vergegenwärtigung nicht bedarf; sie verflüssigt es damit aber auch, indem sie es immer wieder anders umschreibt und ausschreibt; dabei erscheint das der permanenten Figurierung zugrundeliegende Blut in seiner Materialität" (Such poetological self-reflection is typical for a religious literature, which is in the truest sense of the word

superfluous: it visualizes the Word, which requires no such realization; it liquefies its message in doing so, but also through its constant revision and rewriting in full; thus, the blood [of Christ]—with its basis in a process of permanent figuration—appears in its materiality). Weidner, "Körper des Wortes," 105.

29. In the medieval tradition, the passion story is organized according to the path of the *vita Christi*, the pause and meditation on individual elements of the salvation narrative, itself an old meditative technique, and then is deployed as poetic amplification: "die syntagmatische Achse der Erzählung wird so von einer paradigmatisch organisierten Paraphrasen- und Metaphernrede durchbrochen, sodass der in seiner Makrostruktur linear organisierte Text in seiner Mikrostruktur ins Kreisen gerät" (the syntagmatic axis of narration is thus perforated by a paradigmatically organized language of paraphrase and metaphor, such that the linearly organized text of the macrostructure follows a circular pattern in its microstructure); see Günter Butzer, "'Scribe, ut dum scribis legas'—Schreiben als Selbsttechnik," *Sprache und Literatur* 41, no. 2 (2010): 2–18, here 12.

30. Dohm emphasizes the "außerordentliche sinnlich-affektive Wirkungsqualität der Abendmahls-'unio' in ihrer Darstellung" (extraordinarily hermeneutically affective quality of the communion-*unio* on the recipient in its representation) through Greiffenberg and her ability "die sinnliche Wirkung dieses Geschehens in stets wiederholbarer Weise affektiv zu vergegenwärtigen" (to visualize affectively the sensuous impact of this event in ever-repeatable ways); see Dohm, *Poetische Alchimie*, 116; at the close, he writes: "Nach der Konzeption der Autorin wird in ihrer Poesie die spirituelle Realität des Göttlichen sinnlich erfahrbar gestaltet" (according to the author's conception, the spiritual reality of the divine is given sensuously tangible form in her poetry) (129). In opposition to this view, I follow Michael Schoenfeldt in his arguments for an understanding of the literature of the age, specifically its references to affects, from the perspective of conceptions of the body. Michael C. Schoenfeldt, *Bodies and Selves in Early Modern England: Physiology and Inwardness in Spenser, Shakespeare, Herbert, and Milton* (New York: Cambridge University Press, 1999); idem, "Eloquent Blood and Deliberative Bodies: The Physiology of Metaphysical Poetry," in *Renaissance Transformations: The Making of English Writing, 1500–1650*, ed. Thomas Healy and Margaret Healy (Edinburgh: Edinburgh University Press, 2010), 145–60.

31. The empty space before the word *erstummen* is not a double space, but rather a letter "v" that has slid into the form of type during the printing process.

32. Johann Schröder, *Medicin-Chymische Apotheke / Oder Höchstkostbarer Arzeney-Schatz* (Nuremberg: Hoffmann, 1685), facs. ed. s.a. & t. [ca. 1965], 290. A solid substance is *maceriert* (macerated) in a liquid, which draws its active ingredients from the liquid after a sometimes longer application.

33. Burkhard Dohm, "Die Auferstehung des Leibes in der Poesie: Zu einem Passionsgedicht Catharina Regina von Greiffenbergs," *Daphnis* 21 (1992): 673–94, here 684f.; Tatlock, "Empathic Suffering," 44f.

34. See Peter M. Daly, *Dichtung und Emblematik bei Catharina Regina von Greiffenberg* (Bonn: Bouvier, 1976).

35. Ruth Liwerski, *Das Wörterwerk der Catharina Regina von Greiffenberg, Teil II: Deutung*, 2 vols. (Las Vegas: Lang, 1978), 1:193.

36. Weidner, "Körper des Wortes," 112.

37. For example, Gryphius's "Threnen des Vatterlandes / Anno 1636" and Lohenstein's "Thränen." See Liwerski, *Wörterwerk*, 456n21.

38. Song of Songs 2:16f.; similarly 6:2. The enduring frequency and intelligibility of the metaphor extend even to the irreverent humor of *Faust I*, v. 3336f.: "*Mephistopheles*: Gar wohl, mein Freund! Ich hab Euch oft beneidet / Um's Zwillingspaar, das unter Rosen weidet." (Quite so, my friend! My envy often closes / On that pair of twins that feed among the roses.)

39. Johann Christian Günther, "Aria: An seine erzürnte Schöne [Louise] (MEin Vergnügen geht zu Grabe)," in *Werke*, ed. Reiner Bölhoff (Frankfurt am Main: Deutscher Klassiker Verlag, 1998), 774f.

40. "Albanie," V. 31ff. (nr. 43), in Christian Hofmann von Hoffmannswaldau, *Der galante Stil 1680–1730*, ed. Conrad Wiedemann (Tübingen: Max Niemeyer, 1969), 83f.

41. See entry for *beperlen* in *Deutsches Wörterbuch von Jacob und Wilhelm Grimm*, 16 vols. (Leipzig: S. Hirzel, 1854–1961), 1:1479.

42. Kathleen Foley-Beining, *The Body and Eucharistic Devotion in Catharina Regina von Greiffenberg's "Meditations"* (Columbia, S. C.: Camden House, 1997), 53, and *Menschwerdung* (Dritte Betrachtung), SW 3, 119.

43. Judg. 6:36–40.

44. Foley-Beining rightly observes: "There exists almost no metaphorical tension in the use of the words 'dew' and 'little drops' for God's involvement in the conception. The images directly coincide with the actual fluidity of semen in human fertilization." Foley-Beining, *Body and Eucharistic Devotion*, 54.

45. Dohm emphasizes Greiffenberg's writing program, "sich selbst auch in ihrer Leiblichkeit Christus anzuverwandeln" (to adapt herself also in her corporeality to Christ). Dohm, *Auferstehung des Leibes*, 675. Foley-Beining investigates the physical participation of the writer in her contemplative process en route to a textual simulation of a physical interaction with Christ: "she textually stages a physical interaction with Christ." Foley-Beining, *Body and Eucharistic Devotion*, 130. Lynne Tatlock has argued for a relationship of tension between the writing woman and the male-coded textual culture of the time: "I consider Greiffenberg's textual investigation and re-creation of flesh as the deliberate negotiation between a female writer and a typographic, scientific, learned high culture." Lynne Tatlock, "Scientia divinorum: Anatomy, Transmutation and Incorporation in Catharina von Greiffenberg's Meditations on the Incarnation and the Gestation of Christ," *German History* 17, no. 1 (1999): 9–24, here 11. She has also investigated the *Passionsbetrachtungen* in terms of the performance of gender as writing strategy; see Tatlock, "Empathic Suffering,"

29. The same positions also figure in the analysis of Ursula Kundert, "'O himmlische Schattirung,' 'Meßkunst unseres Heils!' Medialität der göttlichen Heilsbotschaft in Greiffenbergs Betrachtung 'Von der Empfängnis Christi,'" in *Text—Bild—Karte. Kartographien der Vormoderne*, ed. Jürg Glauser and Christian Kiening (Freiburg im Breisgau: Rombach, 2007), 435–56, especially in her connection of the "sexuelle Metaphorik in Text und Bild" (sexual metaphorics in text and image) with contemporary beliefs about procreation, as does Foley-Beining, but whose analysis of the linguistic staging fails to advance beyond identifying an irritating effect in the text; see 448–52 and 456.

46. Kemper, *Deutsche Lyrik*, 90. Kemper's psychoanalytic reading of the spiritual love in Greiffenberg's poetry as the "Entwurf einer Gegen-Welt . . . in welcher die Dichterin offenbar eine als real erfahrene Möglichkeit weiblichen Genießens fand" (model of an alternate world . . . in which the poet clearly found in her experience the real possibility of female enjoyment) should be taken with a grain of salt (252); instead, a closer inquiry into those discursive markers points to contemporary concepts of femininity.

47. See Dohm, *Poetische Alchimie*, 95. I investigate the consequences of this concept for the perception of the self and others in Franz M. Eybl, "Typus, Temperament, Tabelle. Zur anthropologischen und medientheoretischen Systematik der Völkerstereotypen," in *Frühneuzeitliche Stereotype: Zur Produktivität und Restriktivität sozialer Vorstellungsmuster*, ed. Miroslawa Czarnecka, Thomas Borgstedt, and Tomasz Jablecki (Bern: Lang, 2010), 29–43. Andrea Sieber attributes Greiffenberg's "schwermütige Gefühlsdisposition" (melancholic disposition of emotions) as found in her letters to gender, but without going into the anthropological model responsible for this concept of melancholy. See Andrea Sieber, "Melancholische Attitüden? Eine Skizze zu Catharina Regina von Greiffenberg," in *Melancholie—zwischen Attitüde und Diskurs: Konzepte in Mittelalter und Früher Neuzeit*, ed. Andrea Sieber and Antje Wittstock (Göttingen: V. & R. Unipress, 2009), 237–55, here 254.

48. Tatlock views the poet's desire to make Christ "zum brunnen meiner begierden / und zum meer aller meiner vergnügungen" (Siebende Betrachtung, SW 9, 395) as outdoing traditional bridal mysticism: "Speaking of Christ here not so much in the role of the soul as in the role of a desiring woman, she brings about a textual amplification with decidedly erotic overtones climaxing in Christ as the sea of all her pleasures." Tatlock, "Empathic Suffering," 37.

49. "Der Heilige Geist wird über dich kommen / nicht nur in diesem Werk / in deinen Geist / sondern über deinem Leib: der wird dein Geblüt reinigen / und den allerheiligsten Leib des Sohns GOttes daraus und darinn formiren / auf die allerheiligste / reineste / und unbegreiflichste Art." *Menschwerdung*, Zweite Betrachtung, SW 3,103, also quoted in Foley-Beining, *Body and Eucharistic Devotion*, 53. This is not to say that Greiffenberg forgets to al-

lude to the spiritual means of procreation. See in this respect Kundert, "Medialität der göttlichen Heilsbotschaft."

50. The woman, herself "colder" by nature, had to be first warmed and then heated through affection and endearing words until she was capable of procreation, until her bodily fluids poured out and combined with those of the man: procreation could only take place once the female seeds joined with the male. Cf. Thomas Laqueur, *Making Sex: Body and Gender From the Greeks to Freud* (Cambridge: Cambridge University Press, 1990). For the present German discussion, see Rüdiger Schnell, *Sexualität und Emotionalität in der vormodernen Ehe* (Cologne: Bohlau, 2002), and Heinz-Jürgen Voß, *Making Sex Revisited: Dekonstruktion des Geschlechts aus biologisch-medizinischer Perspektive* (Bielefeld: Transcript-Verlag, 2010).

51. Even cultural-historical analyses of the artwork miss the intricate connections with historical concepts of the female body; see, for instance, chapter 8, "Ekstatische Ästhetik: Bernini metaphert," in Mieke Bal et al., *Kulturanalyse* (Frankfurt am Main: Suhrkamp, 2002), 224–62. The statue is said here to document "daß Theresia bereits penetriert worden ist, und zwar von dem Flammenpfeil" (that Theresa has already been penetrated, namely by the arrow of flames), 248, because according to Bal, fire becomes a metaphor for passion. Contemporary discourse on the body, however, understood being inflamed as a precondition for procreation and posits a reverse chain of causality. See also Sabine Kyora, "Erotischer Genuß, religioses Ergriffensein: Korperinszenierungen in barocker Lyrik," *Euphorion* 97 (2003): 405–17.

52. Quoted in Liwerski, *Wörterwerk*, 1:179.

53. Kemper, *Deutsche Lyrik*, 268.

54. Günter Butzer has called attention to this point and has discounted the potential of ethopoietical writing in diaristic and meditational literature using the example of Greiffenberg. Textual hermeneutics are not the goal here, but rather "die im schriftlichen Meditationsakt selbst hervorzurufende dichterische Inspiration" (the poetic inspiration that can be aroused itself in the writing act of meditation); see Butzer, *Schreiben als Selbsttechnik*, 12. The author-centric thesis that inspiration can be "auf Dauer gestellt und letztlich habitualisiert werden" (set to permanence and eventually habituated) through perpetuated verbal stimulation (13) does not capture the specific oscillation between presence effect and performance in Greiffenberg's poetry.

55. Kemper, *Deutsche Lyrik*, 258–59.

56. Mysticism scholarship has not yet explored the full scope of Gumbrecht's concept; see Hans-Ulrich Gumbrecht, *Diesseits der Hermeneutik. Die Produktion von Präsenz* (Frankfurt am Main: Edition Suhrkamp, 2004); see also the chapter "Präsenz in der Sprache" in Gumbrecht, *Unsere breite Gegenwart* (Berlin: Suhrkamp Verlag, 2010), 20–32; idem, *Präsenz* (Berlin: Suhrkamp Verlag, 2012).

57. Kemper, *Deutsche Lyrik*, 252. See also Hartmut Laufhütte, "Der Heterodoxie-Verdacht gegen Catharina Regina von Greiffenberg," in *Heterodoxie in der Frühen Neuzeit*, ed. Hartmut Laufhütte and Michael Titzmann (Tübingen: de Gruyter, 2006), 325–36.

58. Liwerski, *Wörterwerk*, 1:456, quotes Johann Caspar Wetzel's *Analecta hymnica, das ist: Merckwürdige Nachlesen zur Lieder-Historie* (Gotha 1752–56) mentioning Hedinger; Wetzel knows only his 1716 edition. Wolfgang Schöllkopf, *Johann Reinhard Hedinger* (1664–1704) (Göttingen: Vandenhoeck & Ruprecht, 1999), 130–31, refers to Reinhard Wittmann, *Ein Verlag und seine Geschichte: Dreihundert Jahre J. B. Metzler Stuttgart* (Stuttgart: Metzler, 1982), 91, where the "Zugabe" is addressed as of hitherto unexplored relevance for the "Textgeschichte der bedeutendsten deutschen Barockdichterin" (textual history of the most important German baroque poetess).

59. Dünnhaupt, *Personalbibliographien*, 4:2633. Dünnhaupt names Hedinger only at this one point in his handbook and not in connection with Greiffenberg.

60. Johann Reinhard Hedinger, *Passions-Spiegel / Oder Zwölff Andächtige Betrachtungen / Uber So viel merckwürdige Umstände des blutigen Leidens und Sterbens JESU CHRISTI unsers HErrn* (Stuttgart: Metzler, 1702); the inter-title here is quoted from 253. Consequent editions appeared at the same publisher in 1706 and 1716.

61. Erdmann Neumeister, *De Poetis Germanicis*, ed. Franz Heiduk, trans. Günter Merwald (1695; Bern: Francke Verlag, 1978), 41; Neumeister comments critically on the *Sonnetten / Lieder und Gedichten* (1662): "Vocabulis certe inusitatis plane et luxuriem Noricam supergressis tantum non scatet" (it, that is, the little book is without doubt entirely full of unusual words and it is almost teeming with ones that exceed even the efforts in Nuremberg) (175).

62. Zedler, *Universal-Lexicon*, 11:815, quoted in Lohse, "Poetische Passionstheologie," 290.

63. Christian Franz Paullini, *Hoch- und wohl-gelahrtes teutsches Frauen-Zimmer, abermahl . . . vermehrt* (Frankfurt: Stössels Erben, 1712), 72 f.

64. Hedinger, *Passions-Spiegel*, 253. Expanding Greiffenberg's iambic pentameter to the Alexandrine form often led to weak adjectives.

65. In the sense of Aleida Assmann, "Schriftliche Folklore: Zur Entstehung und Funktion eines Überlieferungstyps," in *Schrift und Gedächtnis: Beiträge zur Archäologie der literarischen Kommunikation*, ed. Aleida Assmann, Jan Assmann, and Christof Hardmeier (Munich: W. Fink, 1983), 175–93.

66. Schöllkopf, *Johann Reinhard Hedinger*, 129.

67. Kemper, *Deutsche Lyrik*, 260.

68. In this sense also Luther and the orthodox contingent. See Tatlock, "Scientia divinorum," 21.

10

Sister Marcella, Marie Christine Sauer (d. 1752), and the Chronicle of the Sisters at Ephrata

BETHANY WIGGIN

> I hope you will allow the Sisters a Paragraph . . . They have so far transcended the limits of their Sex, that they joined among themselves in a visible Body, independant of any mans Government upon earth, except that they are under a fathers Tutorship. And altho' enclosed into their Appartment, yet their odoriferous fragrancy broke out every where. If I say that they are upon a Level with the Brethren, I do no Justice to their Character, I could say more, if I did not abhor all flattery. Let this be as it will, they have either more zeal for the life to come, or are naturally more inclined than we to a retired life, whilst on the contrary, in our Male-Breasts the revolting faculties of the Lapse are so abundantly collocated, that from thence hardly proceedeth anything else but rebellion and disobedience.
>
> —*Peter Miller, Letter to Benjamin Franklin, 1761*

On May 13, 1745, the celibate sisters of the mystical community at Ephrata cloister in colonial Pennsylvania completed their illuminated sisterbook, *Die Rose Oder: Der angenehmen Blumen zu Saron geistliche*

Eheverlöbnüs mit ihrem himmlischen Bräutigam, welchem sie sich als ihrem König, Haupt, Mann, Herrn, und Bräutigam, aufs ewig hin verlobt (*The Rose or: The Spiritual Wedding Vows Made by the Pleasant Flower of Sharon to Her Heavenly Bridegroom, the King, Head, Husband, Master, and Bridegroom to Whom She Promises Herself in Eternity*).[1] The volume, some four hundred octavo pages composed horizontally and bound in linen-covered boards, begins with two illuminated pages, known vernacularly in Pennsylvania German as *Frakturen*. Stylizing the traditional bridal imagery of the Rose of Sharon from the Song of Songs, the first *Fraktur* exemplifies the perfect harmony symbolized by the rose. A floral and vine garland enwreaths the title word "Rose," while each of its letters is formed by lilies of the valley, more roses, and tulips. Flowers on the title page *are* quite literally the word, "Rose," neatly representing not only the sisters' "spiritual wedding vows" pledged to their "heavenly bridegroom," but providing a particularly apt symbol of the God who was the word made flesh (fig. 10.1).

Two decades after the sisters dated their book, dedicating it to their spiritual mother, Mother Maria (Maria Eicher), and as Ephrata's founder and "Father," Friedsam Gottrecht (literally: Peaceful Right-with-God) (Conrad Beissel), grew old, Peter Miller (or Müller, known as Brother Agrippa at Ephrata) praised these lilies of the field for their "retired life." Despite their enclosure, Miller wrote, "their odoriferous fragrancy broke out every where." Miller, who would become the community's leader after Beissel's death in 1768, worked hard to remove any whiff of disrepute from Ephrata in his letter to Franklin, by then the colony's most influential public figure. It was a project on which Miller would labor for the rest of his life and which culminated in his editing and publishing of Ephrata's internal history, the *Chronicon Ephratense*, in 1786.[2] Miller's efforts to secure Ephrata's reputation from those motivated by "disobedience and rebellion" had prompted his letter to Franklin. But the letter, with its language of confinement and escape, also recapitulates events of the 1740s, an earlier and more important chapter in the cloister's history.

Ephrata was a monastic community of celibate men and women known as Solitaries (*Einsamen*), a semi-enclosed community in colonial Pennsylvania that cultivated a more or less close relationship with

Die
Rose
Oder:
Der angenehmen Blume
zu Saron geistliche Ehe-verlöbnis
mit ihrem himmlischen Bräutigam, welchem sie sich als ihrem König, Haupt,
Mann, Herrn, und Bräutigam, aufs ewig
hin verlobt.

Fig. 10.1. Illuminated title page, *Fraktur*, from the Ephrata sisterbook *The Rose*. Image reproduced courtesy of the Historical Society of Pennsylvania.

surrounding "Householders" (*Haushalter*). Founded in the 1730s by the German mystic Conrad Beissel, Ephrata flourished until his death in 1768, guided by his devotions that eclectically mixed Böhmist teachings on the divine Sophia and bridal mysticism with bodily askesis. While the last sister died in 1813, the community remained inhabited by diminished numbers of Beissel's followers into the twentieth century. The extensive property—with its large dormitories, meeting house, printing office, bakery, and workshops for copyists, carpenters, tanners, and for spinning, weaving, and sewing—was purchased in 1941 by the Commonwealth of Pennsylvania. After extensive archeological investigation and historic restoration, Ephrata is today administered by the Pennsylvania Historical and Museum Commission.[3] The community grew particularly rapidly in the 1740s, a decade that saw dramatic changes both at Ephrata and in the surrounding

British colony of Pennsylvania where migrants were arriving in increasing numbers; many—church people and non-conformists, Lutherans, Reformed (Calvinists), Pietists, Dunkers (Brethren), Mennonites, Schwenkfelders, Moravians, and Separatists—came from Germany.[4] At its largest, Ephrata housed more than three hundred men and women.

With the increase in Ephrata's numbers came dramatic changes to the built landscape that surrounded the members as well as to the rules that governed their movements within it. A thorough reorganization of the sisters' order in the first half of the 1740s occasioned the composition of the sisterbook the *Rose*. The manuscript shaped the sisters' history and daily life in three main sections: an account of the order's beginnings; a list of the sisters' names and their division into seven classes; and an explanation of the many rules governing the sisters' lives, from their clothing ("Ordens Kleider"), to their virginal discipline ("Jungfräuliche Zucht regeln"), to the rules about their work and gathering ("die Ordnungen der Stuben Gesellschafften").

This essay sets the sisterbook the *Rose* amid Ephrata's ambitious efforts in the 1740s to reconcile the body with the word. I devote particular attention to the circumstances surrounding Beissel's only programmatic statement of belief, the *Mystisches und Kirchliches Zeuchnüß* (*Mystical and Churchly Testimony*) of 1743.[5] Read in counterpoint with the *Testimony*, omissions from the *Rose* take on new meaning, and it is one prominent absence from the *Rose* that centrally occupies this essay: the lack of any account of the "renegade" sister Marie Christine Sauer (d. 1758).[6] While the visual and verbal rhetoric of the *Rose* asserts a perfect communion of the body with the word and an ideal harmony of the letter with the spirit, Marie Christine Sauer's story, available to us only in fragments, reveals how that perfect harmony was accomplished only via the strictest censorship. Her absence from the Ephrata sisters' chronicle, I argue by way of conclusion, is very different from the absence influentially described by Michel de Certeau in *The Mystic Fable*.[7] Bringing these two absences into dialogue, however, can help us to delineate de Certeau's mystical silence from the silence of the archives.[8] While de Certeau's absence points to a longed for presence, to the incarnation of the word, the absence of the former nun from the sisterbook points only to more loss, to an inadmissible trauma.

Recent scholarship on German Pietist women has made important interventions into our understanding not only of the lives of women such as Johanna Eleonore Petersen, Eva Butler, and others, but it has yielded invaluable insight particularly into radical Pietists' innovative thinking about sex and gender.[9] In their wake, a reconsideration of Marie Christine's life, and of the sisters' order at Ephrata more generally, is overdue. Bach has suggested the importance of a more detailed study of the *Rose* in light of our revised understanding of the relevance of sex and gender to Pietism as well as of women's leadership roles, particularly within Pietism's more radical strains. He writes of the sisterbook, "Its importance cannot be overestimated as a source in women's voices, describing the reorganized sisters' order."[10] The present essay with its focus on the absence of Marie Christine is intended as a prolegomena to a fuller account of the sisters' order.

The following pages proceed in two steps. A first section considers the little we *do* know about Marie Christine Sauer, and then offers a brief sketch of her life and its intersections with that of her husband, Christoph Sauer, and of her longtime spiritual advisor, Conrad Beissel. The subsequent section explores the varied, but increasingly troubled, interactions between the Ephratensians and Moravians in the early 1740s. I devote particular attention to Ephrata's reaction to the departure of Solitaries who chose to join the Moravians as those events figure in the *Mystical Testimony* and in the *Rose*.

Marie Christine Sauer, Christoph Sauer, and Conrad Beissel

In recent decades, historians have gleaned a sketchy account of Marie Christine Sauer's life from three main sources: her brief mention in the *Chronicon Ephratense* as redacted by Peter Miller; a more racy account of her movements provided by the "disgruntled monk" Ezechiel

Sangmeister in his *Leben und Wandel* (printed in 1825); and a passing remark made in a letter to Germany written by an acquaintance of Christoph Sauer from Springfield Manor.[11] Durnbaugh, whose knowledge of the radical German Pietist milieu in Pennsylvania remains unsurpassed, warns against the unreliability of these sources as well as the difficulty of their interpretation and frequent ambiguity.[12] As Durnbaugh notes, since at least Sangmeister's account, all accounts of Marie Christine have been overdetermined by her proximity to two of colonial Pennsylvania's most prominent residents: Conrad Beissel and the Separatist printer and publicist Christoph Sauer, her husband. In their shadows, her life has been reduced to another object over which they quarreled; and, in turn, their disagreement has been hopelessly interpolated with her biography.[13]

The most reliable accounts we have about Marie Christine's life yield the following brief portrait.[14] In Germany in 1720 the widowed Marie Christine married for a second time. Both she and her new husband, Christoph Sauer, were native to Wittgenstein, an area of relative tolerance and Pietist leanings.[15] The couple wed in the village of Schwarzenau, birthplace of the Anabaptist Church of the Brethren (*Neu-Täufer*, Dunkers) and not far from the town of Berleburg, by 1720 a refuge for the scholar and Pietist Johann Friedrich Haug, the *causa movens* behind the famous Berleburger Bible, published six years after Marie Christine and Christoph married. On August 3, 1724, the young couple, with their two-year-old son, Christoph II, were shipboard, packed onto a vessel out of Rotterdam whose course to Philadelphia went through Dover.[16] They reached Philadelphia after eight weeks and, within two years, moved to Conestoga country, in present-day Lancaster County, and a farm on Mill Creek (Mühlbach). There, they soon met Conrad Beissel, another recent migrant from southwestern Germany.

Beissel had arrived in Philadelphia in 1720, joining the household of the Brethren (or Dunker) minister and baker Peter Becker.[17] By 1724, Beissel had been in Conestoga country for three years and would be chosen that year by the small community of Anabaptist Dunkers to be their leader.[18] In 1726, when Marie Christine and Christoph Sauer attended a meeting of Beissel's Conestoga group, controversies surrounding the group's leader had begun to swell. Leaving questions of Beissel's personality aside, Bach describes how Beissel's inventive amalgamation of various traditions rooted in the "left wing," or Radical Reformation, made ruptures—from any group—virtually inevitable. Although Beissel had received baptism from Becker in 1724, as Bach describes him,

> [Beissel] brought with him the Radical Pietist longing for spiritual love among believers. He had drunk from the spring of Boehmist thought in Heidelberg, mingled with Inspirationists, the loosely knit Philadelphians, the Dunker preacher Becker, adherents of [the hermit] Kelpius, the fading Labadists [in Maryland], and the Mennonites. Yet he also held the separatist distrust in organized religious groups. Many groups influenced Beissel, but he never embraced any fully. This unresolved tension ran through Beissel's career and the Ephrata community.[19]

In 1726, when Marie Sauer first met Beissel, the controversy—stemming from his turn to Sabbatarianism, rejection of marriage, and embrace of celibacy—had only just begun.

Stories, rumors, and gossip have long swirled around Beissel and the community at Ephrata.[20] Even the laudatory *Chronicon Ephratensis* edited by Miller could not go so far as to omit the many controversies in which Beissel became embroiled. Miller's redaction reports that at the conclusion of a 1726 meeting in Conestoga,

> Da nun der Verdacht nach geendeter Versammlung sich mercklich gegen ihn vermehret hatte, glaubten viele, er müßte ein Zauberer seyn, und waren besorgt, ihre Weiber möchten auch verführet warden, ja ein sonst redlicher Bruder *M. U.* umarmte sein Weib und sprach: O mein liebes Weib! ich bitte dich um Gottes willen, verlaß mich nicht: solche Arbeit gibts, wann Gott einen Eingriff thut in Adams Kirche.[21]
>
> ———
>
> The suspicion against the Superintendent [Beissel] had notably increased . . . , many thought that he must be a sorcerer, and were in

> fear lest their wives be seduced. One otherwise upright brother, M[artin] U[rner], embraced his wife and exclaimed, "O my dear wife! I pray you for God's sake, do not leave me!" . . . Such is the effect when God reaches forth into the church of Adam.[22]

Martin Urner's fear that his wife would leave him to join Beissel in the celibate life was hardly idle. God, as Miller phrases it in the passage above, worked through Beissel to reach into the surrounding community—prompting women, notably the sisters Anna and Maria Eicher, to leave their families to join Beissel. As the *Chronicon Ephratensis* reports, "sie entflohen aus ihres Vaters Haus, im Jahr 1726, und begaben sich unter des Vorstehers Führung, welches im Land viel Aufsehens machte, sonderlich weil er ihnen mußte viel Gemeinschaft geben" (they fled from their father's house in 1726 and placed themselves under the prior's leadership, an event that gave rise to a lot of talk in the country, especially because he often had to keep company with them).[23]

The early Ephrata community was described sympathetically by a member of the Germantown Brethren, then estranged from Beissel, Stephen Koch (later known at Ephrata as Brother Agabus). In a letter reprinted in Germany in 1738, Koch provided one of the best contemporary descriptions of the nascent community, noting its daily rituals and disciplinary practices, registering its division into two parts: the Solitaries, in turn divided according to sex, and the Householders:

> About twenty hours distance [from Philadelphia] in the wilderness . . . about forty unmarried people have been living a communal life for several years now. They have everything in common, and live very secluded from the world. The place where they live is called Ephrata. Sometimes two or three live in one house; however, each has his separate lodging. Now [by 1738] they have built two large houses; in one there are only single women; in the other, some distance away, there are only brethren who are unmarried, and each has a small room to himself. They all help one another build their own

> houses. They have neither horses nor cows. Whatever they sow and plant in the fields, they till by hoeing. They insist very much on an austere life. Their clothing and food are humble. They also think highly of continence and of the unmarried state. Therefore they are very despised and many lies are told about them. They also observe the seventh day, but not to the letter, as I have seen and also heard from them. They also observe baptism, the love feast, and feetwashing like the other Brethren whom you know.
>
> There is also a very large congregation of householders, who belong to them. They, however, live each on his own land together with his family. They participate only in the spiritual life of the community. As regards keeping house, etc., they take care of themselves. They have their own cows and horses, and sow and plant each on his own land as he thinks best, still, in such a manner that they all strive for a humble life, and even continence.[24]

Marie Christine joined the nascent Sabbatarian community sometime around 1730. We know nothing about why the family did not join the Householders, nor do we know why she chose to join the female solitaries, necessitating separation from her husband and nine-year-old son. The gossipy Sangmeister claims that Marie Christine wanted to be with Jacob Weiss, whom Sangmeister alleges to have become her "second husband" at Ephrata.[25] In any case, at the same time Marie Christine joined the celibate women's community, father and son left the farm on Mill Creek and went to Germantown.

At this point, the traces of Marie Christine's life begin to fade. Sometime in the 1730s, she had become Sister Marcella and made one of two sub-prioresses under Marie Eicher, who had been selected by Beissel to be *Äbtissin* (abbess) sometime prior to 1741.[26] Yet it seems that despite Marie Christine's decision to join the Solitaries, she maintained some manner of working relationship with her husband. Longenecker asserts that in 1738, Christopher Sauer spent two days at the cloister, where "Marie was friendly and arranged for a formal love feast [*Agapas*] attended by 150 people." Echoing a description offered by Durnbaugh, Longenecker describes "the personal relations between the separated husband and wife [as] cordial, [although Christopher] Sauer kept his guard up lest the Cloister gain some advantage over him" (33).[27]

Sauer established his press in Germantown in that same year, 1738, and completed several jobs from Beissel until the cloister established its own printing press around 1745.[28] The first commission Sauer took on from Beissel, the *Zionitischer WeyrauchsHügel Oder: Myrrhen Berg* (*Zion's Incense Hill or Myrrh Mountain*), a collection of 650 hymns composed by Beissel and other Solitaries, stalled on Sauer's objections to Beissel's self-aggrandizement, particularly in the four-hundredth hymn.[29] The dispute grew heated—and increasingly public—after Sauer printed an account of the quarrel, *Ein Abgenöthigter Bericht* (*A Forced Report*), including letters he had written to Beissel laying out his objections as well as an unsigned letter, purportedly from Beissel, that Sauer says he had received in return.[30] Despite the heated language, Sauer completed printing the huge hymnal the following year.

It is tempting to see Marie Christine mediating the dispute between Sauer and Beissel recorded in the *Forced Report*. Perhaps she had even channeled this important print commission to Christoph Sauer. Before they began doing business with Sauer, Beissel and his English translator, Michael Wohlfahrt (1684–1741), had sent poetry, songs, mystical riddles, and other works to Philadelphia printers Andrew Bradford and Benjamin Franklin. The large Ephrata job would have been critical to the initial success of Sauer's business.[31] Five years would pass before another commission came to Sauer from Ephrata. This was the *Mystical and Churchly Testimony*, a document whose publication history is essential to understanding the *Rose* and its excision of Sister Marcella.

"Renegades" and the Moravian "Challenge" to Ephrata's Brothers—and Sisters?

In the summer of 1741 the spiritual leader of the Moravians, Count Nicolaus Ludwig von Zinzendorf, arrived in Pennsylvania. The faith was rooted, as was Beissel's, in Böhmist mysticism, radical Pietism, Quietism, and the Philadelphia movement and the teachings of Jane Lead. Zinzendorf, his wife and daughters, as well as other followers had come to evangelize in the British colonies after a stay in London where the count had preached on several occasions, arriving with the express intention of uniting the fractious German religious communities.[32] The Moravians presented what Aaron Fogleman has called the "Moravian Challenge" to the colony's various religious communities: German Lutheran and Reformed (Calvinist) churches as well as "sectarians." In Pennsylvania, both German Lutheran and Reformed churches lacked preachers despite congregations' appeals for pastors to be sent. The ecumenical Moravians on the other hand had already "sent dozens of men and women as preachers to the colonies," before Zinzendorf himself and his delegation had even arrived.[33]

The Moravians' "challenge" provoked violence both symbolic and real. Fogleman reports, for example, that Moravian Pastor Johann Christoph Pyrlaeus was greeted on Mulberry Street in Philadelphia on a Sunday in 1742 with threats by German Calvinists, "Schlagt den Hund todt!" (Beat the dog to death). The calls then escalated into bodily injury when Pyrlaeus was "dragged from the pulpit into the street and beaten by the crowd."[34] Moravian preachers, including Zinzendorf's family, nevertheless made preaching tours up and down the eastern seaboard. One daughter and several of her companions came to stay at Ephrata. While Beissel and the Ephrata community seem initially to have welcomed their guests and Zinzendorf's invitation to dialogue, they soon turned against him. A media circus ensued. Whatever differences had prevented Beissel from doing further business with Sauer, they were put aside when the Ephrata community found itself compelled to break their preferred silence and speak their differences.

Zinzendorf had already been attacked in 1742 in the colony's press by Calvinist Johann Philip Böhm (1683–1749), whose *Getreuer Warnungs Brief an die Hochteutsche Evangelisch Reformirten Gemeinden und alle deren Glieder, in Pensylvanien* (*True Letter of Warning to the High German Evangelical* [Lutheran and] *Reformed Parishes and All of Their Members, in Pennsylvania*) had been brought out by the Bradford press.[35] Zinzendorf, in return, worked with the Franklin press to launch a counteroffensive. His direct reply to Böhm, the *Aufrichtige Nachricht ans Publicum* (*Honest Report to the Public*), appeared in 1742.[36]

Beissel and other members of the Ephrata community made their own foray into the media frenzy, ineluctably drawn, they explained, to answer the Moravians. Indeed, their disheartening involvement with the Moravians—moving quickly from their initial welcome to a deep and bitter disillusionment—provoked the Ephrata community of male Solitaries into composing the single document that comes closest to what might be called their articles of faith. Specifically, Ephrata faulted the Moravians for their tireless efforts at conversion and for "seducing" former Ephrata brothers to abandon their spiritual vows and their celibacy.

Ephrata shared with the Moravians a devotion to Christ's side wound, which provided both faiths a privileged metaphor to contemplate the soul's union with the divine. Unsurprisingly, their interpretations of the metaphor failed to coincide. Ephrata accused "the Moravians of merely accepting Christ's merit and not 'undertaking the self-chosen process of suffering' in self-denying repentance." For their part, the Moravians came to believe that "Ephrata's emphasis on repentance and self-denial smacked of righteousness through works."[37]

To answer the Moravians, the Ephrata brothers returned to Sauer and his press to publicize their articles of faith in *The Mystical and Churchly Testimony*.[38] The *Testimony* was authored collaboratively. Bach identifies the Ephrata brother Johannes (Hans) Hildebrand as the lead author;[39] Israel Eckerlin and Beissel himself almost certainly also had a hand in its composition. The foreword explains:

> Wir seynd durch wichtige Ursachen beweget worden / in gegenwärtiger Schrifft ans Licht zu tretten / und ein Zeugnuß abzulegen von den wichtigen Puncten der Christlichen Religion und des Weges zu Gott / wie er unter uns belebet und bewandelt wird: Wiewohl solches gegen unsere Lebens-art scheinet zu seyn / als die wir uns die Sprache des Stillschweigens zu unserm Theil erwählet haben.[40]

We have been moved by significant reasons to step into the light with this present text and to bear witness to the most important points in the Christian religion and to the path to God, how we inhabit and walk that path: Even though it seems to contradict our way of life since we have chosen for our part the language of silence.

Exactly what the "significant reasons" were that forced them into print remain unexplained, although they are not hard to glean from the publications printed and appended to the *Testimony*.

The *Testimony* explains the meaning of the true church, attempting to lay out the preferred metaphors for church:

> Nicht setzen wir die Kirch in einem Hauffen Menschen, Männer, Weiber, Junger und Alten, dann wann wir von der Kirche reden in einem eigentlichen Sinn, so haben wir mit Menschen nichts zu schaffen, ohne in so weit sie durchs Chreutz bewährt, daß sich die Kirche bey ihnen hat nieder lassen können. Sonst bleibet die Kirche ein **Jungfräuliches Weib** und ihr Mann ist Christus Jesus, derselbe hat sie bey seiner Creutzigung in seine offne Seite eingenommen, und in Ihm wird Sie fruchtbar, daß Sie kan ihre Kinder ausgebären wie der Thau aus der Morgenröthe. (boldface original, 11)[41]

> We do not locate the church in a crowd of people, men, women, youths, or the old, for when we speak of the church in its actual meaning, it has nothing to do with people except in that degree that they have proven themselves in the cross that the church can find a place of rest in them. Otherwise the church remains a **virginal woman** and her husband is Christ Jesus who took her into his open side at his crucifixion and in him she will be fruitful so that she might bear her children like the dew on the dawn.

They borrowed this bridal mysticism from the writings of Böhme, particularly as edited and interpreted by Gichtel. In the Garden, Sophia, wisdom, had been Adam's "spiritual bride." But Adam had betrayed her when he desired a physical companion. Even before eating from the tree, humanity had become spiritually impotent, disabled from further participation in the "paradisical birthing work" that divine wisdom alone makes possible. But on the cross, Sophia had been reunited with man when she entered Christ, impregnating him through the side wound.

The true church, the *Testimony* specifies, is divided into two estates as Koch's sketch of the Ephrata community quoted above elaborated: the Solitaries and the Householders. The celibate Solitaries are its vanguard; only they are capable of attaining the gender neutrality figured in Jesus's union with Sophia, a sexual balance necessary to perform the "paradisical birthing work." The new covenant had in fact rendered "natural birthing work" a heathen practice:

> Dann wann Christus erscheinet, so geschiehet ein hefftiger Eingriff in Das, wo Adam mit seiner Eva eins worden ist, woraus die grosse Feindschafft aller Adams-Kinder gegen das Zeugniß Gottes urständet. Also hat dann dieses Gebährungs-Werck in der Christlichen Kirche sein Recht verlohren, und ist durchgehend der Heidenschafft überlassen worden.[42]
>
> ———
>
> Then when Christ appears, a fierce attack occurs against that by which Adam was one with his Eva and whence originated the enmity of all Adam's children against the testimony of God. Thus this kind of birthing work has lost its right in the Christian church and has been completely left to heathens.

Once a brother—or a sister—had committed himself to life as a Solitary and to the birthing of spiritual children, he must not turn back. A "renegade," one who committed "spiritual adultery," could only be described by the *Testimony* as "einen unbeschreiblichen Verlust" (an indescribable loss).[43] And yet, as two short pamphlets printed with it make clear, the loss of Solitaries was precisely the reason why Ephrata had broken its vow of silence. The *Testimony* traces a particular path from vows of silence into mystic writing. The absence, although "indescribable" and so purportedly outside the discourse it produces, nevertheless haunts its margins. Tales of apostate Ephrata brothers who had joined the Moravians lurked, in the case of the *Testimony*, literally at its edges—easily legible in the virulent attacks launched in two short appended texts to the *Mystical Testimony*.

Already on the title page, the Ephrata authors promote their *Testimony* "Nebst einem Anhang darinnen dieselbe ihr unpartheyisches Bedencken an Tag gibt von dem Bekehrungs-Werck der sogenanten **Herrenhutischen Gemeine** in **Pennsylvanien** / und warum man ihnen keine Kirche zustehen könne" (Together with an appendix in which the authors give light to their impartial concerns about the missionizing of the so-called **Herrenhuters** in **Pennsylvania**, and why they cannot be entrusted with a church [boldface in original]). Despite the authors' claims to impartiality, the two short appended texts were anything but. A typical passage from the first appended text, *Unpartheyisches Bedencken* (*Impartial Concerns*), claims of the Moravians, "Man ist dessen versichert, daß in unsern Tagen keine Secte auferstanden, die diese an Blindheit und Unverstand übertroffen" (You can be sure that in our times no other sect has arisen which surpasses their blindness and ignorance).[44] The title of the second text appended to the *Testimony* partially masks its program. Entitled *Ein kurtzer Bericht von den Ursachen, warum die Gemeinschafft in* Ephrata *sich mit dem Graffen* Zinzendorff *und seinen Leuten eingelassen: Und wie sich eine so grosse Ungleichheit im Ausgang der Sachen auf beyden Seiten befunden* (*A short report of the reasons why the community at Ephrata associated with Count Zinzendorff and his people: And how such a great difference between both sides was the result*), it culminates in a strong condemnation of those who had had too much to do with the count and his people. These were brothers who had, in fact, left Ephrata to join the Moravians at their new settlement at the Forks of the Delaware, near today's Bethlehem. After an account of the various visits Zinzendorf and his daughters paid to Ephrata, as well as the theological points discussed in their conferences, the text oscillates between fear and threat. It turns squarely to the remaining members of the solitary brothers, "wann auch noch Einige unter uns sich finden sollen, die der Zucht Gottes müde seyende, durch eine lose Lehre gereitzet, sich zu ihnen wenden würden, so wolten wir ihnen solche (als ihr erworbenes Gut) fest auf gebunden haben: Dann wer auf eine solche Weise von uns auszugehen hat, ist ja freylich nicht von uns gewesen" (if there are still some other among us who are tired of God's discipline and are lured to turn to them by their loose teachings, then so would we want to see it tied firmly to them: For anyone who leaves us in such a manner was surely never among us).[45]

Two years after the brothers bore witness to their faith in the *Testimony* and reminded their rank and file of the necessity of "God's discipline" in no uncertain terms, the Ephrata sisterhood authored their sisterbook, the *Rose*. Unlike the articles of faith produced by the men's order, the chronicle has never been published. Yet, although they strictly controlled the chronicle's circulation, effectively cloistering it until the late nineteenth century, the sisters, like the brothers two years earlier, expressed a great reluctance to speak. The chronicle begins with the same presentation of the turn to writing as ineluctable, unavoidable:

> Wie wol unser Sin Gantz nicht darauf aus, diese unser wehrte gesellschafft alhier zu Saron, die Rose genand, viel in Worten aus zustreichen, so können wir doch nicht vorbey gehen etwas weniges meldung zu tuhn, von ihren Tugenden, Eingezogenheit, Nüchternheit, Mässigkeit u. verachtung aller scheinbahren dingen die sich ausser der christlichen und kirchlichen Disciplin finden. [46]
>
> ———
>
> Although our intent is in no way to distinguish our worthy society here at Saron called the Rose with a great number of words, we cannot avoid brief mention of its virtues, its withdrawal, sobriety, continence, and scorn for all apparent things which are beyond Christian and church discipline.

Here too, I contend, an "indescribable loss" is at work—this time of an apostate sister. If Maria Christine Sauer had been an "unruly wife," as Bach supposes,[47] she was no less an unruly Solitary. For her son reported that his mother left the Solitaries and joined him at his house in Germantown sometime between Sauer's printing of the *Testimony* in 1739 and the sisters' completion of their chronicle in 1745. Within a year after arriving at her son's house, Marie Christine and Christoph (the elder) had apparently reconciled, and she died some seven years later in her husband's home.[48]

Look as one might, no trace of Marie Christine, Sister Marcella, is visible in the pages of the sisters' chronicle. She has been excised from the sisters' own history in an act of willful forgetting. Prior to the record of each solitary sister's name and her chosen words of blessing, a carefully composed prayer is offered to help the sisters "remember in a holy manner":

> Ehe und bevor wir nun in dieser gantzen Sach weiter gehen, wollen wir unsere Zuflucht nehmen zu den Flügeln der Göttlichen Barmherzigkeit, und um Gnade, Beistand, und Hülfe anrufen, daß er gebe weißlich zu handeln und heilig zu gedencken, wir flehen dann einhellig zu dir. O Du Mutter aller Dinge! Verwahre diese deine Dienerinnen von aller betrüglichen Nachstellung dieser Welt, u. würdige sie in den Chor der Ewigen Jungfrauschaft auf und eingenommen zu werden, wir befehlen dir auch diese unsere Geistliche Führerin und vorsteherinnen samt allen die vor uns sorge tragen, daß wir den himmelischen Braut-Schmuck erlangen und ihnen gegeben werde weißlich zu reden und klüglich zu handeln, daß wir durch ihren Unterricht unter deine Fesseln, Bande und Hals-Eisen gebracht werden seine Treue Dienerinnen und Schülerinnen seyen und bleiben in zeit und ewigkeit, Amen.[49]
>
> ———
>
> Before we proceed with this whole matter, we desire to take refuge under the wings of divine mercy where we appeal for grace, support and help that he allows us to act wisely and to remember in a holy manner, we beseech you then in one voice. O You Mother of all things! Protect these your servants from all deceptive tricks of this world and consider them worthy to be taken into the chorus of eternal virginity; we also commend to you our female spiritual leader [Mother Maria] and female guardians as well as all of those who care

> for us so that we might attain the heavenly bridal jewels. Grant them wise speech and intelligent action so that by their teaching we might be brought under your chains, bands, and neck irons to be their true servants and pupils now and forever.

The work of memory, it seems, will be done in shackles.

The sisters were as eager to confine their own movements as they were to restrict the circulation of their chronicle. Page after page of the chronicle is devoted to new and complex rules governing their enclosure. At the time of the chronicle's composition, the sisterhood was undergoing a thorough reorganization led by their spiritual "father," Beissel, and "mother," Maria Eicher, those superiors who the sisters prayed would bind them in "chains, bands, and neck irons." In the order's current condition, the chronicle lamented, complete enclosure was not possible. Yet it was something for which they must strive. The order's reorganization was meant to help them achieve this goal. For, the chronicle emphasized, the consequences of leaving their house for any reason exceeded description, "wor aus dann so viele unordentliche Dinge entstehen, das es nicht alles gesagt noch geschriben kann werden" (from which then so many disorderly things arise that it can neither all be spoken nor written).[50]

Conclusion

Michel de Certeau has described the history of mysticism as a history of absences. He writes, "Thus it is that the historian of the mystics, summoned, as they are, to *say the other*, repeats their experience in studying it: an exercise of absence defines at once the operation by which he produces his text and that which constructed theirs . . . He seeks one who has vanished, who in turn sought one who had vanished, and so on."[51] *The Mystic Fable* is a compelling account of mysticism as a language created to experience the divine, as a " 'nostalgia' connected with the progressive decline of God as One, the object of love."[52]

Absence ineluctably structures this essay. But Marie Christine Sauer's absence from the sisterbook the *Rose* is not that assigned by de Certeau to mystics. The absence of de Certeau's mystics describes only some of the things missing from the brothers' *Testimony* and the sisters' chronicle. Both, I have argued, are motivated and structured by loss—the loss of apostate brothers and sisters to the missionizing Moravians. But these losses, unlike the absence for which the mystics longed, remain outside the language the Ephrata community borrowed and invented to express their desire for spiritual union with the One who was also Nothing, the word that was also flesh. Instead, the imagined crimes of these departed brothers, their "spiritual adultery," remained at the very edges of discourse from where it elicited the clearest articulation of the community's articles of faith.

The crimes of a renegade sister, however, remain outside Ephrata's speech entirely. Her path had led between worlds, between this world and the next, from "natural" to "spiritual marriage" and back again. Such a path had to be censored entirely from the sisterbook. It was not, in de Certeau's words, an act of vanishing committed to find another who had vanished. Marie Christine's departure was pure loss.

Had losing Marie Christine Sauer caused the disorder that the *Rose* deems never to "be spoken nor written"? Did her departure necessitate the order's radical reorganization and the cries they raised for more "chains, bands, and neck irons"? Can we recover her story only as trauma, visible only in the non-figure of the unsayable around which the chronicle tirelessly circles? At this crossroads, it would seem to be so, for only in the chronicle's circular loops around that which cannot be said does the absence of Marie Christine Sauer take on any presence.

At last, we return to Peter Miller and the epigraph provided by his letter to Franklin. By absenting themselves from the world, in Miller's words, the Ephrata sisters' "odoriferous fragrancy" nonetheless "broke out every where." Within their enclosure, the sisters turned themselves into flowers, and there, the flowers produced still more flowers via their "paradisical birthing work." Their "fragrancy" is also the presence hinted at by the visual rhetoric of the sisterbook's first

Fraktur, signified by its powerful overlap of word and image, of the rendering of *Rose* by roses and by the suggestion of the bounty of tulips, lilies, and roses sprouting from the *Rose* they surround. Overcoming the duality of embodiment, their absence, like that absence described in *The Mystic Fable*, produced their mystical presence, or, to use another set of metaphors from which the sisters drew, their chains, bands, and neck irons set them free. Yet, to become present via their own absence, they could not acknowledge a different kind of absence: the departure of their former sister Marcella from the ranks of the solitaries. Their censorship of her story has precluded nearly any kind of presence for Marie Christine, mystical or otherwise. We can only guess at her life's outlines from the near total silence it produced.

Notes

1. All translations mine unless otherwise noted. An English translation of the sisterbook is available in Peter C. Erb, ed. and trans., "The Rose or the Spiritual Betrothal of the Pleasing Flower of Sharon to Her Heavenly Bridegroom," in *Johann Conrad Beissel and the Ephrata Community: Mystical and Historical Texts* (Lewiston, Maine: Edwin Mellen, 1986), 265–90. Jeff Bach cautions against Erb's "serious translation errors that alter the meaning" of the sisters' original German." Jeff Bach, *Voices of the Turtledoves: The Sacred World of Ephrata* (University Park: Penn State University Press, 2002), 199. Bach's "Bibliographical Essay" in this volume provides the best guide into the tangle of primary and secondary sources for Ephrata's history and includes a rich section on Ephrata's important manuscript art (213–15). A second manuscript copy of the *Rose* exists: the nineteenth-century "Snow Hill" copy. This copy is currently being digitized, and a preliminary digital edition is now available at http://digitallibrary.hsp.org/index.php/Detail/Object/Show/object_id/6379 (accessed January 23, 2012). The original 1745 *Rose* and the Snow Hill copy are today in the possession of the Historical Society of Pennsylvania. I would like to thank Hillary S. Kativa there for her assistance with reproductions.

2. The title page of the *Chronicon* states that it was "Zusammen getragen" (compiled) by Brothers Lamech (Jacob Gaas, d. 1764) and Agrippa (Peter Miller). The German-language *Chronicon* is the cloister's internal history published by its own press and highly favorable to the controversial mystic Beissel. While the *Chronicon* offers partial accounts of the many controversial events in which Ephrata and Beissel found themselves, it nevertheless remains historians'

primary source for the convent's founding and history. For a discussion of the sources needed to round out the *Chronicon*, see Bach, *Voices*, 197–207.

3. A virtual tour of the site is available at http://www.ephratacloister.org/virtualtour.htm (accessed January 24, 2012).

4. For a discussion of these demographic changes, and the arrival of more "church people" in particular, see Bethany Wiggin, "'For Each and Every House to Wish for Peace': Christoph Saur's *High German American Almanac* and the French and Indian War in Pennsylvania," in *Empires of God: Religious Encounters in the Early Modern Atlantic*, ed. Linda Gregerson and Susan Juster (Philadelphia: University of Pennsylvania Press, 2011), 154–71 and 295–302.

5. Erb translates the title, incorrectly in my opinion, as the *Document*, thereby obscuring the express intent to bear witness, to testify to the mystical church. Across languages, Pietists shared a language; I have used *Testimony* in part to remind us how the vocabulary of German Pietists overlaps with that of English Quakers. Sauer seems to have remained neutral in the dispute between Ephrata and the Moravians, taking work from both. See entries 55 to 57 in Karl John Richard Arndt and Reimer C. Eck, eds., *The First Century of German Language Printing in the United States of America*, vol. 1 (1728–1807) (Göttingen: Niedersächsische Staats- und Universitätsbibliothek Göttingen, 1989), 28–30.

6. The Sauer family name is variously spelled: as Saur, and, particularly in older literature, in an Anglicized form, Sower.

7. Michel de Certeau, *The Mystic Fable* (Chicago: University of Chicago Press, 1992).

8. I am grateful to Tekla Bude, who helped me refine my account of the different types of silences at play in this essay.

9. Especially important in this regard are Ruth Albrecht's biography, *Johanna Eleonora Petersen: Theologische Schriftstellerin des frühen Pietismus* (Göttingen: Vandenhoeck & Ruprecht, 2005), as well as Willi Temme's masterful discussion of Eva Butler and her group in Willi Temme, *Die Krise der Leiblichkeit: Die Sozietät der Mutter Eva (Buttlarsche Rotte) und der radikale Pietismus um 1700* (Göttingen: Vandenhoeck & Ruprecht, 1998). See also Ruth Albrecht, "Frauen," in *Geschichte des Pietismus*, vol. 4, *Glaubenswelt und Lebenswelt*, ed. Hartmut Lehmann (Göttingen: Vandenhoeck & Ruprecht, 2004), 522–55; Lucinda Martin, "Female Reformers as the Gatekeepers of Pietism: The Example of Johanna Eleonora Merlau and William Penn," *Monatshefte* 95, no. 1 (2003): 33–58; as well as Jeff Bach's consideration of Ephrata's "Mother" or prioress in idem, "Maria Eicher of Ephrata: A Case Study of Religion and Gender in Radical Pietism," *Brethren Life and Thought* 43, nos. 3–4 (1997): 117–57, "a case study for examining whether an alternative construal of gender in an alternative religious community enhanced or restricted the possibilities for at least celibate women" (117). Less successful in this regard is the brief essay by Wendy Everham, "The Recovery of the Feminine in an Early

American Pietist Community: The Interpretive Challenge of the Theology of Conrad Beissel," *Pennsylvania Folklife* (Winter 1989–90): 50–56.

10. Bach, *Voices*, 198.

11. Peter Miller, ed., *Chronicon Ephratense. Enthaltend den Lebens-Lauf des ehrwürdigen Vaters in Christo Friedsam Gottrecht, Weyland Stiffters und Vorstehers des geist. Ordens der Einsamen in Ephrata in der Graffschaft Lancaster in Pennsylvania. Zusammen getragen von Br. Lamech u. Agrippa* (Ephrata, Pa.: Ephrata Cloister, 1786); Ezechiel Sangmeister, *Das Leben und Wandel des in Gott ruhenten und seligen Br, Ezechiel Sangmeister: Weiland ein Einwohner von Ephrata* (Ephrata, Pa.: Joseph Bauman, 1825).

12. Donald Durnbaugh, "Christopher Sauer and His Germantown Press," *Der Reggeboge (The Rainbow): Quarterly of the Pennsylvania German Society* 4, no. 2 (June 1970): 3–16, here 8–13.

13. The letter, cited by Donald Durnbaugh ("Christoph Sauer, Pennsylvania-German Printer," 329), is reprinted in Gustav Mori, *Die Egenolff-Luthersche Schriftgiesserei in Frankfurt am Main und ihre geschäftlichen Verbindungen mit den Vereinigten Staaten von Nordamerika* (n.p.: Stempel A.-G., 1926), 36–37. Durnbaugh's "Christopher Sauer and His Germantown Press" provides the most fulsome account of Marie Christine's life.

In his otherwise excellent anthropological history of Ephrata, *Voices of the Turtledoves*, Bach quickly assumes an antagonistic relationship between Marie Christine and Christoph Sauer based on shaky conjectures (111). Bach makes much of the 1739 letter from Springfield Manor and quotes it via Durnbaugh. Durnbaugh cites the letter to state, "He can spare his wife easily, and lives now much more quietly than when she was with him" ("Christopher Sauer and His Germantown Press," 11). But Bach cites only the second clause in the sentence (*Voices*, 111), thus misrepresenting the source. Bach fails, too, to see the interpretive flag Durnbaugh threw down about the letter: that it "could also be the jaundiced attitude of a Radical Pietist who frowned on conjugal bonds" ("Christoph Sauer and His Germantown Press," 11). Another recent example of how Marie Christine's biography is made to provide the key to the relationship between Beissel and Sauer is Hans-Jürgen Schrader, "Conrad Beissels Ephrata-Gemeinschaft und seine Poesie. Ein philadelphisch-mystisch-arkanes 'Vorspiel der Neuen Welt,'" in *Transatlantische Religionsgeschichte 18. bis 20. Jahrhundert*, ed. Hartmut Lehmann (Göttingen: Wallstein, 2006), 31–63. In this important contribution to our understanding of Beissel's poetry, Schrader takes pains not only to rehabilitate Beissel's poetry but is concerned, too, for his reputation. Discussing allegations of Beissel's sorcery, Schrader plays them down: "Kein Wunder, daß dadurch geschädigte Ehemänner die so verführerischen Ephrata-Leute, den Anführer vor allem, der Magie ziehen und das Ideal der Enthaltsamkeit beargwöhnen, gar 'eine neue Evische Rotte' voll geistlicher Promiskuität heraufziehen sehen" (50–51). Schrader continues in the note appended to this passage, "Die prominenteste Stimme unter solchen Verdächtigern war der Druckerpoinier Christopher Sauer, dessen Frau über Jahre hin den eigenen Haushalt verlassen und sich der Klostergemeinschaft angeschlossen hatte" (50n35).

14. My portrait synthesizes information about Christine Marie Sauer presented in three essays by Donald Durnbaugh: "Christopher Sauer: Pennsylvania-German Printer," *The Pennsylvania Magazine of History and Biography* 82, no. 3 (July 1958): 316–40; "Christoph Sauer and His Germantown Press"; and "Ephrata: An Overview," in *Rezeption und Reform. Festschrift für Hans Schneider zu seinem 60. Geburtstag*, ed. Wolfgang Breul-Kunkel and Lotha Vogel (Darmstadt: Verlag der Hessischen Kirchengeschichtlichen Vereinigung, 2001), 251–65; in Longenecker's group portrait of the Sauer family in his short history of the Sauer press, Stephen L. Longenecker, *The Christoph Sauers: Courageous Printers Who Defended Religious Freedom in Early America* (Elgin, Ill.: Brethren Press, 1981); and in Bach's brief account in *Voices*.

15. Hans Schneider, "Der radikale Pietismus im 18. Jahrhundert," in *Geschichte des Pietismus*, vol. 2, *Der Pietismus im achtzehnten Jahrhundert* (Göttingen: Vandenhoeck & Ruprecht, 1995), 107–97, here 123–32.

16. Financial considerations seem to have dominated the couple's decision to migrate. In this respect, they are examples of what Fogleman identifies as a third phase of German immigration to British North America, one much larger than the previous two, beginning in 1717 and not ending until 1775. Aaron Fogleman, *Hopeful Journeys: German Immigration, Settlement, and Political Culture in Colonial America, 1717–1775* (Philadelphia: University of Pennsylvania Press, 1996), 6.

17. Brethren history long viewed Beissel as the origin of an irreparable rift within their community. A useful survey of the origins of the Church of the Brethren, replete with a wealth of primary documents, is provided by Donald Durnbaugh, ed., *European Origins of the Brethren* (Elgin, Ill.: Brethren Press, 1958). A companion volume, Donald Durnbaugh, ed., *Brethren in Colonial America* (Elgin, Ill.: Brethren Press, 1967), carefully weaves the story of Beissel's disagreement with Becker and the Germantown Brethren, alternating the pro-Beissel version of events in the *Chronicon Ephratense* with the alternative history offered by Sangmeister. Durnbaugh, *Brethren in Colonial America*, 61–111.

18. Bach, *Voices*, 18–19.

19. Bach, *Voices*, 18.

20. Thomas Mann's portrait of Beissel as a "wackeren Mann" (a solid, brave man) in *Doktor Faustus* is among the most positive. Schrader, "Conrad Beissels Ephrata-Gemeinschaft," 39–44, discusses Mann's portrayal.

21. Miller, *Chronicon Ephratense*, 29–30.

22. Durnbaugh, *Brethren in Colonial America*, 77.

23. Miller, *Chronicon Ephratense*, 28.

24. Durnbaugh, *Brethren in Contemporary America*, 97–98. Koch's letter was printed with the *Lebens-Beschreibung von Conrad von Beunigen, Gewesenen Bürgermeister in Amsterdam; Als auch eine Ernstliche Ermahnung an Junge und Alte . . . Nebst einem Anmercklichen Brieff ausz Pensylvanien in America* (Krefeld, 1739). I have been unable to consult a copy of this German original on which the English translation provided in Durnbaugh's *Brethren in Colonial America* is based.

25. Quoted in Bach, *Voices*, 111.

26. Bach, *Voices*, 85.

27. Durnbaugh quotes an account by Christopher Sauer of his attendance at the love feast. Durnbaugh writes that Sauer "was invited to a special love feast and communion at Ephrata, which rite was extended until midnight in the hope that Sauer might be won to the cause. Sauer held firm in his Separatist position, stating that just as he did not wish to join their ranks, he did not expect them to join his" ("Christopher Sauer and His Germantown Press," 12). Durnbaugh's source for this account of the love feast remains unclear.

28. Sauer also printed the hymnal on paper made in Ephrata, hardly a sign of any permanent state of antagonism between Christoph Sauer and Conrad Beissel. Before Sauer's press went into operation, Beissel had published with Benjamin Franklin in English translations done by Michael Wohlfahrt (or Michael Welfare).

29. *Zionitischer WeyrauchsHügel Oder: Myrrhen Berg* (Germantown, Pa.: Christoph Saur, 1739). Gottfried Arnold's "Jerusalem, Du Mutter-Stadt," for example, was included in the 1739 hymnal. Arnold's hymn may have provided a model for Brother Lamech, one of the authors of the *Chronicon Ephratense*, when composing his "Jerusalem, die dort oben ist" (1755) and for Maria Eicher's hymn, "Jerusalem das droben ist," which first appeared in 1762. Bach, "Maria Eicher," 128.

30. *Ein Abgenöthigter Bericht, Oder: Zum öfftern begehrte Antwort, Denen darnach fragenden dargelegt. In sich haltende; zwey Brieffe und deren Ursach . . .* (Germantown, Pa.: Christoph Saur, 1739). Schrader discusses Sauer's letter polemics against Beissel, and notes that it was reprinted in Berleburg as "Abruck einiger wahrhafften Berichte und Briefe" in 1738. Schrader, *Literaturproduktion und Büchermarkt*, 59–61n35.

31. Longenecker quotes an acquaintance of Sauer in Germantown who commented that Ephrata was a tough customer: "Sauer's newly established printing office is very irksome to him, and he must pay more dearly for his experience here than in any venture he has thus far tried. He must print for the Seven-dayers . . . a large hymn-book. They are sharp and particular enough, as one hears: Therefore it makes him much trouble." Longenecker, *The Christoph Sauers*, 45.

32. Fogleman summarizes early Moravian history and teachings, explaining that in the mid-eighteenth century, "the center of the Moravian movement was in Herrnhaag (not Herrnhut) and in a number of surrounding communities in an area near Frankfurt am Main loosely referred to as Wetteravia. There, under the leadership of Count Nicolaus Ludwig von Zinzendorf, the group reformulated gendered notions of power and authority, by feminizing the Trinity, the model for power and authority in the community. They used that model to justify actual practices in their community, including allowing women to preach, sacralizing and promoting marital sex, and dissolving the patriarchal, nuclear family." Aaron Fogleman, "Jesus Is Female: The Moravian Challenge in the German Communities of British North America," *The William and Mary Quarterly* 60, no. 2. (2003): para. 7.

33. Fogleman, "Jesus Is Female," para. 5.

34. Fogleman, "Jesus Is Female," para. 1. Fogleman locates the roots of this and other extreme reactions to the "Moravian challenge" in the group's unorthodox and highly controversial teachings on sex, gender, marriage, and patriarchal authority, but he also correctly emphasizes the importance of the volatile demographic situation into which the Moravians inserted themselves. They arrived "during a period of heavy migration into the German-speaking settlements of North America, where there was no church establishment and a significant level of religious freedom." Fogleman, "Jesus Is Female," para. 8.

35. Johann Philip Böhm, *Getreuer Warnungs Brief an die Hochteutsche Evangelisch Reformirten Gemeinden und alle deren Glieder, in Pensylvanien, Zur getreuen Warschauung, vor denen Leuthen, welche unter dem nahmen von Herrn-Huther bekandt seyn* . . . (Philadelphia: A. Bradford, 1742).

36. Nikolaus Ludwig Zinzendorf, *Aufrichtige Nachricht ans Publicum, Über eine Von dem Holländischen Pfarrer Joh. Phil. Böhmen bei Mr. Andr. Bradford edirte Lästerschrift Gegen Die so genannten Herrnhuter, Das ist, Die Evangelischen Brüder aus Böhmen, Mähren, u.s.f.* . . . (Philadelphia: Benjamin Franklin, 1742). In the same year, the Franklin press began to issue the reports of the various meetings. The first was published under the title *Congregation of God in the Spirit. 1st Conference* (*Authentische Relation Von dem Anlass, Fortgang und Schlusse Der am 1sten und 2ten Januarii Anno 1741 /2 in Germantown gehaltenen Versammlung*). For a bibliography of the reports of the ecumenical meetings urged by Zinzendorf and the Moravians as well as other Zinzendorf essays published by Franklin, see items 34 to 46 in Arndt and Eck's bibliography, *The First Century of German Language Printing in the United States of America*, 17–23.

37. Bach, *Voices*, 59.

38. *Mistisches und Kirchliches Zeuchnüß der Bruderschaft in Zion* (Germantown, Pa.: Christoph Saur, 1743).

39. Bach, *Voices*, 202.

40. *Mistisches und Kirchliches Zeuchnüß*, Vorrede, 1.
41. *Mistisches und Kirchliches Zeuchnüß*, Vorrede, 11.
42. *Mistisches und Kirchliches Zeuchnüß*, Vorrede, 12.
43. *Mistisches und Kirchliches Zeuchnüß*, Vorrede, 15.
44. *Mistisches und Kirchliches Zeuchnüß*, Vorrede, appendix 1, 25.
45. *Mistisches und Kirchliches Zeuchnüß*, Vorrede, appendix 2, 44.
46. *Die Rose* (1745?), n.p.
47. Bach, *Voices*, 111.
48. Durnbaugh, "Ephrata," 254–55.
49. *Die Rose*, 48.
50. *Die Rose*, 78.
51. De Certeau, *Mystic Fable*, 11.
52. De Certeau, *Mystic Fable*, 4.

11

A Battle for Hearts and Minds

The Heart in Reformation Polemic

Jeffrey F. Hamburger and

Hildegard Elisabeth Keller

The essays gathered in this volume pose a fundamental question concerning periodization and, hence, of historiography. How should we construe the relationship between mysticism and modernity? At issue are conceptions of periodization and progress, interiority and subjectivity, all of which, in turn, underpin genealogies of mysticism and, no less, of modernism itself. We approach this complex set of interconnected issues by asking about the relationship between images and interiority. The history of interiority as it was constructed and cultivated in the Western mystical tradition grants images a critical role. There is, however, no consensus as to what the role of images and, more broadly, the imagination, should be. On the one hand, the image, specifically, the *imago Dei*, provides the essential ground on which the *homo interior*'s likeness to God is founded. On the other hand, as exterior idols that occupy space that ideally should be left vacant for God, images fall prey to the iconoclast's ire. Within the context of this spectrum of possibilities, the Reformation is often construed as an assault on the imaginative culture of late medieval Catholicism, and it is on this basis that it becomes possible to construe connections between Protestantism and some of the more radical forms of medieval mysticism.

To oppose the iconic and aniconic in this fashion, however, is too simple. The two conceptions of the image—inner as well as outer—remained as inseparably intertwined in Reformation polemic as in medieval mysticism. Building on a small selection of primary sources—sermons by Meister Eckhart, the debates of the Second Zürich Disputation, and some early modern emblems—we focus on the transition from the Middle Ages to modernity. We do so in order to highlight issues of historiography. The semantics of inner and outer image provide a critique of the concept of interiority as it has been deployed in the historical discourse on mysticism.

The Medieval Image

In the beginning was the image. Or so the legends that link authenticity, authority, and antiquity would have it. Whenever one defines the starting point of our story (and it would differ from one region to another), cult images (defined, for our purposes not simply as images used in the cult, that is, the liturgy, but images that were the object of cult) came in the course of the Middle Ages to function as a means of providing presence. The cult image and the subject of cult (one might speak of the signifier and the signified) came to be perceived as a unity. Images served as "go-betweens" between the human and divine: they provided comfort and power for collective and individual purposes. Precisely because images acted as animated beings, some were tagged with variants of a prophylactic titulus that cautioned: "It is neither God nor man, which you discern in the present figure, / But God and man, which the sacred image represents."[1]

Images, however, could not be controlled by words. Extending what Jacques Le Goff called the history of the imagination and Jean-Claude Schmitt has characterized as the "culture de l'*imago*," proponents of the new anthropology of the image such as Hans Belting and

David Freedberg have, despite their differences, argued that images themselves assume various incarnations, whether physical or mental, and that this practice of projection, far from being a relic of a medieval mentality, is a cross-cultural constant in human behavior involving images.[2] In this way of thinking, the image takes on a life of its own. Depending on a host of political and cultural factors, the animation of the image is both affirmed and denied as various groups seek to define, exploit, channel, or confine their powers. The complex dynamics governing the status of images resists generalizations. In summary, however, and in all too schematic a fashion, it can be said that whereas some view the debate over images as a constant struggle between advocates of images (iconophiles) and their opponents (iconoclasts), others see an oscillation over time between the two tendencies, with the Reformation marking one of several salient moments in the history of European culture in which the tension between them tipped toward iconoclasm. To the first group belong those anthropologists of the image who see attitudes toward images as rooted in response mechanisms that, while not beyond the ken of culture, are deeply engrained in human psychology across time and space. To the second group belong those historians who insist on the conditioning effects of culture. The debates between these two schools at times resemble the struggles between iconodules and iconoclasts. In these debates, modern as well as medieval continuities are played off against discontinuities. Protestants (and Protestant scholarship) emphasize discontinuities (necessarily cast as restoration or reform in order to secure the mantle of authenticity). Catholics (and Catholic scholars), in turn, appeal to continuities. Regardless, however, with which camp one's sympathies lie, attitudes toward images remain central to definitions of the transition from the Middle Ages to modernity.[3] Our focus is less the nature of this epochal transition per se as a matter of fact than on how it has come to be defined in writing about and stemming from the Reformation. In short, we seek to write the history of mysticism from the present as well as from the past. In so far as "mysticism" itself is a modern, not a medieval, term, there is nothing radical in this proposition. Mysticism has always been what we make of it.

Images of Interiority

Images—whether statues or sense impressions—were variously construed as being both indispensable, yet inimical to "true" interiority. The mystical tradition, especially in the post-Victorine era (i.e., from the early twelfth century on), was broad enough to encompass both these tendencies: images were seen as a necessary part in the process of memory and imaginative meditation, yet, at the same time, contemplation was construed as a rigorous process of forgetting and erasure.[4]

Meister Eckhart pushes erasure to an extreme. His writings provide a clear indication that there were powerful iconoclastic tendencies in pre-Reformation spirituality. God, he declares, lies beyond any mediation in forms or images: "Götlich wesen enist niht glîch, in im enist noch bilde noch forme" (God's being is like nothing: in it is neither image nor form).[5] Man may be formed in God's image, but in view of God's formlessness, man's destiny also lies beyond form. By way of making this clear, Eckhart speaks of the *homo interior* as a temple that should be emptied out in the most radical way:

> Dirre tempel, dâ got inne hêrschen wil gewalticlîche nâch sînem willen, daz ist des menschen sêle, die er sô rehte glîch nâch im selber gebildet und geschaffen hât, als wir lesen, daz unser herre sprach: "machen wir den menschen nâch unserm bilde und ze unser glîchnisse." Und daz hât er ouch getân. Als glîch hât er des menschen sêle gemachet im selber, daz in himelrîche noch in ertrîche von allen hêrlîchen crêatûren, diu got sô wünniclich geschaffen hât, keiniu ist, diu im als glîch ist als des menschen sêle aleine. Her umbe wil got disen tempel ledic hân, daz ouch niht mê dar inne sî dan er aleine.[6]

———

> This temple, in which God would rule with authority, according to his will, is man's soul, which he has made exactly like himself, just as we read that the Lord said: "Let us make man in our image and likeness." And this he did. So like himself has God made man's soul that nothing else in heaven or earth, of all the splendid creatures that God has so joyously created, resembles God so much as the human soul. For this reason God wants this temple cleared, that he may be

> there all alone. This is because this temple is so agreeable to him, because it is so like him and he is so comfortable in this temple when he is alone there.

Multiple Mysticisms

To which mysticism is one appealing when one construes continuities between the medieval and the modern? Scholars of the Reformation before and after Steven Ozment have often seen in aspects of Eckhart's and Tauler's thought antecedents of Luther and the Radical Reformation.[7] Eckhart's attack on images and the language of experience, however, must be evaluated against the foil of what McGinn calls the "mystical language of embodied sensation."[8] The "culture of the image" encompassed everything from sense impressions, dreams, and visions to the ineluctable *imago Dei.*[9] By definition, the *Deus absconditus* was beyond all imagining, but according to Christian theology, within the Trinity, Christ was the perfect image of the Father, and in his incarnation, he could, according to iconodules, be represented as fully human as well as fully divine. The balance between these two poles was always difficult to maintain. Nonetheless, the tension between the image and the imageless was inherent from the start in any system that sought to span the difference between God and man. This is even more so in the incarnational piety of the later Middle Ages in which, as McGinn has observed, the "sharp distinction between the two sensoria, the outer and the inner," diminishes, even disappears.

The doctrine of the incarnation made theology and anthropology inseparable.[10] Argument by analogy spanned the gulf that separated God and man within the *regio dissimilitudinis*, yet prevented the two poles from collapsing. Eckhart, for example, employs analogy to underscore the fundamental difference between God and the creature, yet, at the same time, to provide a link between the two.[11] The Reformation sought to accomplish what Eckhart had always demanded, namely an indifference to images that views them as, at best, a means of underscoring difference as opposed to instruments of presence.

"Aus den Herzen reissen": The Struggle in Zürich

The reformers themselves, however, could not agree on where and how images had to be eradicated. As artifacts, from the churches? Or rather as imagined images, from the heart? As a former monk, Luther would have known the medieval discourse on interiority, without which the Reformation debate would probably never have taken place.

Although Zürich experienced iconoclasm, it was hardly uncontrolled. Isolated acts of violence against images were immediately suppressed. At Pentecost 1524, however, as the riots threatened public order, city authorities approved the supervised destruction of the city's works of sacred art (figs. 11.1–11.2).[12] Between June 20 and July 2, the destruction was carried out behind closed doors with the express intention "zu verhüeten, dass die götzen nit m<uo>twillenklich zergent werden" (to prevent that the idols be wantonly destroyed).[13] The civic leaders of Zürich, humanists such as Heinrich Bullinger among them, imagined continuity between themselves and the origins of Christianity. They fashioned the political structures of their city, not only after Roman *res publica*,[14] but also the Byzantium of the iconoclasts. The Second Disputation, in which more than nine hundred scholars and clerics participated, took place in the town hall of Zürich in the fall of 1523 under the direction of the mayor (fig. 11.3).[15] Ulrich Zwingli served as a theological presider, Ludwig Hätzer recorded the proceedings. In contrast to the dispute between Luther and Karlstadt, the Zürich Disputation presents us with a lively back and forth lasting three days. Key issues in the Second Disputation were the images in the church and the Mass. Konrad Schmid, one of Zwingli's first followers, who acquired a master's degree in philosophy and a baccalaureate in theology at the University of Basel, qualifies the necessity of abolishing (*abzutun*) outer images (a key term that refers to Karlstadt's pamphlet). After advocating the erasure of false images of Christ, he wonders *where* such false images do most harm—whether on the walls of churches or in man's heart. Noting that Christ's kingdom is foremost in the heart of men, he concludes that whoever drives him out of that place, by any means (including *höltzinen bilden*) commits an even bigger crime than driving a just ruler out of his kingdom:

> So man aber hie von der abthueung der bilden handlen will, ist min radt, daß besser sye, die erst und gröste abgöttery und schädlichen bild im hertzen, so man Christum und die heyligen anderst im hertzen macht und bildet, dann sy darinn sollend sin nach ußtruck götlichs worte, werde zuo vor abgethon uß dem hertzen, ee und man die ussere bild abthueege, an denen die menschen noch hangend . . . Man sol ie dem schwachen einen stab, daran er sich hept, nit uß der hand ryssen, man gebe im dann ein anderen, oder man fellet inn gar ze boden . . . Und wo Christus also in des menschen hertz durch Ware erkantnus wäre, da wurdind dann alle bild on ergernus hynfallen . . . Darumb ich wölte, das man die innerlichen bild zuo vor hynweg und hindan taty durch starcke verkündung götliche wortes . . . Ja, sag ich, welcher das also hat in einem hertzen, ob er dann glych an ein tüfelsch, abgötisch bild gebunden were, schadt es im wenig, sunder er ist ein guotter, frommer Christ.[16]
>
> ———
>
> If one wants thereby to speak of doing away with images, it appears more advisable to me, not to do away with those outward images, to which people are still attached, but rather, above all, to destroy and do away with those most important idols of Christ and the saints, namely those in the heart, for they ought to be there only on account of the expression of God's words . . . So long as one has not given him anything else with which to support himself, one should not take away from the weak the cane that he uses to support himself; otherwise, he will fall to the ground . . . So where Christ is present in men's hearts on account of true knowledge, there all images will be destroyed without excitement . . . I therefore wish that one first clear out and do away with inward images through the powerful dissemination of God's word . . . Yes, I say to you, whose heart has been secured in this way would suffer no harm, even were he tied to a demonic idol, but would be a good, pious Christian.

Fig. 11.1. Johannes Stumpf: *Gemeiner loblicher Eydgnoschafft Stetten, Landen vnd Volckeren Chronick wirdiger thaaten beschreybung*. Zürich: Christoph Froschauer d.Ä., 1548, part 1, fol. 203r. Image copyright © Zentralbibliothek Zürich, Res 61.

Fig. 11.2. Thomann's transcription of Bullinger's *Reformationsgeschichte*, 1605. Image copyright © Zentralbibliothek Zürich, ms. B 316, fol. 75v.

Fig. 11.3. Thomann's transcription of Bullinger's *Reformationsgeschichte*, 1605. Image copyright © Zentralbibliothek Zürich, ms. B 316, fol. 337r.

For Schmid, the removal of false images from the heart, not the church, is primary. To his surprise, however, he is interrupted with a call to order, at which point Zwingli indicates that he does not agree. Schmid can only protest that they are not bound to the Law as strictly as the Jews and the heathens.[17]

The formula, "to tear from the heart," stems, not from Zwingli, but rather from Luther. It is a battle cry directed against the iconoclast Andreas Karlstadt and his pamphlet, *Von abtuhung der bilder*.[18] In 1525, under the rubric *Von dem Bildsturmen*, Luther attacked Karlstadt in his tract, *Wider die himmlischen Propheten*.[19] Luther accused his rival of being more interested in wanting to protect images than God's word. In this way, he sought to claim for himself the more radical position. It was in this context that Luther devised the formula with which to counter Karlstadt's attack: "Aus den Herzen will ich sie gerissen haben, verachtet und vernichtet, aber ohne die von den Eiferern an den Tag gelegte Gewalt" (I will have them [images] torn from the heart, despised, and destroyed, but without the violence that the zealots applied on the day).[20] In the divisive debate among the reformers, the formula "to tear from the heart" serves to both expose and defame. It comes as no surprise that Luther, in the spirit of the scriptural distinction between wheat and chaff, draws attention to the inversion of the inner (the essential) and the outer (the secondary or disposable). As a former monk, he knew the long tradition of employing edifying architectural metaphors to frame the *homo interior* and, building on this foundation, insists, no less than a medieval mystic, that only one *imago* can occupy this space: the *imago Dei*.

Hearts and Minds: Pictorial Propaganda

Of all the spaces fought over by Protestants and Catholics, none was more fiercely contested than the interior of the heart. Both confessions sought to claim the heart's inner chambers as a space to be cleansed and filled with edifying images. The metaphorics of the heart, which were easily assimilated to more concrete conceptions associated with the physiology of memory and recollection as it was conceived until well into modernity, lay in Paul's message that the word of God was written, not on the Mosaic tablets of stone but rather in the flesh of the heart (2 Cor. 3:3: "Being manifested, that you are the epistle of Christ, ministered by us, and written not with ink, but with the Spirit of the living God; not in tables of stone, but in the fleshly tables of the heart"). Heart imagery proliferated in the late Middle Ages. It carried over into Catholic as well as Protestant emblems, which play a critical role in the early modern period as both expressions of interiority and instruments of its formation (fig. 11.4). In the emblem, image and identity formation, *Bild* and *Bildung*, come together. Protestant and Catholic emblem books demonstrate that well into the seventeenth century, the heart, not the head, continued to be regarded as the principal seat of the soul.[21] As noted by Henrik von Achen, by the seventeenth century, the *Theologia Cordis* emerges as "an interconfessional entity."[22] The heart, however, doubled as an open book (fig. 11.5).[23] Although the heart represented the innermost recesses of the soul, it also ensured that worshipers, as it were, wore their hearts on their sleeve. No less important, it laid their hearts open to scrutiny by confessors or inquisitors. Whether in theories of memory, imagination, devotional practice, or human physiology, the heart provided the space in which exterior imagery was interiorized. As a result, the trope of "painting the interior walls of the heart" became widespread in a variety of literary genres, from sermons to devotional tracts.[24]

This relationship between image and object, the inner and outer, the subjective and the objective, changes with the Reformation. What previously had largely remained invisible becomes visible. Exteriorized images of the heart proliferate and take on a public dimension (figs. 11.6–11.7).[25] Luther adopted the heart as part of his personal emblem, which is closely akin to the peculiar heart-shaped Lutheran altarpiece crafted by Lucas Cranach the Younger, which opens to reveal a scene of Christ on the cross. The vastly influential series of prints produced by the Wierix in Antwerp (figs. 11.8–11.9), which were adopted by Catholics and Protestants alike, testify to the ability of both sides to adopt the rhetoric of the other and lay claim to authentic interiority as an instrument of confessional warfare.[26] If anything is truly modern

Fig. 11.4. Dirck Volckertsz Coornhert after Maarten van Heemskerck, *The Devil Painting the Heart with Idle Thoughts*, engraving, 1550. Image © Rijksmuseum-Stichtung. Amsterdam, Rijksprentenkabinet, Inv. Nr. RP-P-1984-8.

Fig. 11.5. Master of the View of Sainte Gudule (fl. 1470–90). *Young Man Holding a Book*. Ca. 1480. Bequest of Mary Stillman Harkness 1950 (50.145.27). Image copyright © The Metropolitan Museum of Art. Source: Art Resource, NY.

Fig. 11.6. Lucas Cranach the Younger, *Altarpiece of the Incarnation and Passion in the form of a heart*, 1584, exterior. Nuremberg, Germanisches Nationalmuseum, Gm 116, Leihgabe Wittelsbacher Ausgleichsfonds.

Fig. 11.7. Lucas Cranach the Younger, *Altarpiece of the Incarnation and Passion in the form of a heart*, 1584, interior. Nuremberg, Germanisches Nationalmuseum, Gm 116, Leihgabe Wittelsbacher Ausgleichsfonds.

Fig. 11.8. Antoine Wierix, *Cor Iesv Amanti Sacrvm*, title page, Mauquoy-Hendrickx 429. By permission of the Royal Library of Belgium, Brussels.

Fig. 11.9. Antoine Wierix, *Cor Iesv Amanti Sacrvm*, Christ Child reading in the heart's interior, Mauquoy-Hendrickx 444. By permission of the Royal Library of Belgium, Brussels.

here, it lies less in any continuity with medieval traditions, however construed, than in the systematic orchestration of pictorial propaganda to impress carefully constructed conceptions of "interiority" on the body politic.[27]

The History of Mysticism Inside-Out?

Before, however, one can pass judgment on ostensible continuities or discontinuities between medieval and modern mysticism, one first has to establish to what degree modern concepts of mysticism remain rooted in a Protestant cult of "interiority" and the vernacular.[28] More important than any residue of Catholic mysticism in modernity is Protestantism's contribution to modern understandings of medieval mysticism.[29] The insistence on radical, apophatic erasure at the expense of experience persists, for example, in the work of Denys Turner.[30] The debate, however, has deep roots that extend beyond Blumenberg to Weber and beyond.[31] Sarah Beckwith addresses the ideological foundations of all such formulations, arguing that mysticism, in so far as it is identified as "radically individualistic," "is a construct crucially tied up with a protestant (post-reformation) view of the spirit."[32] According to Weber, in severing the link between image and incarnation, Protestants participated in a broader "disenchantment" (*Entzauberung*) of the world that Weber identified as a critical component of modernization.[33] In a famous footnote, Weber argued: "the 'deepest community' (with God) is henceforth found not in institutions or corporations or churches but in the secrets of a solitary heart."[34] In this construction, which makes mysticism modern, Protestantism pits the isolated, inward individual against the ossified, outward institutions of late medieval Catholicism.[35] Closely linked to oppositions such as this are related conceptions of periodization and progress, interiority and subjectivity, which in turn underpin genealogies of mysticism and modernism.

In any genealogy of interiority, Augustine's inward turn provides the critical point of departure.[36] Luther began his own search for truth as an Augustinian monk—but can we speak of Lutheran mysticism prior to the seventeenth century?[37] The revival and reception of authors such as Tauler and Suso in the sixteenth century is only beginning to attract serious study.[38] The Pietist lyrics of Bach's cantatas are unimaginable without the precedent of late medieval mystical imagery.[39] Piecemeal survivals and revivals, however, do not in themselves constitute adequate indicators of continuity.[40] The concept of continuity is problematic insofar as it easily lends itself to constructions of development. Often construed as a cross-cultural constant that stands outside of history, institutional contexts, and social practices, mysticism itself is largely a modern construct.[41] Its history needs to be written backward, from the present, not forward, from the past.[42] Otherwise, like the closely related histories of the "individual" and the "self," it is all too easily accommodated to perhaps the most powerful teleological account of modern subjectivity, namely Hegel's.

Innerlichkeit

Eckhart's writings had an impact on the young Hegel (although Hegel himself prompted the ire of orthodox Lutherans).[43] Hegel defines modernization in terms of interiorization.[44] In his words, "in romantic [i.e., modern] art . . . inwardness withdraws itself into itself, the entire material of the external world acquires freedom to go its own way and maintain itself according to its own special and particular character . . . Subjective inwardness of heart becomes the essential feature to be represented" (II.iii.594).[45] The Reformation, Hegel maintains, accounted for Germany's distinctive spiritual character, which he in turn links to the quality of *Innerlichkeit*: "Since Luther, German thought has been characterized by an increasingly introspective and soulful inner life, by a constant deepening of inwardness."[46] German *Innerlichkeit* becomes a precondition of Germany's modernity.[47] We find a similar strain in Hans Martensen's pioneering study of Eckhart, published in 1840: "The spiritual freedom which announced itself here (in Eckhart's writings) as a Christian antinomianism has many features in common with the picture Luther sketched in his essay, 'On the Freedom of the Christian.' Moreover, it is akin to the joviality and expressive inwardness which has evolved in such rich measure in the Protestant, especially Lutheran, church."[48]

Large though the leap might seem, Wittgenstein, who has been called a mystic, brings us to the heart of modern debates about the character and construction of mystical experience. In the conclusion of his *Tractatus logico-philosophicus*, "a *summa* of the aftermath of German mysticism," Wittgenstein insists on the outer as the basis of the inner, stating: "The human body is the best picture of the human soul" and, still more forcefully: "This simile of 'inside' or 'outside' the mind is pernicious."[49] As noted by Owen Thomas, "all human language and thought derive from and are dependent on what is really the given, the primary, the ultimate background of all human thought and consciousness, namely, what Wittgenstein calls the 'facts of living' or the 'forms of life' . . . customs, traditions."[50] What we have here is akin to what since has come to be called cultural construction, allied in turn with what Steven Katz has argued regarding the character of mystical language.[51] This view of mysticism may be anathema to some in that it tends to drain mystical experience, however defined, of truth. It is consonant, however, with a history of mysticism written with regard to context and community.[52] Far from being inherently rebellious, which is how Protestant historiography has described it, medieval mysticism was often orthodox or suborned to the service of orthodoxy.[53] If anything is modern about mysticism, at least as it has come to be defined in modernity, then it is the desire to see in it a reflection of our own desires for freedom, liberation, and transgression.[54] Mysticism could embody resistance (ask any poor soul declared a heretic). Only, however, when modern scholars shed any vestiges of romanticism regarding the Middle Ages and, in particular, the politics of mysticism, which often (at least as manipulated by religious authority) is deeply conservative, will we arrive at a truly modern view of mysticism and of mysticism's contribution to modernity.[55]

Conclusion: Battles over Inner Space

In all these debates, modern as well as medieval, the heart as the seat of true interiority provides the battleground. Interiority becomes something of a cipher, an empty space that both sides seek to occupy by expelling, not only images, but also their opponents, whose placement outside the "truth" permits one to claim that interior space for oneself. Just as the early Christians claimed that Jews saw only the letter, not the spirit, so too Protestants characterized Catholics as "Judaizers" mired in empty, exterior rituals. Protestants, in turn, quarreled among themselves as to who was the Judaizer and what was more important: eradicating exterior images or expelling them from the interior space of the heart. In all these debates, each side paradoxically laid claim to and reused imagery inherited from the other. Abandoning images was the watchword, yet the image of the heart persisted, indeed, proliferated.

If we stand back, we can see that what is at issue here is not simply the "truth" of one set of confessional claims over another, but also, as famously argued by Hans Blumenberg, the "legitimacy of the modern age" itself. Pope Benedict XVI's repeated pronouncements on Europe's Catholic foundations and the "dictatorship of relativism" represent only the latest chapter in this ongoing struggle over the right roots of modernity.[56] These are the unacknowledged stakes in asserting "continuity in discontinuity." The battle over inner space continues to this day.

Notes

1. "Nec Deus est nec homo, praesens quam cernis imago, / Sed Deus est et homo quem sacra figurat imago." See Herbert L. Kessler, *Neither God nor Man: Words, Images, and the Medieval Anxiety about Art*, Rombach Wissenschaften, Reihe Quellen zur Kunst 29 (Freiburg im Breisgau: Rombach Verlag, 1997). See also Norbert Schnitzler, "Illusion, Täuschung und schöner Schein: Probleme der Bildverehrung im späten Mittelalter," in *Frömmigkeit im Mittelalter: Politisch-soziale Kontexte, visuelle Praxis, körperliche Ausdrucksformen*, ed. Klaus Schreiner (Munich: Fink, 2002), 221–42.

2. Jean-Claude Schmitt, "La Culture de l'*Imago*," *Annales ESC* 51 (1996): 3–36; David Freedberg, *The Power of Images: Studies in the History and Theory of Response* (Chicago: University of Chicago Press, 1989); Hans Belting, *Likeness and Presence: A History of the Image before the Era of Art*, trans. Edmund Jephcott (Chicago: University of Chicago Press, 1994), originally published as *Bild*

und Kult: Eine Geschichte des Bildes vor dem Zeitalter der Kunst (Munich: C. H. Beck, 1990).

3. See James Simpson, *Burning to Read: English Fundamentalism and its Reformation Opponents* (Cambridge, Mass.: Belknap Press of Harvard University Press, 2007). We are very much indebted to James Simpson for a careful and constructive reading of this essay. Some historians, for example Alain Besançon, *The Forbidden Image: An Intellectual History of Iconoclasm*, trans. Jane Marie Todd (Chicago: University of Chicago Press, 2000), have traced the origins of twentieth-century abstraction in art to ancient debates over the possibility of representing the divine.

4. For the role of sensory experience in mystical hierarchies, see Jeffrey F. Hamburger, "Speculations on Speculation: Vision and Perception in the Theory and Practice of Mystical Devotions," in *Deutsche Mystik im abendländischen Zusammenhang: Neu erschlossene Texte, neue methodische Ansätze, neue theoretische Konzepte*, Kolloquium Kloster Fischingen, ed. Walter Haug and Wolfram Schneider-Lastin (Tübingen: Niemeyer, 2000), 353–408.

5. *Meister Eckhart, Werke: Texte und Übersetzungen*, 2 vols., ed. Niklaus Largier (Frankfurt: Deutscher Klassiker Verlag, 1993), sermon 6, line 10, 1:82. For the translation, see *Meister Eckhart: Sermons & Treatises*, trans. and ed. M. O'Walshe (London: Watkins, 1979), 2:134.

6. *Meister Eckhart, Werke*, sermon 1, lines 13–22, 1:10. For the translation, see *Meister Eckhart*: *Sermons & Treatises*, 1:55.

7. Stephen E. Ozment, *Mysticism and Dissent: Religious Ideology and Social Protest in the Sixteenth Century* (New Haven, Conn.: Yale University Press, 1973).

8. Bernard McGinn, "The Language of Inner Experience in Christian Mysticism," *Spiritus* 1 (2001): 156–71, esp. 161. See also Gordon Rudy, *Mystical Language of Sensation in the Later Middle Ages* (New York: Routledge, 2002). For feminist critiques of exterior-interior distinctions, see Sarah Beckwith, "Passionate Regulation: Enclosure, Ascesis and the Feminist Imaginary," *South Atlantic Quarterly* 93 (1994): 803–24, and Amy Hollywood, *Sensible Ecstasy: Mysticism, Sexual Difference, and the Demands of History* (Chicago: University of Chicago Press, 2002), esp. chapter 7.

9. For Luther on the *imago Dei*, see Johann Anselm Steiger, "Luthers Bild-Theologie als theologisches und hermeneutisches Fundament der Emblematik der lutherischen Orthodoxie," in *Die Domänen des Emblems: Außerliterarische Anwendungen der Emblematik*, Wolfenbüttler Arbeiten zur Barockforschung 39, ed. Gerhard F. Strasse and Mara R. Wade (Wiesbaden: Harrassowitz, 2004), 119–33.

10. See Giles Constable, "The Imitation of Christ," in *Three Studies in Medieval Religious and Social Thought* (Cambridge: Cambridge University Press, 1995), 143–248.

11. Mauritius Wilde, *Das neue Bild vom Gottesbild: Bild und Theologie bei Meister Eckhart*, Dokimion 24 (Fribourg: Universitätsverlag, 2000).

12. A decisive impetus to iconoclasm in Zürich came from Ludwig Hätzer's tract: *Ein urteil gottes unsers eegemahels / wie man sich mit allen goetzen vnd bildnussen halten sol / uß der heiligen gschrifft gezogen durch Ludwig Haetzer. Getruckt zuo Zürich Durch Christopherum Froschouer* (1523; Leiden, 1976 [microfiche ed.]).

13. Emil Egli, ed., *Aktensammlung zur Geschichte der Zürcher Reformation in den Jahren 1519–1533* (1879; Nieuwkoop: De Graaf, 1973), 236.

14. Cf. Rémy Charbon, "*Lucretia Tigurina:* Heinrich Bullingers Spiel von Lucretia und Brutus (1526)," in *Antiquitates Renatae. Deutsche und französische Beiträge zur Wirkung der Antike in der europäischen Literatur*, ed. Verena Ehrich-Häfeli, Hans-Jürgen Schrader, and Martin Stern (Würzburg: Königshausen & Neumann 1998), 35–47; Anja Buckenberger, "Heinrich Bullingers Rezeption des Lucretia-Stoffes," *Zwingliana. Beiträge zur Geschichte Zwinglis, der Reformation und des Protestantismus in der Schweiz* 33 (2006): 77–91. For the iconographic context, see Hildegard Elisabeth Keller, "God's Plan for the Swiss Confederation: Heinrich Bullinger, Jakob Ruf and Their Uses of Historical Myth in Reformation Zürich," in *Orthodoxies and Heterodoxies in Early Modern German Culture: Order and Creativity 1500–1750*, ed. Randolph C. Head and Daniel Christensen (Leiden: Brill, 2007), 139–67.

15. Huldreich Zwingli, *Die Akten der zweiten Disputation vom 26.–28. Oktober 1523*, in *Sämtliche Werke*, 2 vols., ed. Emil Egli and Georg Finsler (1908; Munich: Kraus Reprint, 1981), 2:664–767 (trans. H. E. Keller and J. F. Hamburger).

The Second Disputation was a large exegetical congress. The participants were, above all, the clergy of the Zurich region, but also the bishops of Constance, Chur, and Basel; members of the university; the confederates from the other twelve remaining provinces; various ambassadors and representatives; and anyone in the city and beyond who wished to take part. None of the bishops came; the remaining provinces of the Swiss Confederation were represented by only Schaffhausen and St. Gallen. Nonetheless, the Disputation was well attended; it has been estimated that more than nine hundred people were present, of whom three hundred were priests. Included were ten doctors, many "masters," and other learned and well-known people. On the first morning prior to the opening of the discussions, a sermon was heard, followed by meetings of both civic councils. As presiders over the discussions, they appointed three doctors, Joachim von Watt of St. Gallen, Sebastian Hofmeister from Schaffhausen, and Christoph Schupper of St. Gallen, at the time in Memmingen, and charged them with making sure that the speakers did not depart from what was prescribed by scripture. In addition, Zwingli and Leo Jud were charged with responding to each speaker from Holy Scripture.

16. Zwingli, *Die Akten der zweiten Disputation*, 703–5.

17. In 1537 Ambrosius Blarer, the Reformer of Constance, revisits the issue in his decree, *Vom abth(uo)n der bilder*, in which he argues that images should be torn out of men's hearts so that Christ can be planted there. Blarer implies an antithesis between the interior space of the church and the space of interiority, made concrete in the heart. See Rainer Henrich, "Das württembergische Bilderdekret vom 7. Oktober 1537—ein unbekanntes Werk Ambrosius Blarers," *Blätter für Württembergische Kirchengeschichte* 97 (1997): 9–21.

18. Andreas Karlstadt, "Von abtuhung der bilder und das keyn bedtler vnther den christen seyn sollen (1522) und die Wittenberger Beutelordnung," in *Kleine Texte für theologische und philosophische Übungen* 74, ed. Hans Lietzmann (Bonn: Marcus and Weber, 1911).

19. Martin Luther, *Wider die himmlischen Propheten, von den Bildern und Sakrament*, in Martin Luther, *Werke*, Kritische Gesamtausgabe (Weimarer Ausgabe), vol. 18, 37–214, here 62 ff.

20. Luther, *Wider die himmlischen Propheten*, 9.

21. See Thomas Fuchs, *Die Mechanisierung des Herzens: Harvey und Descartes, der vitale und der mechanische Aspekt des Kreislaufs* (Frankfurt am Main: Suhrkamp, 1992), translated as *The Mechanization of the Heart: Harvey and Descartes*, trans. Marjorie Grene (Rochester: University of Rochester Press, 2001).

22. Henrik von Achen, "The Sinner's Contemplation: Protestant Heart Symbolism and the Meditation on the *Via poenitentiae*: A Protestant Meditation on the *Ordo salutis*: 'Rembrandt's Mother' by Gerard Dou related to One Aspect of Scandinavian Mid-17th-Century Use of the Series of Copper Engravings by Anton Wierix, titled *Cor Iesv amanti sacrvm*," in *Images of Cult and Devotion: Function and Reception of Christian Images in Medieval and Post-Medieval Europe*, ed. Soren Kaspersen and Ulla Haastrup (Copenhagen: Museum Tusculanum Press, 2004), 283–304, esp. 283.

23. See Eric Jaeger, *The Book of the Heart* (Chicago: University of Chicago Press, 2000), who notes in chapter 7 ("Picturing the Metaphor") that the earliest examples of the pictured metaphor date to the late fifteenth century.

24. See Fritz Oskar Schuppisser, "Schauen mit den Augen des Herzens: Zur Methodik der spätmittelalterlichen Passionsmeditation, besonders in der Devotio Moderna und bei den Augustinern," in *Die Passion Christi in Literatur und Kunst des Spätmittelalters*, Fortuna vitrea 12, ed. Walter Haug and Burghart Wachinger (Tübingen: Max Niemeyer Verlag, 1993), 169–210, and Jeffrey F. Hamburger, *Nuns as Artists: The Visual Culture of a Medieval Convent* (Berkeley: University of California Press, 1986).

25. To cite only a few examples from the vast literature: Anne Sauvy, *Le miroir du coeur: Quatre siècles d'images savantes et populaires* (Paris: Cerf, 1989); Hsiaosung Kok, "'Mein Hercz leidet schmercz': Über das Herzmotiv in der

religiösen Graphik," in *Das Kleine Andachtsbild: Graphik vom 16. bis zum 20. Jahrhundert, Museum Schnutgen: Auswahlkatalog*, ed. Manuela Beer and Ulrich Rehm (Hildesheim: Olms, 2004), 31–42; Sabine Mödersheim, "Herzemblematik bei Daniel Cramer," in *The Emblem in Renaissance and Baroque Europe: Tradition and Variety. Selected Papers of the Glasgow International Emblem Conference 13–17 August, 1990*, Symbola et Emblemata: Studies in Renaissance and Baroque Symbolism 3, ed. Alison Adams and Anthony J. Harper (Leiden: Brill, 1992), 90–103; Bernhard F. Scholtz, "Religious Meditations on the Heart: Three Seventeenth-Century Variants," in *The Arts and the Cultural Heritage of Martin Luther*, Special Issue of *Transfiguration: Nordic Journal for Christianity and the Arts* (Copenhagen: Museum Tusculanum Press, 2002), 99–35; and Joseph F. Chorpenning, ed., *Emblemata Sacra: Emblem Books from the Maurits Sabbe Library, Katholieke Universiteit Leuven* (Philadelphia: St. Joseph's University Press, 2006), 49–54.

26. In addition to von Achen (as in note 22), see Marie Mauquoy-Hendrickx, *Les Estampes des Wierix conservées au Cabinet des Estampes de la Bibliothèque Royale Albert Ier*: Catalogue raisonné enrichi de notes prises dans diverses autres collections, 3 vols., intro. Louis Lebeer (Brussels: Bibliothèque Royale Albert Ier, 1978), 1:68–79 (nos. 429–46); Dietmar Spengler, "Die *Ars jesuitica* der Gebruder Wierix," *Wallraf-Richartz-Jahrbuch* 57 (1996): 161–94; *The Jesuit Series*, 5 vols., Corpus librorum emblematum, ed. Peter M. Daly and Richard Dimler (Montreal: McGill-Queen's University Press, 1997–2007), vol. 4, and, for Jesuit image theory as it relates to imagery of this kind, Ralph Dekoninck, *Ad imaginem: Status, fonctions et usages de l'image dans la littérature spirituelle jésuite du XVIIe siècle*, Travaux du Grand Siècle 26 (Geneva: Droz, 2005), 194–97. For one of many examples of the influence of the Wierixes on Protestant emblems, see Karl Josef Höltgen, *Aspects of the Emblem: Studies in the English Emblem Tradition and the European Context, with a Foreword by Sir Roy Strong* (Kassel: Edition Reichenberger, 1986), esp. 31–66 ("The Devotional Quality of Quarles's *Emblemes*"). Karl Josef Höltgen, "Henry Hawkins: A Jesuit Writer and Emblematist," in *The Jesuits: Cultures, Sciences, and the Arts, 1540–1773*, ed. John W. O. Malley, Gauvin Alexander Bailey, Steven J. Harris, and T. Frank Kennedy (Toronto: University of Toronto Press, 1999), 600–626, esp. 620, notes that "*Cor Iesu amanti sacrum* is the first fully developed series of cardiomorphic emblems." There are, however, medieval precedents, far more extensive in devotional literature than in the pictorial arts. See Hamburger, *Nuns as Artists*, chapter 4 ("The House of the Heart"), and idem, "'On the Little Bed of Jesus': Pictorial Piety and Monastic Reform," in *The Visual and the Visionary: Art and Female Spirituality in Late Medieval Germany* (New York: Zone, 1998), 383–426.

27. On the role of early modern emblematic and devotional images in producing conformity, see Frédéric Cousiné, "Poétique de l'image de dévotion: Image et méditation dans les traités illustrés d'oraison du XVIIe siècle

français," in *Emblemata Sacra: Rhétorique et herméneutique du discourse sacré dans la littérature en images/The Rhetoric and Hermeneutics of Illustrated Sacred Discourse*, Imago Figurata 7, ed. Ralph Dekoninck and Agnès Guiderdoni-Bruslé (Turnhout: Brepols, 2007), 83–107, and, in the same volume, Christine Goettler, "'Impressed on Paper and on Hearts': David Tenier's *Portrait of Bishop Triest* (1652) and the Virtue of the Image of Christ's Wounds," 569–92.

28. For example, Otto Langer, "Zur Begriff der Innerlichkeit bei Meister Eckhart," in *Abendländische Mystik im Mittelalter: Symposium Kloster Engelberg 1984*, Germanistische Symposien: Berichtsbände 7, ed. Kurt Ruh (Stuttgart: J. B. Metzlersche Verlagsbuchhandlung, 1986), 7–32, takes the term for granted without inquiring into what terms Meister Eckhart himself employs.

29. McGinn, *Foundations*, 267–72, takes a different view from that presented here, arguing that "the powerful tradition of German Protestant theology has been on the whole more negative than positive in its evaluation of the place of mysticism, however defined, in the Christian religion, frequently seeing it as an essentially Greek form of religiosity whose emphasis on the inner experience of God is ultimately incompatible with the Gospel message of salvation through faith in the saving word mediated through the church" (267).

30. Denys Turner, *The Darkness of God: Negativity in Christian Mysticism* (Cambridge: Cambridge University Press, 1995), 259: "Experientialism is, in short, the 'positivism' of Christian spirituality. It abhors the experiential vacuum of the apophatic, rushing to fill it with the plenum of the psychologistic . . . It is happy with the commendations of the 'interior' so long as it can cash them out in the currency of experienced inwardness and of the practices of prayer that will achieve it." For criticism of Turner's construction, see Bernard McGinn's review of Turner, *Journal of Religion* 77 (1997): 309–11.

31. Hans Blumenberg, *The Legitimacy of the Modern Age*, trans. Robert M. Wallace (Cambridge, Mass.: MIT, 1985). The critical debate surrounding Blumenberg's thesis has been enormous. See, for example, Lee Patterson, "The Place of the Modern in the Late Middle Ages," in *The Challenge of Periodization: Old Paradigms and New Perspectives*, ed. Lawrence Besserman (New York: Garland, 1996), 51–66; Felix Heidenreich, *Mensch und Moderne bei Hans Blumenberg* (Munich: Fink, 2005), esp. chapter 8 ("Die Moderne als Säkularisierung und Verhängnis"); and Jean-François Kervégan, "Les ambiguities d'un théorème: La sécularisation, de Schmitt à Löwith et retour," in *Modernité et sécularisation: Hans Blumenberg, Karl Löwith, Carl Schmitt, Leo Strauss*, ed. Michael Foessel, Jean-François Kervégan, and Myriam Revault d'Allonnes (Paris: CNRS, 2007), 107–17. Laurence Dickey, "Blumenberg and Secularization: 'Self-Assertion' and the Problem of Self-Realizing Teleology in History," *New German Critique* (Special Issue on Critiques of the Enlightenment) 41 (1987): 151–65, esp. 154, summarizes Blumenberg as follows: "The overall strategy of *The Legitimacy* is twofold: first, to call into question 'the logic of

continuity' that enabled Löwith et al. to explain 'modernity' in terms of the 'secularization of Christianity'; and second, to demonstrate with specific reference to the concept of secularization just how the secularization theorists came to mistake an 'alienation' of the content of Christianity for a 'transformation' of it." Dickey, "Blumenberg and Secularization," 165, takes Blumenberg to task for not "dealing with issues that would require him to discuss the role [that] Protestantism, in its liberal accommodationist mode, played in the emergence of the 'modern' idea of gradual (i.e., moderate) progress in history." For an argument analogous to Blumenberg's that, like his, identifies nominalism instead of Calvinism as the fundamental point of departure with the past within the Western tradition, but that, unlike Blumenberg, does so in the context of a call for a return to a viable concept of transcendence, see Louis Dupré, *Passage to Modernity: An Essay in the Hermeneutics of Nature and Culture* (New Haven, Conn.: Yale University Press, 1993). For further discussion, see Jürgen Goldstein, *Nominalismus und Moderne: zur Konstitution neuzeitlicher Subjektivität bei Hans Blumenberg und Wilhelm bon Ockham* (Freiburg im Breisgau: K. Alber, 1998).

32. See Sarah Beckwith, *Christ's Body: Identity, Culture and Society in Late Medieval Writings* (London: Routledge, 1993), 11–14. Scholars of late medieval English religious literature have been particularly vocal in their criticism of early modernists' claims that "self-fashioning" as defined by Steven Greenblatt is a peculiarly early modern phenomenon; see David Aers, "A Whisper in the Ear of Early Modernists; Or, Reflections on Literary Critics Writing the 'History of the Subject,'" in *Culture and History, 1350–1600: Essays on English Communities, Identities, and Writing*, ed. David Aers (Detroit: Wayne State University Press, 1992), 177–202; Katherine C. Little, *Confession and Resistance: Defining the Self in Late Medieval England* (Notre Dame, Ind.: University of Notre Dame Press, 2006); Jennifer Brian, *Looking Inward: Devotional Reading and Private Self in Late Medieval England* (Philadelphia: University of Pennsylvania Press, 2008); and, for a polemical critique of concepts of periodization per se, see James Simpson, "Diachronic History and the Shortcomings of Medieval Studies," in *Reading the Medieval in Early Modern England*, ed. Gordon McMullan and David Matthews (Cambridge: Cambridge University Press, 2007), 17–30. See also Jan Frans van Dijkhuizen and Richard Todd, eds., *The Reformation Unsettled: British Literature and the Question of Religious Identity, 1560–1660* (Turnhout: Brepols, 2008).

33. See Hans G. Kippenberg, "Religious Communities and the Path to Disenchantment: The Origins, Sources, and Theoretical Core of the Religion Section," in *Max Weber's 'Economy and Society': A Critical Companion*, ed. Charles Camic, Philip S. Gorski, and David M. Trubek (Stanford, Calif.: Stanford University Press, 2005), 164–82, kindly brought to my attention by Guenther Roth. Robert W. Scribner, "The Reformation, Popular Magic, and

the 'Disenchantment of the World,'" in *Religion and Culture in Germany (1400–1800)*, Studies in Medieval and Reformation Thought 81, ed. Lyndal Roper (Leiden: Brill, 2001), 346–65, argues that "it may . . . turn out that the 'disenchantment of the world' played a marginal role in both the developing history of Protestantism and in advance toward 'the modern world'" (365). For further skepticism, see Philip M. Soergel, "Miracle, Magic, and Disenchantment in Early Modern Germany," in *Envisioning Magic: A Princeton Seminar and Symposium*, Numen: Studies in the History of Religions 75, ed. Peter Schäfer and Hans G. Kippenberg (Leiden: Brill, 1997), 215–34, and for a perspective that looks beyond Protestantism to early modern Catholicism, Moshe Sluhovsky, "Discernment of Difference, the Introspective Subject, and the Birth of Modernity," *Journal of Medieval and Early Modern Studies* 36 (2006): 169–99. For an interpretation of Eckhart's mysticism in terms of "Entzauberung," see Frank Tobin, "Die Entzauberung der Sprache durch die Mystik: Eckhart und Seuse," in *Entzauberung der Welt: Deutsche Literatur 1200–1500*, ed. James F. Poag and Thomas C. Fox (Tübingen: A. Francke Verlag, 1989), 147–64. Walter Haug, "Kulturgeschichte und Literaturgeschichte: Einige grundsätzliche Überlegungen aus mediävistischer Sicht," in *Kultureller Austausch und Literaturgeschichte im Mittelalter/Transferts culturels et histoire littéraire au Moyen Âge: Kolloquium im deutschen historischen Institut Paris 16. –18.3.1995*, Beihefte der Francia 43, ed. Ingrid Kasten, Werner Paravicini, and René Pérennec (Sigmaringen: Jan Thorbecke Verlag, 1998), 23–33, criticizes the application of the Weberian model to the study of medieval literature.

34. Max Weber, *The Protestant Ethic and the Spirit of Capitalism*, trans. Talcott Parsons (New York: Routledge, 2001), 177 (note 16), quoting Edward Dowden, *Puritan and Anglican: Studies in Literature* (London: K. Paul, Trench, Trubner, 1900), 234. See also Roland Robertson, "On the Analysis of Mysticism: Pre-Weberian, Weberian and Post-Weberian Perspectives," *Sociological Analysis* 36 (1965): 241–66.

35. For trenchant discussions of Weber vis-à-vis the medieval, see the following three essays by Brian Stock: "Rationality, Tradition, and the Scientific Outlook: Reflections on Max Weber and the Middle Ages," in *Science and Technology in Medieval Society*, Annals of the New York Academy of Sciences 441, ed. Pamela O. Long (New York: New York Academy of Science, 1985), 7–19; "Schriftgebrauch und Rationalität im Mittelalter," in *Max Webers Sicht des okzidentalen Christentums: Interpretation und Kritik*, ed. Wolfgang Schluchter (Frankfurt: Suhrkamp, 1988), 165–83; and "Max Weber, Western Rationality, and the Middle Ages," in *Listening for the Text: On the Uses of the Past* (Baltimore: Johns Hopkins University Press, 1990), 113–39 and 135–38.

36. Witness his famous prayer in the *Confessions* (X, 27, 38): "Late have I loved you, O Beauty ever ancient, ever new, late have I loved you! You were within me, but I was outside, and it was there that I searched for you." Cf. *Con-*

fessions, III, 6, 11: "You are more intimately present to me than my inmost being and higher than the highest element in me," a formulation that neatly collapses the distinction between inside and outside or, more accurately, identifies the depths of the soul with the height of the divinity. For Augustinian conceptions of self, see Phillip Cary, *Augustine's Invention of the Inner Self: The Legacy of a Christian Platonist* (Oxford: Oxford University Press, 2000); Brian Stock, *After Augustine: The Meditative Reader and the Text* (Philadelphia: University of Pennsylvania Press, 2001); and Ronald J. Ganze, "The Medieval Sense of Self," in *Misconceptions About the Middle Ages*, ed. Stephen J. Harris and Bryon L. Grigsby (New York: Routledge, 2008), 102–16. See further Charles Taylor, *Sources of the Self: The Making of Modern Identity* (Cambridge, Mass.: Harvard University Press, 1989), which, however, largely skips over the Middle Ages, as does his *A Secular Age* (Cambridge, Mass.: Belknap Press of Harvard University Press, 2007), esp. chapter 15 ("The Immanent Frame"), which discusses "the Inner/Outer distinction in a whole range of epistemological theories of a meditational type from Descartes to Rorty" and "the growth of a rich vocabulary of interiority, an inner realm of thought and feeling to be explored" (539–40). According to Taylor, these "inner depths," which once were located in the "enchanted" world, "are now more readily placed within." Like Blumenberg, whom he mentions only in passing, Taylor criticizes what he calls "subtraction stories" of secularization, but from a more nostalgic, communitarian perspective.

37. For Luther's debt to Augustinian theology, see Heiko Oberman, *Werden und Wertung der Reformation: Vom Wegstreit zum Glaubenskampf* (Tübingen: Mohr, 1977). The literature on Luther and mysticism is large; see, for example, Heiko Oberman, "*Simul gemitus et raptus*: Luthur und die Mystik," in *Kirche, Mystik, Heiligung und das Natürliche bei Luther: Vorträge des dritten internationalen Kongresses für Lutherforschung, Järvenpää, Finnland, 11. –16. August 1966*, ed. Ivar Asheim (Göttingen: Vandenhoeck & Rupprecht, 1967), and idem, "Die Bedeutung der Mystik von Meister Eckhart bis Martin Luther," in *Von Eckhart bis Luther: Über mystischen Glauben*, Herrenalber Texte 31, ed. Wolfgang Böhme (Baden: Evangelische Akademie, 1981), 920; Karl Dienst, "Mystik und Protestantismus—ein Widerspruch?" and Markus Wriedt, "Martin Luther und die Mystik," both essays in *Hildegard von Bingen in ihrem Umfeld—Mystik und Visionsformen in Mittelalter und früher Neuzeit/ Katholizismus und Protestantismus im Dialog*, ed. Änne Bäumer-Schleinkofer (Würzburg: Religion & Kultur Verlag, 2001), 227–48 and 249–73 respectively. For the later period, see Johannes Wallmann, "Johann Arndt und die Protestantische Frömmigkeit: Zur Rezeption der mittelalterlichen Mystik im Luthertum," in *Frömmigkeit in der frühen Neuzeit: Studien zur religiösen Literatur des 17. Jahrhunderts in Deutschland*, Chloe: Beihefte zum Daphnis 2, ed. Dieter Breuer (Amsterdam: Rodopi, 1984), 50–74. A critical figure in all such discussions is Sebastian Franck; see Otto Langer, "Inneres Wort und inwohnender Christus:

Zum mystischen Spiritualismus Sebastian Francks und seinen Implikationen," in *Sebastian Frank (1499–1542)*, Wolfenbütteler Forschungen 56, ed. Jan-Dirk Müller (Wiesbaden: Harrassowitz, 1993), 55–69.

38. Dieter Breuer, "Zur Druckgeschichte und Rezeption der Schriften Heinrich Seuses," in *Frömmigkeit in der frühen Neuzeit: Studien zur religiösen Literatur des 17. Jahrhunderts in Deutschland*, Chloe: Beihefte zum Daphnis 2, ed. Dieter Breuer (Amsterdam: Rodopi, 1984), 29–49, and Henrik Otto, *Vor- und frühreformatorische Tauler-Rezeption: Annotationen in Drucken des späten 15. und frühen 16. Jahrhunderts*, Quellen und Forschungen zur Reformationsgeschichte 75 (Heidelberg: Verein für Reformationsgeschichte, 2003).

39. Susan C. Karant-Nunn, "'Gedanken, Herz und Sinn': Die Unterdrückung der religiösen Emotionen," in *Kulturelle Reformation: Sinnformationen im Umbruch 1400–1600*, Veröffentlichungen des Max-Planck-Instituts für Geschichte 145, ed. Bernhard Jussen and Craig Koslofsky (Göttingen: Vandenhoeck & Ruprecht, 1999), 69–95.

40. For a nuanced discussion of the Reformation as either a break or a continuation of certain trends in late medieval piety and theology, see Berndt Hamm, "The Place of the Reformation in the Second Christian Millennium," in his *The Reformation of Faith in the Context of Late Medieval Theology and Piety*, Studies in the History of Christian Thought 90 (Leiden: Brill, 2004), 273–300.

41. Sarah Beckwith, *Christ's Body: Identity, Culture and Society in Late Medieval Writings* (London: Routledge, 1993), esp. chapter 1.

42. An approach rarely taken; the appendix to Bernard McGinn, *The Foundations of Mysticism: Origins to the Fifth Century*, The Presence of God: A History of Western Christian Mysticism 1 (New York: Crossroad, 1994), represents a notable exception. Otto Langer, "Über einige Probleme der Geschichtsschreibung der Mystik," *Zeitschrift für deutsche Philologie: Sonderheft* 113 (1994): 83–155, rests within the Middle Ages.

43. See Rufus M. Jones, *The Flowering of Mysticism: The Friends of God in the Fourteenth Century* (New York: Macmillan, 1939), 66–67; Ernst Benz, *The Mystical Sources of German Romantic Philosophy*, trans. Blair R. Reynolds and Eunice M. Paul (Allison Park, Pa.: Pickwick, 1983), esp. 5–10; and Jeff Mitscherling, "The Identity of the Human and the Divine in the Logic of Speculative Philosophy," in *Hegel and the Tradition: Essays in Honour of H. S. Harris*, ed. Michael Baur and John Russon (Toronto: University of Toronto Press, 1997), 143–61. For an introduction to a key figure in the history of Eckhart's rediscovery and reception, Hans L. Martensen, as well as a translation of his *Mester Eckart: Et Bidrag til at oplyse Middeladerens Mystik* (Copenhagen: Reitzel, 1984), see *Between Hegel and Kierkegaard: Hans L. Martensen's Philosophy of Religion*, American Academy of Religion Texts and Translations Series 17, intro. Curtis L. Thompson, trans. Curtis L. Thompson and David J. Kangas (Atlanta, Ga.: Scholars, 1997).

44. See Harold Mah, "The French Revolution and the Problem of German Modernity: Hegel, Heine, and Marx," *New German Critique* 50 (1990): 3–20, esp. 8.

45. Georg Wilhelm Friedrich Hegel, *Aesthetics: Lectures on Fine Arts*, 2 vols., trans. T. M. Knox (Oxford: Clarendon, 1975), 1:594.

46. Harold Mah, *Enlightenment Phantasies: Cultural Identity in France and Germany, 1750–1914* (Ithaca, N.Y.: Cornell University Press, 2003), 166.

47. In addition to Mah, "French Revolution," see Erzsébet Rózsa, "Hegel über die Kunst der 'neueren Zeit' im Spannungsfeld zwischen der 'Prosa' und der 'Innerlichkeit,'" in *Die geschichtliche Bedeutung der Kunst und die Bestimmung der Künste*, ed. Annemarie Gethmann-Seifert, Lu de Vos, and Bernadette Collenberg-Plotnikov (Munich: Fink, 2005), 121–42; Klaus J. Schmidt, "Der Rückzug der Kunst aus dem Äußeren in die Innerlichkeit," in *Das Geistige und das Sinnliche in der Kunst: Ästhetische Reflexion in der Perspective des Deutschen Idealismus*, ed. Dieter Wandscheider (Würzburg: Königshausen & Neumann, 2005), 95–112; and Jörg Träger, "Gretchens Gebet und Pygmalions Erhörung: Das Goethe'sche 'Andachtsbild' als protestantische Kategorie der Kunstgeschichte," in *Kunst—Geschichte—Wahrnehmung: Strukturen und Mechanismen von Wahrnehmungsstrategien*, ed. Stephan Albrecht et al. (Berlin: Deutscher Kunstverlag, 2008), 295–310, esp. 298 on *Innerlichkeit* and German Pietism.

48. Martensen, *Between Hegel and Kierkegaard*, 235. Martensen qualifies his enthusiasm by noting, "A closer scrutiny of this contrast shows that mysticism, though having disconnected itself from Catholicism in many ways, yet coheres with its deepest root. A spiritualized Catholicism is therefore not yet authentic Protestantism" (237). How paradoxical, then, that *Innerlichkeit* became a hallmark of Germany's most emphatic rejection of some aspects of modernity, namely National Socialism. Consider the characterization of Meister Eckhart in Ulrich Christoffel's, *Deutsche Innerlichkeit*, published in Munich in 1940, in which, claims the author: "'Nur soweit lebt man, als man aus innerlichem Bewegnis wirkt.' Die deutschen Lieder, Bilder und Gedanken können weithin als ein Widerhall dieser einen Wahrheit aus dem Munde des Meisters Ekkehard angesehen werden, denn sie haben sich alle aus der innerlichen Bewegnis der Seelen abgelöst und wenn die Welt tief in die Empfindung hineingezogen wird, strahlt diese wieder einen milden Schein auf alle Wirklichkeit zurück" (One only lives in so far as one acts from inner movement. German songs, pictures, and thoughts can to a great extent be seen as an echo of this truth from the mouth of Meister Eckhart, in that they all originate from the inner movement of the soul, and if the world is drawn deeply into feeling, then this [feeling] projects in a gentle reflection onto all reality). For the application of the category to German medieval art in ways that are untenable, see Ulrich Christoffel, *Deutsche Innerlichkeit* (Munich: R. Piper & Co. Verlag, 1940), 109, as well as the caustic commentary of Willibild Sauerländer, "Die

Naumburger Stifterfiguren: Rückblick und Fragen," in *Cathedrals and Sculpture*, 2 vols. (London: Pindar, 1999–2000), 2:593–711, esp. 614.

49. See B. F. McGuiness, "The Mysticism of the *Tractatus*," *Philosophical Review* 75 (1966): 305–28; Rolf-Albert Dietrich, "Untersuchungen über den Begriff des 'Mystischen' in Wittgensteins *Tractatus*" (Ph.D. diss., University of Göttingen, 1971); and Andrew Weeks, *German Mysticism from Hildegard of Bingen to Ludwig Wittgenstein: A Literary and Intellectual History* (Albany: State University of New York Press, 1993), 235.

50. Owen C. Thomas, "Interiority and Christian Spirituality," *Journal of Religion* 80, no. 1 (2000): 41–60, esp. 50.

51. See Steven T. Katz, ed., *Mysticism and Philosophical Analysis* (New York: Oxford University Press, 1978), and idem, ed., *Mysticism and Language* (Oxford: Oxford University Press, 1992). Ramie Targoff, *Common Prayer: The Language of Public Devotion in Early Modern England* (Chicago: Chicago University Press, 2001), esp. 86–87, makes a similar argument regarding the "language of devotion" in early modern England, stressing instead the poetry's public parameters as defined by shared liturgical modes of expression.

52. See Jeffrey F. Hamburger, "Seeing and Believing: The Suspicion of Sight and the Authentication of Vision in Late Medieval Art," in *Imagination und Wirklichkeit: Zum Verhältnis von mentalen und realen Bilder in der Kunst der frühen Neuzeit*, ed. Alessandro Nova and Klaus Krüger (Mainz: Philipp von Zabern, 2000), 47–70.

53. See, for example, Steven T. Katz, "The 'Conservative' Character of Mystical Experience," in *Mysticism and Religious Traditions*, ed. Steven T. Katz (Oxford: Oxford University Press, 1983), 3–60.

54. See, for example, Elizabeth A. Dreyer, "Whose Story is It? The Appropriation of Medieval Mysticism," *Spiritus* 4 (2004): 151–72. For a nuanced account of "modernity and the critique of the ascetic self," with reference to Blumenberg, see Gavin Flood, *The Ascetic Self: Subjectivity, Memory and Tradition* (Cambridge: Cambridge University Press, 2004), 235–57.

55. Cf. James Simpson, "The Rule of Medieval Imagination," in *Images, Idolatry, and Iconoclasm in Late Medieval England: Textuality and the Visual Image*, ed. Jeremy Dimmick, James Simpson, and Nicolette Zeeman (Oxford: Oxford University Press, 2002), 4–24, esp. 23–24: "Historiographies of cultural rupture, which blacken the repulsed past by identifying it with the imagination, fail to recognize the imagination's 'free citizenship' in the psyche." How free, however, is the imagination, especially in a period, such as the sixteenth century, of incessant visual propaganda in various media?

56. See *A "Dictatorship of Relativism?" Symposium in Response to Cardinal Ratzinger's Last Homily*, special issue of *Common Knowledge* 13, nos. 2–3 (2007).

12

The Rhetoric of Mysticism

From Contemplative Practice to Aesthetic Experiment

Niklaus Largier

Joris-Karl Huysmans, the nineteenth-century French decadent writer, begins his novel *Against Nature* (*À rebours*, 1884) with the following epigraph: "I must rejoice beyond the confines of time . . . though the world be repelled by my joy, and in its coarseness know not what I mean."[1] With this quote from a medieval mystical text, Jan Ruysbroeck's *The Spiritual Espousals*,[2] Husymans's novel evokes a moment of mystical experience in overwhelming joy. The moment of joy Huysmans makes reference to, a mystical encounter with the divine, is alien to the ordinary world and will forever be unknown to it. Its trace, however, re-emerges in the experience of the decadent protagonist of Huysmans's novel, Jean des Esseintes, who reproduces the very alienation from the world in his retreat from it and the very joy of the mystic in his artful enactment of and in his experimentation with moments of intense aesthetic experience.

One of these moments is to be found in Jean des Esseintes's contemplation of the books in his library. After the works of Baudelaire, for whom his "admiration . . . was boundless,"[3] des Esseintes reviews a number of Catholic writers, among others Ernest Hello, who was in fact the nineteenth-century translator of Ruysbroeck's work into French. Huysmans writes: "Des Esseintes felt drawn to this unbalanced yet subtle mind; no fusion had been achieved between the skilled psychologist and the pious pedant, and it was these jarring collisions, these very incongruities that formed the essence of Hello's personality."[4] Among other things, Ernest Hello was the translator and commentator of medieval mystics, of "Angela da Foligno's *Visions*, a book flowing with unparalleled inanity," and "of the selected works of Jan van Ruysbroeck the Blessed, a thirteenth century mystic, whose prose offered an incomprehensible but appealing amalgam of mysterious ecstasy, sentimental effusions, and scathing outbursts."[5] Like Baudelaire, "close to those frontiers which are the dwelling-place of aberrations of the mind," Hello had—according to Huysmans's protagonist—uncovered or rediscovered "the tetanus of mysticism"[6] and prepared the readings that fascinated Jean des Esseintes most, namely the ones from a medieval mystical tradition that gave him the joy he was looking for.

As I argue here, Huysmans's fascination with the mystics and the rediscovery of medieval mysticism in the nineteenth century does, however, not lie primarily with mystical theology or with anything the 'mystics' *believed* or *taught* in dogmatic or theological terms. Instead, it lies with the experiences they *produced* and *explored* in their contemplative practices, and with the very language and texture of their discourse. In the eyes of the character Jean des Esseintes—and of the author Huysmans—the essence of mysticism is to be found in what the mystical writers shared with Baudelaire, namely the fact that he "had gone further" than any other poet, that "he had descended to the very bottom of the inexhaustible mine, had journeyed along abandoned or uncharted tunnels, eventually reaching those regions of the soul in which the nightmare growths of human thought flourish."[7]

Thus, Huysmans puts a form of rhetoric and poetic practice at the center of his engagement with medieval mysticism—a rhetoric and poetic practice that can be understood in terms of a literary and spiritual exercise at the same time. It is an exercise that focuses—to use the words of Georges Bataille who will follow Huysmans's line of thought—on the "possible," on pushing the "limits of the possible,"[8] and on exploring those very limits of human experience. In fact, many of the moments of pleasurable experience in Jean des Esseintes's life are conceived in ways that follow this tradition. They are inspired by Ignatius of Loyola, his spiritual exercises,[9] and the medieval practices of contemplation and of production of mystical experience that lie at the basis of the Ignatian model of reading and contemplation.

As for Georges Bataille, whose references to medieval mystical traditions in his book *Inner Experience* resonate deeply with the quoted passages from Huysmans's *Against Nature*, the focus of this poetics of experience does not consist in the construction of a body of knowledge but in an experiential exploration that goes from "knowledge" and "values" to "non-knowledge"[10] and intensities "unknown" to this world. Bataille writes:

> For some time now, the only philosophy which lives—that of the German school—tended to make of the highest knowledge an extension of inner experience. But this *phenomenology* lends to knowledge the value of a goal which one attains through experience. This is an ill-assorted match: the measure given to experience is at once too much and not great enough. Those who provide this place for it must feel that it overflows, by an immense "possible," the use to which they limit themselves. What appears to preserve philosophy is the little acuity of the experience from which the phenomenologists set out. This lack of balance does not weather the putting into play of experience proceeding to the end of the possible, when going to the end means at least this: that the limit, which is knowledge as a goal, be crossed.[11]

Quoting the mystical tropes of "non-knowledge" and of "unknowing," Bataille evokes in these lines a specific kind of phenomenology. It is not the type of philosophical phenomenology known to us from early twentieth-century German thought, but a phenomenology that emerges in mystical texts that explore and "cross" the limits of knowledge, opening up the "uncharted" territory with which Huysmans is fascinated. In Bataille's understanding the mystical texts do so in a response to the challenges of negative theology, focusing on the very practices that allow for the production of experience and for a phenomenology of experience where knowledge fails and always has to fail. Thus, the production of experience moves to center stage, as it does in the late medieval author Bataille loves most, namely Angela of Foligno.[12] This production of experiential moments happens, however, not in the form of an experience that allows for us to "know" something and to build a body of knowledge (something Thomas Aquinas and his *Summa theologiae* stand for in Bataille's ironic juxtaposition of Thomas and Angela), but as a practice of phenomenological exploration that acknowledges the impossibility of knowing and that moves the boundaries of the possible time and again from within this utter acknowledgment of finitude and "nakedness." According to Bataille, this takes place in exemplary form in the *Liber de vere fidelium experientia* of Angela of Foligno, a text that he puts in opposition to the enterprise of Thomas Aquinas and other scholastic theologians.[13]

Dionysius the Areopagite, whom Bataille quotes in this context as well, stands for a starting point of this rhetoric of experience with his treatises on *Mystical Theology* and on the *Divine Names*. Dionysius is both the inspiration for the strong notion of apophatic speech—the "joy unknown to the world" in Huysmans and the "non-knowledge" in Bataille—and for the kataphatic speech, for a poetics of praise and abandonment, an experimental poetics of affirmation and negation, and thus a poetics of pushing the limits of the possible that allows for the production and the exploration of ever new experiential states. These states—moments of utter absorption in many guises—compensate for the impossibility of knowing the divine (or any kind of absolute truth) and provide an experiential "voyage to the end of the possible of man."[14]

In the following pages I portray a few moments—actually not much more than snapshots—in the history of this phenomenology of experience from which Huysmans and Bataille draw in their readings of medieval and early modern mystics. I am, however, not presenting a linear history that unfolds in time—as the title of my essay might wrongly suggest. What I am trying to argue for is a history and a historiography of mysticism that traces certain moments, certain elements and tropes, and their transformation in specific contexts. Thus, I focus on five moments in this history, which, as I see it, are intimately connected and move in the foreground or background in a number of stages and ways from medieval times up to today. In other words, what I portray in the first and second short parts, focusing on medieval practices of prayer and meditation, already contains the elements that will be important for the other parts, for Baroque mysticism, which I call experimental mysticism here, for a certain understanding of aesthetic experience in Alexander Gottlieb Baumgarten and Johann Gottfried Herder, and for the readings of the mystics in Joris-Karl Huysmans and in a number of other modern authors, including Georges Bataille. What holds these moments together is indeed, as Bataille points out, a specific form of phenomenology, or, more precisely and in my terms, a phenomenology of rhetorical effects.

Prayer, Rhetoric, Mysticism

Throughout the Middle Ages the mystical tradition was part of a tradition of prayer and contemplation in a monastic setting. It was a matter of general recognition to monks and nuns that intense experience and overwhelming grace, be it in the form of visions or other experiential states, did not happen without preparation and training. Prayer, the "ascent of the mind to God" according to John of Damascus and to a medieval tradition that follows his teaching, is the very technique that prepares and forms the soul, that moves it from reading to contemplation, and that leads it from a state of aridity and desolation into a state where mystical experience as an experience of union with the divine in affect, sensation, and cognition seemed possible—and often became real. Thus, the classic path in prayer from *lectio* to *meditatio*, from *oratio* to *contemplatio*, could easily be transformed into a model of mystic ascent as we find it in elaborate forms in the later Middle Ages, especially in the works of David of Augsburg, Rudolf of Biberach, and Hendrick Herp, who exercised a strong influence on the Spanish mystics of the *Siglo de Oro* and on their theories and practices of prayer and contemplation.

Following this tradition, we read in Guigo the Carthusian's *Scala claustralium*: "Beatae vitae dulcedinem lectio inquirit, meditatio invenit, oratio postulat, contemplatio degustat" (Reading looks for the sweetness of the blessed life, meditation finds it, prayer asks for it, and contemplation tastes it). Or, in other words: "Quarite legendo, et invenietis meditando; pulsate orando, et aperietur vobis contemplando" (You look for it in reading and you find it in meditation; you knock on the door in prayer, and in contemplation it opens to you).[15] Thus, the monastic form of spiritual practice leads from reading to meditation and to contemplation and sensual experience (often expressed in terms of intense love, overwhelming taste of sweetness, and intimate touch).

I am choosing one short twelfth-century discourse on prayer in order to illustrate the basic character of this understanding of prayer and its orientation toward the production of experiential states and, more broadly, toward a phenomenology of rhetorical effects. As Hugh of Saint Victor demonstrates in his treatise *De virtute orandi*, the practice of prayer is highly informed by rhetorical tradition and training. Prayer, meant to lead into a state of *excitatio* and *inflammatio*, of intense and overwhelming love, is first and foremost an art of arousing affects and emotions that forgets its own intention: "Pura oratio est, quando ex abundantia devotionis mens ita accenditur, ut cum se ad Deum postulatura converterit, prae amore ejus magnitudine etiam petitionis suae obliviscatur" (Pure prayer happens when the mind is inflamed by the abundance of devotion, so that in turning toward God in overwhelming love it forgets even what it is asking for).[16] Thus, prayer is to be understood in terms of a spiritual exercise that arouses the affects. It does so in a way that not only evokes the affect of overwhelming love but that lays out and deploys from the ground of the soul the "innumerable" forms of affects that humans are able to experience. As Hugh points out, the "number of these affects is infinite," making it impossible for him to "count them all."[17] These affects emerge in a practice that moves from a state of unexcited reading or remembering of the sacred texts to moments of intense perception and emotional arousal. The transition to this state of arousal happens in meditation, the "yoke" of the soul, which exercises a shaping force on the ways of perception. Meditation produces arousal ("excitatio") through "frequent mental re-evocation" ("frequens cogitatio"), a process of rumination and mastication that includes sensual and emotional perception as well as the imagination and intellectual evaluation.[18]

The basis of this form of meditative "cogitation" is a rhetorical practice, namely enumeration, the construction of lists, and the configuration of tropes drawn from the scriptures, from life experience, from lives of saints and martyrs, from memory, and from other available sources. Thus, Hugh argues, a list of pains and an enumeration of all possible evils will produce the effect that the soul experiences a number of affects of pain and suffering. The more impressive and comprehensive the list, the more the soul will "sigh and groan" ("tanto amplius suspirat et gemit")[19] and experience the broad range of affects of suffering. In a similar way the soul can move itself into a state of admiration, pleasure, and praise when it evokes tropes of divine beauty and happiness.[20] What Hugh emphasizes in this short treatise is not only the production of specific sites and states of affective experience but also the very transition from one affect to another one. Often, he writes, the singing of the psalms means exactly that, namely the production of affects and the transition from one affect to another one, then another one, and so on.

In other words, meditation as a rhetorical practice of evocation with the help of lists, enumerations, textual configurations, and reconfigurations produces textures of affective arousal that can be savored, experienced, and phenomenologically explored. In addition to the rhetorical technique of enumeration the technique of narration is an important tool in the construction of these textures of experience. As many medieval authors demonstrate, biblical narratives—the Song of Songs, the passion of Christ—can serve this purpose as well as *Lives of Saints*—one thinks of the story of the temptations of Saint Anthony—or even personal experiences. The function of both the enumeration and the narration does not consist in telling God something he would not know already but in shaping the life of the soul.

As Hugh points out, the very function of the rhetorical techniques of enumeration and narration consists in the production of affective states that help to overcome the understanding of prayer as a means of petitioning God. Instead, the forms of prayer he has in mind produce a complex and comprehensive state of arousal that can be explored, enjoyed, and suffered—and that then makes the intensity of overwhelming love emerge in which a taste of the divine will be savored. Thus, meditation as the production of a dense texture of both terrifying and consoling affects opens the path toward purgation, toward illumination, and finally toward contemplative union in an experience of the taste of the divine—an experience that a broad range of authors after Hugh will be speaking about.

The most remarkable aspect of Hugh's treatise about prayer is its rhetorical character. It uses the scriptures and the body of religious texts and personal experience as an archive that can be mobilized in the practice of meditation in the form of rhetorical stimuli. Based on techniques of amplification—partition, enumeration, narration, construction of lists—these stimuli are used in order to produce a dense texture of affects, which in turn can be focused in additional steps toward the experience of overwhelming love that forms the ultimate experiential goal of the very practice of prayer. As we will see in the following part of my sketch, this production of moments of absorption includes not only emotional but also sensual states of perception. Together, they form the key elements of a medieval rhetorical practice that serves both prayer and mystical experience.

Sensation and the Phenomenology of Rhetorical Effects

Traditionally, the most prominent place for the treatment of the experiential qualities of the encounter with the divine is not only teachings about prayer and affects but also teachings about the five "inner senses." Going back to Origen's and Gregory of Nyssa's exegetical writings,[21] the concept of five "inner senses" is in fact a phenomenological understanding of sensation as it happens in and through practices of reading, prayer, meditation, and contemplation. Thus, in his hermeneutics Origen puts the emphasis on *aisthesis*, the sensual perception of the divine. This form of sensation is produced not in a "natural" way but artificially through a specific use of the words of the scriptures and—again—through a rhetorical amplification that we are meant to perform in the acts of reading and contemplation.

Using the Greek term *aisthesis*, Origen indicates that he speaks about a faculty or an experience that transcends the rational and discursive operations of our intellect. In fact, Origen translates the biblical verse Proverbs 2:5 (King James Version: "Then shalt thou understand the fear of the Lord, and find the knowledge of God") in a specific way, introducing the term *aisthesis* where other translations, including the Septuagint and the Vulgate, use *gnosis* or *scientia*.[22] Thus, Origen emphasizes that the text of the scriptures is the object of each sense of the soul, such as light for the eyes, word for the ears, bread for the taste, tactile sensation for the touch.[23] Origen emphasizes that the practice of reading the scriptures necessarily involves the practice of sensation. In his words, practice and exercise are key elements leading to the constitution of this realm of experience. Where this happens is above all in reading and prayer. Prayer is the place, as well, where the rational, discursive, and practical level of the life of the soul is left behind in favor of the contemplative aesthetic experience of the divine.

In many cases, starting with Gregory of Nyssa and essentially based on a number of biblical verses, the emphasis of this contemplative prayer lies not on the inner *vision*—as one might expect from a modern perspective and from the Greek philosophical basis of a large part of Christian theology—but on inner *taste* and finally on inner *touch* as well. As we might expect, taste refers above all to the sweetness that is experienced in the perception of the divine. Honey is the expression used in many of these cases, quoting from the Bible and its uses of "milk and honey" with regard to the experience of paradise or eternal life, but reference is also made to bitterness and other terms, evoking the entire realm of possible sensation and allowing for the exploration of a variety of experiences of taste.[24] Innumerable authors who use this terminology could be quoted here, especially those who comment on the Song of Songs, the text that is at the basis of most elaborations on the sensory and emotional experience of the divine. Among these, William of Saint-Thierry plays an important role in the medieval tradition, and a Middle High German text that illustrates the importance of the theory of the inner senses is to be found in the *St. Trudperter Hohelied*.[25] Both William and the *St. Trudperter Hohelied* testify to the significance of this form of aesthetic exploration.

Often the approach chosen by the medieval and late medieval authors is not systematic. It does not take shape in the form of a clearly elaborated theory of the hierarchy of the senses, but rather in the form of comments on different approaches to the divine that have their reality in the perfume, the sound, the touch, or the taste that is perceived by the soul while praying, that is, in other and more concrete words, while it is "chewing" and "ruminating" the words. In most cases, biblical verses expressing such moments of taste figure prominently in these texts, which are used as the stimuli, the rhetorical means that call forth specific sensations and emotions. In meditative practice the effect of memorizing and ruminating—akin to Hugh's notion of *cogitatio*—can thus result in the production of complex inner worlds of multiple layers of sensation.

Major attempts to systematize this practice of prayer and contemplation can be found in Albert the Great and in Bonaventure. Albert relates sight, hearing, and odor to knowledge of truth, that is, to the more cognitive intellectual realm; he relates taste and touch to the experience of the good, that is, to the realm of love and will. Inspired by Dionysius the Pseudo-Areopagite, he emphasizes the passivity of this form of experience and the fact that the soul is "suffering" it and that the inner sensory phenomena are aspects of the reality of this suffering of the divine. Speaking of *tactus* and *sapor* with regard to the divine he accentuates the "experiential," purely "receptive," and "passive" character of this kind of perception.[26]

The perception of the divine in terms of an experience of taste and touch becomes most significant in Franciscan traditions, in David of Augsburg's *Septem gradus orationis*, in Bonaventure's *Itinerarium mentis ad Deum* and *Breviloquium*, but even more so in later medieval texts—for example, in Rudolf of Biberach's *De septem itineribus aeternitatis*. Other examples where the gustatory and tactile experience is very important could be added; among those are the late medieval works by Peter of Ailly and the *Imitatio Christi* by Thomas à Kempis. *Delectatio* (pleasure) and *suavitas* (sweetness) are the key words these authors use when discussing the ways by which man can reach the divine in an experiential way, referring to a sensation of taste. Peter of Ailly expresses it in this way: "divinas aeternorum praemiorum delectationes jam quodammodo experimentaliter attingere, et eorum suavitatem delectabiliter sapere" (to reach already in this life the pleasures of the eternal rewards in an experiential way, and to taste their sweetness with delight).[27] Rudolf of Biberach, in the treatise entitled *De septem itineribus aeternitatis*, uses the following words, largely inspired by Alcher and Bernard of Clairvaux's, Hugh of Saint Victor's, and Saint Bonaventure's treatment of the inner senses: "attingens gustum interioris mentis, aperit eum ad aeternorum dulcedinem gustandam" (reaching the inner sense of taste, it opens it up toward the tasting of eternal sweetness).[28]

The eschatological structure of this concept is often obvious since it is in the inner experience[29] that the senses are supposed to be rehabilitated and dignified in a way unknown since the loss of paradise. Such experiences are characterized as an anticipation of the eternal and a reconciliation with the ideal existence of man beyond the state of sin. However, it is more than that. In the Franciscan tradition this rehabilitation of the senses and of experience leads to a new affirmative mode with regard to sense experience itself and to an aesthetic justification of the world as it is to be found in Franciscan poetry and science of the late Middle Ages.

Thus far I have emphasized a model of sensory perception that can and indeed must be explained in what we would call today *constructivist* terms. The five inner senses are in my argument not only related to the outer senses as some form of spiritual allegory. Rather, they focus on the observation that the discursive grasp of the divine—and, one might want to add, of the world in its pre-lapsarian state as well—is always limited and that in Origen's understanding the so-called *inner* sensory experience as such transcends this limited grasp. This inner sensory experience is produced on the basis of a practice of reading and prayer. It results from a specific rhetorical procedure that is meant to liberate from the naïve natural sense-experience and that inserts biblical verses in a specific way into the practice of prayer with the goal that they should unfold an arousing effect and evoke an experiential knowledge of the divine. Ultimately—this is Origen's emphasis—the experience through the inner senses reconstitutes, on the way of human pilgrimage and through grace, the way in which Adam and Eve perceived the world and God in nature. In other words, through the experience of the inner senses an originary sensory experience is reconstituted beyond the limits of nature. This is the view shared also in the theories of the medieval authors I have mentioned. Inheriting Origen's teaching and its various retextualizations, they stress not only the necessity of inner experience but even more—especially in the Franciscan tradition—the close connection between inner and outer senses and the significance of the production of sensory and emotional experience itself.

Often, one key biblical text plays a major role in the production of sensation. It is the Song of Songs, which is used as a blueprint for the application of the senses. It provides us with something we could call a dramatic script. Medieval authors draw from this script both in view of quotes that serve to evoke specific moments of sensation and in view of a paradigmatic model that allows for a dramatization of sense experience and concomitant emotional states. We know from the rewriting of the Song of Songs, from complex prayer texts, for example, in Mechthild's *Flowing Light of the Godhead*, and from the use she makes of it as a blueprint for the staging of the life of her soul, that the text not only produces sweetness and delight, but also bitterness and desolation. In other words, the *aisthesis* she produces includes more than an evocation of feelings of divine sweetness. Instead, it is deployed in a dramatic way as an evocation of the diversity of *possible* experience, or, maybe better: prayer—understood in Hugh's way—serves as a means to *explore* the realm of *possible* sensual experience and to intensify it. Thus, Mechthild uses the Song of Songs as a dramatic script, embedding a series of prayers that allow for a rich staging of moments of sensation and emotional arousal. In doing this, some writers, among them again Mechthild of Magdeburg and Hadewijch of Antwerp, combine in audacious ways the text of the Song of Songs with elements taken from contemporary love poetry (*Minnesang*), amplifying further the impact of the text and playing with the aesthetics of sweetness and desolation in Minnesang and in religious contexts.[30]

Let me point to two other such scripts that have played a major role in monastic contexts and that have served as blueprints for specific forms of the application of the senses: the *creation narrative*, the Hexameron, and the legend of the temptation of Saint Anthony. Two twelfth-century texts, *On the fourfold exercise of the cell* (*De quadripertito exercitio cellae*) by Adam of Dryburgh (Adam Scotus)[31] and Balduin of Canterbury's *On the twofold resurrection* (*De duplici resurrectione*)[32] can illustrate this in exemplary ways. Both texts emphasize again—as does Hugh of Saint Victor—that prayer in the cell cannot be a form of prayer that asks for something or prayer that could be seen as a gesture of petitioning. Rather, they both point out that prayer has to be understood as a technique that puts the soul in a position in which it can be touched by the text, so that it is receptive to its rhetorical effects of emotional and sensual arousal. Balduin's notion of a twofold resurrection refers to the fact that "ordinary people" can be content with the resurrection and the experience of the paradise at the end of time. Monks, however, he writes, know the practice of how to evoke this experience as an actual state of emotional and sensual perception.[33] In this context, he invokes musical imagery, imagining the soul as a musical instrument that resonates (a *psaltherium* or *cithara*) and the senses as the chords that are put in movement through the use that is made of the biblical text in prayer and contemplation. Thus, specific quotes from the creation narrative are used to stimulate the senses, to produce moments of sensation that must be qualified as aesthetic since they are in fact nothing else than the sense experience of the world in light of the redemption. The words Adam and Balduin use are *stupor* and *admiratio*, expressing the translation of the creation narrative into phenomena of overwhelming sensual and affective experience. Paradoxically, we might want to add, all this happens in the solitude of the cell where the direct experience of the world is being replaced by this art of aesthetic animation and by the artificial reconfiguration of the original beauty of nature—something we would want to call a form of virtual reality today and something that comes very close to the experience of Huysmans's protagonist Jean des Esseintes in his country retreat.

However, as all monks since the desert fathers knew, this intense experience is not unproblematic. There is no pure sweetness even in the life of the cell, and wherever pure sweetness appears there has to be the suspicion that it has its origin not with the divine but with the demon who disguises himself. This tension is in most cases evoked through the third script I mentioned, namely the model of the life of Saint Anthony, especially the scenes of his temptation. This model, too, serves as a blueprint, on one side for a dramatization of the sensation that is produced, on the other side for a never-ending process of purification in light of a discernment of the spirits. Each moment of sensation and emotional intensity has to be evaluated and justified, that is, each moment of sensation is in itself the place of a drama where the good has to confront the evil and where the exemplary scenario of discernment, the life of Saint Anthony, has to be enacted. In other words, and this is maybe the most important aspect of the significance of the life of Anthony in medieval monastic life, each moment of sensation has to be confronted by its demonic other, which has to be actively evoked as well. Each moment of meditation turns thus into a scene of martyrdom, evoking not only sensation of consolation, but the demons in disguise as well. Thus, the model of *aisthesis* that we encounter here not only produces a world of sweetness in the cell, but also a world of terror and an aesthetics of terror and disfiguration. It is the aesthetics of terror that we will encounter not only in the texts, but also in the paintings of late medieval and early modern artists who deal with the topic of the temptation of Saint Anthony. The drama that we encounter in these texts and images is not just an allegory of temptation, but the drama that unfolds necessarily in the logic of the application and the rhetorical stimulation of the senses as it was introduced by Origen.

The five senses Origen is talking about are "inner" and "spiritual" insofar as they are not to be identified with the "outer" senses, with the faculties and their ways of being bound up with and determined by the empirical world. Instead, they are malleable, they can be given shape, and they are being given shape in the acts of reading and contemplating the scriptures. They are not just metaphorical, though, since the names of the inner senses refer to real sensation, the sensations of touch and taste, seeing and hearing, and smell insofar as they happen in our mind and soul. In other words, Origen and the traditions that build on him present us here with a phenomenological understanding of sensation (and, mutatis mutandis, also of emotions). In addition, the authors who refer to the concept of the "inner senses"—above all William of Saint-Thierry, Bernard of Clairvaux, and Rudolf of Biberach—develop a keen sense for notions and practices of sense-stimulation that are part of their phenomenological understanding of sensation. Since sensation is not necessarily bound up with sense-faculties, sensation can also be produced by other means, namely with the help of rhetorical stimuli, with words, with images, with music, and with other means.

The same is true, as we have seen in Hugh's understanding of prayer, for emotions and affects. Both affect and sense experience can thus be guided in the practice of meditation and contemplation through the introduction of artificial stimuli; through the use of specific scriptural quotes; and through configurations of word, sound, and image in the practice of daily prayer. This practice of prayer is meant to form a new and previously unknown life of the soul, which is intrinsically linked to the experience and the phenomenological exploration of emotional and sensual arousal in medieval spirituality. Thus, I want to suggest, the invention and the rhetoric of the inner or spiritual senses allowed for the creation of an inner space of *experience*, *exploration*, and *amplification* of the emotional as well as of the sensory life of the soul. I use these three terms because they refer to three aspects of this theory of prayer: an experiential instead of a conceptual understanding of the divine, the discovery of new states of emotional arousal against the "aridity" of the soul, and finally a technique of excitement, that is, of an amplification of the affective and sensual life. This amplification, which follows the use of rhetorical techniques, includes the production of feelings of intense desolation, hope and hopelessness, as well as joy, but also of overwhelming sense-experience of sweetness and bitterness, and finally of intense desire and excessive love that is mostly seen in terms of an experience of touch.

Ultimately, this theory and practice of prayer and contemplation attempts to transcend, or, to put it more precisely, inherently transcends the common and universally emphasized disjunction of inner and outer man in medieval spirituality. This is the case because the evocation of the inner senses in the practice of prayer opens up a realm of emotions, an affective and sensual life that compensates for the lack of the intellectual understanding and for the necessary and most common dissociation of inner and outer man in medieval anthropology. The movement through which this is reached can be characterized as a de-naturalization of the senses by artificial means—the techniques of prayer—and a re-naturalization, a return to the intensity of sensory and emotional experience of the world in the form of an aesthetic experience that is constructed with the help of rhetorical means and artifacts and that is explored in the phenomenology of rhetorical effects.

The Discernment of Spirits, Frameworks of Control, and Experimental Mysticism

As we know from medieval and early modern religious authors, the production of religious states of experience is never unproblematic. Thus, the phenomenology of rhetorical effects always had to be framed in several ways. Such frameworks are provided by the monastery, the monastic community, the confessor, and above all by the individual practice of discernment of spirits. It would go far beyond the scope of this essay to analyze the development of the practice and theory of the discernment of spirits in the later Middle Ages.[34] In order to understand later developments, however, I have to point to two major aspects of its history. The propagation of the rhetorical techniques of contemplative prayer in vernacular contexts has led to a broad range of responses in form of treatises about the discernment of spirits in the later Middle Ages.[35] These treatises make attempts to provide for normative frameworks for the evaluation of religious experience beyond the traditional frameworks, namely the monastery and the spiritual guidance and pedagogy of the monastic community.

Thus, manuals of discernment increasingly focus on exercising control over the techniques of phenomenology of rhetorical effects as they spread out in vernacular languages during the fourteenth and fifteenth centuries.

On another level, Martin Luther will engage deeply with what he sees as the threats of mystical enthusiasm (*Schwärmerei*) in the early sixteenth century. Luther provides a frame for references to the mystical tradition within his own theology, above all with his own reception of the *Theologia deutsch*. At the same time, however, he neutralizes both the significance of the emotional and sensual tradition of the mystical rhetoric as well as the political implications of mystical spiritualism with a strong hand.[36]

This does not mean that the mystical tradition and its phenomenology of rhetorical effects disappear. When modern authors, among them Martin Heidegger and Jacques Derrida, refer to mystical traditions, they often refer not directly to the medieval texts but to the way in which the medieval tradition presents itself in seventeenth-century thought and poetry.[37] This is the case with Huysmans and Bataille as well. They refer to medieval mysticism through the lens of its transformations in Ignatius of Loyola and traditions that built on this transformation in seventeenth-century thought on the one hand. On the other hand, the repositioning of mysticism in Reformation thought and its rediscovery in Pietist spirituality[38] against orthodox Lutheranism had a significant impact on the role of mystical traditions in Baroque and Enlightenment thought.[39]

What I want to mention here is just one aspect of this transformation, namely the emergence of an experimental mysticism that builds on medieval traditions of the phenomenology of rhetorical effects discussed above. It can be seen most clearly in a line of thought that leads from the reconfiguration of the phenomenology of rhetorical effects in seventeenth-century German spirituality to the formulation of a philosophical concept of aesthetics in Baumgarten and Herder. In its Baroque form it draws on both the reconfiguration of prayer in Ignatius's notion of spiritual exercises and the vein of mysticism that opposes orthodox Lutheranism and that leads to Pietist culture and spirituality. The hallmarks of German Baroque mysticism are a stronger emphasis on a systematic approach to the phenomenology of rhetorical effects—as it is to be found in the *Spiritual Exercises* of Ignatius of Loyola with its configuration of a space of the imagination and the application of senses and emotions—and a broad range of practices of poetic experimentation. The latter can be found most prominently in the writings of Angelus Silesius and Catharina Regina von Greiffenberg, but also in the thought of Johann Arndt, Philipp Jakob Spener, and in Gottfried Arnold's *Theologia experimentalis*. What characterizes these forms of experiential religiosity is not only an opposition to orthodox Lutheranism and a return to medieval forms of affective piety. More than that it is a rediscovery of the phenomenology of rhetorical effects in a context that goes far beyond the framework of monastic life and that connects with some aspects of late medieval vernacular theology. In other words, in the works of Angelus Silesius, Daniel von Czepko, Catharina Regina von Greiffenberg, and Quirinus Kuhlmann—to name just a few[40]—the tradition of the production of mystical experience turns into an art of poetic experimentation that is intimately connected with—as Goethe's Pietist friend Katharina von Klettenberg will call it—a new "art of living" where religious experience and aesthetic experience converge.[41]

The Emergence of Aesthetic Experience

It is in this broad context of redeployment of mystical tropes that a key term from medieval mystical traditions re-emerges in a very prominent place in eighteenth-century writings on aesthetics. Both Alexander Gottfried Baumgarten, the "founder" of the modern philosophical discipline of aesthetics, and Johann Gottfried Herder in his discussion of contemporary aesthetics make reference to the mystical notion of the "ground of the soul."

Baumgarten introduces the concept of the "ground of the soul" in a chapter on "aesthetic enthusiasm" of his *Aesthetica* (sectio V). In the original Latin he speaks of the "impetus aestheticus" and the "pulcra mentis incitatio, inflammatioque, . . . ecstasis, furor, enthousiasmós, pneuma theou" (the beautiful arousal of the soul, its inflammation, . . . ecstasis, furor, enthusiasm, divine spirit, or inspiration).[42] This arousable character of the soul, he says, is a fundamental quality that is required in successful aesthetic experience.

Experience means here the way in which the soul takes shape under the specific influence of stimuli that awaken the "lower faculties of the soul," that is, the faculties that have been "lying dead" until now. When I say the soul "takes shape," we have to think of the soul in a somewhat Aristotelian way as a realm of potentialities that are brought into emergence and into form in specific interactions with the world. Beyond Aristotle, however, the notion of the "ground of the soul" points to a different concept of possibility and potentiality, which has been elaborated in the history of late medieval mysticism, especially in the writings of Meister Eckhart and his follower Johannes Tauler, an author who was most influential in Pietist circles of the eighteenth century. Here, the ground is often understood as a pure and empty mirror,[43] a realm of utter possibility to "be" or "become everything" in breaking through the intentional, instrumental, teleological, and rational order of the world, and to experience the world in light of the divine. Under the condition of this breakthrough in "enthusiasm," Baumgarten writes in a similar way, the "ground of the soul" rises up, is aroused, and informs the higher faculties in unexpected ways, shaping the whole apparatus of perception and representation, including the senses and the affects.[44] In this ecstatic state, in this aesthetic experience, body and soul affect each other mutually and the soul—better: the unity of soul and body—takes on a new shape and appears as something new. "Compare this," Baumgarten writes in order to illustrate his point, to the experience and the pleasure of "otium" ("leisure") during a leisurely walk. When the spirit "leaves behind all sorrow," Baumgarten goes on, when the soul leaves behind the hardship of work and of business, and when it moves without plans and goals along a pleasant alley of blooming trees, it opens itself up to aesthetic perception and pleasure. This, he concludes, "is possibly the experience of the Helicon, the dream of Parnassus" that now informs the soul and the body, giving shape to it in a way that we call aesthetic experience of itself and the world.[45]

Since many philosophers, Baumgarten writes in these passages of his *Aesthetica* further, "ignore" the "ground of the soul," people usually point to the "gods" and a model of divinization when they try to identify the origin of this extraordinary state of experience. They usually do so, he writes, in evoking "the poets" and their divine "inspiration." Baumgarten himself, however, introduces the term "fundus animae," the "ground of the soul" instead, indicating that he draws on a tradition that, as he argues, "is currently ignored by the philosophers."[46] He thus points to a tradition that puts the emphasis on the one hand on the immanence of the divine principle, of its identity with the soul itself, and on the other, on the soul as the very ground of possibility that is virtually everything in sensation, affect, and imagination. At the same time he brings back the concept of a phenomenology of rhetorical effects when he focuses on the very production of aesthetic experience and enthusiasm. In Baumgarten's understanding of aesthetic experience the notion of a "ground of the soul" is equivalent to the notion of the excitable soul in Hugh of Saint Victor's theory of prayer. In both cases the soul emerges in its ground as a horizon of possibility that is open to and receptive of rhetorical stimulation. And in both cases this stimulation shapes the soul, produces emotional and sensual states of arousal, and gives human experience a new intensity and texture that can be phenomenologically explored.

This line of thought becomes even stronger in Herder. Herder is famous for his rehabilitation of the sense of touch as a basis for the modern concept of aesthetic experience.[47] When he thinks about touch he does so, as do some late medieval authors,[48] again in connection with the "ground of the soul," the "fundus animae." For Herder, too, the "ground of the soul" is not just a negative counterpart of our discursive and intellectual activity and knowledge. It constitutes a complex intersection of sensuality, affect, perception, feeling, and imagination, and forms thus the basis for an alternative way of cognition where the dualism of soul and body, spirit and matter, is being replaced by a monism of sensual, emotional, and cognitive experience.

This notion of the soul resonates with elements of contemporary philosophy of nature and aspects of French sensualism Herder is drawing on. However, he never entirely covers up the provenience of the mystical trope of the ground of the soul. Thus, he writes in his *Metakritik der sogenannten Transzendental-Ästhetik* that "das Nichts im Nichts . . . offenbaret sich im dunklen Seelengrund der Mystiker" (nothingness in nothingness . . . reveals itself in the dark ground of the soul of the mystics) "um die einzig-mögliche Bedingung aller Offenbarung des sinnlichen sowohl als verständlichen Weltalls zu werden" (in order to become the only possible condition of the revelation of the sensual as well as the comprehensible world.)[49] In other words, the ground of the soul is not only the natural and generic ground of our becoming and of all our abilities, it is also the "dark ground" of all our feelings, and it is "the dark ground of the soul of the mystics," the nothingness and the abyss that we find in medieval texts and—much closer to Herder—in Baroque mysticism and Pietist thought.

It is on this basis that Herder figures and reconfigures the sense of touch in a new way, namely as a correlation between the "darkness" of the ground of the soul, that is, the soul taken as realm or possibility, and its very expression in *Gefühl*, that is, in the way the soul takes shape in perception. This emphasis on touch in Herder's thought has been extensively analyzed, for instance, in the discussion of touch in French philosophy, especially in Condillac. In my focus on the notion of the ground of the soul I am adding one aspect that has been ignored, namely that in rehabilitating touch Herder rehabilitates a notion of "darkness" and of the mystical tropes that go with it. At the same time he makes use of the rhetoric of animation I mentioned above.

What Herder describes in his analysis of aesthetic experience is the transformation of the eye into an organ of touch.[50] For Herder this happens literally, not metaphorically. He does not describe ways in which the eye, as we sometimes say, touches a surface or a body, using the notion of touch in order to express the intensity of seeing. Instead, he describes a transformation that happens while we see and observe, a transformation in which the eye loses its specificity, the determinate ways of looking at form, surface, color, shape, and perspective. In this transformation the eye turns into touch and the visual is "reduced," so to speak, to the tactile, which is the very ground of possibility of all sensation and feeling and which takes shape in aesthetic experience. It is touch that moves along the object and that in moving along gets absorbed in the very perception, making the experience one of a replication of the sculpture in the soul and of a communication between the soul and the object. In its encounter with the sculpture the soul animates its possibilities of sensation, affect, and cognition, starting necessarily with the most basic one, namely touch.

It is important to take Herder's argument seriously that we are not dealing with metaphorical language here. He does not present us with an allegorical or metaphorical explanation of the act of viewing and the ways in which emotions and affects are involved in it and in which they are seduced by the object. What happens instead is to be described as a kind of transfiguration of seeing into touch whereby the ground of the soul with all its possibilities is being aroused in the experience of the work of art, the plasticity of the figure, and where something new takes shape in this experience—a new object, a new soul, and a new sphere of experience. The eye sees determined, limited, defined shapes, forms, and colors. Touch, however, appears as a moment of liberation from this determination, as the condition of possibility of transcending the determined vision and the level of meaning, and as the level of experience where object and subject, sculpture and viewer, merge in a slow temporal process.

In other words, the plasticity of the ground of the soul, its receptivity and openness, is informed by the effects of the work of art, that is, the effects of figuration, of a product of invention, and takes shape in a tactile exchange with it. Or, to put it differently, the "tactile" is the name for an experience that allows a sculpture to fully deploy its rhetorical effects on the soul and allow it to act on the soul and unfold its potential of experience. Through this process the soul is increasingly absorbed in the very experience of the effects that take place in this exchange between the viewer and the sculpture, and this in Herder is aesthetic experience as an exploration of possibility. The sculpture, one has to add, turns thus into an artifact or a figure that stimulates the soul, that makes it emerge as a specific site of affect, sensation, and cognition, allowing time and again for an experimental exploration of its very possibilities.

Conclusion

Let me return to the beginning of this essay and to the notions of phenomenology and experience Georges Bataille and Joris-Karl Huysmans refer to when they talk about mysticism. What I tried to analyze here in a number of more or less elaborate descriptions of historical moments are a few aspects of the genealogy of this notion of phenomenology and its function in the context of what Huysmans calls the "frontier" and Bataille the "limits of the possible." The two modern authors bring to our attention that mysticism is based on a set of practices and that, in fact, these practices are meant to produce certain forms of intense experience. Thus, they evoke a specific aspect of a medieval tradition of spiritual exercises, an aspect that I call the phenomenology of rhetorical effects. As I have tried to show, this phenomenology forms the basis of meditative prayer and of certain techniques of reading that focus on the active stimulation of the soul and the animation of its experiential possibilities. In doing so, meditative prayer and contemplation use rhetorical techniques in order to produce sensual and emotional states of experience. Late medieval mystics make extensive use of these techniques, experimenting with them increasingly also beyond the borders of monastic communities. Thus, they prepare the field for later uses of this technique both in experimental mystical poetics of the Baroque era and in the conception of notions of aesthetic experience in the eighteenth century. In all these cases we encounter the type of phenomenology Bataille and Huysmans are asking for, namely a phenomenology of rhetorical effects invested in an alienation from the known world, in addressing the "limits of the possible," and in crossing these limits in absorbing experience time and again.

Notes

This essay is based on a range of preliminary work published during the past few years. I have presented some of this material at a number of occasions and want to thank all the participants and interlocutors. References to my other publications with more extensive treatments of specific aspects can be found in the notes. This is a first—and still quite sketchy—attempt at producing a synthetic view of these materials.

1. Joris-Karl Huysmans, *Against Nature* (Oxford: Oxford University Press, 1998), 1.

2. Huysmans quotes from the French translation by Ernest Hello, *Rusbroek l'Admirable* (Paris: Poussielgue frères, 1869).

3. Huysmans, *Against Nature*, 117.

4. Huysmans, *Against Nature*, 129.

5. Huysmans, *Against Nature*, 128.

6. Huysmans, *Against Nature*, 117.

7. Huysmans, *Against Nature*, 117.

8. Georges Bataille, *Inner Experience*, trans. Leslie Anne Boldt (Albany: State University of New York Press, 1988), 8.

9. See Joris Karl Huysmans, *À rebours*, ed. Marc Fumaroli (Paris: Gallimard, 1977), 101 and 394.

10. Bataille, *Inner Experience*, 8–9.

11. Bataille, *Inner Experience*, 8.

12. Cf. Amy Hollywood, "Bataille and Mysticism: A 'Dazzling Dissolution,'" *Diacritics* 26, no. 2 (1996): 74–87; idem, "'Beautiful as a Wasp': Angela of Foligno and Georges Bataille," *Harvard Theological Review* 92 (1999): 219–36.

13. Bruce Holsinger, *The Premodern Condition: Medievalism and the Making of Theory* (Chicago: University of Chicago Press, 2005), 33–34.

14. Bataille, *Inner Experience*, 7.

15. Guigo V. the Carthusian (?), *Scala claustralium, sive tractatus de modo orandi*, in *Patrologia latina*, vol. 184, ed. Jacques-Paul Migne (Paris: Migne, 1862), 476.

16. Hugh, *De virtute orandi* 7, in *L'ouvre de Hugues de Saint-Victor*, vol. 1, ed. H. B. Feiss and P. Siccard (Turnhout: Brepols, 1997), 136.

17. *L'ouvre de Hugues de Saint-Victor*, 152.

18. Compare the commentary of Thomas of Aquinas on Richard of Saint Victor and his use of the term *cogitatio*: "cogitatio secundum Richardum de sancto Victore videtur pertinere ad multorum inspectionem, ex quibus aliquis colligere intendit unam simplicem veritatem. Unde sub cogitatione comprehendi possunt et perceptiones sensuum ad cognoscendum aliquos effectus, et imaginationes et discursus rationis circa diversa signa vel quaecumque perducentia in cognitione veritatis intentae" (*Summa Theologiae*, II II, 180, 3, ad 1).

19. Hugh, *De virtute orandi* 14, 158.

20. Hugh, *De virtute orandi* 14, 158.

21. Bernard McGinn, "The Language of Inner Experience in Christian Mysticism," *Spiritus* 1 (2001): 157–60.

22. See Karl Rahner, "Le début d'une doctrine des cinq sens spirituels chez Origène," *Revue d'ascétique et de mystique* 13 (1932):113–45, here 116 (Origenes: *kai aísthäsin theían heuréseis*. Septuagint: *kai epígnosin theou heuréseis*; Vulgate: *et scientiam Dei invenies*). Compare also Niklaus Largier, "Inner Senses—Outer Senses: The Practice of Emotions in Medieval Mysticism," in *Codierungen von Emotionen im Mittelalter / Emotions and Sensibilities in the Middle Ages*, ed. C. Stephen Jaeger and Ingrid Kasten (Berlin: de Gruyter, 2003), 3–15.

23. Origenes, *Commentarium in Canticum Canticorum* II 9, 12, in *Commentaire sur le Cantique des cantiques*, 2 vols., ed. Luc Brésard, Henri Crouzel, and Marcel Borret (Paris: Cerf, 1991), 1:442.

24. Gregory of Nyssa, *In Canticum Canticorum homilia* 14, in *Patrologia Graeca*, 44:1084c; in *Gregorii Nysseni Opera*, vol. 6, *In Canticum canticorum*, ed. Hermannus Langerbeck (Leiden: Brill, 1960), 425–26.

25. *Das St. Trudperter Hohelied. Eine Lehre der Liebenden Gotteserkenntnis*, ed. Friedrich Ohly, in collaboration with Nicola Kleine (Frankfurt am Main: Deutscher Klassiker Verlag, 1998), 922–23. See also Hildegard Elisabeth Keller, *Wort und Fleisch. Körperallegorien, mystische Spiritualität und Dichtung des St. Trudperter Hoheliedes im Horizont der Inkarnation* (Bern: Lang, 1993).

26. Albert the Great, *In quattuor libros Sententiarum* III d. 13 a. 4, in *Opera omnia*, vol. 28, ed. Stephanus Borgnet (Paris: Vivès, 1894), 240: "Si autem objicitur contra hos duos sensus, quod sensus est vis cognitiva: istud autem non ordinatur ad apprehendere, sed potius ad affici: dicendum, quod est cognitio per modum receptionis quasi ab extra: et est cognitio experimentalis, sicut dicit Dionysius quod Hierotheus patiendo divina, didicit divina: et haec cognitio est per gustum et tactum spirituales" (If someone argued against these two senses that sense experience is a cognitive power, one should stress that this does not refer to active apprehension but rather to passive perception. One should reply that it is a form of cognition in the mode of an influence as if from outside. It is experiential cognition, to be understood in the way Dionysius said of Hierotheus that he knew the divine through suffering the divine. This is cognition through the spiritual senses of taste and touch). For Albert's understanding of the inner senses, see also *De caelestis hierarchia* c. 15 n. 5, in *Opera omnia*, vol. 14, 414.

27. Peter of Ailly, *Compendium contemplationis* III 11, in *Opuscula spiritualia* (Douai, 1634), 134.

28. Rudolf of Biberach, *De septem itineribus aeternitatis* VI dist. V, in *De septem itineribus aeternitatis*, Nachdruck der Ausgabe von Peltier 1866 mit einer Einleitung in die lateinische Überlieferung und Corrigenda zum Text, ed. Margot Schmidt (Stuttgart: Frommann-Holzboog, 1985), 467.

29. In his long treatment of the inner senses, Rudolf makes this experiential aspect very explicit: "Ex quo ergo gustum illum nemo potest exprimere, sed solum per experientiam noscitur, ideo oportet viam quaerere,

qualiter spiritus noster ad istam gustus experientiam possit pertingere" (This explains why nobody can express this taste. It can only be known through experience, and this is why we have to look for the way in which our mind can reach the experience of this taste) (467).

30. See also Niklaus Largier, "Praying by Numbers: An Essay on Medieval Aesthetics," *Representations* 104 (2008): 73–92.

31. *Patrologia Latina*, vol. 153, ed. Jacques-Paul Migne, 799–884.

32. *Patrologia Latina*, vol. 204, ed. Jacques-Paul Migne, 429–42.

33. *Patrologia Latina*, vol. 204, ed. Jacques-Paul Migne, 429: "Simplae morti simpla congruit resurrectio. At nobis una resurrectio sufficere non potest" (Simple mortals are satisfied with one resurrection. We, however, are not satisfied with one resurrection).

34. Compare the recent treatment of this topic by Rosalynn Voaden, *God's Words, Women's Voices: The Discernment of Spirits in the Writing of Late-Medieval Women Visionaries* (Rochester: Boydell & Brewer, 2000). See also Nancy Caciola, *Discerning Spirits: Divine and Demonic Possession in the Middle Ages* (Ithaca, N.Y.: Cornell University Press, 2003); Carol Thysell, *The Pleasure of Discernment: Marguerite de Navarre as Theologian* (Oxford: Oxford University Press, 2000); Niklaus Largier, "Rhetorik des Begehrens: Die 'Unterscheidung der Geister' als Paradigma mittelalterlicher Subjektivität," in *Inszenierungen von Subjektivität in der Literatur des* Mittelalters, ed. Martin Baisch (Königstein, 2005), 249–70.

35. See Niklaus Largier, "Die Phänomenologie rhetorischer Effekte und die Kontrolle religiöser Kommunikation," in *Literarische und religiöse Kommunikation in Mittelalter und Früher Neuzeit. DFG-Symposion 2006*, ed. Peter Strohschneider (Stuttgart: Metzler, 2009), 953–68.

36. Niklaus Largier, "Mysticism, Modernity, and the Invention of Aesthetic Experience," *Representations* 105 (2009): 37–60, esp. 39–45.

37. See Largier, "Mysticism."

38. For a recent and very comprehensive study, see Hermann Geyer, *Verborgene Weisheit. Johann Arndts 'Vier Bücher vom wahren Christentum' als Programm einer spiritualistisch-hermetischen Theologie*, 2 vols. (Berlin: de Gruyter, 2001).

39. Cf. Hans-Georg Kemper, *Gottebenbildlichkeit und Naturnachahmung im Säkularisierungsprozeß* (Tübingen: Niemeyer, 1981).

40. For an overview of the life and work of these poets, see Hans-Georg Kemper, *Deutsche Lyrik der frühen Neuzeit*, vol. 3, *Barock-Mystik* (Tübingen: Niemeyer, 1988).

41. See Largier, "Mysticism," 50–52.

42. Alexander Gottlieb Baumgarten, *Aesthetica*, ed. Dagmar Mirbach (Hamburg: Meiner, 2007), §78.

43. For a history of this trope, see Bernard McGinn, *The Harvest of Mysticism in Medieval Germany* (New York: Crossroads, 2005), 83–93, 118–24, 254–64; Niklaus Largier, "Vernunft und Seligkeit. Das theologische und philosophische Programm des 'Paradisus anime intelligentis,'" in *'Paradisus anime intelligentis': Studien zu einer dominikanischen Predigtsammlung aus dem Umkreis Meister Eckharts*, ed. Burkhard Hasebrink, Nigel F. Palmer, and Hans-Jochen Schiewer (Tübingen: Niemeyer, 2009), 1–15; idem, "Spiegelungen: Fragmente einer Geschichte der Spekulation," *Zeitschrift für Germanistik*, new series 3 (1999): 616–36.

44. Baumgarten, *Aesthetica*, §80.

45. Baumgarten, *Aesthetica*, §84.

46. Baumgarten, *Aesthetica*, §80 and §511.

47. For a more comprehensive discussion of this issue, see Niklaus Largier, "The Plasticity of the Soul: Mystical Darkness, Touch, and Aesthetic Experience," *Modern Language Notes* 125 (2010): 536–51.

48. See Niklaus Largier, "Tactus. Le sens du toucher et la volupté au Moyen Age," *Micrologus 13: La peau humaine* (2004): 233–49.

49. Johann Gottfried Herder, *Werke in zehn Bänden*, ed. Hans Dietrich Irmscher (Frankfurt am Main: Deutscher Klassiker Verlag, 1991), vol. 8, 368.

50. See Largier, "Plasticity of the Soul," 546–49.

Contributors

Sarah Apetrei is Fellow in Ecclesiastical History at Keble College, Oxford. She has worked in teaching and research at the Faculty of Theology and Religion, Oxford; the Institute of Historical Research, London; the British Academy; and Goldsmiths College, London. She published her monograph, *Women, Feminism and Religion in Early Enlightenment England* with Cambridge University Press in 2010.

Euan K. Cameron is Henry Luce III Professor of Reformation Church History at Union Theological Seminary, New York and holds a concurrent part-time appointment in the Department of Religion at Columbia University. He has previously held positions at All Souls College, Oxford, and the University of Newcastle upon Tyne. He is the author of a number of works on early modern religious history, including *Enchanted Europe: Superstition, Reason and Religion 1250–1750* (2010) and *The European Reformation* (2nd ed., 2012). For 2014–15 he holds a Luce Fellowship in Theology to develop a research project entitled "The Biblical View of World History 1250–1750: Rise, Refinement, and Decline."

Kirsten M. Christensen is Associate Professor of German at Pacific Lutheran University, where she teaches all levels of German language and culture. Christensen's publications examine late medieval and early sixteenth-century mystical literature and devotional writings, particularly by women, from Germany and the Low Countries. She also has an abiding interest in and has published a number of articles on labor issues in higher education.

Franz M. Eybl is Professor of Modern German Literature at the University of Vienna. His research interests include Heinrich von Kleist, the history of the book industry, media theory, and religious literature, especially of the early modern period. In addition to numerous essays on these topics, Eybl is the author of *Kleist-Lektüren* (WUV, 2007), coauthor of *Geschichte des österreichischen Buchhandels*, in collaboration with Norbert Bachleitner und Ernst Fischer (Harrassowitz, 2000), and coeditor of *Delectatio. Unterhaltung und Vergnügen zwischen Grimmelshausen und Schnabel*, with Irmgard M. Wirtz (P. Lang, 2009), and *Elementare Gewalt. Kulturelle Bewältigung. Aspekte der Naturkatastrophe im 18. Jahrhundert*, with Harald Heppner and Alois Kernbauer (WUV, 2000).

Genelle C. Gertz, Associate Professor of English at Washington and Lee University, teaches courses in medieval and early modern literature and directs the Writing Program. Her book, *Heresy Trials and English Women Writers, 1400–1670* (Cambridge, 2012), offers the first full-length study of the writings of women on trial for heresy. She is currently working on a book-length project about medieval and seventeenth-century women prophets. An essay on a seventeenth-century English nun "Barbara Constable's *Advice for Confessors* and the Tradition of Medieval Holy Women" appears in *The English Convents in Exile, 1600–1800: Communities, Culture and Identity* (Ashgate, 2013).

Jeffrey F. Hamburger is the Kuno Francke Professor of German Art & Culture at Harvard University. A member of the American Academy of Arts and Sciences and American Philosophical Society, as well as a Fellow of the Medieval Academy of America, he has published widely on medieval manuscript illumination, the art of female monasticism, and medieval mysticism. Current projects, all collaborative, include books on the Prayer Book of Ursula Begerin, the liturgical manuscripts from Paradies bei Soest, and a major international exhibition on German manuscript illumination in the age of Gutenberg.

Hildegard Elisabeth Keller is a specialist in both German and Spanish literature and has since 2008 held the chair for medieval German literature at Indiana University in Bloomington, Indiana. She also teaches at the University of Zurich. Active as an independent author, she has collaborated on exhibitions, most recently, the exhibition on mysticism at the Museum Rietberg in Zurich. In 2011 she published the "Trilogie des Zeitlosen," three audio books dealing, inter alia, with Meister Eckhart, Zhuangzi, Heinrich Seuse, Hildegard of Bingen, and Etty Hillesum. Her biography of Jakob Ruf and edition of his collected works appeared in 2008. Since 2009 she has been a member of the jury for the Bachmann Prize in Klagenfurt, and since 2012, a critic in the "Literaturclub" on the Swiss television station SRF. In 2013, Keller also published an edited anthology of the stories and columns by Alfonsina Storni, an Argentinian writer with Swiss roots, entitled *Meine Seele hat kein Geschlecht* (My Soul has no Sex).

Alana King completed her Ph.D. in German literature at Princeton University in December 2013. Her dissertation, advised by Sara S. Poor, examines the legacy of medieval mysticism in early modern Germany (sixteenth and seventeenth centuries), is entitled *Mysticism and Confessional Conflict in Post-Reformation Germany: The Mystical Theology of Valentin Weigel (1533–1588)*, and was the basis for her receiving a DAAD research fellowship in 2009–10. Other research interests include medievalism (particularly early modern perspectives on the Middle Ages), medieval and early modern historiography, philology, religious activism and Quietism, and medieval mystical writers.

Niklaus Largier is the Sidney and Margaret Ancker Professor of German and Comparative Literature at the University of California, Berkeley. His most recent books explore the relation between bodily ascetic practices (in particular flagellation), eroticism, and the literary imagination (*Lob der Peitsche: Eine Kulturgeschichte der Erregung* [Beck, 2001], American translation: *In Praise of the Whip: A Cultural History of Arousal* [Zone, 2007]), and the fascination of decadent literature with such religious practices (*Die Kunst des Begehrens: Dekadenz, Sinnlichkeit und Askese* [Beck, 2007]). He is currently finishing a book on practices of figuration.

Arthur F. Marotti, Distinguished Professor of English Emeritus at Wayne State University, is the author of *John Donne, Coterie Poet* (1986); *Manuscript, Print and the English Renaissance Lyric* (1995); and *Religious Ideology and Cultural Fantasy: Catholic and Anti-Catholic Discourses in Early Modern England* (2005) and the co-author of *Ink, Stink Bait, Revenge and Queen Elizabeth: A Yorkshire Yeoman's Household Book* (2014). He has edited or co-edited ten collections of scholarly essays, most recently (with Chanita Goodblatt) *Religious Diversity in Early Modern England: Catholic, Judaic, Feminist, and Secular Perspectives* (2013). He served as the Editor of the journal *Criticism* from 1986 to 1996. His current research deals both with early modern English Catholic culture and with manuscript poetry collections.

Sara S. Poor is Associate Professor of German Literature and Director of the Program in Medieval Studies at Princeton University. She is the author of *Mechthild of Magdeburg and Her Book: Gender and the Making of Textual Authority* (Penn, 2004), co-editor of *Women in Medieval Epic: Gender and the Limits of Epic Masculinity* (Palgrave, 2007), and author of a number of recent essays dealing with the relationship between gender, learning, and the production and circulation of devotional books in late medieval Germany.

Kees Schepers is Associate Professor at the Ruusbroec Institute of the University of Antwerp. He has published critical editions of several late medieval mystical texts, both in the vernacular and in Latin translation, as well as of a Middle Dutch miscellany. His research now focuses on the sixteenth-century mystical renaissance in the Low Countries and the neighboring Rhineland. He is preparing a critical edition, with an English translation, of the *Arnhem Mystical Sermons*.

Alison Shell is Professor of Early Modern Studies in the Department of English at University College London. She is the author of *Catholicism, Controversy and the English Literary Imagination, 1558–1660* (1999), *Oral Culture and Catholicism in Early Modern England* (2007), and *Shakespeare and Religion* (2010), as well as a number of articles dealing with literature and religion in early modern England.

Nigel Smith is William and Annie S. Paton Foundation Professor of Ancient and Modern Literature at Princeton University. His major works are *Andrew Marvell: The Chameleon* (Yale University Press, 2010), *Is Milton Better than Shakespeare?* (Harvard University Press, 2008), the Longman Annotated English Poets edition of Andrew Marvell's *Poems* (2003, 2006), *Literature and Revolution in England, 1640–1660* (Yale University Press, 1994), and *Perfection Proclaimed: Language and Literature in English Radical Religion 1640–1660* (Oxford University Press 1989). New work involves the comparison of English with literatures in other European vernaculars in the context of religious, political, and scientific transformation between 1500 and 1800.

Bethany Wiggin is Associate Professor in the Department of Germanic Languages and associate Faculty in English Literatures at the University of Pennsylvania. She is the author of *Novel Translations: The European Novel and the German Book* (Cornell University Press, 2011) as well as of the forthcoming *Germanopolis: Utopia Found and Lost in Penn's Woods* (Penn State University Press, 2015). She has edited *Babel of the Eighteenth-Century Atlantic* (Penn State University Press, 2015), co-edited another, *UnTranslatables: New Maps across Germanic Literatures* (Northwestern University Press, 2014), and is at present editing an issue of *The Germanic Review* devoted to translation, multilingualism, and world literature in pre-modern Germany. Wiggin is the founding director of the Environmental Humanities Fellows Program at the University of Pennsylvania and will direct the Penn Humanities Forum in 2015–16 in a year devoted to the theme of Translation.

Index

Page numbers in italics refer to illustrations.